Schools for Talent Development: A Practical Plan for Total School Improvement

Joseph S. Renzulli
The University of Connecticut

When one door closes another opens. But we often look so long and so regretfully upon the closed door that we do not see the one which has opened for us.

–Alexander Graham Bell

Printed in the United States of America
ISBN 0-936386-65-7

To Liza, Sara, Scott, and Mark.
From preschool to graduate school,
they have helped me keep in touch
in a personal way with the education system...

And to Sally,
Whose extraordinary insights about the balance
between excellence and equity served
as the motivation for this book.

Consulting editor
Jeanne H. Purcell

Table of Contents

List of Figures

List of Tables

Preface

The Shape of the Things to Come: The Systemic Change Pipeline

Most efforts to make major changes in schooling have failed. Although there is endless speculation about why schools are so resistant to change, most theorists and policy makers have concluded that tinkering with single components of a complex system will give only the appearance of school improvement rather than the real and lasting change so desperately sought by educational leaders. Examples of single component tinkering are familiar to most educators. More rigorous curriculum standards, for example, without improved curricular materials and teachers able to use the materials effectively negates any potential value that new standards may have for improving academic performance. Similarly, single component tinkering designed to force change in classrooms (e.g., high-stakes testing) may create the illusion of improved achievement, but the reality is increased pressure on schools to expand the use of compensatory learning models that, so far, have contributed only to the "dumbing down" of curriculum and the lowering of academic standards. Teacher empowerment, school-based management, an extended school day and year, and revised teacher certification requirements are merely apparitions of change when state or central office regulations prescribe the curriculum by using tests that will determine whether schools get high marks for better performance.

Disillusionment with single component tinkering has resulted in a new and promising approach to school improvement that has been popularized in the literature under the heading of systemic change or systemic educational policy (Smith & O'Day, 1990). Systemic change simply means that the focus of change must be on the entire system, rather than on fragmented components of the system. There is almost unanimous agreement that a systemic approach to change is more promising that past efforts. However, a good deal of disagreement about the ways systemic educational policy should be developed and implemented. The arguments center around the extent to which educational policy should be standardized and centralized on one hand, or differentiated and decentralized on the other (Clune, 1993). Persons favoring a standardized/centralized approach point out that local control of schools, especially those serving students in urban areas, has not produced impressive results; local authorities have been unable to produce high standards and rigorous curricula. They believe that curricular decision making is a job for experts rather than local teachers and administrators. Proponents of centralized control argue that:

> ...the existing system of school governance is seen as incapable of producing a major upgrading of instruction. The present system is characterized by multiple power centers issuing fragmented control over various components of the curriculum-guidance system....The essence of [centralized] systemic policy is to replace this fragmented

nonsystem with a coherent system of curriculum controls at the level of national and state governments. (Clune, 1993, p. 244)

The arguments against a standardized/centralized approach to systemic change are equally compelling, especially when we acknowledge the fact that America has two school systems that are separate and unequal. Urban schools and rural schools that serve economically poor students face problems that are fundamentally different from the problems facing schools in suburban and financially stable communities. Dictatorial management procedures, insufferable regulations, and politicized state and central office bureaucracies, it is argued, are exactly what has brought about the degeneration of urban schools, and the same regulations have been capriciously applied to all schools. Furthermore, the competence of educational leaders has been an ongoing criticism of persons who favor decentralization. These persons argue that concentrating power in ineffective and unimaginative administrators will only result in more tedious and largely ignored regulations.

The strongest argument for a differentiated/decentralized approach to systemic policy is that local needs must be the first consideration and driving force for change initiatives. Proponents of this position insist that policies designed to guide practice for all schools end up being far too general for any particular school. To support their position, proponents cite the immense diversity of school populations, dissimilar financial and human resources, varying ideologies and the idiosyncrasies of the twin bureaucracies, administrations and unions. The reaction of practitioners to these "top down" mandates is predictable. Unless large amounts of money or compliance reviews accompany the directives, local mandates are complied with in minimal ways, or simply ignored once the classroom door is closed.

How, then, do we establish an effective change process—one that overcomes the long record of failed attempts? The leverage for meaningful change depends upon breaking two mindsets: (1) that one person or single group knows the right answer, and (2) that change is linear. If we agree there is merit in both a standardized/centralized approach and differentiated/ decentralized approach, and if we further agree that real and lasting change can come about only if changes occur in all components of the system, how can we develop a plan that incorporates the best of the top-down and the bottom-up approaches? The only reasonable solution is to develop a process whereby the adoption of policy and the adoption of practice proceed simultaneously! Policy makers and practitioners in schools need to collaborate during all phases of the change process by examining local capacity and motivation in conjunction with the desired changes. Thus, neither policy makers nor practitioners, by themselves, can reform schools; instead both must come together to shape a vision and develop the procedures that will be needed to realize and sustain that vision. Senge (1990) compares "visioneering" to the hologram, a three-dimensional image created by interacting light sources:

When a group of people come to share a vision, ...each sees his or her own picture. Each vision represents the whole image from a different point of view. When you add up the pieces of the hologram, the image does not change fundamentally, but rather becomes more intense, more lifelike, more real in the sense that people can truly imagine achieving it. The vision no longer rests on the shoulders of one person [or one group], but is shared and embodies the passion and commitment of all participants. (Senge, 1990, p. 312)

Experience and common sense support Senge's metaphor because we know that ownership and involvement are far more effective in promoting the motivation to succeed than external pressure and regulations.

Currently, many believe educational change is a simple, linear movement from where we are to where we want to go. This mindset is based on the premise we know what we want and the interventions necessary to take us there. Restructuring, however, is a multifaceted and complex task that is frequently unpredictable; many of the solutions cannot be known in advance. Accordingly, change is no longer a linear progression, but is an evolving process. This concept was perhaps best stated by H. L. Mencken who said, "For every complex question, there is a simple answer—and it is wrong."

What, then, is the new shape of the metaphorical change pipeline? First, the pipeline is no longer narrow; rather, it is a wide route to accommodate the shared vision of all the new stake holders and the resulting commitment and passion that will fuel educational change. Second, the pipeline is no longer a straight line leading from one point to another; instead, its configuration is unknown, taking its shape as the stake holders create and implement solutions to the complex problems inherent in educational change. Stacy (1990) articulated clearly the nature of the task ahead of those who share a vision for educational renewal, "Route and destination must be discovered through the journey itself if you wish to travel to new lands...the key to success lies in the creative activity of making new maps" (p. 3).

The Reason for This Book: Dreaming in Another Language
This book is based on a shared vision that my colleagues in The Center for Talent Development at the University of Connecticut and I have had for a number of years. This vision is also embraced by thousands of teachers and administrators with whom we have worked in academic programs and summer institutes that date back to the early 1970s. *Simply stated, this vision is that schools are places for talent development.* Academic achievement is, indeed, an important part of the vision and the model for school improvement described in this book; however, we believe a focus on talent development places the need for improved academic achievement into a larger perspective about the goals of education. The things that have made our nation great and our society one of the most productive in the world are manifestations of

talent development at all levels of human productivity. From the creators and inventors of new ideas, products, and art forms, to the vast array of people who manufacture, advertise, and market the creations that improve and enrich our lives, there are levels of excellence and quality that contribute to our standard of living and way of life.

This vision of schools for talent development is based on the belief that *everyone* has an important role to play in societal improvement, and that everyone's role can be enhanced if we provide all students with opportunities, resources, and encouragement to aspire to the highest level of talent development humanly possible. Rewarding lives are a function of ways we use individual potentials in productive ways. Accordingly, this book is a practical plan for making our vision of schools for talent development a reality. We are not naive about the politics, personalities, and financial issues that often supersede the pedagogical goals that are the focus of this book. At the same time, we have seen this vision manifested in schools ranging from hard core urban areas and isolated and frequently poor rural areas to affluent suburbs and combinations thereof. We believe that the strategies described in this book provide the guidance for making any school a place for talent development.

There are no quick fixes or easy formulas for transforming schools into places where talent development is valued and vigorously pursued. Our experience has shown, however, that once the concept of talent development catches on, students, parents, teachers, and administrators begin to view their school in a different way. Students become more excited and engaged in what they are learning; parents find more opportunities to become involved in all aspects related to their children's learning, rather than "around the edges" activities; teachers begin to find and use a variety of resources that, until now, seldom found their way into classrooms; and administrators start to make decisions that affect learning rather than "tight ship" efficiency. When a teacher was asked how she made such remarkable changes in her involvement with students, she replied, "Now I see everything as an opportunity, resource, or procedure for engaging, or re-engaging, students with their important work. Last night I taped a TV program, cut out three articles from the newspaper for different projects students were completing, and convinced a parent to offer an enrichment cluster in Japanese for a group of interested sixth graders...It's like dreaming in another language because I'm not thinking about what page in the textbook I am on."

A Word About the Format of This Book

We have punctuated the text with outtakes and sidebars that call attention to important issues, words of wisdom, and practical experiences. All were selected and edited carefully. It is our hope that the outtakes and sidebars capture the essence of thoughts in the book, elaborate on ideas to help bring a sense of reality to ideas, and provide opportunities for reflection on particularly compelling issues.

We also will make reference to "companion volumes" that contain ways for implementing the practices recommended in the chapters that follow. The plan described in this book has been field tested by practitioners and refined over a period of fifteen years. To capitalize on the practical strategies refined by practitioners and to avoid repeating material that is already in print, readers are referred occasionally to other related books and articles.

Finally, throughout the chapters we will occasionally use the phrase, "high-end learning". We want to emphasize that this phrase reflects our emphasis on *labeling services rather than students*. Accordingly, high-end learning should *not* be misinterpreted to mean that the focus of this book is on high achievers. The practices set forth herein are designed to promote high performance and talent development opportunities for all students.

Acknowledgments

Many people are responsible for the development of this book. Persons at The Center for Talent Development who contributed to the manuscript and reviewed endless drafts are Deborah Burns, E. Jean Gubbins, Sally Reis, Karen Westberg, and Jann Leppien. Staff members who reviewed the manuscript, tracked down references and resources, and provided assistance are Diana Whitton, Cathy Suroviak, Karen Logan, Dee Korner, Dawn Guenther, and JoAnn Easton. Del Siegle and Siamak Vahidi provided invaluable assistance in the thoughtful development of graphic displays that help clarify concepts in the narrative and the interrelationships among the various parts of the model. Special thanks are also extended to Carolyn Cooper for her careful editorial review of the manuscript. Finally, sincere appreciation is extended to Jeanne Purcell, who contributed most of the material included in the resource guides, provided endless feedback on the substance and technical qualities of the text, and served as the overall production manager of this book. Without her assistance the book would not have "come together" as a unified whole. It is because of the contributions of these many people that I have used the collective "we" rather than "I" when putting forth points of view and descriptions of experiences.

Furthermore, appreciation is extended to all persons whose works are cited and included in both the text and the sidebars. Finally, sincere appreciation is extended to the many persons in schools throughout North America and overseas who were willing to take a chance on implementing the suggestions put forth in this book. They have provided the "reality check" that resulted in the motivation to write this book.

Chapter 1

A Bridge to Halfway There

Introduction

THIS BOOK DESCRIBES A plan that has already demonstrated its effectiveness in bringing about significant changes in schooling. The plan, entitled the Schoolwide Enrichment Model (SEM), is a systematic set of specific strategies for increasing student effort, enjoyment, and performance, and for integrating a broad range of advanced level learning experiences and higher order thinking skills into any curricular area, course of study, or pattern of school organization. The general approach of the SEM is one of infusing more effective practices into existing school structures rather than layering on additional things for schools to do. This research-supported plan is designed for general education, but it is based on a large number of instructional methods and curricular practices that had their origins in special programs for high ability students.

Everyone has a stake in schools that provide all of our young people with a high-quality education. Parents benefit when their children lead happy and successful lives. Employers and colleges benefit when they have access to people who are competent, creative, and effective in the work they do and in higher educational pursuits. Political leaders benefit when good citizens and a productive population

The cumulative effect of the test score decline on standards of living is quite large. The social cost is now [1989] $86 billion annually....If the forecasted shortfalls in output up to the year 2010 are cumulated..., the total present discounted costs of the test score decline is $3.2 trillion or roughly three-fourths of the 1987 gross national product.

John H. Bishop, 1989

Rarely do outside-of-school remedies work their way into the fabric of the school or into educators' lives, and even more rarely into classrooms. Therefore, they offer only modest hope of influencing the basic culture of the schools.

Roland Barth, 1990

contribute to a healthy economy, a high quality of life, and respect for the values and institutions in a democracy. And professional educators at all levels benefit when the quality of schools for which they are responsible is effective enough to create respect for their work and generous financial support for the educational enterprise.

Everyone has a stake in good schools because schools create and *re*create a successful modern society. In a study of the relationship between test scores and national productivity conducted by the New York School of Industrial and Labor Relations, Bishop (1989) examined the unprecedented test score decline that began around 1967. Productivity growth and test scores declined almost simultaneously; and Bishop concluded "that the effects of general intellectual achievement on wage rates and productivity is larger than heretofore believed" (p. 193). Researchers (Flynn, 1987; Husén & Tuijnman, 1991) who studied the relationship between effective schools and national productivity in several countries report that schools produce the intellectual and creative capital of modern, technological societies; expanded capital, in turn, increases both the number of young people who can benefit from formal education and their career prospects for successful working lives. But the quality and effectiveness of formal education, as it takes place in individual schools and classrooms on a day-to-day basis, must change. Schools that were largely designed to feed the factories of an industrialized nation are no longer workable in a highly technological society where information and ideas are replacing the coal, steel, and other raw materials that created employment and prosperous standards of living. Renewed and sustained economic growth and the well-being of all citizens means investing in high-quality learning the same way that previous generations invested in machines and raw materials. Our schools are already dumping millions of functionally illiterate young people into the workforce; more and more colleges are teaching remedial courses based on material formerly taught in high school; and college graduates in almost all fields are experiencing difficulty entering career areas of choice.

Although everyone has a stake in good schools, America has been faced with a "school problem" that has resulted in declining confidence in schools and the people who work in them, drastic limitations in the amount of financial support for education, and general public apathy or dissatisfaction with the quality of education our young people are receiving. The parents of poor children have given up hope that education will enable their sons and daughters to break the bonds of poverty. And the middle class, perhaps for the first time in our nation's history, is exploring government supported alternatives such as vouchers and tax credits for private schools, home schooling, charter schools, and summer and after-school programs that enhance admission to competitive colleges. A great deal has been written about America's "school problem," and studies, commissions, reports, and even a Governor's Summit Conference have been initiated to generate solutions to problems facing our schools. But the hundreds if not thousands of conferences, commissions, and meetings, and the tons of reports, proclamations, and lists of goals, have mainly generated only one thing — a new species of educator called "the school reformer!" The habitats of this species are institutions of higher education, federal and state educational agencies, consultant hutches, and, occasionally, the central offices of school districts. Noticeably absent from the new species are the within-school personnel who are expected to carry out recommended practices, the students upon whom the practices are targeted, and parents who are the proxy holders of their children's education. So accustomed have we become to this top-down arrangement, that most people who live and work in schools do not even speculate about alternative approaches to changing even the smallest *modus operandi* of daily classroom activity. The groups and individual members of the new reformer species all have their own suggestions for improving schools. And, while it is not our intention to pass judgment on the many recommendations that have emerged from the school reform movement, we will comment briefly on some of the approaches that have failed to improve schools because this book is based on a fundamental belief that *schools can change only from within.*

How Not to Improve Schools

State agencies, regulations, guidelines, lists of goals and standards, and yet another rally-round-the-flag report will not improve schools. Under the best of circumstances, these external forces, admonitions, and affirmations have only resulted in minimal, but reluctant compliance, and involuntary completion of more and more needless paperwork. Less favorable circumstances have resulted in antagonism between school personnel and external agencies, deceptive reporting, and malaise on the parts of teachers and building principals which often robs them of the kinds of energy necessary to take enthusiastic steps to serve students in an exceptional way.

Obviously, the great danger of the current admixture of schizophrenia and ignorance in educational reform policy is that bally-hooed, but misguided top-down reforms may backfire. If they do, the result will be further disillusionment with public education, increasing sentiment to abandon the public schools and support [for] policies facilitating the privatization of education. Whether we can sustain the momentum of the current reform movement, or whether we are destined to return to neglect, is the critical question confronting us.

William Lowe Boyd, 1987

Teachers...often described negative effects associated with mandated standardized tests on curriculum or student learning. They stated, for example, that a state or district testing program caused narrowing or fragmenting of the curriculum, limited the nature of thinking, or forced them to rush too much for students to learn well. The interviews also confirmed the finding of the national survey that instruction by teachers facing high-stakes testing pressures is often heavily oriented toward testing preparation.

George Madaus, Mary West, Mary Ellen Harmon, Richard Lomax, & Catherine Viator, 1992

And in the worst of circumstances, regulations have simply been ignored once the classroom door is closed. No one questions the noble intent of externally imposed regulations, but like the barnacles on a ship, they have proliferated and attached themselves to schools in such proportions that they have actually slowed down the progress of school improvement.

State-level testing programs that are intended to make schools and teachers "accountable" will not improve schools. The well-documented results of increased testing include more pressure on teachers to concentrate on basic skills, a slow-but-steady movement toward a national, one-size-fits-all curriculum, and what teachers have described as coercion to engage in admittedly poor teaching practices. The irony of what has been called "high-stakes" testing programs is that economically poor students, those who traditionally have scored lower than the general population, end up receiving ever increasing amounts of drill on the low level skills that these tests measure. This practice is clearly inconsistent with fluff pieces and admonishments that warn us about our post-industrial society's need for creative thinkers and problem solvers. Some reports do, indeed, tell of test score increases resulting from highly regulated compensatory programs. What the reports fail to mention are concomitant increases in dropout rates, the lack of preparedness for anything but the lowest level jobs, no increases in the percentages of students who can perform at the highest levels of reading, mathematics, and science, and virtually no increase in the number of disadvantaged students entering higher education (Educational Testing Service, 1991). Also not mentioned is that low achieving students have sometimes been excluded from post-testing because they have been declared learning disabled or students in need of other forms of special education! Testing has not only failed to improve school; it has actually been counterproductive. Consider the almost schizoid policies that have resulted from test-driven decision making. Schools with large numbers of low scoring students have routinely received additional funding through compensatory education programs. A worse-case scenario is that school districts actually profit from poor performance by receiving increased funds. Some recent policies, on the other hand, are offering financial rewards for improved test scores. Since socioeconomic level is the only consistent factor that correlates with test scores, we may have devised yet another way of punishing young people because they are poor!

Outside consultants and the "innovations" they peddle will not improve schools. Consultants have blitzed in and out of schools at least since the advent of regularly scheduled airlines; we are always being entreated by cover story articles in professional journals that herald the latest flavor-of-the-month innovation. Almost every major effort to reform American education has been met with limited and temporary success. Progressive education, programmed instruction, discovery learning, open education, and a host of other "innovations" lie battered and broken on the roadside of educational reform. Goodlad (1984) and other analysts tell us that in spite of massive efforts and billions of dollars expended to bring about significant changes in the education process, present day schools bear a striking resemblance to the structure of education at the turn of the century. Whole group instruction, prescribed and didactic curriculum, and an emphasis on basic skills and minimum competencies have turned our schools into dreary places that can't begin to compete with out-of-school interests, extracurricular activities, and endless hours in front of the television set. We sometimes adopt the jargon of these movements, and occasionally, we even fool ourselves into believing that we have taken a giant step forward. Consider the school district that made much fanfare about a recent decision "to do away with textbooks" in reading and language arts. A visit to schools in that district revealed that the textbooks had been replaced with a prescribed set of trade books for each grade level, teachers were still under pressure to teach the achievement test-related skills that were in the basals, and students were not allowed to progress at different rates through the new books.

Finally, and perhaps most surprisingly, parents, school boards, and central office administrators cannot change schools. These groups *are* essential players in the overall process of school improvement, but without the genuine participation of principals and teachers, these groups play the same role as that of the state agencies and external regulations discussed above. And even principals and teachers cannot change schools unless they are willing to cooperate with one another and to compromise when differences of opinion occur. In this day of job actions, work-to-rule, involuntary transfers, and placing "a letter in your file," almost everyone who works in schools knows that maintaining the *status quo* may not be the best way to serve all of our students, but it certainly is the easiest way to survive in complex and bureaucratic

As a parent of several young ones struggling through a system that provides them not much more than a minimal education, I find this recent odyssey into the real world of education reform extremely discouraging. Here is a large number of parents who want to be a vital part of their children's education being told, albeit politely, not to bother, butt out, stick to the bake sales, don't really get involved....There is little parents can do to influence the kind of entrenched resistance I have encountered. We have scant leverage or clout. Why should teachers and principals listen when they do not have to account to parents for school policies and practices, when they have a captive audience, save for those willing and able "to go private"?

Mary R. Blanton, 1992

The level of concern and amount of energy being expended in thinking about public schooling are more intense now than at any previous time. Proposals have been put forward at the national, state and local levels, setting out new standards to which educators, schools, and students should be held accountable in order to halt what one commission deemed 'the rising tide of mediocrity that threatens our very future as a nation and as a people' (National Commission on Excellence in Education)....All are well-intended and sincerely proposed. Not one of these proposals, however, takes into account the most fundamental variables in the educational process: the nature of the relationship between educators and their students and the extent to which students are actively engaged in the learning process.

Michael Sedlack, Christopher Wheeler, Diana Pullin, & Phillip Cusick, 1986

organizations. If we lived in an ideal world in which noble goals guided all of our actions, school improvement would become the *status quo*. But personalities, politics, vested interests, and a struggle merely to survive in a demanding and underfunded enterprise must be taken into consideration when we think about a plan for school improvement.

Schools won't improve in substantial and lasting ways unless what happens in classrooms changes. It is for this reason that the focus of this book is on the act of learning, as it takes place in classrooms where teachers, students, and curriculum interact with one another in a variety of learning situations. And it is also for this reason that schools can change only from within. School systems at large can be improved only to the extent that classrooms change, and classrooms can change only when individual school principals and faculties make dedicated and specific plans together. In other words, schools change one at a time; and only as a result of what people *inside* a given school do with their students and with each other. It is for this reason that the main audience for this book is what we will call the "nuclear school family." The principal and faculty are key players in this family, but parents and students are also important members.

How to Start a School Improvement Process

As is always the case with any change initiative, a person or small group becomes interested in something they believe will be good for their school. It is our hope that persons reading this book will fulfill this role. If this happens, the following series of actions are recommended for using the material in this book.

The principal and representatives of groups in the nuclear family should form a steering committee. There are only three guidelines for the steering committee as it embarks on a process for *exploring* the plan presented in this book. (The word exploring is emphasized because consensus must be reached at each step of the process in order for the plan to work.) First, all steering committee members should be provided with information about the Schoolwide Enrichment Model so that they are well informed and can engage in an intelligent discussion and debate about whether or not they are interested in the plan. All steering committee members should have equal rights and opportunities to express their opinions. If a majority decision is reached to recommend the plan to the school community at large, information should be made available to all faculty and parents. Older students (middle grade and above) should also be asked to participate in the discussions.

Second, the steering committee should arrange a series of discussion group meetings that are open to and include members of all subgroups in the school's nuclear family. In setting up the discussion groups, it is important to avoid separate parent groups, teacher groups, and administrator groups. Grouping by role is a classic error that has plagued understanding and communication in the school community, and it is the main contributor to the "Us-And-Them" mentality that pits one group against another. Printed information, key diagrams and charts, and the results of steering committee deliberations should be brought to the attention of the discussion groups. The discussion groups should elect a chairperson and recorder, they should remain intact for the duration of the examination process, and they should set a mutually acceptable schedule of meeting dates and times. The meetings should continue until everyone has had a chance to express his or her opinions, after which a vote should be taken as to whether or not to proceed with the plan. Voting results from each discussion group should be reported to the steering committee, and a report of all the votes should be issued to the nuclear school family. The report should also contain each group's suggestions and concerns. If at least two-thirds of the persons voting express an interest in going ahead with the plan, the steering committee should make arrangements to meet with the superintendent or appropriate central office personnel. Once again, descriptive material about the model should be provided, and the model characterized as a pilot or experimental venture. Assurances should be given that there is no intention to replace any of the programs or initiatives that the district has already adopted. The fastest way to get a polite but firm rejection from the central office is to threaten existing programs or policies to which decision makers already have already made a commitment.[1] It is worth repeating that our goal is to *infuse* exemplary learning and teaching opportunities into the existing school frameworks.

A third guideline is concerned with strategies for overcoming roadblocks that might occur during one of the above stages of the examination process. Any plan for school change is a lightning rod for naysayers, self-proclaimed experts, and people who are reluctant to endorse almost anything involving thinking or doing something differently. The problem is an especially sticky one if these persons occupy positions of authority or informal status in the school

"In setting up...discussion groups, it is important to avoid separate parent groups, teacher groups, and administrator groups. Grouping by role is a classic error that has plagued understanding and communication in the school community, and it is the main contributor to the 'Us-And-Them' mentality that pits one group against another."

[People need to] open their eyes to the only processes that are realistically available for dealing with the long term: the process of real-time learning in groups....These processes direct your attention away from imaginary obstacles such as lack of information, techniques or prescriptions and toward the real obstacles, which have to do with the way power is used and the impact this has on group dynamics and the effectiveness of your organization's political system.

Ralph Stacy, 1992

community, or if they are particularly adept at creating negative energy that is not easily overcome. Such persons, like all others, should have an opportunity to express their opinions in a democratic process. But in order for a majority opinion to be the deciding factor in determining whether or not the model is adopted, it may be necessary to pursue strategies that ensure majority rule.

Putting on Our Thinking Hats

Change strategies based on consensus building must also provide enough guidance to avoid the usual kinds of conflict and frustration frequently present in group decision-making situations. One of the best strategies for examining school change through group discussion and analysis is an easy-to-use plan developed by Edward de Bono (1985). De Bono argues that the main difficulty of thinking about new things and translating intentions into performance is confusion. "We try to do too much at once. Emotions, information, logic, hope and creativity all crowd in on us. It is like juggling with too many balls" (p. 2). De Bono's plan, which is built around a metaphor of six "thinking hats," allows people to conduct an examination of a proposed plan such as SEM in much the same way that a conductor leads an orchestra. Certain kinds of information or emotion are selectively called into play by the conductor, and this approach helps to clarify the rationale for decision making.

A distinct type of thinking is associated with each color hat in de Bono's plan. The white hat represents objective facts and figures; the red hat gives the emotional view; the black hat covers negative aspects; the yellow hat connotes optimism, hope, and positive thinking; the green hat indicates creativity and new ideas; and the blue hat is concerned with organization of the thinking process. De Bono's plan provides a set of "rules" for approaching a problem and numerous suggestions for using the different types of thinking to solve problems. Specific strategies help to focus information, ideas, and emotions. By asking people to change hats, a non-threatening procedure for switching thinking is provided. Thus, for example, a statement such as, "Let's take off our black hats for a moment and examine [this] with our white hats on...," is less threatening or confrontational than asking a person to "stop being so negative." Working on a plan or new idea becomes a process with defined rules rather than a matter of exhortation or condemnation.

Between the idea and the reality,
Between the motion and the Act,
Falls the Shadow.

T. S. Eliot,
"The Hollow Men"

What's in It for Me?

Although everyone has a stake in good schools, it would be naive to assume that already overburdened professionals, or parents who have had a limited impact on school change historically, will make a commitment to a new initiative which requires time, energy, and participation in activities that are a departure from the *status quo*. Each person examining the SEM should ask himself or herself: What's in it for me? What will I have to do? What will I have to give or give up? What will I get out of it? Policy makers and administrators should examine these questions with an eye toward the kinds of public support necessary for adequate, and perhaps even generous financial commitments to public education. The tide of criticism that is constantly being directed toward our schools has taken its toll in the extent to which the public is willing to pay for public education, and it has also resulted in low morale at all levels of the profession. Education is rapidly becoming a profession without an ego because of this criticism. Schools in other nations are constantly being held up to us as mirrors for pointing out our own inadequacies; hardly a month passes without someone writing yet another article or news story about the crisis in educational leadership. It would be nice to think that some magical force will "save us," but the reality is that leadership for better schools can come only from people who are responsible for schools at the local level.

More than any other group, teachers will have to ask themselves these hard questions. Almost every teacher has, or at one time had, an idea about what good teaching is all about. And yet, it is not an exaggeration to say that most teachers are dissatisfied with their work and with the regulations and regimentation imposed on their classrooms. A recent report (McLaughlin & Talbert, 1993) on teachers' response patterns to classroom practices indicated that teachers who adapt to traditional practices "...become cynical, frustrated, and burned out. So do their students, many of whom fail to meet expectations established for the classroom" (p. 6). We still, however, must raise the questions: Are there benefits for teachers who are willing to take on the challenge of variations in traditional practice? Can we avoid the cynicism, frustration, and burnout that seems to be so pervasive in the profession? The SEM is designed to provide opportunities for a better "brand" of teaching through the application of more engaging teaching practices.

But it is important to mention here that we are not asking teachers "to go it alone." This model requires that

**DATELINE:
MINNEAPOLIS, 1993**

Company Seeks to Link Pay to Student Improvement

Minneapolis may be the first public school system to hire a private, for-profit firm to manage the entire district on a long-term basis.

**DATELINE:
HARTFORD, 1993**

Finding Profit in Public Schools

Private industry is seeing there is big money in schools. In most communities, schools spend more money than anything else. Industry is waking up.

Whittle is confident that his concept for new schools will be able to survive even without government assistance, and stay ahead of any potential competitor. "Twenty years from now, there will be three or four major private providers of education," he says. "We will just be the first to get there."

Whittle, in Ellis, 1992

---

administrators provide clear and unequivocal support for specific implementation strategies, and that teachers be involved in all aspects of decision making that relate to their work. Support for a better brand of teaching is also available in the form of a comprehensive instructional materials data base, numerous planning guides, specific strategies for curricular modification, and several other resources that have been developed over the years. This better brand of teaching is the subject of this book, and it is our hope that participation in this kind of teaching will return to the profession some of the creative opportunities, dignity, and other rewards that regimented school structures have minimized in so much of the daily work of teachers.

Finally, parents must examine the above questions with an eye toward the kind of education they want for their sons and daughters. The SEM is not intended to replace the schools' focus on traditional academic achievement, but it does emphasize the development of a broader spectrum of the multiple potentials of young people. Schools do not need to be places to which so many of our young people dread going, but in order to make schools more enjoyable places, parents must have an understanding of and commitment to an education that goes beyond the regimentation and drill that is designed only to "get the scores up." Schools are places for developing the broadest and richest experiences imaginable for young people.

> *"Schools do not need to be places to which so many of our young people dread going....Schools are places for developing the broadest and richest experiences imaginable for young people."*

How to Use This Book

This book can be used for two purposes by educators and parents at local, state, and national levels. First, the material can be used as the focal point for a discussion between and among professional groups and parents seeking a vehicle for developing a comprehensive school improvement initiative, or a vehicle that will add higher levels of challenge to already-adopted school improvement strategies. In this regard, the plan might be considered a proposal that can be brought forward to the several constituencies that must reach consensus before any real and lasting changes can take place in a school or district. When this plan is used as a proposal to school boards, to funding agencies, or to garner general faculty support, users of the book are encouraged to recommend modifications that will accommodate existing resources, current commitments to already-adopted school improvement plans, and the sum total of present school, faculty, and community strengths.

A second purpose of this book is to provide schools, districts, and agencies that adopt the plan with a rationale, overview, and public awareness piece that can serve as starting points for examining the large number of resources that are currently available for implementing the Schoolwide Enrichment Model. This book is designed to capture people's interest by providing a comprehensive picture of the SEM in a relatively small number of pages. The large number of existing resources available for implementing the model can be found in companion books and materials referenced throughout the text and listed in the Resource Guides at the end of Chapters 5, 6, 7, and 8. In this regard, the book might be viewed as a management plan for using the several already-existing planning guides, instruments, curriculum modification procedures, enrichment materials, and teacher training activities that we have developed, adapted, or adopted over the years. The material that follows is divided into the following seven chapters:

- Chapter 2 provides background information about the model and a rationale for this approach to general school improvement.
- Chapter 3 presents the five major goals of schoolwide enrichment and a rationale for why these goals have been selected as the central themes of the model.
- Chapter 4 presents an overview of the model, descriptions of the school structures targeted by the plan, and brief descriptions of the organizational and service delivery components.
- Chapters 5, 6, and 7 describe in greater detail the service delivery components which consist of: The Total Talent Portfolio, Curriculum Modification Techniques, and Enrichment Learning and Teaching.
- Chapter 8 describes the following seven organizational components: the Schoolwide Enrichment Team; the Professional Staff Development Model; Curricular Materials and Resource; the Schoolwide Enrichment Teaching Specialist; the SEM Network; Parent Orientation, Training, and Involvement; and a Democratic School Management Plan.

Preparing a book that attempts to present both a rationale and a plan causes certain kinds of logistical problems. We wanted to keep the book short enough so that its size would not prevent it from being read! At the same time, we wanted

Changing the Frame of Reference

The most daunting task facing [organizations] today lies at a far deeper and more disturbing level than the obvious one of coping with turbulent change. Most [organizations], preoccupied with stability and obvious forms of control, are not taking sufficient account...of the dynamics of success. The real challenge, therefore, is to develop a more appropriate frame of reference...to understand creative actions. It is the mental models that we employ, not some bag of tools or techniques, that determine our ability to deal with the unknowable. This book is, therefore, concerned with mental models–with different ways of thinking....Robust mental models [enable us] to devise prescriptions as we go along.

Ralph Stacy, 1992

the reader to know that there is a large amount of very specific implementation information in companion books and manuals already written about the Schoolwide Enrichment Model. Because some of the early versions of this model gained their initial acceptance in programs that serve high ability students, the companion volumes to which we will refer may use terminology related to special populations and programs that serve high ability youth. In a later chapter, we will point out why and how the present model evolved from its early beginnings in special programs to a vehicle for total school improvement.

Crossing Over the Bridge

"But this bridge will only take you half way there— The last few steps you'll have to take alone."

Shel Silverstein, 1981

Books about educational change are cascading off the press at an unprecedented rate. Some of these books dwell on all that is wrong with our schools; others tell us how we can make schools better. Still others focus on the change process independently of a specified plan or model to improve schools. Almost all of these books build their arguments around a need to achieve greater excellence or greater equity in education. Although obligatory comments are devoted to the importance of achieving both excellence and equity, it is a rare case indeed when preference is not shown for one side of the issue or the other. These mixed messages have resulted in battle lines being drawn between representatives of the greater education community. Books and articles that deal with a need to challenge our most able students are greeted with cries of elitism and of insensitivity to frightful conditions that exist in many schools that serve at-risk populations. And material that focuses on equity issues gets a bad rap from people who believe that school programs are being watered down to less-than-mediocrity quality. We do not view these debates as unproductive, because even admittedly biased points of view promote dialogue that will focus the issues, keep schools in the forefront of national concerns, and help us to search for solutions that will embrace concerns about *both* excellence and equity.

Encompassing all that has been included in this book and related companion volumes is a twofold mission that we hope the reader will embrace. The first part of this mission is to present a feasible change process within the context of a concrete and creditable model for program improvement. In other words, we have tried to present both what we want a school to do and how we should go about doing it. The second part of our mission is to address, head on, both the excellence and equity issues. This is a difficult, but not impossible, task. Our experiences in many schools that have used our work have shown that people of good will and dedication to a common cause can make school a better place for all who enter.

But we also realize that this or any other book, by itself, can't do anything! People make changes, and the advice that Shel Silverstein gives in the poem below, is meant to point out that *you* have an important role to play in school improvement. If you believe there is value in the plan presented here, any payoff so far as school improvement is concerned will depend on the steps that you and your colleagues take to put the plan into action in ways that capitalize on your own energy, commitment, creativity, leadership skills, and use of local resources.

"But we also realize that this or any other book, by itself, can't do anything! People make changes, and the advice that Shel Silverstein gives in the poem, 'This Bridge,' is meant to point out that you have an important role to play in school improvement."

This Bridge
**This bridge will only take you halfway there
To those mysterious lands you long to see:
Through Gypsy camps and swirling Arab fairs
And moonlit woods where unicorns run free.
So come and walk awhile with me and share
The twisting trails and wondrous worlds I've known.
But this bridge will only take you halfway there—
The last few steps you'll have to take alone.**

Shel Silverstein
A Light in the Attic

---

[1] A later section will discuss the "gentle and evolutionary" approach to change recommended in this model.

Chapter 2

Rationale Underlying the Schoolwide Enrichment Model

The Secret Laboratory of School Improvement

IN MANY RESPECTS, SPECIAL programs of almost any type have been the true laboratories of our nation's schools because they have presented ideal opportunities for testing new ideas and experimenting with potential solutions to long-standing educational problems. Programs for high potential students have been an especially fertile place for experimentation because such programs are usually not encumbered by prescribed curriculum guides or traditional methods of instruction. It was within the context of these programs that the thinking skills movement first took hold in American education, and the pioneering work of notable theorists such as Benjamin Bloom, Howard Gardner, and Robert J. Sternberg first gained the attention of the education community. Other developments that had their origins in special programs are currently being examined for general practice. These developments include: a focus on concept rather than skill learning, the use of interdisciplinary curriculum and theme-based studies, the use of student portfolios, performance assessment, cross-grade grouping, alternative scheduling patterns, and, perhaps most important, opportunities for students to exchange traditional

If we always do what we've always done, we will always get where we've always got.

Adam Urbanski

Instead of embracing structural change that may or may not enhance student learning, schools should look behind classroom doors and determine factors that contribute to the kinds of interactions between students and teachers that promote student achievement.

Heckman, in Rothman, 1990

roles as lesson-learners and doers-of-exercises for more challenging and demanding roles that require hands-on learning, first-hand investigation, and the *application* of knowledge and thinking skills to complex problems.

Research opportunities in a variety of special programs allowed us to develop a model (Renzulli, 1977a; Renzulli & Reis, 1985) that emphasizes the need (1) to provide a broad range of advanced-level enrichment experiences for *all* students, and (2) to use the many and varied ways that students respond to these experiences as stepping stones for relevant follow-up on the parts of individuals or small groups. This approach, called performance-based identification, is not viewed as a new way of identifying who is or is not "gifted!" Rather, the process simply identifies how subsequent *opportunities, resources, and encouragement* can be provided to support continuing escalations of student involvement in both required and self-selected activities. This approach to the development of high levels of multiple potentials in young people is purposefully designed to sidestep the traditional practice of labeling some students "gifted" (and by implication, relegating all others to the category of "not-gifted"). The term "gifted" is used in our lexicon only as an adjective, and even then, it is used in a developmental perspective. Thus, for example, we speak and write about *the development of gifted behaviors* in specific areas of learning and human expression rather than giftedness as a state of being. This orientation has afforded many students opportunities to develop high levels of creative and productive accomplishments that otherwise would have been denied through traditional special program models. Over the years, a remarkable number of student products have been developed in schools with widely varying demographic characteristics and at all age and grade levels.

There is both good news and bad news about having the origins of this work in programs for high ability students. The good news is that the amount of academic freedom usually associated with gifted programs[1] allowed us to have *carte blanche* in experimenting with the model. In spite of state guidelines that rigidly restricted special program services to a small percentage of high scoring students, once we got our foot in the door and began accruing many favorable results, opportunities to expand services to a broader range of the student population were made available to us. These expansions were sometimes carried out with permission from regulating officials who allowed us to implement the model under special experimental clauses in state guidelines. The bad news about the gifted education roots of the SEM is that even though the model has emphasized providing enrichment services for *all* students, it is still viewed by some as a gifted program model. Because of these perceptions, many students who can profit from a broad range of enrichment services have been excluded from the kinds of learning experiences recommended by the model.

Assumptions Underlying the Schoolwide Enrichment Model

WHILE EDUCATORS scramble to find ways to improve their schools, a quiet plan for school change that began in the late 1970s has emerged into a very successful model for school improvement. It was at this time that many of the strategies for challenging our most able learners were engineered into a plan called the Schoolwide Enrichment Model. The model is practical and realistic, and it takes as its point of departure an honest appraisal of the ways most schools exist and operate. The discourse of the model is not on radical reform or long lists of worthwhile school objectives, however desirable such objectives might be. Rather, the focus is on specific and attainable ways in which school improvement can be achieved through a gentle and evolutionary, but realistic, approach to change.

Although this model had its roots in programs for high achieving students, several research studies and field tests in schools with widely varying demographics resulted in modifications and adaptations that have made the model effective as a general school improvement plan. The several years of research and development also resulted in an accumulation of know-how that provides practical tactics and techniques for putting this plan into action.

Many ideas and proposals are being put forth for school improvement, so it might be worthwhile to point out how the Schoolwide Enrichment Model differs from the multiplicity of approaches being recommended by persons interested in school reform. Although each reform proposal has its own intentions and merits, consideration of three crucial points is not being emphasized in many of the current reform initiatives. The three crucial points are the focus of the Schoolwide Enrichment Model and include: (1) the central role of learning, (2) the issue of time, and (3) a gentle and evolutionary approach to the process of school improvement.

Remediation in Business

THEN:

Amount spent annually by U.S. businesses on basic literacy skills training for employees, early 1980s: **Millions of dollars.**

NOW:

Amount spent annually by U.S. businesses on basic literacy skills training for employees, late 1980s: **$240 million to $260 million.**

Sources: Testimony in public hearings, National Commission on Excellence in Education, Denver, September 16, 1982; *Workplace Basics: The Skills Employers Want,* American Society for Training and Development, 1988.

The Central Role of Learning

Improving schools must begin by placing the *act of learning* at the center of the change process. Organizational and administrative structures such as site-based management, school choice, ungraded classes, parent involvement, and extended school days are important considerations, but they do not address *directly* the crucial question of how we can improve the act of learning. *An act of learning takes place when three major components interact with one another in such a way as to produce the intellectual or artistic equivalent of spontaneous combustion.* These three components are a learner, a teacher, and the material to be learned (i.e., curriculum). A figural representation of an act of learning is shown in Figure 1.

Each of these three major components of an act of learning has its own important subcomponents. Thus, for example, when considering the learner, we must look at his or her abilities and present achievement level in a particular area of study, the learner's interest in the topic and ways in which we can enhance his or her present interests or develop new interests, and the preferred styles of learning that will improve the learner's motivation to pursue the material being studied. Similarly, we must consider the teacher's role in learning by examining his or her knowledge of the discipline, instructional techniques, and the extent to which the teacher has developed a "romance" with the material being taught. Finally, the curriculum must be examined in terms of the structure of the discipline, the content and methodology of the discipline, and the extent to which the material appeals to the imagination of students. The intersecting circles in Figure 1 are intended to emphasize the *dynamic interactions* rather than linear relations between and among the components. This representation of the act of learning does not assume equity among all components and subcomponents. The circles undoubtedly vary in size from one learning situation to another, and variations exist even within a single learning situation. But the theory that is summarized in this diagram (Renzulli, 1992) does argue that all acts of learning can be optimized by organizing experiences that result in interaction among the several parts of this conception of the learning process.

The Structured to Unstructured Continuum

All learning and teaching exists along a continuum ranging from highly structured situations to situations that are totally unstructured. The structured end of the continuum consists

Inspiration, hunger; these are the qualities that drive good schools. The best we educational planners can do is to create the most likely conditions for them to flourish, and then get out of the [teachers' and students'] way.

Theodore Sizer, 1984

of prescribed material based largely on the use of predetermined textbooks and didactic teaching methods. Structured learning is almost always geared toward carefully-specified student outcomes that are usually expressed in terms of content mastery. Although attention has been given in recent years to process outcomes such as thinking skills, structured models of learning continue to be the predominant method of instruction used in most classrooms. Pressures placed upon schools and teachers to "get the scores up," and

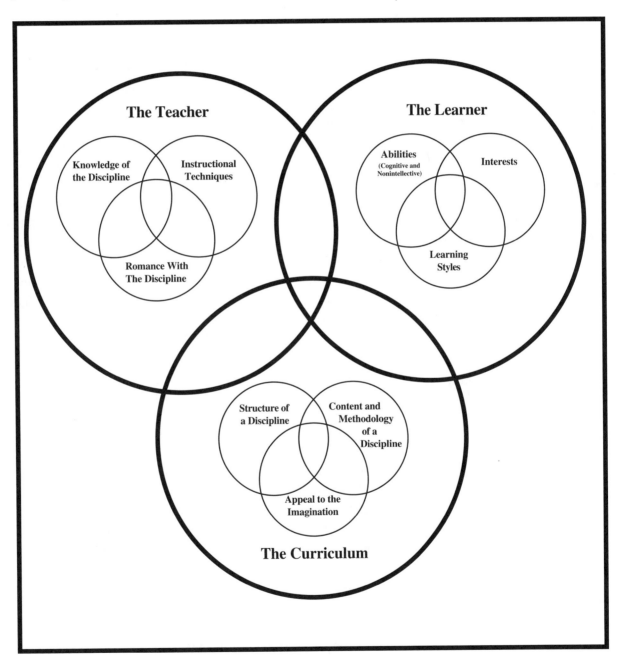

Figure 1. Figural representation of the act of learning.

Chapter 2

test score comparisons between and among schools, districts, and states have increased the use of mastery and outcome based models. These pressures have resulted in squeezing the less structured learning activities out of the curriculum. Although we are not arguing against the value of a certain amount of structured learning, we believe that schools dominated by such approaches have become mechanistic, dreary places that have lost sight of innumerable opportunities to make schools and classrooms inviting places that students *want* to attend, places that have at least some of the excitement and challenge typically found in club programs, self-selected extracurricular activities, or "on the street." We need not look far to find evidence supporting this assertion. In spite of the billions of dollars that have been spent on highly structured compensatory education programs designed to improve the achievement of at-risk students, test scores have shown negligible gains, dropout rates in our inner cities continue to climb, SAT scores are at their lowest levels in decades, and international comparisons place the achievement of U.S. students at or near the bottom of most of the industrialized nations (Applebee, Langer, & Mullis, 1988; Educational Testing Service, 1991; Singal, 1991; Stevenson, Chen, & Lee, 1993; Stevenson, Lee, & Stigler, 1986). It is almost ironic that many of the proposed solutions to these problems are based on increasing the structure and rigidity of the learning models that gave rise to the problems in the first place. What is equally ironic is that the multiplicity of state-level policies designed to improve the education of low achieving students, policies that emphasize standardization, compulsion and regulation, have also forced a more structured curriculum on even our most high achieving schools.

One of the alternatives to an over-regulated, structured curriculum is a method of schooling that we call *enrichment learning and teaching*. This perspective about learning evolved after several years of studying the three factors depicted in Figure 1 and consideration of practical factors such as school organization and management. Our knowledge about these factors, and, therefore, how learning occurs, has increased substantially over the past several decades. We also now know that the role of the learner is central to effective growth, both in terms of achievement and the motivation to put forth one's greatest effort. We know that all learning improves when schools are perceived as being enjoyable, relevant, friendly places where students have some role in at least part of the process of deciding what they will learn and how they will pursue topics in which they may have a special interest. We know that teachers can create effective learning environments by balancing structured teaching with less structured experiences that are more personalized because they use student interests and learning styles as points of departure for classroom activities. We know that motivation and the enjoyment of learning increase when at least some of the prescribed curriculum is replaced with self-selected, open-ended real-world problems that allow students to assume roles as first-hand investigators. We know that cooperativeness and mutual respect among students increases when teacher- and textbook-dominated activities are replaced with group investigation models of learning. We also know that alternatives to traditional classroom organization and management procedures can produce remarkable results in academic, personal, and social development—alternatives such as cross-grade grouping, interest and common-task grouping, and specially designated time blocks during which the *highest* premium is placed on talent development and creative productivity. Finally, we know there are many alternatives to the traditional testing and grading procedures which have dominated school life and served as *de facto* curriculum decision makers. These alternatives include authentic assessment techniques such as product evaluation and feedback procedures, post-learning analysis sessions, portfolio review and analysis, and portfolio "engineering" (i.e., taking specific steps to guarantee that student products are carried forward to subsequent teachers, college admission officers, and prospective employers).

These things that we know about learning are part of the rationale for enrichment learning and teaching, which is, in turn, the core of the Schoolwide Enrichment Model. The essence of this approach to learning is that it follows the ways in which learning takes place in the natural (i.e., non-school) environment. In almost all fields except pedagogy, scientists look to nature for the solutions to complex problems. *Learning is a natural phenomenon,* and thus, the concept of enrichment learning and teaching is based on organized common sense about how people learn naturally. If we assembled any group of persons with a common problem to solve, whether they be young people or adults, they would instinctively fall into a *modus operandi* of problem solving that approximates enrichment learning and teaching. We have engineered much of what is known about this type of learning into the Schoolwide Enrichment Model in order to emphasize the

Regardless of subject, students reported that they liked to do activities that involved them actively or in which they worked with others. These included going on field trips, making films, building or drawing things, making collections, interviewing people, acting things out, and carrying out projects.

John Goodlad, 1984

makeup, dimensions, and purpose of enrichment learning and teaching, and to give direction to implementation considerations such as teacher training, resource needs, and organizational structures. The natural and common sense orientation of this approach to learning makes it especially easy for teachers to use in a variety of school situations.

Two Dimensions of the Issue of Time
Students' Time

Although it would be interesting to speculate about why schools have changed so little over the centuries, at least part of the reason has been our unwillingness to examine critically the issue of time. At some point in history, between the time when Socrates met with young people in the marketplace in Athens and the advent of formal schools, the complexities of educating large numbers of students gave rise to a formal organizational pattern that has come to be known as "the schedule." The arrival of textbooks, with their ramifications for "coverage," and, eventually, state regulations requiring prescribed amounts of time for various subjects further locked the school day and week into a formula for orderliness that has remained virtually unchanged since the turn of the century. If the ways in which we currently use school time were producing remarkably positive or even adequate results, there might be an argument for maintaining the traditional schedule. But such is not the case.

Although it is acknowledged that schools without schedules would probably be chaotic, the almost universal pattern of school organization that has emerged over the years has contributed to our inability to make even the smallest changes in the overall process of learning. This universal pattern is well known to educators and lay persons alike. The "major" subject matter areas (Reading, Mathematics, Language Arts, and Social Studies) are taught on a regular basis, five days per week. Other subjects (sometimes called "the specials") such as Science,[2] Music, Art, and Physical Education are taught generally once or twice a week. So accustomed have we become to the rigidity of this schedule that even the slightest hint about possible variations is met with a storm of protest from administrators and teachers. "We don't have time *now* to cover the regular curriculum." "How will we fit in the specials?" "They keep adding new things [Drug Education, Sex Education, etc.] for us to cover." Our uncontested acceptance of the elementary and secondary school schedule causes us to lose sight of the fact that at the

---

The school schedule is a series of units of time; the clock is king. The base time block is about 50 minutes in length. Some schools, on what they call modular scheduling, split that fifty minute block into two or even three pieces....The flow of all school activity arises from or is blocked by these time units.

Theodore Sizer, 1984

---

college level, where material is ordinarily more advanced and demanding, we routinely drop from a five-meeting-per-week schedule to a three-day- (and sometimes even two-day) -per-week schedule of class meetings. And our adherence to the more-time-is-better argument fails to take into account research that shows quite the opposite. For example, international comparison studies report that 8 of the 11 nations that surpass U.S. achievement levels in mathematics spend less time on math instruction than do American schools (Jaeger, 1992).

Some of the current reform proposals have indeed recommended changes in the schedule, but most of these proposals suggest extending the school day and year. These recommendations ignore the fact that extending school time *without primary attention to the quality of learning* will only increase the number of students who are bored to the point of refusing to learn what they already perceive to be irrelevant material taught by pedantic methods, methods that place primary emphasis on the needless repetition of vast amounts of material already covered. Numerous commentaries on textbooks have summarized large numbers of research studies about the repetitiveness of a widely acknowledged, "dumbed down" curriculum in our schools. It is this research that has given rise to procedures in the Schoolwide Enrichment Model about specific ways for making modest alterations in the school schedule. The purpose of these alternative options for scheduling is to guarantee that some time will be available in each school week during which enrichment learning and teaching will take place. It is further argued that participation in these types of learning situations will provide teachers with experiences that are more valuable to their overall professional development than the thousands of hours they typically spend in traditional educational workshops. Our experience has shown that a small amount of time devoted to learning situations that focus on non-structured enrichment learning and teaching, and small amounts of time devoted to analyzing the circumstances and impact of these situations, has a spill-over effect on all teaching contingencies.

Teachers' Time

There is a second dimension of time that plays an extremely consequential role in school improvement. This dimension is the amount of time that teachers have to work collaboratively with one another. Studies dealing with school improvement have revealed that the ways in which teacher

The American high school is an enduring institution. For three-quarters of a century, a period characterized by immense social, political, economic, and technological change, the high school has not changed its basic form of organization. Whether observed in 1920 or 1980, whether in an inner city school in Boston or a small country high school in the West, a common pattern characterized our high schools.

The school day is usually divided into seven periods, plus a homeroom and lunch period. Classes average approximately 45 minutes, whether the subject is English literature or auto mechanics....Lecture, questions and answers, and homework dominate instruction.

Joseph Carroll, 1989

Chapter 2

Creative Strategies for Finding Teachers' Time

Mohegan Elementary School in the Bronx:

Teachers piloting a new curriculum are scheduled for the same daily lunch period and a common preparation period thereafter.

Gardendale Elementary Magnet School, Merritt Island, Florida:

Teachers have adopted a year-round calendar, with three-week intercessions between quarters. The intercessions permit concentrated, two-or-three-day meetings for teacher planning.

In Rhode Island:

A superintendent lengthened the school day by 20 minutes for four days in order to dismiss students at noon on the fifth. He made Wednesdays teacher meeting days and persuaded local churches to hold their religious education meetings on Wednesday afternoons, and scouts and other youth activities then.

Mary Anne Raywid, 1993

time is utilized are more important than equipment, facilities or staff development, and that "successful schools are distinguishable from unsuccessful ones by the frequency and extent to which teachers discuss practice, collaboratively design materials, and inform and critique one another" (Raywid, 1993, p. 30). Fullan and Miles (1992) report that the ways in which teacher time is used is the *major* issue in every study of school improvement that has appeared during the last decade. International studies by Stigler and Stevenson (1991) report that in highly effective Asian schools, teachers spend 30 to 40 percent of their school hours in activities other than teaching.

In a study dealing with how schools are finding the time for teachers to work collaboratively, Raywid (1993) describes fifteen examples of specific methods through which time can be made available. These examples fall into three general categories: taking time from that which is now scheduled for instruction or staff development; adding time to the school day and/or year; and altering staff utilization patterns. The fifteen examples that Raywid provides are both creative and feasible. For example, a school district in New York reallocated time from staff development days in such a way that two-hour collaborative sessions for teachers were made available every two weeks throughout the school year. Some schools used time gained when students were involved in community internship activities; and others trimmed some instructional time in exchange for voluntary contributions of equal amounts of teachers' time. "According to the superintendent of New York City's alternative high schools, the secret to finding collaborative time during the school day lies in 'creative interpretation' of state requirements for instruction. He discovered that the time requirements could be met in four, rather than five, classes per week, permitting the blocking of 'specials' on the fifth day....This configuration frees other teachers for regular, extended collaborative sessions" (Raywid, 1993, p. 32).

The challenge of reallocating even small proportions of teachers' time is fraught with bureaucratic regulations, collective bargaining issues, and the willingness of teachers to make adjustments in what has become a very standardized way of viewing their work. It is clear that everyone will have to "give a little" and to compromise on vested interests in order for collaborative time for teachers to be made available. Present day school schedules and work rules were not divinely inspired; therefore, they should be open to the kinds of examination that allow both imagination and experimentation to be brought to bear on the process of modifying them. Information related to restructuring the way schools use time is included in the Resource Guide in Chapter 8.

A Gentle and Evolutionary Approach To School Improvement

The change process recommended in this model begins with an examination of the major factors affecting the quality of learning in a school (see Figure 2). These factors exist along a continuum of internal (to the school) to external, and each factor is interdependent with the others. Thus, for example, an internal factor such as the building principal may be externally influenced if the principal is assigned by central administration; and an external factor such as a state regulation may be internally influenced by the ways in which it is interpreted (or possibly ignored) by teachers and administrators. All of these factors have three salient characteristics. First, they are always present, and regardless of micro or macro change initiatives, they always will be present! Second, each factor exists along a continuum of negative to positive influence on the quality of learning that takes place within a given school. Third, each factor is almost always going through a process of change, for better or worse.

Our goal in the Schoolwide Enrichment Model is not to replace these essential factors, but, rather, to apply the strategies and services that define the model to the various factors that represent the "givens" of school life. We do not aspire to the wholesale elimination of textbooks, standardized tests, or recently adopted initiatives such as heterogeneous grouping or outcome based educational models. We do, however, recommend specific strategies for modifying and adapting the factors in Figure 2 in ways that will help to accommodate individual students' interests, abilities and learning styles. Thus, for example, an SEM component called curriculum compacting provides a research-proven method for modifying the regular curriculum for students who have already mastered prescribed outcomes. A related part of the method provides the teachers of these students with a systematic procedure for substituting material that is more challenging and personally meaningful to the students. Similarly, a three-phase staff development model described in Chapter 8 is designed to overcome the relatively low yield in school improvement that has resulted from the traditional workshop approach to teacher training. We view this process

Creative Strategies for Finding Teachers' Time (continued)

Kentucky:

The State Board of Education sought legislative permission to convert five of the required instructional days into staff development time.

Central Park East Secondary School, Manhattan:

One morning each week, the lower division students engage in community service. Teachers meet together until noon.

Mary Anne Raywid, 1993

as an *infusion approach* to systemic school improvement, and the main targets of the change process are those factors that have a direct bearing on the process of learning.

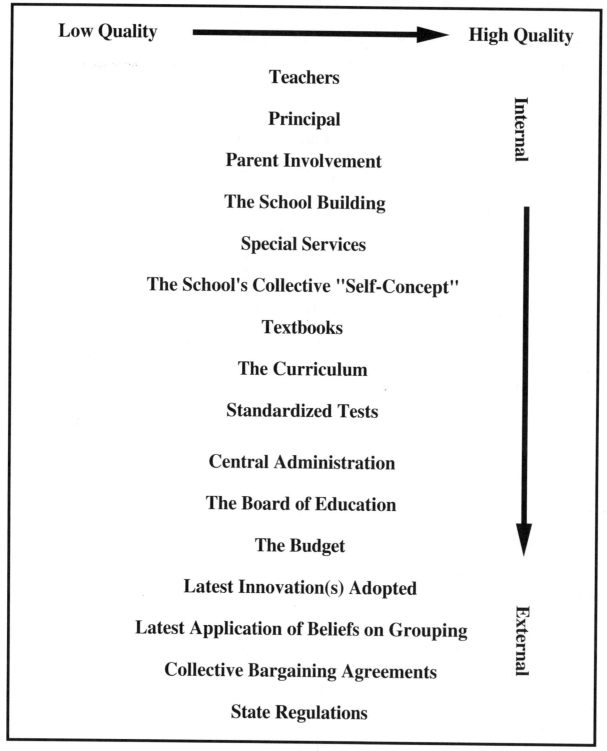

Low Quality ➜ **High Quality**

Teachers

Principal

Parent Involvement

The School Building

Special Services

The School's Collective "Self-Concept"

Textbooks

The Curriculum

Standardized Tests

Central Administration

The Board of Education

The Budget

Latest Innovation(s) Adopted

Latest Application of Beliefs on Grouping

Collective Bargaining Agreements

State Regulations

Internal

External

Figure 2. Factors affecting the quality of learning.

Some of the factors listed in Figure 2 are more powerful than others in determining the quality of learning that takes place in a school. Standardized tests, for example, have become the "elephant in the room" so far as initiatives on school reform are concerned. Standardized testing may always be a dominant influence in schooling; however, emerging procedures such as performance-based assessment and practices that we will recommend regarding *how* standardized tests can be used to improve curriculum and instruction are examples of the ways in which the SEM can influence factors as powerful as state and local testing policies.

A Realistic Approach to School Improvement

Schools are being bombarded with proposals for change. These proposals range from total, systemic reform to tinkering with bits and pieces of specific subjects and teaching methods. Oftentimes the proposals are little more than lists of intended goals or outcomes, but limited direction is provided about *how* these outcomes can be achieved; even less information is provided about the effectiveness of recommended practices in a broad range of field test sites. Worse are the mixed messages that policy makers and regulators are beaming at schools at an unprecedented rate, messages that are often incompatible with one another. One state, for example, mandated a core curriculum for students, but then evaluated teachers on the basis of generic teaching skills that had nothing to do with the curriculum. Schools are encouraged to raise their standards, and advocates of site-based management encourage teachers to become more active in curriculum development. But these same schools are rated on the basis of test scores tied to lists of state specified, outcome-based competencies. A recent study (Madaus, West, Harmon, Lomax, & Viator, 1992) reported that the most widely used tests measure low level skills and knowledge rather than problem-solving activities, and that teachers are under pressure to emphasize low level material because it will enhance test scores. The study also reported that teachers and administrators believed the tests forced them to compromise their ideals about good teaching. Schools spend approximately half a billion dollars annually on standardized testing (Paris, Lawton, Turner, & Roth, 1991), and approximately 100 hours of class time are spent practicing for and taking tests (Smith, 1991). The demands placed on schools for increased testing also increase the likelihood that schools will continue to offer a curriculum that prepares

High Ability Secondary Students' Perceptions of the Degree of Challenge in Their Educational Programs

Students who find their school:

Very Challenging......19%
Somewhat or Not
  Very Challenging...79%
Not at All
  Challenging.............2%

Who's Who Among American High School Students, *1991*

students for nonexistent "factory work" rather than one that prepares students for the modern, complex, and rapidly changing technological world (McCaslin & Good, 1992).

It would be easy to jump on the restructuring bandwagon with yet another grand design or string of rhetoric for radical and revolutionary school reform: "Throw out all the textbooks!" "Replace or retrain all the teachers." "Let the parents select the building principal." "Set world class standards and develop curriculum frameworks." "Replace the existing curriculum with interdisciplinary, multicultural, theme-based units." "Bring technology into the schools and form school/business partnerships." "Build magnet schools to achieve racial balance." All these things make for exhilarating speeches, but the realities of school life, coupled with an already overburdened system of regulations, inadequate funding, vested interest groups, and recent commitments to new initiatives would inevitably lead to more of the fragmentation and chaos discussed above. It is easy to "talk a good game" about school improvement, and on rare occasions we throw uncommonly large amounts of money at staff development, curricular revision, or projects that promise to start yet another showcase school. We have been doing these things for years, but in the overwhelming majority of America's classrooms *nothing changes*. Little wonder that a recent review of research from the Center on Organization and Restructuring of Schools (Prager, 1992) indicated that current school restructuring recommendations are not being widely adopted. When researchers asked educators how they would evaluate educational reforms, they said, "There's nothing but chaos. Our best strategy is to ignore them and close our doors and go about our business" (Palaich, in Olson, 1992).

In spite of this gloomy scenario, we believe that school improvement can be initiated and strengthened through gentle and evolutionary strategies for change. These strategies must first and foremost concentrate on the act of learning as represented by the interactions that take place between and among learners, teachers, and the curriculum. In the early stages of the change process, these strategies should make minimal but specific suggestions for change in existing schedules, textbook usage, and curricular conventions. And these strategies should be based on practices that have already showed demonstrated results in places where they have been used for reasonable periods of time. We also believe that the individual school building is the unit of change for addressing

"Schools spend approximately half a billion dollars annually on standardized testing, and approximately 100 hours of class time are spent practicing for and taking tests."

school improvement, and that effective and lasting change can occur only when it is initiated, nurtured, and monitored from within the school itself. Outside-of-school regulations and remedies have seldom changed the daily behaviors of students and teachers or dealt effectively with solutions to inside-of-school problems (Barth, 1990). A simple but sincere waiver of top-down regulations, a plan that involves consensus and shared decision making on the parts of administrators, parents, students, and teachers, and incentives for specific contributions to the change process are the starting points and the only "big decisions" policy makers need to make in order to initiate a gentle and evolutionary school improvement process. Details regarding the specific procedures for change recommended in this model are described in Chapter 3 (see Goal 5) and Chapter 8.

The Role of a Model in Systemic School Improvement

A model is an interrelated set of ideas and practices that are directed toward a common set of goals and outcomes. A model serves three important roles in promoting change in organizations (Paine, Bellamy, & Wilcox, 1984). The first role is to establish functional relationships between a theoretically-defined and research-supported set of intervention procedures and a desired set of practical outcomes. Second, a model should demonstrate that a specified set of procedures can produce results in schools that are ethnically, economically, organizationally, and demographically diverse, and that these results can be attained by persons not associated with the development of the model. If a set of procedures cannot be exported with a fairly high degree of integrity to a desired set of outcomes, then the procedures are idiosyncratic to a particular situation and, therefore, do not qualify as a model. For example, the "model school" approach to widespread educational improvement has met with limited success because factors such as supplementary funding, a hand-picked faculty, media fanfare, and the leadership of a "patron saint" have frequently been the essence of the model, and these factors are usually not exportable to schools that do not have similar resources.

The third role of a model is that it should facilitate communication through "user-friendly" language. Underlying theory and research are necessary foundations for effective models, but adoption and replication are a function of the ✓ clarity of description, the practicality of recommended

Significant educational improvement of schooling, not mere tinkering, requires that we focus on entire schools....If we are to improve [a school], we must understand it. If we are to improve schooling, we must improve individual schools.

John Goodlad, 1984

A program model illustrates that a significant social problem can be solved in a particular way, **and provides a prototype or pattern for replication in other settings where similar services could be provided.**

Stan Paine & Thomas Bellamy, 1982

"[T]he 'model school' approach to widespread educational improvement has met with limited success because factors such as supplementary funding, a hand-picked faculty, media fanfare, and the leadership of a 'patron saint' have frequently been the essence of the model, and these factors are usually not exportable to schools that do not have similar resources."

"In order for a model to be practical, it must establish a harmonious relationship between the structural and theoretical concerns related to the operation of a school."

procedures, the feasibility of gaining broad based support, and the flexibility of the model in accommodating local differences while still maintaining integrity to major goals. Models provide integrity in other important ways that will be considered throughout this book. Consider, for example, the almost random approach that is often used to select speakers for in-service workshops. Even if the speaker is informative, exciting, and entertaining, the time may not be well spent if the topic does not fit into an organized plan that is part of a larger and more harmonious structure. It's like buying drapes without considering the color of the carpet or the walls!

Any discussion of a plan to develop a schoolwide enrichment program must begin with a recognition of the difference between structural and theoretical models. Structural models consist of patterns of organization and procedures for dealing with such issues as: how we group students, develop schedules for the time spent in various activities, deploy school personnel, and arrange for the delivery of services. Theoretical models, on the other hand, consist of principles that guide the instructional process and give direction to the content, thinking processes, and the outcomes of learning experiences that might take place within any given administrative pattern of organization. Theoretical models are mainly influential in determining the *quality* of learning experiences, whereas administrative models are more concerned with the efficiency and smoothness of overall school operation and the ways that learning activities fit into the total school program. In order for a model to be practical, it must establish a harmonious relationship between the structural and theoretical concerns related to the operation of a school. Recommendations for the most exotic kinds of learning activities imaginable will bear no fruit unless a place can be found for such activities in an already-saturated school schedule. Similarly, an organizational change such as cross-grade grouping, for example, will not produce improvements in learning without accompanying modifications in the ways we teach in newly organized structures.

The Need for Both Structure and Flexibility

In order for a model to produce results, it must also straddle the thin line that exists between structure and flexibility. Without structure, the implementation of a model is likely to be a hodgepodge of whatever any individual or group wants it to be. Too much structure, on the other hand, results in a strait jacket that discourages local initiative, creativity and ownership.

Although we believe that schools using the SEM should strive to accomplish all of the goals set forth in this model, we also believe that any plan for program development must allow for a great deal of flexibility in the achievement of its goals. This flexibility is necessary because no written plan or set of procedures can take into account the many variations that exist at the local school level. Differences in school populations, politics, personnel, variations in financial resources, community support and involvement, and a host of other local variables must be considered in the implementation of this or any other approach to school improvement. A model that does not allow for such flexibility could easily become a facade that simply will not work when one or more of the local considerations is not taken into account. Some schools will have supplementary resource teachers for managing an enrichment program while others will not. Some school districts will have an abundance of community resources readily available, and others, perhaps more geographically isolated, will have limited access to museums, planetariums, colleges and universities, etc. Some schools may serve larger proportions of culturally diverse students than others, and in some places, excessive state regulations may be in effect.

Three steps are necessary for achieving harmony between structure and flexibility. First, a school community (parents, teachers, and administrators) should study the model and reach consensus on the recommended goals and outcomes. Second, through reading, discussion, and other professional development activities, all persons should reach a *common* understanding of the model's components. If, for example, a "real problem" means three different things to three different people, then these people will be working at cross purposes with one another. Third, all persons involved in the delivery of services must be willing and able to build their own specific implementation activities within the context of the model's components and directed toward the agreed-upon goals. If a model does not encourage this type of local building process, chances are another round of canned procedures or activities are being rammed down a school's throat! This third step is the one that unleashes the imagination and energy of dynamic individuals and results in programs that achieve both uniqueness to the local school, and integrity to the goals and components of the model.

The guiding principle being put forward here is that the school must become largely self-directing. The people connected with it must develop a capacity for effecting renewal and establishing mechanisms for doing this.

John Goodlad, 1984

Chapter 2

There is another reason why program development models must maintain a large degree of flexibility. Educators tend quickly to lose interest in "canned" programs and models that do not allow for local initiative, creativity and teacher input. New and better ways to serve students at the local level will be discouraged if our approach to program development does not allow for local adaptation and innovation. This book provides a certain amount of general direction in both the goals and procedures for pursuing these goals. At the same time, however, the specific types of activities that you select and develop for your program, and the ways in which you make these activities available to various populations of students will actually result in the creation of your own programming model. You will, in effect, be developing your own resource guide because the actual content of recommended services will be determined locally by *your* program and school personnel. We believe that so long as the goals are maintained, even if in slightly modified form, your program will achieve the integrity that is sought in the SEM. In this regard, our orientation attempts to achieve the best of two worlds! First, your school will benefit from the theoretical and research developments as well as the many years of field testing and practical application that have led to the advice put forth in this book. Second, the ideas, resources, innovations and adaptations that can grow only out of the local situation become legitimate aspects of your program and the very factors that contribute to its uniqueness and practicality in meeting local needs. Throughout this book we consistently recommend that program developers make whatever procedural modifications and adaptations that are necessary to accomplish program tasks. So long as the integrity of the goals for each type of service delivery component is maintained, we believe that there are many pathways and alternatives to reaching desired outcomes.

In addition to providing a common set of goals toward which to work, and a wide degree of flexibility to pursue these goals, the SEM also provides a common vocabulary through which we can communicate. By putting a "handle" on a small set of key components, everyone in the school speaks the same language and understands how various components fit into the overall framework of the model. In a certain sense, the vocabulary of the model is the glue that holds together the major concepts around which the overall plan is built.

Assets Available for the Implementation of SEM

FOR THE past 15 years, we have been developing, field testing, and carrying out research on the Schoolwide Enrichment Model in numerous schools throughout the United States, Canada, and several nations overseas. For at least four reasons, the model "caught on," and user satisfaction can be documented through evaluation and research studies, commendations by educators using the model, and site visits to places where the model is being used.

Practicality and Existing Know-How

The first reason for the success of SEM is its clarity, practicality, and flexibility. The roles and responsibilities of participating teachers, students, and administrators are easy to learn and are described in ways that avoid complex language or ponderous rhetoric. And although the model is directed toward a small number of common goals, each school is encouraged to develop its own unique program within the framework of general goals, guides, and how-to information. This flexibility has produced numerous examples of local pride and ownership, and it has also generated many practitioner-developed contributions to the model that have been shared locally and nationally. Sharing of this type has expanded dramatically the know-how available to networking users of the model, and it has served as a source of motivation for the professionalism objective described in a later chapter.

In order for a model to "work," it must be based on sound ideas and research, but every idea must be backed up with practical information, strategies, and materials. The following list represents categories of the broad array of service delivery components that we have developed and field tested over the years:

- Print and video staff development materials
- Planning guides and worksheets for each major component of the model
- Instruments for assessing students' strengths, interests, and learning styles
- Procedures for developing schoolwide enrichment teams
- A slide presentation and script for parent orientation
- A taxonomy of specific thinking skills

"In addition to providing a common set of goals toward which to work and a wide degree of flexibility to pursue these goals, the SEM also provides a common vocabulary through which we can communicate....In a certain sense, the vocabulary of the model is the glue that holds together the major concepts around which the overall plan is built."

Why the Soviet Union collapsed:

Nobody believes in action any more, so words have become a substitute, all the way up to the top, a substitute for the truth nobody wants to hear because they can't change it or they'll lose their jobs if they change it, or maybe they simply don't know how to change it.

John leCarre, 1989

- Guidelines for preparing interest development centers
- Procedures for developing a scope and sequence for thinking skills
- A directory of within- and across-discipline enrichment materials
- A directory of "how-to" books for first-hand investigative activities
- Sample letters, memos, and pamphlets for parents, students, and faculty
- Guidelines for developing a faculty/community mentor system
- Procedures for establishing a student "research foundation"
- A set of slides and script to train students in the investigative process
- Planning worksheets and documentation forms
- A community resources survey and classification system
- Easy-to-understand charts, diagrams, and summary sheets that facilitate staff development and student and parent orientation
- Evaluation forms and instruments for each major component of the model
- A residential summer staff development institute for advanced training and the training of trainers
- A national network and directory of school districts using the model
- A directory of practitioner consultants who have extensive experience in using the model
- Technical reports verifying the research base underlying the model.

Underlying Theory and Research

A second reason for the success of SEM has been the practicality of the theory underlying the model and the research that has been carried out over the years to support various aspects of the model. The underlying theory is divided into two dimensions. The first dimension focuses on a broadened conception of human potential and creative productivity (Gardner, 1983; Renzulli, 1977a, 1985); the second dimension concentrates on pedagogical issues that are directly related to improving high level acts of learning.

Most proposed changes in educational systems are implemented because of good intentions and desperate needs for improvement in the *status quo.* We have taken the time over the years to examine the effectiveness of the model in a broad range of school settings (Renzulli & Reis, 1994), and this research has been summarized in Appendix A. We have also compiled numerous examples of program materials and documents that point out a broad variety of implementation activities in districts with widely differing demographic characteristics.

Attractiveness to All Types of Schools

The third reason for the success of SEM has been the quality and commitment of persons who have implemented the model at the local level. For a variety of reasons, the model has attracted energetic teachers and administrators who believe that schools can be more effective and caring places. Many of these persons first became involved with the SEM because of their work in special programs for high ability students. They were initially attracted to our written material and summer training programs at The University of Connecticut because of our concerns for equity as well as excellence in learning and teaching, and because of the flexible and common sense features of the model. We have always advocated serving larger proportions of the school population than those served in traditional programs for the gifted. And as the model evolved toward more specific recommendations and procedures for total school enrichment, most of these people "stuck with us," and even became emissaries for change in their local districts. Whereas our annual summer institute formerly attracted only persons who were employed as teachers of the gifted, the majority of persons in attendance during the past several summers have been general classroom teachers and administrators. We attribute this change in persons wishing to study our model to both the activism of our emissaries and the growing national concern for using the technology of gifted education to improve the quality of schools at large.

"We attribute this change in persons wishing to study our model to both the activism of our emissaries and the growing national concern for using the technology of gifted education to improve the quality of schools at large."

Concern for At-Risk Populations

A final reason for the growing popularity of the Schoolwide Enrichment Model is our concern for providing special enrichment opportunities for students from low socioeconomic backgrounds and for students who show potentials for superior performance in areas that are not easily assessed by traditional ability measures. Low achievement among economically disadvantaged students represents the

> *"Low achievement among economically disadvantaged students represents the single most glaring failure of our educational system."*

> *All that is valuable in society depends upon the opportunity for development accorded the individual.*
>
> *Albert Einstein*

single most glaring failure of our educational system. The lack of results from years of compensatory programs and expenditures of billions of dollars have caused a small but growing number of educators at all levels to realize that we must explore alternatives to traditional remedial models. These models have grossly underestimated the potentials of poor children, and it doesn't take a rocket scientist to conclude that we have been using the wrong approach to improve schooling for at-risk youngsters!

New theories are emerging regarding the underachievement of high ability urban youth. Ogbu (1974, 1985, 1987, 1991) argues that two types of minorities—immigrant and involuntary—enter differentially into the process of schooling. Accordingly, he believes these students' academic achievement is affected differentially. He concludes, "...neither the core curriculum approach nor the multicultural education approach will appreciably improve the schooling performance of some minority groups until they and other school interventions, innovations, and reforms are informed by an understanding of *why* children from specific minority groups are experiencing learning and performance difficulty" (Ogbu, 1992, p. 7).

It is for this reason that we devote a later section in this book (Chapter 8) to parent involvement in the schools. Parents of children who exist at the margins of our society have a key role to play in their children's education.

Opening the School Door to Improvement Through Enrichment

THE GENERAL attitude that many educators and educational reform leaders have toward special programs for the gifted has resulted in barriers toward the broader implementation of any set of ideas with "gifted roots." Overt charges of elitism have been directed toward a field that historically has found its greatest support in school districts that serve the white middle class. Some of these criticisms are not unfounded. Quota requirements for the funding of special programs and identification guidelines that are predominantly based on ability test scores are still in effect in most states, and the conservative branch of the field's leadership continues to argue for restrictions on the number of students identified as the "truly gifted." Conservatives in the field also look with suspicion on identification procedures that are alternatives to IQ scores, and models such as SEM have been viewed with particular scorn by gifted education conservatives because they believe the concept of giftedness has been "watered down." The conservative leadership also has criticized our more flexible approach to identification because *our* advocacy for developing thinking skills in all students is viewed as a usurping of their early "discovery" of the process models. These process models were their stock-in-trade; therefore, our recommendation for a broader-based use is viewed as giving away the family jewels!

All of these forces act against the provision of special enrichment opportunities for students who are from low socioeconomic backgrounds or students who show potentials for superior performance in areas that are not as easily assessed as those areas measured by traditional ability tests. These same forces also limit the opportunities of females in areas such as mathematics, science, and engineering. Compounding the problem is the slow but certain movement toward a test-driven, basic skills curriculum that has gained a strong foothold in many states. This movement, which is primarily directed toward "getting the scores up" on state and national wall charts, is already resulting in cutbacks in library and media programs, arts programs, extracurricular activities, and just about anything else that makes school an enriching and inviting place. Increasing test scores is, indeed, an important national priority, and a goal of the SEM. But thirty years of federal and state support for compensatory education has produced negligible results; yet, the present focus on "outcomes" is predicated on the same didactic model of learning. At-risk students have been the major victims of this "drill-and-kill" approach to learning, an approach that has almost become public policy in the nation's schools. It is the children of the poor who suffer most from declining enrichment opportunities. It is the families of these young people who cannot afford the computer camps, the dance lessons, the well-stocked home bookshelves, the summer on-campus science programs, and the SAT prep courses that the middle class uses to compensate for unchallenging schools.

A model that has its historical roots in gifted education also suffers from the cloud of suspicion that has been cast over the entire field of gifted education. At a recent meeting of the American Educational Research Association, a leading reform advocate said that ..."[reformers of general education] should be doing everything 'the gifted people' are doing!" What was implied, however, was that reformers should steer

"At-risk students have been the major victims of this 'drill-and-kill' approach to learning, an approach that has almost become public policy in the nation's schools. It is the children of the poor who suffer most from declining enrichment opportunities."

We do not see in our descriptors, then, much opportunity for students to become engaged with knowledge so as to employ their full range of intellectual abilities. And one wonders about the meaningfulness of whatever is acquired by students who sit listening or performing relatively repetitive exercises year after year. Part of the brain, known as Magoun's brain, is stimulated by novelty. It appears to me that students spending twelve years in the schools we studied would be unlikely to experience much novelty. Does part of the brain just sleep, then?

John Goodlad, 1984

The last ten years since the publication of A Nation at Risk have been a splendid misery for American education. We have suffered many disappointments. But we have not given up the quest to shape education into the enterprise that it must become if America is to keep its proud place of leadership in the marvelous Information Age of this decade and beyond. Perhaps we should have made more progress than we have. But at least we have stayed with the task.

Terrel H. Bell, 1993

clear of "the gifted people." Thus, this cloud of suspicion has excluded even the most liberal of special educators from the reform conversation, and by so doing, it has minimized opportunities to apply proven strategies for general educational improvement. Had it not been for the opportunities for experimentation and research afforded by programs for high ability students, our earlier work with these students would not have emerged into what we now consider to be a model for general school improvement. Nor would we have been able to learn about the leadership potential and potential for professional contributions by hundreds of persons who are implementing the model. Because SEM came into the schools through the back door of gifted programs, there are certain components of the model that still need to be developed or expanded. But a major part of the enrichment teaching know-how and supporting procedures are already completed.

Because so much of the reform movement currently exists in words rather than in deeds, the reformers themselves are already locked in deadly, albeit rhetorical battles, about school improvement. A recent front page story in *Education Week* (Olson, 1992) began with the headline, "Fed Up With Tinkering, Reformers Tout 'Systemic' Approach to School Redesign." We believe that the SEM is a systemic approach to general school improvement because it is based on a model for learning that cuts across all activities that take place in a school. *If we are serious about improving our schools, we must first consider the creation of an enriched learning environment in which young people want to participate.* The Schoolwide Enrichment Model is purposefully designed to create such an environment by blending the kinds of activities that promote challenge, effort, and enjoyment into the entire curriculum. These types of activities have been used for years in special programs, and they can be applied easily to general education if we can pry open the door of entrenched school curriculum and governance.

[1] By academic freedom I mean that special programs have largely avoided being guided by fixed-level textbooks and curricular guides that typify general education.

[2] It is interesting to note that our national commitment to the improvement of science scores has not elevated courses in science to five-day-per-week status in most elementary and middle schools.

Chapter 3

The Goals of Schoolwide Enrichment

THE SCHOOLWIDE ENRICHMENT MODEL is designed to accomplish five major goals. In this chapter, each goal will be described, and a brief rationale will be presented to point out why the goal is a central rallying point for the services and implementation strategies that are recommended in later parts of this book.

Goal 1

TO DEVELOP *the talent potentials of young people by: (a) systematically assessing strengths, (b) providing enrichment opportunities, resources, and services to develop the strengths of all students, and (c) using a flexible approach to curricular differentiation and the use of school time.*

A Focus on Talent Development

Schools should be enriching places, where the mind, body, spirit, and values of every student are escalated in an atmosphere that is maximally enjoyable, interesting, and challenging. While knowledge acquisition is unquestionably an important goal of education, other goals such as know-how, creativity, self-fulfillment, wisdom, and character should

Treat people as if they were what they ought to be, and you will help them become what they are capable of being.

Goethe

Enthusiasm is the match that lights the candle of achievement.

William Arthur Ward

take their place beside the traditional goals of schooling. Schools should not be places where young people merely learn what is already known. Rather, they should aspire to a higher calling that includes creating a learning environment in which present knowledge is viewed as stepping stones to the creation of new knowledge, to the solutions of unsolved problems, and to invention, artistic production, and examination of ways to improve life on Earth. We need only look to other organized learning situations (both in and out of school) to realize that this objective is both realistic and achievable. But in order to achieve this objective, we must be willing to apply some already available learning strategies that have demonstrated their efficacy in a variety of other learning environments. Programs such as 4-H, Junior Achievement, the Foxfire Program, Future Problem Solving, Invent America, and a broad range of extracurricular activities have consistently demonstrated that when the application of knowledge is coupled with the acquisition of knowledge, school problems are solved, or minimized, at least. Observation of 4-H students at work, or of a school newspaper staff rushing to publish the next edition allow us to see genuine motivation, engagement and involvement, as well as see real cooperativeness, enjoyment, and purpose, and it represents the kinds of authenticity in learning that by and large has eluded so much of traditional schooling. We also note that these activities frequently span age levels, socioeconomic backgrounds, demographics, and ability levels of students.

Goal 1 has been placed first in the Schoolwide Enrichment Model because if we are to make any substantial changes in the way that schools operate, we must first examine the predominance that has always been placed on objectives related to raising achievement test scores. Raising standard achievement is, indeed, important, but we simply have been going about it the wrong way! Repeated failures to improve general school achievement through mastery learning models and achievement-test-driven objectives should have taught us that numerous variations on the same unsuccessful approach to school improvement have not served us well. A long list of reform "movements" such as individually prescribed instruction, management by objectives, minimum competency programs, mastery learning, and outcome-based education have all been based on a limited view of the learner-as-assimilator rather than as a problem finder, problem solver, and creative producer. And the latest bandwagon that focuses on specifying and raising standards is yet another variation on the same model. Researchers have already commented about how the testing movement, designed to assess higher standards, not only narrows curriculum, but also creates conditions that are adverse to reform:

> Coping with the pressure to attain satisfactory results in high-stakes tests caused educators to develop almost a "crisis mentality" in their approach, in that they jumped quickly into "solutions" to address a specific issue. They narrowed the range of instructional strategies from which they selected means to instruct their students; they narrowed the content of the material they chose to present to students; and they narrowed the range of course offerings available to students. (Corbett & Wilson, 1990, p. 207)

No one can argue against the need to raise standards for all our schools, but simply stating such a goal and creating lists of standards does not give us specific guidance for improving the performance of students who are unprepared to deal with the advanced material in courses for which standards have been raised. The inevitable result of movements such as mastery learning, raising standards, and high-stakes testing is yet another set of state regulations and another layer of standardized testing with predictable demographic results. These regulations, like the barnacles on a ship, slow down any chance for real progress, and eventually may even sink the entire enterprise.

In order for a *qualitative* change to take place in our schools, Goal 1 has become the centerpiece of this plan. It is based on a reconceptualized role of the teacher, the curriculum, classroom organization and management, and, most of all, the role of the student. These reconceptualized roles, which are summarized in a later section on enrichment learning and teaching (Chapter 7), are neither new nor abstract. They have occurred in learning situations throughout history, in classrooms and non-school learning situations, in extracurricular activities, and in apprenticeships and on-the-job training experiences. We have seen increases in these changing roles of teachers and students as a direct result of applying SEM to a variety of school situations; and our know-how in this regard represents the strength that this model can bring to a proposal for school change. A goal that focuses on developing talent potentials is not a revelation in education, but it has never been an affirmation of any consequence

The first requisite for school reform is the school as a unit, with its approved curriculum based on its own needs and evolved by its own staff. If we fail to secure that, we simply fall from one formalism into another, from one dung-hill of inert ideas into another.

Alfred North Whitehead, 1929

because of the supremacy of the traditional achievement goal. By making this objective the centerpiece of SEM, we hope to emphasize that what has occurred in the past—a series of scattered, random, and infrequent examples of enriched learning—can indeed exist as the standard operating procedure for the majority of schools that make a commitment to this plan.

Goal 2

*T*O IMPROVE *the academic performance of all students in all areas of the regular curriculum and to blend into the standard curriculum activities that will engage students in meaningful and enjoyable learning.*

Indicators and Reasons for Declining Academic Performance

The most obvious problem facing our schools, and the one that has received the most attention is poor academic performance, especially the performance of disadvantaged students. Although recent studies have shown slow but steady gains on standardized test scores for disadvantaged students, the scores for this population are still well below desirable levels, and high school and college graduation rates have shown little or no increase over the past several decades. Improving the performance of disadvantaged students continues to be the single most important challenge facing our schools, but there is also another crisis in American education that needs to be addressed. This quiet, but nevertheless alarming, crisis is that in spite of achievement gains on the parts of disadvantaged students, the *overall* test scores for the nation at large have declined since their historic highs in the 1960s. The reason for this overall decline is that the performance of populations that traditionally have scored at higher levels has gone down (Singal, 1991). According to Herman Rudman, an author of the Stanford Achievement Test, the highest group of achievers has shown the greatest decline across a variety of subjects as well as across age level groups. The most reliable international comparison studies[1] also paint a bleak picture of the achievement of American students. When compared with other industrialized nations, U.S. students are at or near the bottom of almost every educational index imaginable, from academic areas to vocational studies.

Our results indicate a serious gap in instructional emphases between high- and low-minority classrooms that conflicts with our national concern for equity in the quality of education. Such practices reinforce the teaching of low level skills emphasized by these tests and rob time from instruction that could be devoted to the development of skills recommended by curriculum experts. The fact that minority students were shown to be particularly affected by such test-related instructional practices raises concern regarding equity in the quality of education.

George Madaus, et al., 1992

If we are to understand the overall declines in school performance we must examine some of the within-school factors that have influenced the achievement of students across the spectrum of socioeconomic groups. Global finger pointing at a system that has become inefficiently bureaucratized, arrogantly unresponsive, and financially wasteful may call attention to the problem in general, but it does not get down to the daily, within-classroom roots of the problem. These roots are buried in the curriculum adopted by our schools and the instructional methods used to apply this curriculum to student learning.

The Dumbing Down of Textbooks

The organizational bedrock of curriculum and instruction, and, therefore, what takes place in most classrooms is textbooks. For better or for worse, textbooks dominate what students learn, how teachers teach, and how we chart the progress of learning. Similarities among the leading textbooks, and complementary entanglements with the major standardized achievement tests, have had the effect of producing a uniform curriculum throughout the nation. According to Michael W. Apple (1992), a leading analyst of textbook policy and content, "We *do* have a national curriculum, but it is not determined by a democratically-elected body and it is not determined by a central ministry of education. The curriculum is determined by textbooks, and the textbooks — by and large — look the same all over the United States" (p. 3). The omnipotence of textbooks in American education, and the acknowledged inadequacy of these texts have resulted in what Tyson-Bernstein has called an American textbook fiasco:

> Imagine a public policy that is perfectly designed to produce textbooks that confuse, mislead, and profoundly bore students, while at the same time making all of the adults involved in the process look good, not only in their own eyes, but in the eyes of others. Although there are some good textbooks on the market, publishers and editors are virtually compelled by public policies and practices to create textbooks that confuse students with non sequiturs, that mislead them with misinformation, and that profoundly bore them with pointlessly arid writing (Tyson-Bernstein, 1988, p. 3).

Few aspects of education have been subjected to more intense scrutiny and criticism than textbooks. Chall and

Most teachers rely on textbooks. Often, the information teachers disseminate to students is directly aligned with the information offered by textbooks, providing students with only one view of complex issues, one set of truths.

Catherine Twomey Fosnot, 1993

Conard (1991) have documented a trend of decreasing difficulty in the most widely used textbooks over a thirty-year period from 1945-1975. "On the whole, the later the copyright dates of the textbooks for the same grade, the easier they were, as measured by indices of readability level, maturity level, difficulty of questions and extent of illustration" (p. 2). Kirst (1982) also believes that textbooks have dropped by two grade levels in difficulty over the last 10-15 years. Most recently, Altbach (1991), a noted scholar and author on textbooks in America, suggests that textbooks, as evaluated across a spectrum of assessment measures, have declined in rigor.

> Textbooks are a central part of any educational system. They help define the curriculum and can either significantly help or hinder the teacher. The "excellence movement" has directed its attention to textbooks in the past few years. American textbooks, according to the critics, are boring and designed for the lowest common denominator. They have been "dumbed down" so that content is diluted and "readability" is stressed. Textbooks have evolved over the past several decades into "products" often assembled by committees in response to external pressures rather than a coherent approach to education. Most important to many of the critics, textbooks do not provide the knowledge base for American schools in a period of reform, renewal and improvement. (Altbach, 1991, p. 2)

Researchers have discussed the particular problems encountered by students when textbooks are "dumbed down" because of readability formulas or the politics of textbook adoption. Tyson-Bernstein (1989) summarizes the particular problem that current textbooks pose for large numbers of students, "Even if there were good rules of thumb about the touchy subject of textbook adoption, the issue becomes moot when a school district buys only one textbook, usually at 'grade level,' for all students in a subject or grade. Such a purchasing policy pressures adoption committees to buy books that the least-able students can read. As a result, the needs of more advanced students are sacrificed" (p. 465). Chall and Conard (1991) also cite particular difficulties for the above-average student with regard to less difficult textbooks.

Another group not adequately served was those who read about two grades or more above the norm. Their reading

The banal content of elementary social studies books gets children off to a bad start. Young children are bored by these books because they discuss things they already know—that people live in families, that they buy food at a store, that fire engines respond to fires or that rush hour is busy.

Harriet Tyson-Bernstein & Arthur Woodward, 1988

textbooks, especially, provided little or no challenge, since they were matched to students' grade placement, not their reading levels. Many students were aware of this and said, in their interviews, that they preferred harder books because they learned harder words and ideas from them. Since harder reading textbooks are readily available, one may ask why they were not used with the more able readers, as were the easier reading textbooks for the less able readers. This practice of using grade-level reading textbooks for those who read two or more grades above the norms has changed little through the years, although it has been repeatedly questioned (see Chall, 1967, 1983). It would appear, for various administrative reasons, that teachers do not use a reading textbook above the student's grade placement. The reason most often mentioned is really a question: If the third-grade teacher uses fourth grade books, what is the fourth-grade teacher going to do? (p. 111)

Further, Chall and Conard stress the importance of the match between a learner's abilities and the difficulty of the instructional task, stating that the optimal match should be slightly above the learner's current level of functioning. When the match is optimal, learning is enhanced. However, "if the match is not optimal [i.e., the match is below or above the child's level of understanding/knowledge], learning is less efficient and development may be halted" (p. 19). It is clear that the current trend of selecting textbooks which the majority of students can read is a problem for students who can progress at faster rates.

Repetition in Textbooks

Recent findings by Usiskin (1987) and Flanders (1987) indicate that not only have textbooks decreased in difficulty, but also, they incorporate a large percentage of repetition to facilitate learning. Usiskin argues that even average eighth grade students should study algebra since only 25% of the pages in typical seventh and eighth grade mathematics texts contain new content. Flanders corroborated this finding by investigating the mathematics textbook series of three popular publishers. Students in grades 2-5 who used these math textbooks encountered approximately 40% to 65% new content over the course of the school year which equates to new material two to three days a week. By eighth grade, the amount of new content had dropped to 30% which translates

The typical mathematics text seems to assume that all the review at a given grade level must precede any new material....On average, the first half of a grade 1-8 book has 35 percent new content, whereas the second half of the book has 60 percent new content....The net result is that early in the year, when students are likely to be more eager to study, they repeat what they have seen before. Later on, when they are sufficiently bored, they see new material—if they get to the end of the book.

James Flanders, 1987

The mentioning problem, like the bad writing problem, is directly attributable to public policies and procedures. Adoption states that generate excessively detailed textbook specifications seldom take into account the time it would take to teach all of the required items, or the space available in a standard-sized textbook. Typical selection procedures seldom take into account the critical mass of information a student needs to understand a familiar topic.

Harriet Tyson-Bernstein, 1988

to encountering new material once every one and one half days a week. Flanders (1987) suggests that these estimates are conservative because days for review and testing were not included in his analysis. He concludes: "There should be little wonder why good students get bored: they do the same thing year after year" (p. 22).

In light of the findings by recent researchers, a mismatch seems to exist between the difficulty of textbooks, the repetition of curricular material in these texts, and the needs of individual learners. Many students spend much of their time in school practicing skills and learning content they already know. All of these factors are causing many students to learn less and to proceed haltingly in their development, thereby creating or encouraging their underachievement. Rampant boredom resulting from an under-challenging curriculum may be the largest cause of school dropouts and "turnoffs" because students learn at an early age that if they do their best in school, they will be rewarded with an endless array of the same kind of drill and practice materials that produced the boredom in the first place.

Most analysts agree that the low level of current American textbooks is a direct result of two interrelated practices. The first practice is a process called "dumbing down," a term first used in 1984 by Terrel Bell, former U.S. Secretary of Education. Dumbing down simply means that textbook material has purposely been made easier, and, therefore, less challenging. Two forces have influenced the dumbing down process. First, because of national concerns to improve the performance of low achieving students, textbook publishers began in the late 1960s to include more and more practice material in texts while simultaneously lowering reading levels and the depth to which topics are covered. Second, educational conservatives (with a good deal of support from the "fundamental right") exerted influence on textbook publishers, especially in the primary textbook "adoption states" where fundamental beliefs are the most widespread. Fundamentalists successfully argued for a renewed emphasis on the three Rs and the elimination of curricular material that developed skills such as critical thinking, in-depth analysis of contemporary social issues, and the development of creativity.

Mentioning

The second practice that has influenced contemporary textbooks is called "mentioning." Knowledge has expanded dramatically in the past half-century, and the highly competitive textbook market has responded by including more and more material in standard texts. Michael Apple comments on this process: "There's a standard rule in elementary and secondary school curriculum and in texts. Don't drop anything — only add. As a result, we have longer and more expensive texts. There is no doubt that there is a movement to incorporate more and more information. Because of that, there is more fragmentation" (Apple, in Lockwood, 1992, p. 3). When we couple increases in new information in texts with larger amounts of practice material, the inevitable result is that textbooks are only able to "mention" topics and cover them at very superficial levels. In the literature review included in Chapter 6 of this book, we describe in detail an overwhelming number of research studies on mentioning, dumbing down, and problems related to present day textbooks and the politics of textbook adoption. These studies provide compelling support for the need to initiate curricular modification procedures such as the ones described in the section that follows.

How can we deal with the combined problems of dumbing down and mentioning? The unsatisfactory state of textbooks in American education could certainly justify a radical approach to needed change; and therefore, it would be easy to recommend total replacement of textbooks and/or non-text alternatives. But even to hope for changes of these proportions would be romantic at best and totally unrealistic in terms of financial costs, vested interests, political considerations, and practical expediency. Furthermore, if such a total reformation were possible, there would undoubtedly be as much controversy surrounding whatever emerged to replace present textbooks as there is with the present state of textbook use. While most scholars and practitioners would agree that a textbook-based curriculum is not necessarily wise, textbooks are viewed by almost everyone as a practical necessity for mass education, and, therefore, textbooks will continue to be a fact of life in our schools. In keeping with the "gentle and evolutionary" approach to change discussed earlier, we will describe four specific strategies for accomplishing Goal 2. The first strategy, entitled, "Curriculum Compacting," is a systematic process that is designed to modify curriculum for students who are capable of covering regularly-assigned material at faster rates than might ordinarily be pursued in large group teaching situations. The second strategy consists of forming faculty teams that are charged

Every weekday, 25 million children study mathematics in our nation's schools. Those at the younger end, some 15 million of them, will enter the adult world in the period 1995-2000. The 40 classroom minutes they spend on mathematics each day are largely devoted to mastery of the computational skills which would have been needed by a shopkeeper in the year 1940—skills needed by virtually no one today. Almost no time is spent on estimation, probability, interest, histograms, spreadsheets, or real problem solving—things which will be commonplace in most of these young people's later lives. While the 15 million of them sit there drilling away on those arithmetic or algebra exercises, their future options are bit-by-bit eroded.

Mathematical Sciences Education Board, 1986

with the responsibility of examining present curriculum by grade level and subject area, and making recommendations for curricular revision. We call these faculty groups Textbook Analysis and Surgical Removal Teams. The third strategy focuses on specific procedures and resources for blending content and thinking skills activities. The fourth strategy provides teachers with a three-step process for introducing greater depth into curricular topics through the deliberate selection of more challenging content and systematic procedures for teaching complex concepts and material. These recommendations are covered in detail in Chapter 6, Curriculum Modification Techniques.

Goal 3

TO PROMOTE continuous, reflective, growth-oriented professionalism on the parts of all school personnel.

What Does It Mean to Be a Professional?

Schools are only as good as the people who work in them. This goal focuses on the crucial but elusive task of improving the professionalism of teachers, administrators, and other school personnel. Because of endless years of failed attempts to achieve this noble goal, it might be tempting to dismiss an objective about improved professionalism as an idealistic but largely unachievable task. But this objective lies at the heart of school improvement. For this reason we must examine both failed attempts and promising approaches to professional improvement, and we must use our accumulated knowledge, experience, and wisdom to devise a practical plan to improve the professionalism of personnel in schools using the Schoolwide Enrichment Model.

Professionals are people within an occupational category who share a common body of knowledge and standards of practice that allow them to *make decisions* in the best interests of their clients. Whether or not teaching is a "true profession" is not as important an issue in this discussion as are the steps that can be taken to *allow* professionalism to develop in schools. The work of true professionals is characterized by the regular use of judgment and nonroutine activities rather than mechanized or prescribed applications of duties. In order for true professionalism to be achieved, the individual, *and* the institution within which the individual works must be

How can a profession survive, let alone flourish, when its members are cut off from each other and from the rich knowledge base upon which success and excellence depend?

Roland S. Barth , 1990

amenable to change. Many reform proposals have recognized the importance of improved professionalism, but they have failed to respect the "ground rules" of professional work. Professionalism is a social contract that requires individuals to acquire and make use of certain competencies and ethics, but the contract also requires that the institution support the application of these competencies and ethics. Some of the recommended educational reform proposals have failed to examine the interaction between individual improvement and institutional change. Darling-Hammond and Goodwin comment on this dilemma: "Paradoxically, numerous reforms intended to 'professionalize' teaching have included measures that further control and regularize teaching (e.g., externally developed curriculum mandates and tests, regulation of teaching methods, and routinized prescriptions for the curriculum of teacher preparation programs)" (1992, p. 26). Another noted author on school reform also commented about politically motivated change that overlooks the interaction between individual improvement and institutional change:

> Politically motivated change is accompanied by greater commitment of leaders, the power of ideas and additional resources; but it also produces unrealistic time-lines, uncoordinated demands, simplistic solutions, misdirected efforts, inconsistencies and underestimation of what it takes to bring about reform (Fullan, 1991, p. 27).

When all is said and done, the quality of learning that takes place in any classroom depends mostly on the quality of the teacher in that room. But teachers are not "free agents!" They often lack the academic freedom and decision making opportunities accorded other professional; therefore, we cannot consider the professionalism of teachers without examining the other factors that exert influence on school quality. Although these external factors influence within-classroom teaching practices, neither favorable nor unfavorable regulations, textbooks, or standards will compensate for teachers who lack the knowledge base and know-how of effective teaching. And even when teachers have the theoretical background and know-how, the link between knowledge and attitudes about effective teaching and the actual application of these techniques is largely speculative. If teachers lack the freedom to *apply* effective teaching practices in their daily interactions with students,

But the 1980s virtually exploded with state-driven reforms of schooling led by both governors and legislators....State mandates and directives on matters that had usually been left to the discretion of local school boards and superintendents flowed to the district in an ever-broadening stream. Curriculum, testing, textbook selection, evaluation and dozens of other areas were now detailed and aligned to district goals as a major strategy of school improvement. The growing percentage of state funding in district budgets in the 1980s marked further gains in state control over schooling and the relentless shrinking of local interest.

Larry Cuban, 1990

then we must analyze the factors preventing good teaching techniques from being used in their classrooms.

Reasons For Failed Attempts to Improve Schools

Let us begin with failed attempts and what we have learned from them. An examination of the school improvement literature suggests that there are at least two general reasons why proven teaching techniques are not often used by experienced teachers.

External Regulations

The first reason is a proliferation of external regulations that are designed to increase "accountability," and that are subtly but powerfully enforced by standardized tests. These tests are "the elephant in the room" of school improvement, and their influence has become so pervasive that various plans have been put forward to link teacher evaluations with test scores. In keeping with the gentle but evolutionary approach to change recommended in this model, we are not proposing the elimination of standardized tests as part of the criteria by which we should examine the quality of learning that takes place in a school. It is important to know how well our students are progressing on commonly agreed-upon goals, but it is equally important for teachers to be a part of the decision making process that determines both the goals and *the full range of criteria* that can be used to evaluate progress toward these goals. Professionals are people who make decisions rather than receive orders about the work that they do. If we want teachers to be at least willing, and, hopefully, enthusiastic participants in school improvement activities, then it is essential that school governance models allow for shared decision making on goals and evaluative criteria as well as the teaching and curricular practices that are the means for achieving goals. The first step toward achieving true teacher professionalism, therefore, is to invite teachers into the decision-making process as equal partners with administration on the most important decisions to be made. But professionalism also requires informed decision making; therefore, procedures should be developed to provide teachers with relevant information. Thus, for example, a Goals/ Evaluation Committee might be provided with some general literature and briefing material on school improvement issues, and information on recent developments such as performance-based assessment, classroom climate assessment techniques,

I haven't been in long enough to retire, but I've been in too long to quit. I like the children. I want to do a good job, but I don't have room to maneuver. What I think about things doesn't seem to count. My ideas are not important. Nobody asks me what ought to be done or how we could do better. The school board is under pressure to reduce expenditures. All that the board members seem to care about is raising scores on standardized achievement tests, anyway. The central office grinds out curriculum guides and memos that nobody pays attention to, except when the supervisor comes around. The union is more concerned about making noise than about helping me do a better job in my classroom. I'll go to school everyday. I'll go through the motions. I'll put my time in. But my heart is not in it.

Jack Frymier, 1987

student portfolios, and alternate ways of using standardized tests to examine progress toward goals.

The limited use of high quality teaching practices is related to the issue of external regulations and accountability, but it is manifested in the relationships between administrators and teachers. Adversarial relations are the inevitable result of both top-down decision making and a failure on the parts of teachers and administrators to communicate effectively about their respective problems and agendas. Roland Barth portrays the essence of these communication problems by describing what he calls "The Parking Lot Syndrome:"

> As a new principal, I prepared carefully for my first faculty meeting. I arranged the chairs in circles, and encouraged several teachers to contribute. Yet, during the meeting I found I did most of the talking while teachers sat quietly by. A few minutes after the meeting, I looked out my office window at the school parking lot and realized where the real faculty meeting was taking place. Little clusters of teachers were abuzz, expressing their ideas about all the subjects on the agenda. (Barth, 1990, p. 20)

The ways in which we have traditionally approached school improvement through staff development activities illustrates the "us-and-them" attitude that is almost universal between and among teachers and administrators. The process customarily begins with knowledge about a particular idea, teaching technique or curricular "package" that is obtained from one or a combination of three sources: professional reading, attendance at professional meetings, or directives received from state agencies and passed on down the line from central administration. Occasionally, the idea may originate with teachers, but in order for the idea to move forward, approval must be obtained from building and/or district level decision makers. Teacher-initiated ideas are more likely to gain approval for what might be called "micro-skill" improvements; and what follows is yet another replay of "the workshop game." A one-shot workshop is arranged on a specific topic such as thinking skills, assertive discipline, time management, or a broad range of make-it-and-take-it activities that teachers can use with their students. The salient features of micro-skill workshops initiated by teachers is that they pose little or no threat to the *status quo,* and although they may improve individual teaching skills, they seldom have a major

Something is seriously out of whack. The bureaucratic nature of the enterprise seems to have acquired a purpose of its own.

Jack Frymier, 1987

We compiled a substantial amount of data pertaining to teachers' links to sources of influence in their teaching and to one another. The teachers we studied appeared, in general, to function quite autonomously. But their autonomy seemed to be exercised in a context more of isolation than a rich professional dialogue about a plethora of challenging educational alternatives. The classroom cells in which teachers spend much of their time appear to me to be symbolic and predictive of their relative isolation from one another and from sources of ideas beyond their own background and experience.

John Goodlad, 1984

or lasting impact on policy or new directions for a school district.

Major or macro-change initiatives follow a different pathway. State level directives or guidelines are usually the trigger for adopting a systemic change initiative, and central office administrators are almost always the initiators. When a plan is adopted for a comprehensive school improvement process (with or without input from teacher members of a district-level committee), a different workshop scenario is played out. Following introductory remarks about the importance of the topic, the school or district's commitment to implement whatever is being considered, and the marvelous credentials of the visiting speaker(s), the initiators make a graceful exit from the workshop situation and the "toxic details" of implementation. Teachers who are expected to put the new initiative into practice often feel put upon by yet another top-down educational innovation and a lack of support in terms of both time and resources to put the practice into action. Their feelings of alienation from the decision-making process and limited support frequently result in minimal compliance, passive resistance, and a "this-too-shall-pass" attitude. Administrators usually respond to these attitudes by raising the stakes in the accountability game, and test scores become an enforcer that further widens the gulf between teachers and administration.

Teacher Alienation From One Another

A second reason why proven teaching techniques are not easily applied is that the present structure of schools has cut most teachers off from the kinds of professional improvement that can be derived from colleagues as well as the kinds of growth that result when professionals consult with one another. If we observe other groups of professionals at work, whether they be physicians, engineers, plumbers, or any other client-serving group, they talk to one another about problems in need of solution, and use their collective experience, knowledge, and wisdom to come up with potential ways for addressing these problems. The teaching profession, on the other hand, has evolved into a very private set of behind-closed-door domains and competencies. Barth (1990) compares the work of teachers with the "parallel play" that takes place between toddlers playing at opposite corners of the same sandbox, and describes the taboo in teaching that prevents one teacher from observing another teacher at work or the taboo of sharing craft knowledge with one another. In an informal poll among teachers and principals, Barth found that most of the persons he queried had visited schools in countries other than in their own system. He also reported that when teachers *do* interact with one another, the conversation often focuses on criticism of colleagues or administrators rather than the sharing of extraordinary insights or rich experiences.

Breaking down the structural isolation of teachers' work and the us-and-them attitude that currently exists between teachers and administrators is a major part of the professionalism goal of the SEM. This task must be approached in a systematic and non-threatening manner, and it must extend beyond the usual practice of parading one visiting speaker after another through the time blocks devoted to staff development. The professional development model that is described in a later section is built around a three-phase process that includes: (1) substantive examinations of theoretical, pedagogical, and curricular knowledge, (2) skill oriented training that focuses on the know-how of implementing a particular teaching method or set of curricular materials, and (3) opportunities to apply knowledge and know-how in a relatively unrestricted experimental setting. This plan for professional development is also related to issues of democratic school governance that are discussed in connection with Goal 5.

Goal 4

T *O CREATE a learning community that honors ethnic, gender, and cultural diversity, mutual respect and caring attitudes toward one another, respect for democratic principles, and preservation of the Earth's resources.*

Schools for a Better Society

A major conviction among educators, policy makers, and the general public is that schools should play a role in ameliorating important problems in our society. Although our schools were originally invested with the obligation to teach the three Rs and to pass on the accumulated knowledge of the past, a rapidly changing world, dramatic changes in the job market, and a host of increasingly complex societal issues have placed demands on the educational system that require an enlarged role for the schools. This role has been reflected over the

The growth of state and federal authority in solving matters during the last two centuries, then, has been an expression of deep faith in public schooling as an instrument for solving national problems....If alcohol and tobacco abuse inflict harm on individuals and families, then teach children the evils of these habits. If poverty is the enemy, then enlist teachers and schools to fight it by expanding children's knowledge and building marketability skills. If foreign economic competition threatens the country, then promote vocational education as another line of national defense.

Larry Cuban, 1990

years by the inclusion of numerous contemporary curricular issues that range from driver education and a "life adjustment curriculum," to concerns about war and peace, values and character, and sex and drug education. Each of these issues, and the efforts to address them through additions to the school curriculum, have kindled or rekindled the classic controversies between conservative and liberal ideologies. Although this goal does favor a broader set of beliefs about the role of the school, it is included as a major focus of the SEM because of the rapid changes taking place in our society and the declining well-being of young people in America.

Most people would agree that talent development and academic performance are the main responsibilities of schools; however, changes in family structures and a fast-track society have also placed on schools a broader range of responsibilities. Issues such as alarmingly high delinquency rates, substance abuse, racial disharmony, teenage pregnancy, intolerance, wasteful consumerism, and a lack of respect for our fellow human beings has resulted in a generation of young people who are experiencing psychological distress and social alienation as well as declining school performance. Many will argue that school is not the place to address such problems, but the fact remains that these problems and their by-products have ended up on the schoolhouse doorstep. Education, alone, cannot resolve these problems, but schools can play an important role in fostering the intelligence, persistence, and creativity necessary to bring about needed improvements in both the quality of life for young people and the improvement of the social institutions that are necessary for perpetuating our political democracy.

The inclusion of this goal in the SEM is not intended to impose a set of political beliefs or social values on schools that use this model. Although the goal does encourage the examination of societal issues that young people will have to address in one form or another throughout the course of their lives, we believe that the educators, parents, and students of *each* school must come to terms with both the topics that reflect their collective values and beliefs, and the curricular approaches for addressing these values and beliefs. In other words, we believe that contemporary issues should be part of an enrichment program that attempts to bring relevancy and realness into the curriculum. At the same time, we also believe that local decision making must prevail as far as specific topic selection is concerned.

"Education, alone, cannot resolve these problems, but schools can play an important role in fostering the intelligence, persistence, and creativity necessary to bring about needed improvements in both the quality of life for young people and the improvement of the social institutions that are necessary for perpetuating our political democracy."

Because the focus of this model is on the act of learning, we will pursue this goal by concentrating on instructional methods that address more effectively the topics that schools select within broad parameters of this goal. We will also provide references to materials that are available for various kinds of enrichment experiences related to selected topics.

In a comprehensive review of the literature on curriculum that focuses on contemporary issues, Leming (1992) analyzed numerous research studies that dealt with: drug/substance abuse education, suicide prevention programs, death education, sex education, reducing racial prejudice, sex role stereotypes, global education, environmental education, and peace education. Although it is difficult to generalize across the numerous studies reviewed, Leming did find trends that are relevant to implementing Goal 4 of the SEM. His main finding, so far as instructional methods are concerned, is that lecture and "scare tactic" approaches are of limited value in changing attitudes about the topics listed above. The more successful programs usually involved higher degrees of participation on the parts of students. For example, studies of drug abuse programs revealed: "Peer programs that involved positive peer influence through peer teaching and peer counseling and helping, were found to show a definite superiority for the magnitude of the effect size obtained on all outcome measures" (p. 120).

Although didactic presentation of information was generally ineffective with regard to the acquisition of knowledge, Leming reported that increased knowledge about contemporary issues did not result in noticeable changes in attitude or behavior. Positive changes in attitude were, however, reported when curricula were used that involved peer interaction, group discussions, and cooperative learning strategies. Our own experience in enrichment programs also has shown that changes in both attitude and behavior resulted when students were given an opportunity to deal directly with contemporary issues. Students who, for example, conducted original studies on environmental pollution, acid rain, drunk driving, and teenagers' knowledge about and attitudes toward AIDS became "crusaders" for action with regard to their chosen topics of study. In Chapter 7, we will discuss the strategies for promoting this type of direct involvement and provide examples of how these strategies can be applied to this goal of the SEM.

Grounded in lessons from successful corporate enterprises, knowledge of school improvement, and the tenets of professionalism, the following principle rests at the heart of the restructuring schools movement: that the authority to make changes and the control of the resources to do so must reside with those who are the closest to the learners.

Joseph Murphy, 1991

Goal 5

*T*O IMPLEMENT *a democratic school governance procedure that includes appropriate decision-making opportunities for students, parents, teachers, and administrators.*

The Need for Democratic Governance

Educational leaders across the nation have recognized that decentralized management procedures are a major component of school improvement. This type of management, commonly referred to as site- or school-based management (SBM), has a long and successful history in the private sector, and it has been endorsed by many educational organizations, including the National Governors' Association. SBM decreases centralized control and encourages high levels of involvement and control on the parts of persons who are closest to production of products and the delivery of services. Although this goal is considered to be one that evolves and matures over a period of several years, it is also considered to be essential for any real and lasting improvement in the quality of learning that takes place within a school. A number of commentators on the current status of American education have indicated that excessive regulation is the single most contributing factor to our schools' inability to change, and accordingly, many state departments of education are in the process of minimizing the number of regulations placed on school districts. Deregulation at the state level, however, will not produce desired results without an equal concern for transferring decision making power to the building level and to the teachers and parents who are closest to the education of their children. The most important value of democratic governance, and the reason we have included this goal in the SEM, is that if a school decides to adopt this (or any other) model or school improvement initiative, the decision must be protected from the biases or predilections of the always changing personnel who occupy district decision making positions. In one district with which we are familiar, a new assistant superintendent in charge of curriculum wiped out one of the most successful enrichment programs in the country because of a personality conflict with the program coordinator, and her desire to assert authority. Efforts to reinstate the program by a majority of teachers, and even a hue and cry of highly satisfied parents in the community were not strong

There is a destiny that makes us brothers: None goes his way alone; All that we send into the lives of others Comes back into our own.

Edwin Markham

enough to overcome the amount of power vested in a single person.

Studies of decentralization in the private sector indicate that organizations in which complex tasks are carried out can benefit by a collegial or team approach to problem solving (Maeroff, 1993; Wohlstetter & Mohrman, 1993). These studies also point out that control over the following four resources needs to be decentralized in order to maximize the improvement of performance:

1. Power to make decisions that influence organizational practices, policies, and directions.
2. Knowledge that enables personnel to understand and contribute to organizational performance including technical knowledge to do the job or provide the service, interpersonal skills, and managerial knowledge or expertise.
3. Information about the performance of the organization, including revenues, expenditures, unit performance, and strategic information on the broader policy and economic environment.
4. Rewards that are based on the performance of the organization and the contributions of individuals (Wohlstetter & Mohrman, 1993, p. 1).

Democratic school governance represents a fundamental and systemic organizational change. Like all other changes of this magnitude, and especially changes that include a redistribution of power to make important decisions, the process must be approached thoughtfully and cautiously! Training in management and decision making techniques must be provided to personnel who have customarily been in subordinate roles, and central office personnel must also receive training in the potentially enigmatic task of sharing power, knowledge, information, and opportunities to influence the reward structure of the school. Experience from the private sector and from school districts that are using site-based management have resulted in a good deal of know-how about the process of implementing democratic governance procedures. A growing number of print resources and consultants are available for the pursuit of this goal as well as specific systems such as W. Edwards Deming's Total Quality Management approach. Also available are instruments and procedures for assessing parent, student, and teacher attitudes toward present school structures and needed changes. In

[E]mpowerment has its problems and cooperation is required to solve them. Everyone has to learn to take the initiative instead of complaining, to trust colleagues, to live with ambiguity, to face the fact that shared decisions mean conflict....All these stances and skills are learnable, but they take time. It is up to steering groups to learn to work well together, using whatever assistance is required.

Michael Fullan & Matthew Miles, 1992

Chapter 8 we will provide descriptions of these resources and suggestions for using them.

Districts that have been successful in empowering professionals and in decentralizing operations have often taken 5 to 10 years to do so.

Joseph Murphy, 1991

[1] The major studies confirming this distressing fact are too numerous to list. Research based reports identifying the status of U.S. students have been released by The College Board, the Twentieth Century Fund, the National Science Foundation, the Educational Commission of the States, the National Commission on Excellence in Education, and the International Association for Educational Achievement.

Chapter 4

An Overview of the Schoolwide Enrichment Model

THE SCHOOLWIDE ENRICHMENT MODEL consists of three parts. Two of the parts are called *the service delivery components* and *the organizational components*. The third part consists of *the school structures* toward which these components are targeted. Although the model was described by one commentator as "elegant common sense," some care is necessary in describing this plan because it represents a three-way interaction between and among the components and the school structures, which are the settings where learning takes place. These interactions are depicted in the three dimensional diagram in Figure 3. The two types of components in the SEM are shown on the front and side dimensions of the figure, and the school structures are presented on the top of the diagram. The Service Delivery Components consist of three types of direct services to students. These services are: (1) the preparation of a strength-oriented profile called the Total Talent Portfolio; (2) the use of systematic curriculum modification techniques that are designed to make the regular curriculum more responsive to individual student needs; and (3) the use of enrichment learning and teaching techniques that are specifically designed to promote higher levels of motivation, thinking, and authentic engagement with self-selected topics. The Organizational Components consist of a distinct set of resources and procedures that are designed to

That so many of our students work below their potential has grave implications for the nation. The scholarship, inventiveness, and expertise that created the foundation for America's high standard of living and quality of life are eroding.

United States Department of Education, 1993

What is important in education is not so much how we teach but how students learn—for absolutely nothing has happened in education until it happens to a student.

Joseph Carroll, 1989

support the use of the service delivery components. These components are listed on the left-hand side of Figure 3. The three School Structures toward which the service delivery and organizational components are targeted are: the regular curriculum, the enrichment clusters, and the continuum of special services. These structures will be described in the section that follows, and the organizational components of the SEM will be discussed in subsequent chapters.

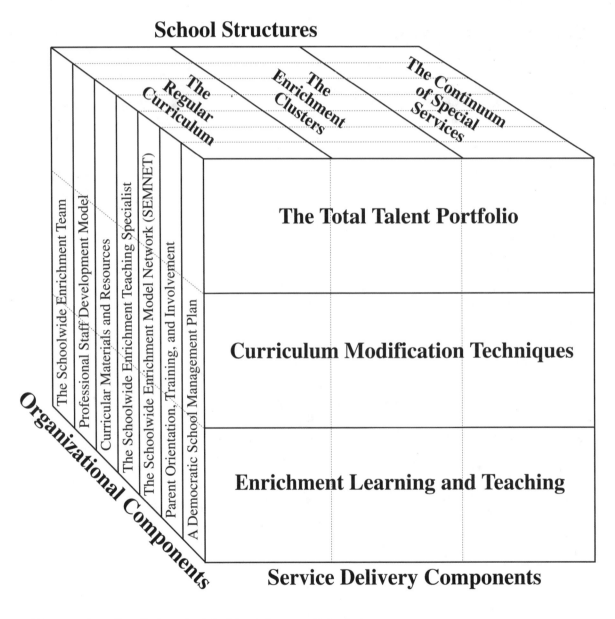

Figure 3. The Schoolwide Enrichment Model.

The School Structures Toward Which the Model Is Targeted

The Regular Curriculum

THE REGULAR curriculum consists of anything and everything that is a part of the predetermined goals, schedules, learning outcomes, and delivery systems of the school. The regular curriculum might be traditional, innovative, or in the process of transition, but its predominant feature is that authoritative forces (i.e., policy makers, school councils, textbook adoption committees, state regulators) have determined that certain outcomes should be the "centerpiece" of student learning. The current emphasis on defining curriculum in terms of outcomes is a favorable development; however, it could easily end up being another ill-fated regression to a minimum competency, basic skills approach to learning. If schools are to capitalize on the impetus of the outcome-based education movement, and the parallel movement toward specifying standards within subject matter areas, it is absolutely essential that the regular curriculum include within each unit of instruction systematic service delivery procedures for: (1) adjusting levels of required learning so that all students are challenged, (2) increasing the number of in-depth learning experiences, and (3) introducing various types of enrichment into regular curricular experiences. Although our goal in the SEM is to influence rather than replace the regular curriculum, it is conceivable that the application of certain SEM components and related staff development activities might eventually result in substantial changes in both the content and instructional processes of the entire curriculum.

Before describing each of the three service delivery components listed in the preceding paragraph, one additional component that overrides all regular curriculum pursuits should be mentioned. This component, which is called "group jumping," is important because in this model a firm distinction is made between grouping and tracking. Regular, systematic reviews of students' progress that result in group jumping is a major safeguard against the negative practice of allowing grouping to become tracking. We consider within-class cluster grouping to be a necessary part of the total repertoire of effective practices for classroom and instructional management. We also believe that there are many kinds of grouping that can be used in addition to, or in place of, ability

You can teach a student a lesson for a day; but if you can teach him to learn by creating curiosity, he will continue the learning process as long as he lives.

Ancient Chinese proverb

Grouping Options:

Within-Class Grouping

- *Interest grouping*
- *Skill-level grouping*
- *Question-based grouping*

Beyond-the-Classroom Grouping

- *Across-grade grouping*
- *Multi-age grouping*
- *Team regrouping*

Acceleration

- *Advanced Placement*
- *Early entrance to school*
- *Concurrent enrollment*
- *Credit by examination*
- *Grade telescoping*
- *Grade skipping*
- *Mentorships*
- *Subject acceleration*
- *Summer or evening courses*
- *Combined accelerative options*

Karen Rogers, 1991

grouping. Such grouping arrangements can be based on common interests, tasks, projects, skill levels, or on complementary skills and talents that enhance total productivity in situations where divisions of labor are called for. In spite of the arguments for and against grouping, and a renewed interest in non-graded schools (which in practice is a very rigid grouping-by-skill configuration), good teachers will always accommodate individual differences and avoid whole group teaching by forming subgroups or clusters in their classrooms. This practice is common in basic skill areas such as reading, mathematics, and language arts. But in order to prevent grouping from becoming tracking, a guaranteed procedure should be built into the instruction/assessment process so that students will not be locked into groups that are below their skill level. The locking in, which is usually a matter of classroom management convenience rather than responsive teaching, is precisely what causes low achieving students to fall farther and farther behind over several years of schooling. A thorough discussion of the grouping issue is included at the end of this chapter.

Adjusting Levels of Required Learning

Two service delivery components have been developed to modify the regular curriculum so that it will be more responsive to individual differences in learning rates and styles. The first component, which is called "curriculum compacting," is designed for use with individuals or small groups who show clearly documented evidence of preexisting proficiency in a unit of study or the potential to cover a defined segment of material at a faster rate than other students will pursue it through the regular instructional process. Curriculum compacting is a systematic procedure for modifying or streamlining the regular curriculum in order to eliminate repetition of previously-mastered material, to upgrade the challenge level of the regular curriculum, and to provide time for appropriate enrichment and/or acceleration activities. Essentially, the procedure involves (1) defining the goals and outcomes of a particular unit or segment of instruction, (2) determining and documenting which students have already mastered most or all of a specified set of learning outcomes, and (3) providing replacement activities for material already mastered through the use of instructional options that enable a more challenging and productive use of a student's time. These options include content acceleration, individual or group research projects, peer teaching, and involvement in non-classroom activities that will be discussed in the section on the continuum of services. A key feature of these options is that students will have some freedom making decisions about both the topic and the methods for studying it. Curriculum compacting might best be thought of as *organized common sense,* because it simply recommends the natural pattern that teachers ordinarily would follow if they were individualizing instruction or teaching in the days before textbooks were "invented." Compacting might also be thought of as the "mirror image" of remedial procedures that have always been used in diagnostic/prescriptive models of teaching. The specific steps for carrying out curriculum compacting in both basic skill and content areas are described in Chapter 6.

Surgical Removal of Repetition and Drill From Textbooks

A second related procedure for making adjustments in regular curricular material consists of examining textbooks in order to determine which aspects of a required text can be economized upon through the textbook analysis and "surgical" removal of repetitious drill and practice. The textbook *is* the curriculum in the overwhelming majority of today's classrooms, and despite the rhetoric about school and curriculum reform, the situation is not likely to change in the near future. Until such time that high quality textbooks are universally available, we must deal with the curriculum situation as it currently exists. Although curriculum compacting is one procedure that can be used to get an unchallenging curriculum "off the backs" of students who are in immediate need of modifications in learning, the procedure is a form of "damage control"; we need to take a more proactive stance to overcome the well-documented low levels of American textbooks. In other words, we must deal directly with the textbooks themselves. Procedures for carrying out this process are also discussed in Chapter 6.

Increasing the Depth of Learning

Adding depth to the curriculum is a particularly troublesome task because teachers have been encouraged to add *more* topics to what they have been teaching rather than to *discontinue* teaching large numbers of prescribed topics in favor of smaller amounts of in-depth material (Floden, Porter, Schmidt, Freeman, & Schwille, 1981). State and district frameworks typically specify outcomes in terms of quantity of material, and the emphasis has generally been on content and process

In the United States, the publishing of textbooks is a billion-dollar enterprise. Textbooks are sold to tens of thousands of schools and used in classrooms by millions of students. By the time most students complete high school, they will have been exposed to over 32,000 pages of textbooks. Almost all of their time in reading instruction and at least three-fourths of their time in content classes will be spent with a textbook.

Jeanne Chall & Sue Conard, 1991

[H]ow in our system of education are we to guard against...mental dryrot? We enunciate two educational commandments, Do not teach too many subjects, and What you teach, teach thoroughly. The result of teaching small parts of a large number of subjects is the passive reception of disconnected ideas, not illuminated with any spark of vitality. Let the main ideas which are introduced into a child's education be few and important, and let them be thrown into every combination possible.

Alfred North Whitehead, 1929

skills rather than conceptual understandings and applications (Porter, 1989). Introducing greater depth into the curriculum is also directly related to the issue of time discussed earlier. If the curriculum is "crowded" by superficial coverage of fragmented or compartmentalized facts and concepts, little time will be available for the in-depth study of highly representative topics in a field, key concepts that unlock deeper understandings of particular areas of study, or the pursuit of broad-based, interdisciplinary themes. Nor will time be available for learning the kinds of first-hand investigative methodologies that allow students to apply what they have learned to real life situations. Using the strategies discussed above (i.e., compacting and the systematic removal of redundant and unchallenging material) opens the door to opportunities for in-depth learning; however, there is a need to develop a plan for topic or theme selection, and for dealing with material in a truly in-depth manner. In the chapter on enrichment learning and teaching (Chapter 7), we will discuss specific strategies for increasing the depth of learning.

The Enrichment Clusters

The second school structure toward which the SEM is targeted consists of a series of interest-based groupings called enrichment clusters. The enrichment clusters are non-graded groups of students who share common interests, and who come together during specially designated time blocks to pursue these interests. The model for learning used in these clusters, which is described in Chapter 7, is called enrichment learning and teaching. It represents a significant departure from traditional didactic approaches to instruction. These clusters cut across grade levels and ability levels, and they exist for various durations of time ranging from one semester to several years. Like extracurricular activities and programs such as 4-H and Junior Achievement, the main rationale for participation in one or more enrichment clusters is that *students and teachers want to be there.* Selection of an enrichment cluster, however, is not a random or spontaneous process. Through the use of an SEM component called the Total Talent Portfolio (Chapter 5), a systematic process is used to help students make meaningful decisions about clusters in which they might want to participate. A similar kind of interest assessment is used with teachers and other adults who might be interested in facilitating[1] a cluster. Interest assessment procedures, examples of previous positive involvement in curricular or non-school activities, and highly positive reactions to purposefully selected interest development activities are all used to help young people and adults (i.e., teachers and community resource persons) make decisions about which enrichment cluster(s) they might like to select for given periods of time.

Developing Talents Through Multiple Enrichment Clusters
The organizational pattern for enrichment clusters is a programmatic application of Gardner's Theory of Multiple Intelligences (Gardner, 1983) and Renzulli's (1978) earlier conception of a developmental theory of human potential. The clusters have been organized around the broad subject areas listed in the left-hand column of Figure 4 because they are more commonly used in schools and they are areas in which students usually develop special interests. For example, it is much more likely for students to say: "We are interested in doing research on child abuse or toy safety" rather than, "We want to develop our logical/mathematical and task commitment skills." We view Gardner's intelligences and Renzulli's three sets of characteristics (Abilities, Task Commitment, and Creativity) as capacities to be developed and as factors that cut across the areas around which the clusters are organized. The differences between this approach and traditional patterns of grouping students together for special activities are that: (1) interests and learning styles rather than ability are major considerations for participation in a particular cluster, (2) all students are involved, and the choice of a cluster(s) is determined by the student, (3) teachers also select the clusters in which they would like to participate (individually and cooperatively with other adults), and (4) the clusters are guided by an enrichment learning and teaching model rather than most of the practices that characterize formal instruction.

   In the right-hand column of Figure 4 are the names of enrichment clusters that we have observed over the years in various schools using the SEM. Although they have been placed in categories according to general subject areas, an examination of the clusters' titles points out the interdisciplinary nature of several groups. It should also be noted that an effort has been made to avoid "schoolish" terms such as "course" or "class." Similarly, the use of the term "club" has been avoided because we want to emphasize the professional nature of the work that will be pursued in the clusters. The types of enrichment cluster titles used in Figure 4 do, however, raise an issue that will be discussed later, but

There can be no mental development without interest. Interest is the sine qua non for attention and apprehension. You may endeavor to excite interest by means of birch rods, or you may coax it by the incitement of pleasurable activity. But without interest, there will be no progress.

*Alfred North Whitehead,
1929*

65

General Areas	Specific Examples of Clusters
Language Arts, Literature, and the Humanities	The Young Authors' Guild The Poets' Workshop The African-American Literary Society The Investigative Journalism Group *The Quarterly Review of Children's Literature*
Physical and Life Sciences	The Save the Dolphins Society The Physical Science Research Institute The Mansfield Environmental Protection Agency The Experimental Robotics Team
The Arts	The Electronic Music Research Institute The Visual Artists' Workshops The Meriden Theater Company The Native American Dance Institute The Video Production Company The Young Musicians' Ensemble The Photographers' Guild
Social Sciences	The Hispanic Cultural Awareness Association The Junior Historical Society The Social Science Research Team The Torrington Geographic Society The Creative Cartographers' Guild
Mathematics	The Math Materials Publication Company The Math Mentors' Association The Female Mathematicians' Support Group The Mathematics Competitions League *The Math Puzzle Challenge Quarterly*
Computers	The Computer Graphics Design Team The Computer Games Production Company The Computer Literacy Assistance Association The Creative Software Society The Desktop Publishing Company
Physical Education	The Experimental Games Research Team The Physiology of Sport Study Group The Physical Fitness Support Group The Institute for the Study of Multicultural Recreation
Industrial Arts/ Home Economics	The Creative Furniture Design Company The Architecture for Learning Research Team The Experimental Dietary Group The Future Fashion Research Institute The Child Care Assistance Group

Figure 4. Sample Enrichment Clusters.

it is worthwhile to mention at this time. In the paragraph above we pointed out that students don't say things like, "We want to develop our logical/mathematical and task commitment skills." Neither do they ordinarily say, "I would like to be in a Desktop Publishing Company." This is especially true if there is no history of these kinds of enrichment clusters in a school. Because of the way that most students have come to view school, they are most likely to say they want to learn something about a particular topic. The only alternative to expressing an interest in "learning about" a preferred topic are the kinds of expressions related to participation in extracurricular activities. The extracurricular option is closer to the ways in which students should select enrichment clusters; however, there is still a certain amount of traditional predeterminism in the selection of extracurricular activities. In a later chapter a procedure will be described that allows students with interests in particular areas, both general and specific, to explore alternatives for applying their interests and selecting a product- or service-oriented vehicle for developing their interests.

The best way to understand an enrichment cluster is to view it in the same way that we view a research laboratory, small business organization, artists' guild, or public service agency. These organizations have certain things in common that make them substantially different from the "organization" that we call a classroom. First and foremost, there is some element of choice in the type of laboratory or agency in which one chooses to participate. Second, there is a common interest and purpose that binds the group together and that is directed toward the production of a product or the delivery of a service. Third, everyone does not do the same job. Rather, there is a division of labor, and everyone contributes in his or her own area of specialization. The group is tied together in a symbiotic way that is guided by the common purpose, and the uniqueness of each person's speciality is valued for what it contributes to the overall enterprise. This real-world conception of productivity, service, and cooperation is the prototype for the enrichment clusters, and it is based on the fundamental belief that each student is special if he or she is a specialist in a specialized group.

Although the multiple enrichment clusters are organized around traditional families of knowledge, there are also opportunities to form overlapping, interdisciplinary clusters. Thus, for example, students with interests in both electronics and music can combine efforts to form an electronic music

What Does 4-H Club Work Aim to Do?

- *To provide boys and girls with an opportunity to "learn by doing" through carrying out certain farm or home projects and demonstrating to others what they have learned.*

- *To teach boys and girls the value of research, and to use its results in solving the problems of the farm and the home.*

- *To arouse in boys and girls worthy ambitions and a desire to continue to learn.*

Helps for 4-H Leaders, 1951

In What Ways do Enrichment Clusters Differ From Classrooms?

- *Choice with respect to the type of activity in which one engages.*

- *A common interest among members which is directed toward the production of a service or product.*

- *Different jobs for participants that promote the development of an individual's unique talents.*

Many educational institutions have spent millions of dollars and untold hours of effort revamping their programs without much apparent long-range success. But with little additional cost, medical schools are starting to put students into small groups and help them solve the real life problems they will face in treating patients. According to the research data, classroom dynamics change fundamentally, students learn as many facts as in traditional classes, they enjoy their studies more, and they become lifelong learners.

It's an approach to learning that can happen without a new course of study, a mandate from the state legislature, or a large budget increase. It's a model that all educators can use.

David Aspy, Cheryl Aspy, & Patricia Quinby, 1993

cluster; students whose interests range across several topics (e.g., acting, writing, cinematography, costume design) can collaborate through the formation of a film or television production company. This type of school structure would be difficult, if not impossible, to organize if the almost universal school practice of grouping by grade was followed. Group members who span two, three, or even four grade levels have a great deal more in common if they share a similar interest than members who may be linked together only because they were born in relatively close proximity to one another. Another consideration regarding the formation of enrichment clusters is that within a general content area, the group may further subdivide into smaller groups that represent more specialized interests within the broader field of study. Thus, for example, a science cluster might include subgroups in physical and biological sciences, and even within a physical science group, further subdivisions might be organized around mechanics, electronics, and chemistry. These sub-subgroups are especially important at upper grade levels where interests become more specialized.

When this type of arrangement is first brought to the attention of teachers and administrators, a few inevitable questions are raised: "Suppose there are more subgroups than there are teachers?" "What happens if some groups are very large and others only have a few students?" "This sounds like a good idea, but does it mean I will have to do an extra preparation?" These are legitimate questions if we are thinking only in terms of the teacher-as-instructor and the student-as-lesson-learner. In later sections a very easy-to-learn, but nevertheless, different role for both the teachers and students who work together in an enrichment cluster will be described.

The enrichment clusters are not intended to be the total enrichment program, but they are one of the major vehicles for pursuing Goal 1 of the SEM. The enrichment clusters are also vehicles for staff development in that they provide teachers with opportunities to participate in enrichment teaching, and subsequently to analyze and compare this type of teaching with traditional methods of instruction. Procedures for this type of analysis will be discussed in connection with a later component of the SEM dealing with the professional growth of teachers. Suffice it to say at this time that a goal of the SEM is to infuse enrichment learning and teaching skills that are developed and practiced in enrichment clusters into the regular curriculum by creating a learning environment based on *direct participation* in this type of learning. In this regard, the goal is to promote a spill-over effect by encouraging teachers to apply some of these techniques to regular classroom situations.

Overview of Enrichment Learning and Teaching

The model for learning used with enrichment clusters is based on an inductive approach to the pursuit of real-world problems rather than traditional, didactic modes of teaching. Entitled the Enrichment Triad Model (Renzulli, 1977a), this approach is purposefully designed to create a learning environment that places a premium on the development of higher order thinking skills and the authentic application of these skills in creative and productive situations. Very briefly, the model consists of three types of enrichment activities designed to increase students' levels of creative productivity: Type I, general exploratory activities; Type II, group training activities; and Type III, students' self-selected, first-hand investigations into real problems. A diagram of the model is included in the sidebar, and a full explanation of the model is included in Chapter 7.

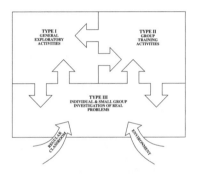

The theory underlying this approach is based on the work of constructivist theorists such as Jean Piaget and Jerome Bruner, and applications of constructivist theory to classroom practice (e.g., Atkin & Karplus, 1962; Lampert, 1984; Lawson, 1978; and Linn, Chen, & Thier, 1977). In this approach to learning, there are no lesson or unit plans, nor do teachers prescribe and present material that has been predetermined by curriculum guides or textbooks. Rather, the process begins by examining the kinds of things that people *do* within the context of common or complementary interest areas, and the types of products that they produce. Persons with an interest in language arts and literature, for example, might explore the types of products created by poets, journalists, literary critics, or authors of children's literature. Product finding and focusing within an interest area become the starting point, after which the processes and resources necessary to pursue product development are brought into play. The role of the teacher (and other adults) is to assist in problem finding and focusing, to help procure necessary resources, to interpret complex information and investigative/creative methodologies, and to provide feedback, editorial assistance, and personal support. In this approach to learning, the teacher's function is more like the role of a mentor or coach than that of an instructor. Although process development is the major outcome of enrichment learning and teaching,

Chapter 4

**Types of Products
Produced by Those
Involved in the
Humanities/Language
Arts**

Displays
Learning Centers
Sculptures
Posters
Exhibits
Museums
Masks
Photo Essays

Audio Products
Lyrics
Folksongs
Symphonies

Leadership Events
Marches
Rallys
Campaigns
Fund Raisings
Legislative Bills

Performances
Oral Histories
Storytelling
Poetry Readings
Choreography

Instruments and Designs
Tools
Toys
Puzzles
Mazes
Experiments
Lighting Design
Blueprints

Print Material
Cartoons
Genealogies
Maps
Greeting Cards
Newspapers
Scripts
Magazine Articles
Comic Books
Advertisements
Legends
Guide Books
Curricula
Dissertations
Recipes
Ethnographies

Philosophy
Essays
Theories

teachers do not even specify processes, nor do they select topics or curricular activities. Rather, they help students to identify a broad range of projects or products that creative persons within a field typically pursue, and they help students explore the ways in which persons with such interest areas organize themselves.

Chapter 7 describes the procedures for using enrichment learning and teaching strategies; however, a good way to gain a general understanding of this concept and its relationship to the concept of enrichment clusters is to examine the sample enrichment clusters listed in Figure 4. We note in this figure that the title of each cluster implies an approximation of the work of professionals within a speciality area, whether that area is product- or service-oriented.

Enrichment clusters are excellent vehicles for promoting cooperativeness within the context of real-world problem solving, and they also provide superlative opportunities for promoting self-concept. A major assumption underlying the use of enrichment clusters is that *every child is special if we create conditions in which that child can be a specialist within a specialty group.* Our experience has shown that common interests and goals related to product development produce much more effective groups than traditional age or ability grouping patterns, and they have the added advantage of creating situations in which authentic divisions of labor can take place. This type of working together to produce a meaningful, real-world product is a far cry from the contrived kind of "cooperative learning" that takes place when we ask groups of students to complete a worksheet or answer questions at the end of a textbook chapter.

When Do the Enrichment Clusters Meet?

Although enrichment clusters have proven to be remarkable vehicles for improving the quality of learning, they do, nevertheless, require some modest changes in the school schedule. Because of the venerable nature of existing school schedules, one might reasonably ask at this point, "Why don't we just apply the know-how of enrichment learning and teaching to the existing curriculum rather than creating a separate time block that has ramifications for changing the school schedule?" It is well known that "messing with the schedule" is the fastest way to get a polite but firm rejection from school persons who might consider adopting the SEM. The answer to this question is simple, but very compelling. We know from experience that nothing *substantially* different will take place in classrooms unless specifically designated time blocks are made available for enrichment learning and teaching. We must, however, proceed cautiously! The requirements of the regular curriculum and entrenched instructional techniques are simply too powerful to legislate an immediate conversion to either a completely restructured schedule or a model that is based on enrichment teaching. As mentioned in the introductory section on "A Gentle and Evolutionary Change Process," realistic approaches to change that have already produced demonstrated results are far more acceptable to educators and parents than yet another rhetorical harangue about "breaking the mold" through wholesale attempts to change a system that has, over the years, become almost totally immune to large scale change. A host of so called educational innovations and change efforts lies battered and broken on the roadside of educational improvement—things like Individually Guided Education, Programmed Instruction, Discovery Learning, Open Education, Learning Centers—the list goes on and on. It is for this reason that we have chosen to pursue a gentle and evolutionary change strategy that infiltrates schools with small but specific beginnings, and that subsequently expands and radiates outward toward total school improvement. The specificity of the approach provides opportunities to evaluate progress and make modifications according to feedback derived from specific learning situations, as well as a rationale for outward extensions based on demonstrated effectiveness.

A second reason exists for beginning with enrichment clusters rather than attempting to change the present configuration of general instruction. The activities that take place during the enrichment clusters provide an immediate vehicle for making young people want to go to school! In carefully documented studies of Asian schools, Stigler and Stevenson (1992) report that a formal and rigorous curriculum is interspersed throughout the day or week with a wide variety of hands-on, extracurricular activity that promotes cooperative attitudes, social interaction, and much more positive attitudes toward school. Stevenson acknowledges that these activities, which make up about one fourth of the time spent during the school day, may not contribute directly to academic success, but they help to make school an enjoyable place. By so doing, they promote positive attitudes toward school that undoubtedly have an indirect influence on improved achievement. By way of contrast, most American students have a general dislike for school. Rising dropout rates,

"A second reason exists for beginning with enrichment clusters rather than attempting to change the present configuration of general instruction. The activities that take place during the enrichment clusters provide an immediate vehicle for making young people want to go to school!"

especially among urban and disadvantaged youth, is testimony to the fact that our schools are viewed as dreary, unenjoyable, and uninviting places. While it would be easy to dwell on cliches about how "*all* learning should be interesting, exciting, and enjoyable," this has been a largely elusive goal rather than a reality in many of our schools. Because of the premium that enrichment clusters place on self-selected, product-oriented activities and a learning environment that promotes cooperativeness and social interaction, we can give more young people a reason for wanting to go to school.

A goal of the SEM is, indeed, to improve all of general education by creating remarkably favorable and enjoyable learning environments in which teachers and students can experiment with and refine the strategies for enrichment learning and teaching. Our experience has shown that working in such an environment, even for relatively small amounts of time, eventually influences all instructional activities because it highlights the effectiveness, feasibility, and satisfaction that can be derived from engaging in a different "brand" of learning and teaching. In this regard, the enrichment clusters are viewed as learning laboratories that have wider application in general education for both students and teachers. In a later section, we will discuss the ways in which participation in the enrichment clusters can be used as a part of the professional improvement of teachers.

Time-Finding Strategies

There are a number of ways to make time blocks available for enrichment clusters. Our preference is for these time blocks to be at least one-half of a school day, and that the enrichment clusters meet at least once a week. A number of patterns for such meetings are presented in Figure 5. Figure 5-a portrays one month of the typical "five-by-five" weekly schedule that is found in most schools. The five major subjects (reading, math, language arts, social studies, and science) ordinarily meet five days per week, and special subjects such as music, art, and physical education meet one or two times per week. Figure 5-b presents a schedule in which one meeting of each major subject per *month* is "borrowed" from the regular schedule. This procedure yields one class meeting per *week* during which enrichment clusters take place. This approach is the least disruptive to the regular school routine, but it has the disadvantage of short time blocks and the types of discontinuity that result when there is a week between enrichment cluster meetings. In one middle school that

On one hand, many teachers verbalize the importance of students increasingly becoming independent learners; on the other, most view themselves as needing to be in control of the decision-making process. The classroom is a constrained and constraining environment. The prospect of this setting slipping from their control is frightening for many teachers, not surprisingly. It is likely that they hold back from giving their students much "space" for fear they will take over, and no doubt students pick up the signals. As one high school student put succinctly, "We're birds in a cage. The door is open, but there's a cat outside."

John Goodlad, 1984

a **THE REGULAR SCHOOL SCHEDULE**

MONDAY	TUESDAY	WEDNESDAY	THURSDAY	FRIDAY
1 READING MATH LANGUAGE ARTS SOCIAL STUDIES ETC...	**2** READING MATH LANGUAGE ARTS SOCIAL STUDIES ETC...	**3** READING MATH LANGUAGE ARTS SOCIAL STUDIES ETC...	**4** READING MATH LANGUAGE ARTS SOCIAL STUDIES ETC...	**5** READING MATH LANGUAGE ARTS SOCIAL STUDIES ETC...
8 READING MATH LANGUAGE ARTS SOCIAL STUDIES ETC...	**9** READING MATH LANGUAGE ARTS SOCIAL STUDIES ETC...	**10** READING MATH LANGUAGE ARTS SOCIAL STUDIES ETC...	**11** READING MATH LANGUAGE ARTS SOCIAL STUDIES ETC...	**12** READING MATH LANGUAGE ARTS SOCIAL STUDIES ETC...
15 READING MATH LANGUAGE ARTS SOCIAL STUDIES ETC...	**16** READING MATH LANGUAGE ARTS SOCIAL STUDIES ETC...	**17** READING MATH LANGUAGE ARTS SOCIAL STUDIES ETC...	**18** READING MATH LANGUAGE ARTS SOCIAL STUDIES ETC...	**19** READING MATH LANGUAGE ARTS SOCIAL STUDIES ETC...
22 READING MATH LANGUAGE ARTS SOCIAL STUDIES ETC...	**23** READING MATH LANGUAGE ARTS SOCIAL STUDIES ETC...	**24** READING MATH LANGUAGE ARTS SOCIAL STUDIES ETC...	**25** READING MATH LANGUAGE ARTS SOCIAL STUDIES ETC...	**26** READING MATH LANGUAGE ARTS SOCIAL STUDIES ETC...
29 READING MATH LANGUAGE ARTS SOCIAL STUDIES ETC...	**30** READING MATH LANGUAGE ARTS SOCIAL STUDIES ETC...	**1** READING MATH LANGUAGE ARTS SOCIAL STUDIES ETC...	**2** READING MATH LANGUAGE ARTS SOCIAL STUDIES ETC...	**3** READING MATH LANGUAGE ARTS SOCIAL STUDIES ETC...

b **THE PERIOD EXCHANGE SCHEDULE**

MONDAY	TUESDAY	WEDNESDAY	THURSDAY	FRIDAY
1 Enrichment Clusters MATH LANGUAGE ARTS SOCIAL STUDIES ETC...	**2** READING Enrichment Clusters LANGUAGE ARTS SOCIAL STUDIES ETC...	**3** READING MATH Enrichment Clusters SOCIAL STUDIES ETC...	**4** READING MATH LANGUAGE ARTS Enrichment Clusters ETC...	**5** READING MATH LANGUAGE ARTS SOCIAL STUDIES Enrichment Clusters
8 Enrichment Clusters MATH LANGUAGE ARTS SOCIAL STUDIES ETC...	**9** READING Enrichment Clusters LANGUAGE ARTS SOCIAL STUDIES ETC...	**10** READING MATH Enrichment Clusters SOCIAL STUDIES ETC...	**11** READING MATH LANGUAGE ARTS Enrichment Clusters ETC...	**12** READING MATH LANGUAGE ARTS SOCIAL STUDIES Enrichment Clusters
15 Enrichment Clusters MATH LANGUAGE ARTS SOCIAL STUDIES ETC...	**16** READING Enrichment Clusters LANGUAGE ARTS SOCIAL STUDIES ETC...	**17** READING MATH Enrichment Clusters SOCIAL STUDIES ETC...	**18** READING MATH LANGUAGE ARTS Enrichment Clusters ETC...	**19** READING MATH LANGUAGE ARTS SOCIAL STUDIES Enrichment Clusters
22 Enrichment Clusters MATH LANGUAGE ARTS SOCIAL STUDIES ETC...	**23** READING Enrichment Clusters LANGUAGE ARTS SOCIAL STUDIES ETC...	**24** READING MATH Enrichment Clusters SOCIAL STUDIES ETC...	**25** READING MATH LANGUAGE ARTS Enrichment Clusters ETC...	**26** READING MATH LANGUAGE ARTS SOCIAL STUDIES Enrichment Clusters
29 Enrichment Clusters MATH LANGUAGE ARTS SOCIAL STUDIES ETC...	**30** READING Enrichment Clusters LANGUAGE ARTS SOCIAL STUDIES ETC...	**1** READING MATH Enrichment Clusters SOCIAL STUDIES ETC...	**2** READING MATH LANGUAGE ARTS Enrichment Clusters ETC...	**3** READING MATH LANGUAGE ARTS SOCIAL STUDIES Enrichment Clusters

c **HALF DAY ENRICHMENT CLUSTER SCHEDULE**

MONDAY	TUESDAY	WEDNESDAY	THURSDAY	FRIDAY
1 READING MATH LANGUAGE ARTS SOCIAL STUDIES ETC...	**2** READING MATH LANGUAGE ARTS SOCIAL STUDIES ETC...	**3** ENRICHMENT CLUSTERS SOCIAL STUDIES	**4** READING MATH LANGUAGE ARTS SOCIAL STUDIES ETC...	**5** READING MATH LANGUAGE ARTS SOCIAL STUDIES ETC...
8 READING MATH LANGUAGE ARTS SOCIAL STUDIES ETC...	**9** READING MATH LANGUAGE ARTS SOCIAL STUDIES ETC...	**10** ENRICHMENT CLUSTERS READING	**11** READING MATH LANGUAGE ARTS SOCIAL STUDIES ETC...	**12** READING MATH LANGUAGE ARTS SOCIAL STUDIES ETC...
15 READING MATH LANGUAGE ARTS SOCIAL STUDIES ETC...	**16** READING MATH LANGUAGE ARTS SOCIAL STUDIES ETC...	**17** ENRICHMENT CLUSTERS LANGUAGE ARTS	**18** READING MATH LANGUAGE ARTS SOCIAL STUDIES ETC...	**19** READING MATH LANGUAGE ARTS SOCIAL STUDIES ETC...
22 READING MATH LANGUAGE ARTS SOCIAL STUDIES ETC...	**23** READING MATH LANGUAGE ARTS SOCIAL STUDIES ETC...	**24** ENRICHMENT CLUSTERS MATH	**25** READING MATH LANGUAGE ARTS SOCIAL STUDIES ETC...	**26** READING MATH LANGUAGE ARTS SOCIAL STUDIES ETC...

d **ONE DAY PER WEEK ENRICHMENT CLUSTERS SCHEDULE**

The Regular Classroom Day

9:00 am — 3:00 pm

| M | 1 | 2 | 3 | 4 | 5 | 6 | 7 |
| T | 1 | 2 | 3 | 4 | 5 | 6 | 7 |

The Enrichment Clusters Day

| W | All Day Cluster 1 |
| | Half-Day Cluster 1 | Half-Day Cluster 2 |

| Th | 1 | 2 | 3 | 4 | 5 | 6 | 7 |
| F | 1 | 2 | 3 | 4 | 5 | 6 | 7 |

Figure 5. Alternative scheduling plans.

Chapter 4

Four-Day School Week Accommodates Enrichment Learning*

School bells ring differently on Fridays at Ma'ili Elementary School, located about 30 miles from Honolulu. On the last day of each school week, teachers and other community experts offer a variety of optional, high interest enrichment courses to students and any community members who wish to enroll. Recent offerings include, for example: computer literacy, Hawaiian language, hands-on mathematics, enrichment language arts and ceramics.

Do students take advantage of the "day off" to play hooky? Not so, says first grade teacher, Kropf, who reports that on a typical Friday about 600 students and parents attend classes from 7:15 AM until 2:30 PM. Part of the secret for the success of the experimental enrichment program in Ma'ili may be the kind of learning opportunities offered to students. Kropf reported that enrichment learning "exposes our students to a type of learning they don't often experience."

Now, after more than a year with the new program, the faculty and community have decided to adopt the experimental program. Faculty members are hopeful that the more flexible school schedule and enrichment learning opportunities will "lead kids to a greater appreciation for learning and, ultimately, to greater achievement in life."

*Source: D. Dismuke, (November, 1992). Four-Day Week Comes to School. NEA Today, p. 15.

experimented with this approach, the teachers said that by the time they "got organized and settled down," the period was over.

Figure 5-c presents a half-day-per-week approach. The instructional advantages of a longer time block are obvious, and this plan also allows time for students to rearrange their classroom environment so that it is more conducive to the type of work they are doing. For example, students in one enrichment cluster that produced a weekly newspaper transformed their room into a "city room," complete with an editorial department, graphics center, layout section, and printing division. Easily movable partitions made from know-how gained in a book on cardboard carpentry, and permission to bring extra computers and graphics design materials into the room, helped create an atmosphere that contributed to the overall professionalism and ambience of the cluster.

Figure 5-d shows a weekly schedule in which one full day per week is devoted to enrichment clusters. Some clusters meet for an entire day, and others are organized so that students can participate in clusters that represent two areas of interest. The material in the side bar summarizes a very successful enrichment program based on the one-day-per-week plan.

Each school will need to examine its own preferences, and develop a schedule that accommodates local needs. Since all teachers, including music, art, physical education, and other special subject teachers should be involved in the enrichment clusters, some accommodations need to be made in order to develop a mutually acceptable schedule. Thus, for example, it might be necessary to double-up certain meetings of special subjects in order to provide equitable time for subjects that do not meet daily. The key issues regarding any modifications in the schedule are experimentation and imagination. Even issues such as the "required minutes game" (in states that regulate instructional time) can be overcome by simply allocating the time spent in a mathematics cluster, for example, to the total mathematics instructional time of a given school. The current national movement toward the specification of outcomes rather than inputs will help to support our concern for a focus on proficiency rather than "seat time."

The Role of Administrators

Time after time, enthusiastic teachers who have expressed a strong commitment to adopt the SEM have expressed equally strong reservations because they feared administrative roadblocks. Arranging time blocks for enrichment clusters obviously requires a commitment from both central administration and building principals. The first question that inevitably is raised by administrators (and in many cases, by teachers) is, "How can we cover the regular curriculum if we 'give up' two or three periods a week?" The answer to this question could entangle us in endless dialogue and debate about larger issues such as the value of the five-day meeting schedule for basic subjects, how we determine the amount of time that should be devoted to any given subject, and the benefits that might be gained by substituting a small portion of regular subject meetings with enrichment opportunities.[2] Since there is no definitive theoretical or empirical rationale for the allocation of time to school subjects, we prefer to deal pragmatically with the time issue by recommending procedures for tightening up the regular curriculum, especially in the basic skill areas. These procedures were discussed in connection with Goal 2, but it might be worthwhile to repeat at this time the reference to Jaeger's (1992) research. He reported that 8 of the 11 nations that surpass U.S. achievement levels in mathematics spend less time on math instruction than do American schools.

The essence of the issue, however, is whether or not administrators are bold enough to exercise their authority over an issue that is clearly necessary for implementing a school change procedure. The most effective and best intentioned teachers cannot improve schools by themselves. Changing complicated and often bureaucratized school systems requires a partnership in which persons in each role make a commitment to do something different within their respective domains of power and operation. Teachers will need to extend themselves in order to deliver high quality services associated with Goal 1 (as well as the other objectives) of this model. Principals and central office administrators will need to extend themselves by supporting and assisting in the development of scheduling options necessary to allow the objective to commence. And superintendents and school boards will need to extend themselves by obtaining waivers (when necessary) for state regulations that, in some cases, still specify instructional minutes per grade and subject!

There are only two "non-negotiables" regarding the scheduling of enrichment clusters. First, in order to keep the focus on talent development, *all* students should be involved in the enrichment clusters. If low achieving students are scheduled for remedial instruction during these time blocks, we will remove the focus on talent development and create

A principal who can help teachers flourish [i.e., take on expanded leadership roles]...is an enabler: a person in authority who opens doors for others with less power so that they can make things happen. The National Education Association along with several corporate partners scoured the country during the 1989-1990 school year to find 115 teachers who were chosen among 20,000 nominees as being the most exceptional in the United States. When the teachers were asked how it was possible for them to perform is such exemplary a manner, they said, one after another, that it was because they had principals who were enablers—principals who let them take risks.

Gene Maeroff, 1993

The political reality repeats itself as governments attempt to plan educational reform on state or national scales. Ask any teacher or administrator. There are at least three responses....One is to become cynical and not initiate any change....A second is to strive to become indifferent to external machinations—a kind of "this too shall pass" attitude. Third, and by contrast, the learning organization sees the environment differently....It realizes that the outside world is always messy, complex and volatile. It picks and chooses its way, attempting to use certain events as catalysts for action, turn constraints into opportunities, and blunt or minimize impositions that do not make sense. The key differences are that such organizations...realize that the environment is not in the business of doing them any favors, and above all have an insatiable inquiry and learning orientation because they know that that is the only way to survive and prosper in complex environments.

Michael Fullan, 1993

yet another set of blue birds, red birds, and crows atmosphere! Second, the time allocated to enrichment clusters must be respected on a par value with regular school subjects. If this time block becomes a catch-all period for scheduling assemblies, taking school photographs, administering standardized tests, or making up classes that were missed because of snow days, students and teachers will learn quickly that talent development is not a highly valued part of the school's overall mission.

The Continuum of Special Services

A broad range of supplementary services is the third school structure that is targeted by the model. The continuum of special services encompasses enrichment and acceleration options that take place: (1) within regular classrooms or clusters of classes from one or more grade levels, (2) during special grouping arrangements within-classrooms, across grade levels, or in after-school and out-of-school programs, (3) in special schools such as magnet schools or high schools that focus on advanced learning opportunities in particular curricular areas, and (4) through arrangements made for individual students at colleges, summer programs, internship opportunities, or special counseling services. The continuum also ranges across both general and targeted groups of students. Thus, for example, a general enrichment experience on a topic such as local history might be presented to all students at a particular grade level(s), or it might be provided on an invitational basis to students who have a special interest in history. In a later chapter we will discuss how general enrichment for all students serves as a stepping stone for more intensive follow-up on the parts of students who develop advanced interest in topics that were originally introduced through general enrichment.

Age and grade levels also play a role in making decisions about special services. Abilities, interests, and learning styles tend to become more differentiated among students and more focused on the parts of individuals as students grow older. There is, therefore, more justification for interest and achievement level grouping as students progress through the grades. It would be inappropriate to have a special class in mathematics, for example, at the primary or elementary grade levels; however, a within-class cluster group or a non-graded cluster group of the highest achieving math students is one way of ensuring advanced levels of challenge for students with unusually high levels of achievement in mathematics.

At the middle and secondary school levels, achievement in various subjects becomes more differentiated, and interests become more focused; thus, there is greater justification for advanced classes or special services such as a math club or competitive math league group.

The nature of the subject matter and the degree to which classroom teachers can reasonably differentiate instruction also play a role in making decisions about grouping students for participation in activities on the continuum of special services. Subjects that are highly structured and linear-sequential in content (e.g., algebra, chemistry, physics) tend to be taught in a more unalterable fashion than subjects than subjects more conducive to variations in speed and level. Language arts and social studies, for example, lend themselves to greater within-topic differentiation of the complexity of the material; therefore, individual differences can be accommodated more easily in heterogeneous groups. And, of course, age/grade level and the subject matter area interact with one another in making decisions about grouping students for special services. Within-class differentiation in literature, for example, is easier to accomplish at the elementary or middle school levels, but an advanced literature class is a more specialized option at the high school level.

Figure 6 provides a graphic representation of the continuum of special services. Options such as special schools at the high school level, the number of Advanced Placement courses that can be offered, and enrollment in college courses are a function of school and district size and geographic location. The continuum of special services can also be expanded as more offerings become available through increased availability of electronic media and distance learning.

Although the enrichment clusters and the SEM-based modifications of the regular curriculum provide services to meet individual and group needs, *a program for total talent development still requires a range of ancillary services that challenge young people who are capable of working at the highest levels of their special interests and abilities.* The continuum of special services might be viewed as the talent development counterpart to the kinds of special services that schools have always made available to students with remedial or compensatory educational needs. These services, which cannot ordinarily be provided in enrichment clusters or the regular curriculum, are familiar to most educators and have been in place in some schools for many years. Some of these

"Age and grade levels also play a role in making decisions about special services. Abilities, interests, and learning styles tend to become more differentiated among students and more focused on the parts of individuals as students grow older. There is, therefore, more justification for interest and achievement level grouping as students progress through the grades."

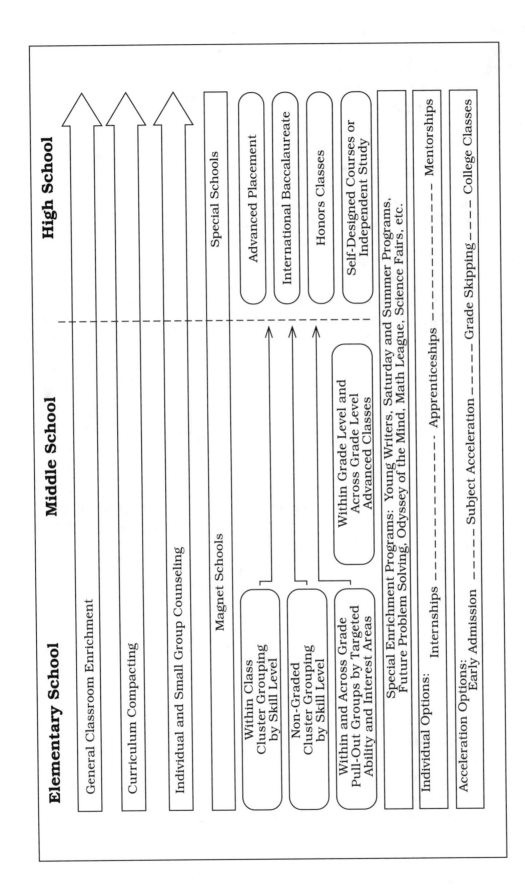

Figure 6. The continuum of special services.

services are represented by the extracurricular program, and in other cases they may be part of special class options or existing internship or work-study programs. A continuum of special services that focuses on talent development typically includes: individual or small group counseling, direct assistance in facilitating advanced level work, mentorships with faculty members or community persons, within and across grade cluster groups for students with extremely advanced performance in a particular area, and making other types of connections between students and out-of-school persons, resources, and agencies. Direct assistance also involves setting up and promoting student, faculty and parental involvement in special programs such as Future Problem Solving, Odyssey of the Mind, the Model United Nations program, the International Artifact Box Exchange Network, and state and national essay, mathematics, and history contests. Another type of direct assistance consists of arranging out-of-school involvement for individual students in summer programs, on-campus courses, special schools, theatrical groups, scientific expeditions, and apprenticeships at places where advanced level learning opportunities are available.

The keys to developing a comprehensive continuum of special services are (1) identifying the types of programs and opportunities that are available for students of varying age levels within certain geographic areas, (2) obtaining information about how schools can access these programs and opportunities, and (3) enlisting school personnel and parent volunteers who are willing to devote some of their time to organizing and managing special service options. Many of the programs and opportunities that are available for young people can be located by contacting professional organizations and societies. *The Encyclopedia of Associations* (Yakes & Akey, annual), which is available in most university and large public libraries, lists thousands of organizations by both topic and geographic area. Some organizations have data bases that list special opportunities for students by category and age/grade levels. The Council for Exceptional Children, for example, will conduct computer searches for special summer program opportunities for a modest fee.[3] An example of an entry from one of the SEMNET data bases, Fairs, Competitions and Product Outlets, is provided in the side bar. In Chapter 8 additional data bases that are a part of the Schoolwide Enrichment Model's data base resources are described.

Young Astronauts Program

The Young Astronauts Program is a national education program for preschool, elementary, and junior high school students designed to promote the study of science, mathematics and space-related subjects. The Young Astronauts Council develops and distributes original, high-quality, space-related curricular materials and hands-on activities to member chapters which are established in schools and communities under the direction of a teacher or a chapter leader. The materials are developed around an annual space theme by curriculum specialists with the support of NASA and other experts who work for industry and government. The program also sponsors contests, conferences and interactive broadcasts to support the program.

Fairs, Competitions, and Student Product Outlets, SEMNET Data Base

Students Do Well at Problem Solving Competition*

After placing second at State level competition, a team of Future Problem Solvers from Hebron Elementary School has qualified for an invitation to represent Connecticut and the Town of Hebron at the International Future Problem Solving Conference. The three sixth grade students—Tom Lewis, Karen Hippe, and Julie Edmonds—will travel to the University of Wisconsin for four days of problem solving and other activities. The students will be accompanied by their coach, teacher Lisa Thomas, their principal, Mrs. Francis Bilodeau, and several parents. The Hebron team is one of only nine teams, out of a total of forty from around the country, to qualify for an "at large" invitation.

The students have worked hard throughout the school year to learn the creative problem solving process and to apply it to such issues as student stress, hunger, ocean abuse, and drug addiction. These children are among the problem solvers of tomorrow—and of today.

*Source: Press release, Hebron Elementary School, Hebron, Connecticut June, 1993

The overall responsibility for organizing a broad based continuum of special services is usually assumed by the schoolwide enrichment teaching specialist working in cooperation with the schoolwide enrichment team. At the middle and secondary school levels, these teams are frequently organized within departments; and the types of special services they focus on represent the individual interests of department members or the department as a whole. Thus, for example, a social studies teacher with a particular interest in world peace encouraged his students to prepare essays and submit them to a contest sponsored by the United States Institute for Peace. An entire mathematics department served as coaches for a Math League team within their school, and an industrial arts teacher, working in cooperation with a local craftsman, assisted a group of interested students in the construction of furniture for display at a state fair. At an elementary school, a group of parent volunteers organized and conducted a series of after school enrichment courses that focused on a wide range of student interests. Some of these courses were so popular that they later were used as the basis for forming enrichment clusters.

The continuum of special services is a marvelous way to use inexpensive and often neglected resources that contribute to talent development. It is also a good vehicle for making use of cultural institutions and private sector resources as well as promoting more community involvement in the schools. A well-planned program of special services may take several years to develop, but as the program expands to include a full range of offerings, all students can benefit from the diversity of resources that are encompassed within this component of the SEM. The self-selection of special services also helps students to work with other young people and adults who share common interests. This factor alone is a powerful force in promoting group acceptance, developing self-concept, and in providing situations in which students develop respect for one another. In this regard, the continuum of special services shares many of the characteristics of the enrichment clusters.

Two Important Issues: Grouping and Funding

GROUPING AND funding are educational matters that are complex and frequently polarizing. The complexity and polarization that surrounds these issues distract us from the central purpose of education which is to provide appropriate and meaningful learning activities for all students. Accordingly, it is important to confront these topics now, clarify their role with respect to this model for talent development, and avoid the confusion they may engender during subsequent explanations.

The Issue of Grouping

Grouping is an intensely debated issue that has always been the subject of much controversy in American education, and the pendulum between homogeneous and heterogeneous grouping has swung back and forth since the beginning of public education. Before presenting recommendations about grouping within the context of the SEM, some of the concerns that make grouping such a controversial issue will be discussed.

Grouping vs. Tracking

Any discussion of grouping must begin by making a very clear distinction between grouping and tracking. We view tracking as the general and usually permanent assignment of students to classes that are taught at a certain level, and that usually are taught using a whole-group instructional model. Tracking is most prevalent at the secondary school level, and there are several features about tracking that have made it a detrimental procedure, especially for students who end up in low tracks. A concentration of low achieving students in one classroom almost always results in a curriculum that emphasizes remediation, isolated and repetitive practice of skills like phonics and computation at the expense of problem solving and comprehension, and very low expectations for all students in the group (Oakes, 1985; Slavin, 1987; Slavin, 1990). Students are frequently locked into all low or "general" track classes; and, unlike college or vocational tracks, they have a dead-end orientation rather than an orientation toward post-secondary education or entrance into the skilled labor market. This lack of purposefulness frequently results in low motivation and self-esteem, underachievement, behavior problems, absenteeism, and school dropouts. Low track classes are usually taught in such a way that they become ends in themselves, rather than as places where students are being prepared to move into higher track classes. Economically disadvantaged students are disproportionately represented in low track classes, and this practice further

*Tracking **includes broad, inflexible programmatic divisions that separate students for all academic subjects over many, if not all of a child's school years***

*Grouping **is the process of organizing and arranging students into classes or subdivisions of classes to maximize their learning, interests, and abilities.***

Group Jumping in Action

Sara: **My teacher moved me to a higher reading group today.**

Mom: **But I thought you just started in A New Day *last* week.**

Sara: **That's right. But my teacher asked me to read to the reading teacher, and then she moved me to Garden Gates.**

Mom: **How long did you read to the reading teacher?**

Sara: **About five minutes.**

Mom: **Did any other kids read to the reading teacher?**

Sara: **Yes. Timmy and Juanita and Michael. Juanita and Timmy moved to Garden Gates, and Michael stayed in A New Day.**

reinforces their sense of failure and feelings about the limited value of a formal education.

In contrast, at the elementary level, within-class instructional groups are common practice, and they serve an important purpose in accommodating different levels of achievement within the classroom. It is essential, however, to have a built-in review process so that students who are ready to progress to a more advanced group do not get locked into a lower group for reasons of mere convenience. Without such a review process, instructional groups can serve as *de facto* tracks; and as such, they play a role in the cumulative development of underachievement. Our first recommendation, therefore, is purposefully intended to prevent grouping from becoming tracking by initiating a systematic practice called *group jumping*. We recommend that, regardless of the types of grouping arrangements a school uses, regularly scheduled formal and informal assessments should be used so students can progress to achievement level groups that are maximally challenging. As the scenario in the side bar illustrates, an observant classroom teacher and a few minutes of a reading specialist's time was sufficient to prevent three children from spending several weeks in a reading book that was below their instructional level. Students and parents should be informed about the group jumping policy (in writing), and information about group placement should be routinely provided to parents and students.

The Politics of Grouping

The argument over grouping has been a long and passionate one, and every faction rattles off its cache of research studies, while simultaneously pointing out the shortcomings of research presented by the opposition. And like all of the armies that ever took up weapons, each group is convinced that rightness is on *their* side. Adversaries even lay claim to the same study by adding their own surplus interpretation or procedure for reanalyzing the data. The only thing certain about the research on ability grouping and its relation to achievement is that there are well-documented arguments on both sides of the issue (Kulik, 1992; Oakes, 1985; Rogers, 1991, Slavin, 1987, 1990). But let us examine how a few studies which report negative social and attitudinal effects of grouping have been blown out of proportion in the popular press and in non-research journals. In an article in *The Middle School Journal* entitled " Tracking and Grouping: Which Way for the Middle School?" (George, 1988), the author uses the results of a questionnaire to draw conclusions that clearly are not justified by the data. Simply stated, the conclusions were that good middle schools were ones that did not group students, and that administrators of non-grouped middle schools were considered to be effective and innovative. This study did not gather any achievement data, nor were any data reported about the criteria for evaluating a school or its administrators. But the most manipulative practice was carried out by the journal's editors who selected outtakes (large type, bold print quotes) that unanimously favored the anti-grouping position and that were in agreement with their own position as set forth in an editor's note preceding the article. A subsequent report sponsored by the National Association of Secondary School Principals (Toepfer, 1990) draws upon this article in a fashion that would lead the casual reader to believe that it is more powerful research than is actually the case; then the report proceeds to highlight yet another string of anti-grouping statements. What has clearly happened is that commentators are using "the research" to support a political issue rather than an educational issue, and "the research" has become little more than a pawn that is being used for political expediency.

The best way to substantiate this accusation about political interpretation of research is to assume for a minute that the research on grouping is inconclusive or neutral, and then examine conclusions drawn from grouping studies. Whenever average or below average students fail to show growth in achievement from grouping studies, the almost universal conclusion is that grouping is at fault. But note how a prominent analyst of grouping research distinguishes clearly between the effect of grouping *per se* and other factors such as curriculum adaptions for students in the group.

> Gifted and special education programs may be conceived of as one form of ability grouping, but they also involve many other changes in curriculum, class size, resources, and goals that make them fundamentally different from comprehensive ability grouping plans....Studies of special programs for the gifted tend to find achievement benefits for the gifted students...and others, would give the impression that ability grouping is beneficial for high achievers and detrimental for low achievers. *However, it is likely that characteristics of special accelerated programs for the gifted account for the effects of gifted programs, not the fact of separate grouping per se....*(Slavin, 1987, p. 307, italics added)

It is not the grouping strategy itself that causes academic gains; rather, it's what goes on in the groups.

Karen Rogers, 1991

Slavin presents a clear message. If positive growth is the result of curriculum adaptations, class size, resources, and goals, why then cannot we apply the same explanation to cases in which growth is not shown? More important, shouldn't we be using the know-how of educational practices that emerges from studies of favorable achievement to explore ways of promoting better performance in lower achieving students? This is exactly the rationale that underlies the SEM. But the grouping issue, rather than a focus on what must be done to create favorable acts of learning, has taken center stage, and it is offered as a quick-fix approach to improving our schools. Slavin, pursuing the same distinctions pointed out above, offers an alternative to traditional forms of ability grouping.

> In the nongraded plan, students are flexibly grouped for major subjects (especially reading and math) across class and age lines, so that the resulting groups are truly homogeneous on the skills being taught. Further, by creating multi-age groups from among all students in contiguous grade levels, it is possible for teachers to create entire reading or math classes at one or, at most, two levels, so that they need not devote much class time to follow-up. (Gutiérrez & Slavin, 1992, p. 339)

The research summarized by Gutiérrez and Slavin (1992) clearly indicates that multi-age grouping based on the skills being taught has proven to be an effective practice. But we also believe that even within a homogeneous, skill level group, provisions must also be made for curriculum compacting and cluster grouping that is based on other considerations (e.g., interests, learning styles) as well as achievement levels. We also believe that group jumping should be the goal of all group assignments. Like the Boy Scout and Girl Scout merit badge program, the goal should be to demonstrate competency in a skill area, after which the individual moves on to a more advanced level of involvement.

Nongraded Instructional Grouping and Within-Classroom Cluster Grouping

In the SEM, grouping is viewed as a much more flexible (i.e., less permanent) arrangement of students than the frequently unalterable group arrangements that characterize tracking. And although we will present recommendations for various types of instructional and cluster groups, it is important to

We should not get stuck or divided on the issue of grouping or tracking. We should concentrate on improving curriculum and instruction to help all youth develop their talents to the highest possible level.

John F. Feldhusen, 1983

point out that there are many other factors about grouping that should be taken into consideration *in addition to* achievement level, and sometimes in place of achievement level. These factors include motivation, general interests (e.g., drama) and specific interests within a general area (e.g., play writing, acting, directing), complementary skills (e.g., an artist who might illustrate the short stories of students in a creative writing group), career aspirations, and even friendships that might help to promote self-concept, self-efficacy, or group harmony. In the real world, which serves as the rationale for many of the procedures that guide the SEM, the most important reason people come together is because they are pursuing a common goal. And in most cases, the effectiveness of the group is a function of the different assets that are brought to bear on a mutual purpose. The major criteria for group effectiveness are commonality of purpose, reciprocal respect and harmony, group and individual progress toward goals, and individual enjoyment and satisfaction. It is these criteria that helped to create the rationale for the enrichment clusters and the enrichment learning and teaching strategies that will be described in detail in Chapter 7.

Another factor that should be taken into consideration is the age level of students and the material being taught. Many elementary age students begin to fall behind and have difficulty catching up when they are placed in lower level groups. And while nongraded instructional groups and cluster groups within the classroom may be necessary to accommodate varying achievement levels in basic skills, variations in teaching style can also be used to deal with diversity in students' knowledge and skills. In studies of Asian teachers, Stigler and Stevenson (1991) point out how Asian teachers thrive in the face of diversity, and indicate that some teaching practices actually depend on diversity for their effectiveness.

> [Asian teachers] typically use a variety of approaches in their teaching, allowing students who may not understand one approach the opportunity to experience other ways of presenting the material. Explanations by the teacher are interspersed with periods in which children work with concrete materials or struggle to come up with their own solutions to problems. There is continuous change from one mode of presentation, one type of representation, and one teaching method to another. (pp. 196-197)

"[I]t is important to point out that there are many other factors about grouping that should be taken into consideration in addition to achievement level, and sometimes in place of achievement level. These factors include motivation, general interests (e.g., drama) and specific interests within a general area (e.g., play writing, acting, directing), complementary skills (e.g., an artist who might illustrate the short stories of students in a creative writing group), career aspirations, and even friendships that might help to promote self-concept, self-efficacy, or group harmony."

5th Grade Japanese Classroom

The teacher walks in carrying a large paper bag full of clinking glass....The children are regarding her with rapt attention. What's in the bag?....She removes a pitcher and vase. A beer bottle evokes laughter and surprise. She soon has six containers lined up on her desk. The children continue to watch intently, glancing back and forth at each other as they seek to understand the purpose of the display....The teacher poses a question: "I wonder which one would hold the most water?" Hands go up, and the teacher calls on different students to give their guesses: "the pitcher," "the beer bottle," "the tea pot." The teacher stands aside and ponders: "Some of you said one thing, others said something different. You don't agree with each other. There must be some way we can find out who is correct. How can we know who is correct? Interest is high and the discussion continues....Finally, the teacher returns to the question she posed at the beginning: Which container holds the most water? She reviews how they were able to solve the problem and points out that the answer is now contained in the bar graph on the board. She then arranges the containers on the table in order according to how much they hold and writes a rank order on each container....She ends the class with a brief review of what they've done. No definitions of ordinate or abscissa, no discussion of how to make a graph preceded the example—these all became obvious in the course of the lesson, and only at the end did the teacher mention the terms that describe the horizontal and vertical axes of the graph they had made.

James Stigler & Harold Stevenson, 1991

Stigler and Stevenson credit the highly skilled professionalism of Asian teachers for their remarkable success and the widespread excellence of their lessons. They also point out that the techniques used by Asian teachers are not foreign or exotic. "In fact, they are the ones often recommended by American educators" (p. 198). Although one of the goals of the SEM is to provide professional training that allows teachers to expand their repertoire of teaching practices, the range of diversity in American schools and our educational traditions will continue to make grouping an issue in school improvement.

Although curriculum compacting and other modification techniques are important procedures within the SEM for meeting individual differences in achievement levels, we also recommend that instructional groups be formed within the classroom and across grade levels. There is both research support (Gutiérrez & Slavin, 1992; Kulik, 1992; Rogers, 1991) and a common sense rationale for forming advanced instructional groups for students who are achieving several years above grade level. Two criteria, however, should guide the formation of advanced instructional groups. First, a course description rather than a group label should be used, and the course should be defined by the level of instruction and the amount of material to be covered. This approach avoids the stigma of calling it an honors or gifted group. Defining advanced classes by the level and amount of material ensures that certain predetermined standards will be met, that we will avoid "watering down" the course, and that success in the course is dependent on certain expectations. A detailed description of the amount of material, the rate of coverage, reading and writing assignments, homework expectations, and evaluation criteria should be provided. The description presented in the side bar on the next page is an example of a course that is designed to attract students who have a strong background in reading, who are willing to cover basic skills at an accelerated rate, and who are interested in alternative opportunities to examine various aspects of literature.

The second criterion for advanced instructional groups is that standardized test scores should *not* be a factor in determining admittance. If, after examining the course description and understanding the expectations of the teacher, a student expresses an interest in enrolling, that student should be given an opportunity, regardless of test scores and previous grades. High motivation on the part of a student, coupled with supplementary assistance from a teacher or other adult, may very well enable a lower achieving student to maintain the level of standards that define the course. A key issue related to this second criterion is that students may volunteer to take a course. Consider the procedure used with Advanced Placement (AP) courses. The content, standards, and examinations are set, but AP is not required. In addition to its attractiveness to some students (and the teachers who offer AP courses), the benefits of such courses are more in the nature of incentives and "bonuses" rather than penalties. Students get course credit for passing an AP course, and there is an additional bonus if they pass the official AP exam at a level that earns them advanced standing in colleges participating in the program.

A good example of how carefully defined standards for rigorously demanding, high level classes can have an impact on at-risk students can be found in the multi-racial San Diego High School. A program based on the International Baccalaureate[4] curriculum was developed at this inner-city school that serves a mainly low-socioeconomic minority population. Students can select from among nine academic requirements that include both traditional courses, an interdisciplinary course in the philosophy of knowledge, participation in a creative, aesthetic, or social service activity, and an extended essay based on independent research. Students' performance is evaluated through written and oral external examinations that are used world-wide, and oral presentations, lab books, portfolios, and research papers are also evaluated externally. Following the inception of the International Baccalaureate Program, the academic performance of all students at San Diego High School improved dramatically, and three years later, 85 percent of the graduating class went on to college. The school became a "hot" recruiting place for many Ivy League colleges seeking to increase their minority student enrollments.

If we are serious about improving the standards of American education and providing greater access to advanced courses for students who traditionally have been locked into lower tracks, it will also be necessary to concentrate on basic skills achievement at lower grade levels. But we also need to have alternative routes to advanced courses for those students who have the motivation to enroll, but who lack some of the skills necessary for high level instruction. Transitional "prep" classes and individual or small group tutoring are ways of helping motivated students prepare for more advanced classes. These approaches, however, should not fall into the remedial

Advanced Placement (AP): Literature and Composition*

The AP course in English Literature and Composition engages students in the careful reading and critical analysis of imaginative literature. Through close reading of selected literary works, students deepen their understanding and enhance their pleasure in literature. They develop critical standards for interpreting the effects writers create by means of the artful manipulation of language. To achieve these goals, students study individual works, their characters, action, structure, and language. They consider both large-scale literary elements such as form and theme, and smaller-scale elements such as figurative language, imagery, symbolism, and tone. Students analyze these and other aspects of literature to derive meaning from their experience in reading. Students consider literary works in their historical context and in relation to their own lives and experience as well....Writing should be an integral part of the AP English course, for the AP examination is weighted toward student writing about literature. Writing assignments focus on the critical analysis of literature and include expository, analytical and argumentative essays. Although critical analysis provides the bulk of student writing in the course, well-constructed creative writing assignments may help students see from the inside how literature is written.

Source: **Advanced Placement Course Description: English Literature and Composition, 1994. The College Entrance Examination Board.*

trap, i.e., reverting to the lowest common denominator of a subject matter area. If, for example, students are preparing for an advanced literature class, the focus should be on literature rather than more practice on grammar or traditional reading instruction.

Managing Within-Classroom Cluster Groups

Although the use of cluster grouping within-classes is a major improvement over tracking or large group instruction, in practice this approach is usually less effective than it could be because students are often placed in clusters on the basis of a single criterion. In most classrooms that use cluster grouping, all high achieving math students or all low achieving reading students are typically members of the same group. The students within this small group are usually given the same instruction and assignments, despite the fact that high achieving or low achieving students can differ from one another with respect to their strengths and weaknesses within the various strands or subdisciplines in a given subject area.

For example, two students who score in the 95th percentile on the math subtest of a norm-referenced achievement test score may be markedly different in their achievement with respect to fractions, decimals, problem solving and/or measurement skills. One student in the high achieving group may need more help on fractions, but less assistance with problem solving. But by using an "average score" to reflect individual achievement in a subject area, and grouping students according to this number, we continue to "wash out" the differences between students and within the subject area. When this happens, the potential benefits of small group teaching as a means of maximizing individual student performance are decreased because individual differences between the students and within each of the ability groups are not addressed. As a result, teachers may not see increased achievement for students who were placed in such groups when compared to students who were taught similar objectives through large group instruction. In other words, the use of small groups for instruction will not, in and of itself, guarantee student achievement (Kulik & Kulik, 1987; Slavin, 1987; Walberg, 1984).

The quality of small group instruction depends as much on what goes on within the cluster groups; more specifically, the achievement of students in these groups depends upon the ability of the teacher to group students flexibly, and then adapt the learning objectives, the teaching strategies, the modeling activities, the practice materials, and pacing to match the students' needs. Flexible cluster grouping allows students to participate in group instruction when the unit pretesting reveals wide differences among students with regard to mastery of learning objectives for a given unit of study. Once groups of students are formed for instruction, characteristics of individuals comprising the cluster dictate the learning objectives, the type of modeling, the type and amount of practice materials, and the pacing.

Although cluster grouping and concomitant instructional changes represent "common sense" with respect to teaching practices, cluster grouping should not dominate classroom instruction. Instead, a balance between whole-class and cluster grouping is determined by the teacher according to the purpose of instruction and the degree to which students differ with respect to various curricular objectives. Large group activities such as storytelling, discussions, debriefings, class meetings, audio visual aids, visitations, lectures and demonstrations are used to motivate students, to introduce or extend a curriculum unit, or to teach content or skills that are new for *all* students. Individual or small group activities are used for intensive study or exploration of specific topics within the unit that reflect strong personal interest or when wide differences exist among students with respect to mastery of learning objectives in a given unit of study.

When teachers implement small group instruction, classroom management issues inevitably arise. "What will I do with the other students in the room?" "How will I know they are meaningfully engaged while I am working with the small groups?" In the 1950s, the answer to these questions was to assign "seatwork" to the students who were not meeting in a small group. In too many cases, worksheets were used as busy work to fill students' time. This seatwork involved ineffective and uninteresting drill and repetition that bore little resemblance to the way the skills were actually used and applied in real world situations. It is no wonder that the research on this form of small group teaching and practice proved to be no more effective than teaching the same objective to all students in the classroom!

Vygotsky's work (1962) provides a possible solution. He suggests that in order to help all students achieve the greatest amount of learning in a limited amount of instructional time, all students should be able to learn and work within their individual "zone of proximal development." Simply put, Vygotsky believed that it is only when a learner is asked to

Grouping is not a single thing. Rather, it comes in a variety of forms and is done for a variety of reasons. It is, therefore, a mistake to think that the different approaches to grouping all have the same effect.

James A. Kulik, 1992

stretch beyond the comfort of his or her present learning levels that maximum learning will be achieved. In order to accommodate this zone of proximal development, Vygotsky recommends that parents and teachers supply students with scaffolding that will support learners as they attempt the difficult learning objectives that are beyond their grasp. Theoretically, we could place all students in their zone of proximal development if we were able to provide each student with his or her own individual tutor. The tutor would adjust the instruction and the practice activities to suit the learner's next desired level of achievement and provide the scaffolding, in the form of feedback, assistance and monitoring, as the student practices and learns these new objectives. This is the same premise behind the very successful Reading Recovery Program (Clay & Cazden, 1992) that is helping so many remedial readers improve their skills in language arts.

A problem arises, however, when we try to provide these same services in classrooms where one teacher is assigned to 25 or more students! Although teachers are unable to act as a private tutor for all of the students in their classes, teachers can increase the amount of time students spend working in their zone of proximal development by increasing the use of small group teaching. Teachers and researchers (Hoover, Sayler, & Feldhusen, 1993) have described the practice of using flexible skill groups in the regular classroom. In these instances, teachers help students in each small group work cooperatively to practice and apply the skill or objective that was the focus of the teacher-led group instruction. By working cooperatively, students provide scaffolding for each other and are not reduced to practicing the kind of repetitive drill that the old "seatwork" approach produced. These cooperative practice groups meet and work with the teacher on a rotating basis; specifically, teachers meet with 2-4 groups a day to evaluate student progress, provide instruction and/or new scaffolding, assess the appropriateness of grouping arrangements and reassign (e.g., "group jump") students accordingly. This application of cooperative learning principles ensures that all students in a small group are supporting and helping one another *and* that they are all striving to achieve a common objective that is appropriate for *all* group members.

While some students are involved in teacher-directed flexible skill groups, and other students are working cooperatively to extend, practice or apply the common objective they were taught in their skill groups, still other

"Vygotsky believed that it is only when a learner is asked to stretch beyond the comfort of his or her present learning levels that maximum learning will be achieved."

students can be allowed to use interest centers, learning centers, classroom libraries, software and technology to pursue individual interests or to extend and enrich a curriculum unit. Students provided with these enrichment options demonstrated mastery of curriculum objectives in the assessment of student knowledge that preceded instruction. Class meetings are used to explain enrichment options and to teach the skills necessary for students to work independently. Student logs can be used to provide the teacher with information about what each student does each day, and contracts can be written by students and teachers, using compromise and consensus, to ensure that each student has a relevant and realistic plan for his/her enrichment time. Of course, teachers can use the enrichment cluster meetings and Type III time (Chapter 7) to mentor and facilitate these student projects.

Concluding Thoughts on Grouping

It is easy to point out the social consequences of grouping, the grouping practices followed in other nations, and the level of professionalism required for teachers to accommodate the diversity that is always present when two or more students come together. Our schools are a reflection of the society at large and the educational traditions that this society has created. Schools do, indeed, play a role in shaping society; however, they have thus far been an abysmal failure at influencing larger societal issues such as housing, health care, and equal job opportunities. These larger societal issues also are forms of "grouping," which must be addressed *at the same time* that we struggle with the most equitable forms of grouping that should take place in our schools. Schools cannot shoulder the entire burden of shaping and improving our multicultural society. Until these larger issues are addressed, and until dramatic changes take place in the funding of education, the levels of preparation of our teachers, and a national commitment to improve standards for all students, grouping will continue to be a practice that helps to accommodate the broad range of diversity that characterizes our school population. We believe that grouping, *per se*, is not the issue. Rather, the issue is what is done *within* groups, regardless of how they are organized, to help all students maximize their potentials and view learning as both a valuable and enjoyable experience. It is for this reason that the *SEM focuses on the act of learning rather than the types of administrative arrangements that have been offered as school*

Observation of modeling alone is not sufficient. Students need to try out thinking themselves and subject their own thinking processes to community reaction and supportive critique. In participating in this social zone of proximal development (Vygotsky, 1962), a child may better envision the new capability he or she would have if only the knowledge the other person had contributed were acquired.

Roy D. Pea, 1988

It would be a loss for all kids if we made schools 'one track' and all kids did the same things at the same time.

James A. Kulik in J. O'Neil, 1992

There's no doubt that a system of education that demands and expects more from all our kids will get more from all or almost all of them. No doubt some will move ahead faster than others. We should do more—much more—for those who start out behind....But we must not apply a kind of reasoning to education that we would reject in every other sphere of life. We must not reject a system of excellence that brings us some inequity in favor of a more equal system in which all are mediocre.

Albert Shanker, 1993

---

reform paradigms. By concentrating on what and how we teach, grouping becomes incidental to the overall process of school improvement.

The Issue of Funding: Investing in an Academic Trophy Case

In order for any program to survive, and to make real and lasting changes in a school, it is necessary to view the costs as an investment rather than an expenditure. Investing in a program that focuses on talent development means that a school district must back up its commitment with dollars as well as noble intentions and a strategic plan for school improvement. The pay-off from such a commitment has been demonstrated in many schools in which we have worked over the years. This pay-off has taken many forms including, for example, improved achievement, heightened motivation and engagement in learning on the parts of both students and staff, and student productivity that has given many schools the equivalent of a well-appointed academic trophy case.

Although SEM programs are not expensive to implement, our experience has shown that separate, line-item funding at the district level is necessary to guarantee the critical mass of resources needed to develop and sustain successful programs. Funds for designated personnel, staff development, and related resources establish the program as a discrete, and therefore, accountable entity within the general educational program. Our experience has also shown that schools that have not made a financial investment in a talent development program end up with little more than a facade that disguises business-as-usual. These schools frequently claim they are doing "good things" to promote high-end learning and talent development, but identifiable services to students are usually spotty, uncoordinated, and of short duration. Without designated personnel, the old cliché, "Something that is the responsibility of everyone ends up being the responsibility of no one," almost always proves itself to be true.

We also have found that state-level funding provides the incentive and support for school districts to make an investment in talent development and high-end learning for all of its students. State funding is especially crucial for financially strapped districts and districts that serve large numbers of at risk students. These districts often view any new program as a potentially desirable, but largely unaffordable "extra," and they frequently rationalize the need for separate expenditures with statements such as: "Our general program takes care of all student needs," or, "We have so many low achieving students that we need to concentrate on the basics." Such statements deny the talent development potential of students who traditionally have been underrepresented in programs for gifted students, and they perpetuate the mistaken belief that a school must be oriented toward *either* basic skill learning or high-end learning. Good schools can and should provide for *both* of these crucial goals of education.

How Does Gifted Program Funding Square With the SEM?

One of the questions frequently raised about the Schoolwide Enrichment Model is concerned with state funding, especially in those states that have allocated separate, state-level reimbursement funds for gifted programs. These funds have been dwindling or eliminated from several state budgets in recent years (Purcell, 1993a), mainly because of financial shortfalls and concerns about elitism and the under representation of minority students in special programs for the gifted. Nevertheless, these hard-fought-for dollars have produced remarkable results for high achieving students, and the last thing that we want to do is create an atmosphere in which the SEM is offered as a rationale for the further reduction or elimination of state or local funding. It has been distressing to learn that some schools have eliminated gifted program funds due to budgetary problems, and then indicated that they would substitute "schoolwide enrichment" (with absolutely no funding). The SEM pursues goals that are compatible with the goals of traditional gifted programs, but it also takes into consideration contemporary research that has resulted in a much broader conception of giftedness (Bloom, 1985; Gardner, 1983; Renzulli, 1978, 1986; Sternberg, 1986). Accordingly, the model has the added advantage of overcoming some of the charges of elitism that have caused the demise of support for gifted programs.

The compatibility of SEM goals with those of traditional gifted programs provides a rationale for recommendations related to funding, at both the state and local levels. Before discussing these recommendations, however, it is necessary to deal with two related questions that are frequently raised about the SEM:

1. Is the SEM a *replacement* for the existing gifted program?

There can be little doubt that our nation's largest untapped source of human intelligence and creativity is found among the vast number of individuals in the lower socioecomonic levels...An invaluable natural resource is being wasted daily by a system of education that has shut its eyes and turned it back on [these children]. The by-products of this waste are evident in unprecedented urban turmoil, in unemployment and underemployment, in rising crime and delinquency rates, and most important, in the human despair that accompanies thwarted expression and creativity.

Joseph S. Renzulli, 1973

2. Does the adoption of SEM mean that we will have an enrichment program for all students and a *separate* program for "the gifted?"

The answer to both of these questions is emphatically no! Rather, the SEM is purposefully designed to provide a continuum of services that increases the challenge level for all students, and at the same time avoids the politically loaded issue of labeling some students and not others. Focusing on developing talents and gifts without labeling "the gifted" does not deny that some students have high levels of achievement, performance, or potential for advanced level performance. We do, indeed, target and nurture specific learning strengths through the use of the Total Talent Portfolio (see Chapter 5). We also believe that schools should *label the services* that are designed to promote high-end learning rather than label students who receive the services. When individual student strengths are identified and nurtured and when services, not students, are labeled, adaptations can be made in any one or a combination of the following school structures: (1) the regular curriculum, (2) the enrichment clusters, or (3) the continuum of services for talent development (see Chapter 4). The following illustration provides clarification:

Anna, a dean's list student at Yale University, began her participation in an SEM program when she was in first grade. High achievement in reading and language arts resulted in curriculum compacting for her throughout her elementary school years. An interest in, and demonstrated talent for writing poetry resulted in participation in cross-grade group enrichment clusters in poetry and creative writing in both elementary school and middle school. By the time she completed fifth grade, she had written and illustrated a book containing more than 180 original poems. Arrangements were made for her to work with a mentor on a one-to-one basis, she participated in state and national writing competitions that were organized by the enrichment teaching specialist, and she was on her school's Future Problem Solving team for several years. In middle school talent pool classes, as well as in high school, she was enrolled in Advanced Placement and honors classes, and her AP literature class teacher arranged for her to join a local authors' guild. Prior to high school graduation, fifteen of her poems had been published in

*The Schoolwide Enrichment Model does **NOT** replace existing programs for high ability students.*

*Furthermore, adopting the Schoolwide Enrichment Model does **NOT** require an enrichment program for all students and a separate program for "the gifted."*

national magazines, and the high school SEM coordinator encouraged her to use her portfolio to gain early admission and a scholarship to Yale. She was the first member of her working class family to go to college. Although her SAT scores were high, they were below the average level for entering Yale students. When her portfolio was forwarded to the English Department by the admissions office, it came back with the comment, "Definitely accept. When she becomes America's Poet Laureate, I would hate to see Harvard or Princeton after her name!"

This brief anecdote points out how we *develop* giftedness and talent, how the Total Talent Portfolio helps us to recognize *specific* dimensions of potential that include interests and learning styles as well as abilities, and how a continuum of *labeled services* played a part in talent development. Anna's parents never asked whether or not their daughter was "gifted!" Rather, they were provided with information about the services that were available or created for their daughter. Information about curriculum compacting helped them to understand why Anna didn't need to do all of the worksheets or regular class activities; they were introduced to the concept of talent development and advanced level school and community opportunities for young people in a parents' orientation program; and they were given assistance in helping complete college financial aid applications.

Accordingly, SEM does not replace existing gifted programs, nor does its adoption signal separate enrichment services for those who have been labeled "gifted" and those who have not. Instead, SEM incorporates all learning activities, including those traditionally targeted for high ability students, into a continuum of services. SEM is an umbrella that embraces many traditional gifted program services. Additionally, it helps to produce true differentiation because targeting specific dimensions of potential creates a rationale for specific services.

If services are labeled rather than students, what, then, becomes of traditional funding formulas that have been based on a "body count" that allocates a specified number of dollars per "identified gifted student?" This approach has resulted in "hard core" identification procedures (a student is gifted or not gifted), which in turn, has placed pressure on school districts to use the single criterion of test scores to select students for special programs. In many states that use hard

*The leaves fall
At the mercy of the wind.
Their stems cracked,
They glide away from the tree,
Softly landing on the ground
Among others,
Who experienced their fate.*

Anna, 8-years old

"The Schoolwide Enrichment Model is an umbrella that incorporates all learning activities, including those traditionally targeted for high ability students, into a continuum of services."

core identification, more state reimbursement money flows to affluent school districts because of the higher scores that characterize students' test results in these districts. Unusual pressures are placed on school officials by parents seeking admission for their children, and instances of "score buying" have been reported in some states where IQ tests administered by private psychologists are accepted by school districts as criteria for certification as a gifted program candidate. Hard core identification almost always results in equally hard core separation of identified students and the invariable criticisms about inequity, elitism and the unequal distribution of resources.

Einstein, once again, points the way toward a solution to the funding question when he comments, "Problems cannot be solved at the same level of consciousness that created them." We must also bring new levels of consciousness to such practical matters as how we go about funding programs such as the Schoolwide Enrichment Model. The best way to avoid all of the problems associated with the body count approach to funding is to allocate state funds *on the basis of total district enrollment*. Many states already use total enrollment formulas for the allocation of other categories of state aid.

Funding for talent development programs based on total district enrollment is not without its own potential pitfalls. Monies could easily be absorbed into the general education program without a clear and specific focus on high-end learning and talent development services. Or the monies could become the school or districts "slush fund" for activities such as field trips, uniforms for the band, or new computers for the math lab. It is for this reason that we recommend state guidelines and a prior approval process for programs. Within these guidelines we further recommend that the personnel and staff development accounts comprise a majority of the allowable expenditures. Equipment and materials should also be allowable categories, but once again, they must be related to specific talent development activities. A particular type of computer, for example, might be necessary for an enrichment cluster that is providing a desktop publishing service, but this purchase should not be used to replace or augment the school's general need for computer equipment. Similarly, field trips are legitimate if they serve specialized, talent development purposes; however, funds allocated for the enrichment program should not be substituted for funds a district allocates for its regularly planned field trips. If we don't earmark and

> *"The best way to avoid all of the problems associated with the body count approach to funding is to allocate state funds on the basis of total district enrollment."*

protect the funds allocated for talent development, financially strapped schools will always find "creative" ways to use money appropriated for talent development for other purposes. Good will and the watchful eye of a Talent Development Committee are necessary to ensure appropriate expenditure of these funds.

Although many factors must be taken into consideration when allocating monies for any school program, we recommend a program budget based on total district enrollment, and calculated at the rate of $100 per student. Thus, a school district of 1,000 students would allocate $100,000. The budget in the sidebar is suggestive of the ways we have found that budgeting can influence quality control.

When it comes to budgeting, there are no magic formulas or easy answers to the many questions that surround resource allocation. Each school and district is different, variations exist among states in both the availability of supplementary funding and the ways in which funds can be used, and district priorities are often subject to intense political pressures. In those districts where programs such as the SEM have attained priority status and in which financial support has been implemented according to the suggestions above, the results have been cost effective. In Chapter 8, a discussion of the organizational components of the model will point out how a combination of designated personnel, a schoolwide enrichment team, and total faculty involvement in the enrichment program can achieve the goals discussed earlier in a cost-effective way.

A Proposed Budget for Implementing the Schoolwide Enrichment Model	
Personnel (including fringe benefits)	*70%*
Staff development (including conference fees, travel to conferences and visitation sites)	*10%*
Materials, Equipment, and Supplies	*15%*
Travel for staff and students	*5%*

---

[1] "Facilitating" is one of those overused and often vague terms that educational writers have a propensity to latch on to! It is used here to avoid the verb, "o teach." In a later chapter, we will clarify the very different role that teachers play when working with young people in an enrichment cluster.

[2] It is interesting to note that massive increases in the amount of time devoted to repetition and drill (euphemistically called "time-on-task") have not significantly increased the general achievement of disadvantaged students. And no one ever seems to question the transition to three (or sometimes even two) class meetings per week when students matriculate from high school to college, where there is an implicit assumption that the material is more difficult and demanding.

[3] For information about this service, contact the Council for Exceptional Children, 1920 Association Drive, Reston, VA 22091.

[4] Information about the International Baccalaureate program can be obtained by writing to: International Baccalaureate North America, 200 Madison Avenue, New York, NY 10016.

Chapter 5

The Total Talent Portfolio

EVERY LEARNER HAS STRENGTHS or potential strengths that can be used as a foundation for effective learning and creative productivity. The Schoolwide Enrichment Model capitalizes on these strengths by developing a portfolio of student assets in the areas of abilities, interests, and learning styles. A model for total talent development requires that we give equal attention to interests and learning styles as well as to the cognitive abilities that have been used traditionally for educational decision making. Assets related to these three clusters of learner characteristics are documented in individual student portfolios; this information is used to make decisions about various types of student involvement in the full range of regular curriculum and enrichment opportunities that are available in schools using the SEM.

Although information obtained from formal assessment is a part of student portfolios, additional information gained through informal, performance-based assessment is equally valuable in maximizing the use of the portfolio. The best way to capitalize on student performance is to (1) provide opportunities for participation in a broad range of activities within and across interest areas, (2) observe and document performance, satisfaction, and enthusiasm, and (3) make decisions about subsequent activities that will capitalize on *positive* reactions to previous experiences. Student portfolios

DATELINE:
RHODE ISLAND, 1993

Rhode Island Girl Wins
National EPA Award

The romance began when Kate W. McCalmont watched Pacific sea turtles laying eggs on a beach one night. When she returned to school, she decided to do a project on her town's endangered turtle, the diamond back terrapin. The project blossomed into a year-long campaign to save the turtle and make people aware that pollution is destroying its only known habitat in Rhode Island, Hundred Acre Cove.

This week, Kate McCalmont's turtle project and public awareness campaign won her a President's Environmental Youth Award, given annually by the EPA to 10 students across the country. In an essay Kate wrote about her project, and said, "I wanted to establish a guardian for the terrapin. I knew no individual could do that, so I thought the whole town would be perfect."

are used to document strength assessment activities, and regularly scheduled meetings with staff members, parents, and students are used to make decisions about appropriate follow-up, needed resources, and the development of future performance assessment situations. Whereas the traditional diagnostic-prescriptive learning model focuses on remediating student weaknesses, this approach "accentuates the positive," because it uses positive reactions to learning experiences as vehicles for attacking deficiencies in basic skill learning. Thus, for example, a child who has developed a spirited interest in dolphins, but who is also experiencing difficulties in reading and basic language skills, is far more likely to read background material and improve written and oral language skills when she or he is working on a research project based on this abiding interest in dolphins. All cognitive behavior is enhanced as a function of the degree of interest that is present in an act of learning, wherever that cognitive behavior may be on the continuum from basic skill learning to higher levels of thinking and creative productivity. It is for this reason that SEM uses performance-based assessment within the context of student interests as well as in basic skill learning.

This chapter is divided into three sections. The first section describes the seven categories of information that make up the Total Talent Portfolio. The second part of the chapter provides practical strategies for using the Total Talent Portfolio, and the third section, The Resource Guide, contains information and resources to assist practitioners implement the Total Talent Portfolio in their classes and schools.

General Features of the Total Talent Portfolio

THE TOTAL Talent Portfolio is a vehicle for gathering and recording information systematically about students' abilities, interests, and learning styles. The major dimensions of the portfolio and the specific items that guide data gathering within each dimension are presented in Figure 7.

A key issue regarding the use of the Total Talent Portfolio and relevant follow-up activities is the creation of learning experiences that will encourage the development of strong interests. How did the student in the above example develop the interest in dolphins that served as a launching pad for subsequent activity? This interest might have been discovered through formal assessment such as responses to

Joseph S. Renzulli

Abilities	Interests	Style Preferences			
Maximum Performance Indicators	Interest Areas	Instructional Styles Preferences	Learning Environment Preferences	Thinking Styles Preferences	Expression Style Preferences
Tests	Fine Arts	Recitation & Drill	Inter/Intra Personal	Analytic (School Smart)	Written
•Standardized	Crafts	Peer Tutoring	•Self-Oriented		Oral
•Teacher-Made	Literary	Lecture	•Peer-Oriented	Synthetic/Creative (Creative, Inventive)	Manipulative
Course Grades	Historical	Lecture/Discussion	•Adult-Oriented		Discussion
Teacher Ratings	Mathematical/Logical	Discussion	•Combined	Practical/Contextual (Street Smart)	Display
Product Evaluation	Physical Sciences	Guided Independent Study *	Physical		Dramatization
•Written	Life Sciences	Learning /Interest Center	•Sound	Legislative	Artistic
•Oral	Political/Judicial	Simulation, Role Playing, Dramatization, Guided Fantasy	•Heat	Executive	Graphic
•Visual	Athletic/Recreation	Learning Games	•Light	Judicial	Commercial
•Musical	Marketing/Business	Replicative Reports or Projects*	•Design		Service
•Constructed	Drama/Dance	Investigative Reports or Projects*	•Mobility	Ref: Sternberg, 1984, 1988, in press	Ref: Renzulli & Reis, 1985
(Note differences between assigned and self-selected products)	Musical Performance	Unguided Independent Study*	•Time of Day		
Level of Participation in Learning Activities	Musical Composition	Internship*	•Food Intake		
Degree of Interaction With Others	Managerial/Business	Apprenticeship*	•Seating		
	Photography	*With or without a mentor	Ref: Amabile, 1983; Dunn, Dunn, & Price, 1975; Gardner, 1983		
Ref: General Tests and Measurements Literature	Film/Video	Ref: Renzulli & Smith, 1978			
	Computers				
	Other (Specify)				
	Ref: Renzulli, 1977b				

Figure 7. The Total Talent Portfolio.

items on an instrument called the *Interest-A-Lyzer* (discussed later in this chapter), or it might have resulted from purposefully planned interest development activities that are a part of the model. But identifying interests through formal or performance-based activities is only a first step. Other strategies in the model deal with specific steps for nurturing interests, examining the ways in which the student might like to pursue interests, and providing the teacher guidance and resources necessary to escalate the level of student productivity. Over the years, a good deal of know-how has been accumulated on identifying strengths and providing appropriate follow-up. Although much of the work on student portfolios and performance-based assessment has concentrated on improving procedures for program evaluation, the same know-how can be readily applied to identifying student strengths and developing related curricular experiences that capitalize on these strengths. Two unique features about the Total Talent Portfolio that distinguish it from other compilations of student records are discussed next.

Status and Action Information

The portfolio consists of both status information and action information. Status information is anything we know or can record about a student prior to the instructional process that tells us something about learner characteristics. Examples of status information are test scores, course grades, teacher ratings of various learning behaviors, and formal and informal assessments of interests and learning styles. We have compiled and developed a number of assessment instruments and techniques over the years that are especially valuable for recording status information, and we have also designed teacher training activities to help ensure the most effective use of this information.

Action information consists of annotated recordings of *events* that take place within the instructional process. Action information, by definition, cannot be recorded beforehand because it is designed to document the ways in which students react to various learning experiences as well as other experiences that take place outside the formal learning environment. Documentation procedures such as the *Action Information Message* (see Figure 8) and staff development techniques related to the use of this form are designed to "capture" episodes in which remarkable interests, unusual insights, or other manifestations of learning are displayed. By "seizing the moment" to record this information, teachers

---

Status Information

Status information is anything we know or can record about a student prior to the instructional process that tells us something about learner characteristics:

Terry's reading w have been consistently high over the last year. Additionally, she scored well on the latest Reading Mastery Tests.

Action Information

Action information consists of annotated recordings of events that take place within the instructional process:

Terry showed great enthusiasm for teaching younger students about her Haiku poetry that she loved to write.

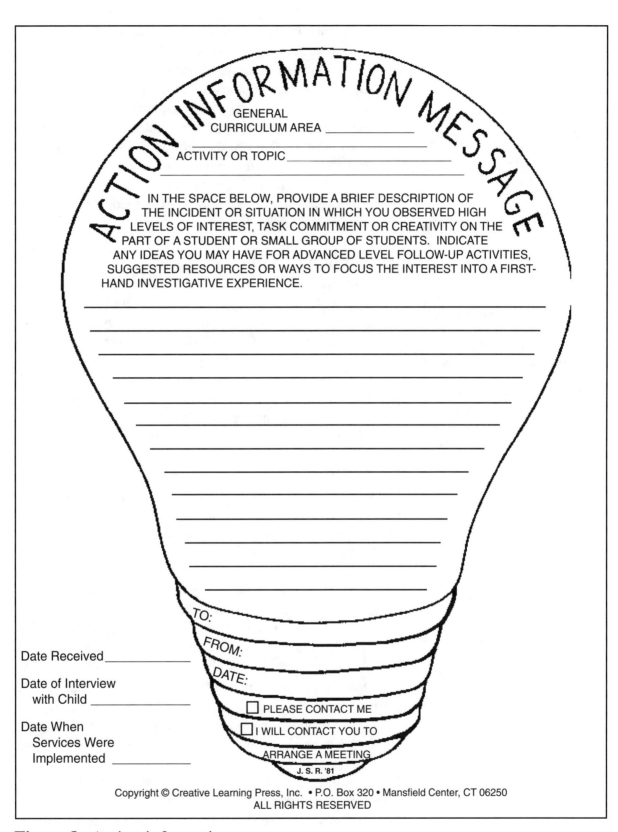

Figure 8. Action information message.

and students have a vehicle for documenting what might be starting points to high levels of follow-up activity. Action information also consists of annotated work samples of completed assignments and other performance-based observations and assessments. These annotations can be both informal notes and more structured analyses of student work such as the type that results from our formative evaluation instrument entitled *The Student Product Assessment Form* (Reis, 1981), which is discussed in Chapter 7. This research-based instrument provides students with feedback on specific dimensions of product quality.

Focus on Strengths

The second unique feature of the Total Talent Portfolio is its focus on strengths and "high-end learning" behaviors. A tradition exists in education that has caused us to use student records mainly for spotting deficiencies. Our adherence to the medical (i.e., diagnostic-prescriptive) model has almost always been pointed in the negative direction: "Find out what's wrong with them and fix them up!" Total talent assessment emphasizes the identification of the most positive aspects of each student's learning behaviors. Documentation based on the categories in Figure 7 should be carried out by inserting in the portfolio any and all information that calls attention to strong interests, preferred styles of learning, and high levels of motivation, creativity and leadership as well as the academic strengths that can be used as stepping stones to more advanced learning activities.

Portfolios of any type are only as valuable as the use to which they are put. Portfolios as exemplars of performance-based assessment are receiving a great deal of attention in the professional literature; they are being considered as supplements to or replacements for traditional evaluation procedures such as standardized tests. Although the information gathered in a Total Talent Portfolio can be used for program evaluation purposes, *the primary use of the portfolio within the context of the SEM is to make educational programming decisions for individual students or for small groups of students who share common abilities, interests or learning styles.* Through a process that might best be described as "portfolio engineering," examples of positive performance are accumulated on a continuing basis, and regularly scheduled reviews are used to make decisions about subsequent talent development activities. These decisions may relate to guidance regarding the selection of enrichment

"Through a process called 'portfolio engineering,' examples of positive performance are accumulated on a continuing basis, and regularly scheduled reviews are used to make decisions about subsequent talent development activities."

clusters, within-class special projects, curriculum compacting, group jumping, or individual learning opportunities that are a part of the continuum of special services discussed earlier. Portfolio engineering also involves conducting conferences among groups of teachers and specialists, meeting with parents, and conveying information about student strengths to subsequent-year teachers, college admission officers, and prospective employers. The "theme" of the Total Talent Portfolio might best be summarized in the form of two questions: What are the very *best* things we know and can record about a student? What are the very best things we can *do* to capitalize on this information? The first question is addressed in the three sections that follow dealing with student abilities, interests, and learning styles. The second question is addressed in the remaining chapters of the book.

Abilities

ABILITIES, OR maximum performance indicators, as traditionally defined in the psychometric literature, deal with competencies that represent the highest level of performance a student has attained in a particular area of aptitude or scholastic achievement. Assessment on this dimension of school performance has traditionally been evaluated by tests or course grades. The first column of Figure 7 includes these conventional assessments, but it also includes a number of additional procedures by which maximum performance can be examined. These procedures may not be as reliable and objective as traditional tests, but they do have the advantage of letting us know how students perform on more complex tasks and on tasks that require the application of knowledge to assigned or self-selected learning activities. The merits of formal testing versus alternative forms of assessment have been debated extensively in the literature, and it is not our purpose here to reexamine this debate or to argue for one approach or the other. We believe that any and all sources of information are valuable if they will improve our understanding of potential for future performance and if they provide direction for enhancing future performance. We do argue, however, that alternative forms of assessment are equal in value to formal tests, and that a Total Talent Portfolio that does not include alternate assessment information will seriously limit the purposes of this component of the SEM.

"The 'theme' of the Total Talent Portfolio might best be summarized in the form of two questions:

- *What are the very best things we know and can record about a student?*

- *What are the very best things we can do to capitalize on this information?"*

In directing the activities of the young, society determines its own future in determining that of the young. Since the young at a given time will at some later date compose the society of that period, the latter's nature will largely turn upon the direction children's activities were given at an earlier period. The future then, depends on children's growth with respect to their abilities— their power to grow.

John Dewey, 1916

Gathering and Recording Information About Abilities

Standardized Tests and Teacher-Made Tests

THE CONCEPT of ability implies the measurement of competencies in terms of maximum performance. The traditional use of the term "ability," at least in educational settings, has almost always been linked with standardized test scores, and expressed in a normative or comparative fashion with the scores of other students in the same age or grade group. Arguments about the value of standardized tests have existed since the time these instruments came onto the educational scene, and it is not our intention to review or take sides in this age-old debate. Nor is it our intention to debate distinctions among various categories of testing instruments, whether they be called achievement tests, criterion-referenced tests, aptitude tests, curriculum-referenced tests, process tests, or any other names that undoubtedly will emerge over time. They often measure the same thing! Standardized tests are a reality in our schools, and in those cases where the tests meet the criteria of reliability, validity, objectivity, and audience appropriateness, they can provide us with useful information if used properly within the context of the SEM. At the risk of dwelling on a cliché, the tests are not as much of a problem as the uses to which they are put.

Although standardized test scores are gathered and recorded in the Total Talent Portfolio, it is important to emphasize that these scores are only one source of information about students' abilities. The fancy trappings and statistical paraphernalia that surround commercially published tests do not make them any more valuable than other types of information about student abilities listed in the first column of Figure 7. The most important use of standardized test scores is simply to identify which general area or areas are a student's greatest strengths. To do this we need only look at *one student's* scores, and we should purposefully avoid comparative information such as percentiles or other norms based on national or even local comparisons. The question that we are raising is: In which curricular areas or aptitudes does this student show his or her greatest strengths?

Teacher-made assessments are usually designed to assess the degree of mastery of a specific unit that has been taught and to evaluate competence in an entire course or segment thereof. Objective teacher-made tests (e.g., multiple

Not everything that counts can be counted and not everything that can be counted counts.

Albert Einstein

choice, matching, short answer) provide information about knowledge acquisition, the mastery of basic skills, and, in some cases, problem-solving strategies. This information is valuable for determining general levels of proficiency, but the most valuable kind of teacher-made assessments, so far as the purposes of the Total Talent Portfolio are concerned, are those that elicit open-ended or extended responses. Responses of this type enable teachers to gain insight into complex student abilities such as: constructing convincing arguments, using expressive written or oral language, generating relevant hypotheses, applying creative solutions to complex problems, and demonstrating deep levels of understanding. Open-ended responses also provide excellent opportunities for students to demonstrate artistic and scientific creativity, and to display advanced abilities such as analysis, generalization, and evaluation. Whenever teacher-made tests result in a student's exemplary manifestations of these more complex learning abilities, the tests should be copied, annotated, and entered into the student's portfolio.

One of the issues that needs to be addressed in connection with the types of open-ended and extended response questions discussed above is their frequency of use in classroom situations. The majority of teacher-made assessments generally fall into the short-answer, recognition and/or recall category. For this reason, there is a need to provide teachers with guidance in constructing and evaluating questions that elicit more complex responses. Fortunately, a good deal of new technology is available for this purpose, mainly as a result of advances that have been made in the area of performance-based assessment. The Resource Guide at the end of this section includes selected examples of publications that provide assistance in developing and evaluating open-ended and extended response questions.

Grades

The grades students have received in previously completed courses can also provide information about particular strength areas. When grades reflect both performance on teacher-made assessments and other accomplishments in less structured situations, they provide a more comprehensive picture of student abilities than can be derived from test scores alone. The advantages and disadvantages of course grades are well documented in the literature on tests and measurements, and all teachers have had experiences related to the grading process and the usefulness of grades. The value of course grades in

Standardized Tests:

- *Highlight student strengths*
- *Focus attention on objectives*
- *Can measure some domains of knowledge accurately*
- *Are cost effective*
- *Are efficient*

Teacher-made and Authentic Assessments:

- *Maximize and highlight student strengths*
- *Do not rely on arbitrary time constraints*
- *May involve an actual audience*
- *Are not always evaluated on a single score*
- *Are representative of the challenges that exist within a discipline*
- *Minimize comparisons among students*

"The value of course grades in the Total Talent Portfolio is similar to standardized and teacher-made assessments in that they all provide a quick overview of general area strengths that may be capitalized upon when making decisions about possible modifications in the regular curriculum, enrichment cluster placement, or access to special opportunities that are available in the continuum of special services."

the Total Talent Portfolio is similar to standardized and teacher-made assessments in that they all provide a quick overview of general area strengths that may be capitalized upon when making decisions about possible modifications in the regular curriculum, enrichment cluster placement, or access to special opportunities that are available in the continuum of special services. Thus, for example, Mark, a sixth grade student who showed consistently poor grades and a lack of interest in all subjects except science, was placed in a science enrichment cluster. This placement may seem obvious, but prior to the initiation of an SEM program, the only supplementary services made available to him related to his deficiencies. Special science opportunities were actually denied to Mark because he didn't "measure up" in other curricular areas. The enrichment program was also the catalyst for curricular modifications. Decisions made in meetings of Mark's middle school teachers provided him opportunities to substitute non-fiction and science fiction reading selections for other required reading in language arts, and creative writing assignments were replaced with writing that focused on scientific interests. The social studies teacher also allowed him to replace regular assignments with reports about scientific persons and events in the countries they were studying, and the enrichment specialist arranged for Mark to assist the computer specialist by repairing equipment.

Teacher Ratings

One of the instruments that has been a long-standing part of the SEM is a series of rating scales used to identify behavioral characteristics reflecting superior learning potentials. *The Scales for Rating the Behavioral Characteristics of Superior Students* (SCRBSS, Renzulli, Smith, White, Callahan, & Hartman, 1977) have been widely used for special program assessment; however, their use in the Total Talent Portfolio is not intended to "label" students. Rather, the purpose of the scales, like all other items in the portfolio, is to contribute information that will result in a comprehensive picture of a student's strengths. The SCRBSS consists of the following ten scales, each of which is named for the specific ability area it is designed to evaluate: Learning, Motivation, Creativity, Leadership, Art, Music, Dramatics, Communication (Precision), Communication (Expressiveness) and Planning. Each scale is composed of a series of items derived from the research literature dealing with specific manifestations of superior abilities within the ten areas. Sample items from five of the ten scales are included in the side bar. Teachers are instructed to read each item carefully and to respond in terms of how frequently the characteristics cited are observed in particular students. The specific response options are: (1) Seldom or Never, (2) Occasionally, (3) To a Considerable Degree, and (4) Almost All of the Time.

When using the SCRBSS, it is important to analyze students' ratings on each of the selected scales separately. The ten dimensions of the instrument represent relatively different sets of behavioral characteristics, and, therefore, *no attempt should be made to add the subscores together to form a total score*. Because of variations in student populations, the range of learning options that may be available in a particular school, and the availability of other types of data, it is impossible to recommend a predetermined set of "superior scores" for the scales. The best "norm" or frame of reference for SCRBSS is the individual student. A teacher training activity based on some of the scales in SCRBSS, and a parallel rating scale for parents entitled *Things My Child Likes to Do* are described in the Resource Guide at the end of this chapter.

Like all information in the Total Talent Portfolio, SCRBSS ratings should be used in conjunction with other information as part of a comprehensive system for identifying student strengths. Every effort should be made to capitalize on individual strengths revealed by the ratings by devising learning experiences that develop these capacities. For example, a student who achieves high ratings on the Motivation Scale will probably profit from experiences that provide opportunities for self-initiated pursuits and an independent study approach to learning. A student with high scores on the Leadership Characteristics Scale should be given opportunities to organize activities and to assist the teacher and his classmates in developing plans of action for carrying out projects. Thus, a careful analysis of scale ratings can assist teachers in their efforts to develop more individualized learning experiences for individual and small groups who share common strengths.

Performance Evaluations of Student Products

Recent developments in the field of educational evaluation have provided large amounts of the know-how necessary to assist teachers in evaluating student products. These developments have benefited from techniques originally developed for special types of evaluation situations such as writing contests, science fairs, artistic competitions, and the

Sample items from **Scales for Rating the Behavioral Characteristics of Superior Students**

Learning Characteristics
- *Has an unusually advanced vocabulary for age or grade level; uses terms in a meaningful way; verbal behavior is characterized by a richness of expression.*
- *Has quick mastery and recall of factual information.*

Motivational Characteristics
- *Becomes absorbed and truly involved in certain topics; is persistent in seeking task completion.*
- *Needs little external motivation to follow through on work.*

Leadership Characteristics
- *Carries responsibility well.*
- *Is self-confident with children of peer group and adults; seems comfortable when asked to show his/her work to the class.*

Artistic Characteristics
- *Likes to participate in art activities.*
- *Incorporates a large number of elements into art work; varies the subject and content of products.*

Communication Characteristics
- *Uses voice expressively.*
- *Conveys information non-verbally through gestures, facial expressions, and body language.*

Examples of Student Products

Audio Tape
Collage
Construction Estimate
Debate
Demonstration
Dramatization
Editorial
Independent Research
Interview
Letter to the Editor
Map
Marketing Strategy
Mathematical Model
Movie Script
Newspaper Investigation
Opinion Poll
Painting
Photo Essay
Poem
Political Campaign
Scientific Instrument
Sculpture
Short Story
Slide Show
Speech
Survey
Video Tape

holistic scoring and primary-trait scoring of written material. In most cases, earlier techniques were associated with academic or artistic competitions, and they frequently depended on expert opinion from specialists within subject matter domains. The more recent developments in performance assessment have attempted to organize analytic procedures into checklists and rating scales that teachers can use to determine the presence or absence of key indicators of product quality. For example, the National Center for Research on Evaluation, Standards, and Student Testing (CRESST), (Gearhart, Herman, Baker, & Whittaker, 1992) has developed a scale for evaluating the quality of narrative, descriptive, and persuasive writing. The instrument contains four 6-point scales for assessing General Competence, Focus/Organization, Elaboration, and Mechanics. For each level of proficiency within these four general areas, specific criteria are provided to help teachers determine the presence or absence of characteristics that should be reflected in good writing. Teachers trained in the use of this assessment technique showed high levels of agreement when the instrument was used in experimental studies.

Similar approaches have been developed by other centers and agencies. The State of Vermont, for example, has developed several analytic assessment guides that are based on scaled criteria of product quality. One guide, the Vermont Writing Assessment uses a 5-point scale and a range of descriptive characteristics to examine Purpose, Organization, Details, Voice/Tone, and Usage, Mechanics, and Grammar (Vermont Department of Education, 1991a). The Vermont Department of Education has also developed a resource book (1991b) and a teacher's guide (1991c) for performance assessment in mathematics. The Connecticut Department of Education, also, has developed performance evaluation strategies in science and other areas in the Connecticut Common Core of Learning (Baron, Carlyon, Greig, & Lomask, 1992). Similar procedures have been used to develop scales in other subjects and in general areas such as interpersonal skills, manual dexterity, and using information systems. At the University of Michigan, Meisles (1993) and his associates have developed a *Work Sampling System* (see the Resource Guide at the end of this chapter) that is designed to be used in preschool through third grade. The system consists of developmental checklists, portfolios, and summary reports that aid teachers in gathering and documenting performance-based information in seven content domains including: personal and social development, language and literacy, mathematical thinking, scientific thinking, social studies, the arts, and physical development.

The work at CRESST and other evaluation centers has focused on program evaluation and the development of scorable portfolios that can be used as alternatives to standardized testing. In other words, the emphasis has been for portfolios to evaluate the effectiveness of instruction at the conclusion of a course, unit, or segment of teaching. These performance evaluation techniques are valuable contributions to the long overdue need for more authentic ways to assess the effectiveness of instruction. But this work also has equal value for the goals we are trying to achieve through the use of the Total Talent Portfolio. By examining existing student products at the "front end" of instruction, we can identify strength areas that can be used as points of entry into challenging assignments, and use these areas as a platform for the development of other skills. Thus, for example, if a student has an interest in science and a flair for creative writing, opportunities for capitalizing on both interest and ability might be pursued by providing opportunities for science fiction writing or adventure stories with a scientific theme. The analytic work that has been done to provide guidance in evaluating students' writing can be used by teachers to make more insightful judgments about strength areas that serve as starting points in talent development, and the scaled characteristics of effective writing such as the ones discussed above and provided in the sidebar can be used to provide students with feedback about specific areas that are in need of improvement.

Another advantage of the work that has been done in performance assessment is that it can be used for staff development activities. Many teachers are adept at evaluating basic skills and assigning grades based on holistic evaluations of more complex assignments; however, additional guidance can be gained by studying the scaled characteristics of proficiency that have emerged from the recent developmental work and research on performance evaluation. The Resource Guide at the end of this chapter lists key references that should be explored by practitioners who want more information about the availability and use of materials used to identify students' ability strength areas.

Sample items from a Story Structure Assessment Rubric

Introduction

4= *Contains a well-described setting, delineates an appropriate time period, and includes rich description of a main character and others who are related in a reasonable way.*
3= *Some description of time and place; includes a main character and others.*
2= *Includes a main character and a brief description of time and place.*
1= *Has only one character and/or little information about time and setting.*
0= *Has no information about characters, time period or setting.*

Conflict

4= *Includes rich detail about the protagonist and his/her problem; elaboration is also provided about the antagonist....*

Resolution

4= *The ending is fully described and makes sense within the context of the story....*

It is hardly necessary to press the point that interests and discipline are connected, not opposed. Parents and teachers often complain that children 'do not want to hear, or want to understand.' Their minds are not upon the subject precisely because it does not touch them; it does not enter into their concerns. This is a state of things that needs to be remedied, but the remedy is not in the use of methods which increase indifference and aversion.

John Dewey, 1916

Interests

THE SECOND dimension of the Total Talent Portfolio is student interests. If there is a "keystone" in the overall structure of the SEM, it is students' interests. *All cognitive behavior is enhanced as a function of the degree of interest that is present in an act of learning, wherever that cognitive behavior may be on the continuum from basic skill learning to higher levels of conceptualization and creative productivity.* The relationship between interest and learning was undoubtedly recognized by the first humans on earth, but it became a topic of scientific inquiry in the 19th century when philosophers recognized the close relationship between interest and learning (Herbart, 1806, 1841; James, 1890). Dewey (1913) and Thorndike (1935) called attention to the important role that interests play in all forms and levels of learning. They also recognized the importance of the *interestingness* of tasks and objects[1] as well as the personal characteristics of the learner. Piaget (1981) argued that all intellectual functioning depends on the energizing role that is played by affective processes such as interests, and he used the term "energetic" to describe this dimension of human information processing. Numerous empirical studies have also demonstrated that individual interests have profound influences on learning (Krapp, 1989; Renninger, 1989, 1990; Schiefele, 1989), and developmental theorists have also acknowledged the importance of interests. Albert and Runco (1986) state that "it is primarily in those areas in which one takes a deep personal interest and has staked a salient aspect of one's identity that the more individualized and 'creative' components of one's personality are energized" (p. 343). Gruber (1986) argued that the main force in the self-construction of the extraordinary is the person's own activities and interests. Research studies that have examined the long-range effects of participation in enrichment-based programs have indicated that the single best indicator of college majors and expressions of career choice on the parts of young adults have been intensive involvement in projects based on early interests (Hébert, 1993). Studies have also shown that students who participated in an SEM program for five years or longer, and exhibited higher levels of creative productivity than their peers, displayed early, consistent and more intense interests (Reis & Renzulli, 1994).

Gathering and Recording Information About Interests

The Interest-A-Lyzer

BUILDING EDUCATIONAL experiences around student interests is probably one of the single most effective ways to guarantee that enrichment practices will be introduced into a school. In numerous evaluation studies of SEM programs, student comments about most favored practices almost always dealt with greater freedom for selecting at least a part of the work they pursued. A planned strategy for helping students examine their present and potential interests is based on an instrument called the *Interest-A-Lyzer* (see sample items in the side bar). This instrument has been used with students in grades 4-9, and it has also been adapted for use with younger children (McGreevy, 1982), secondary students (Renzulli, Hébert, & Sorenson, 1993) and adults (Renzulli, 1977a). The items consist of a variety of real and hypothetical situations to which students are asked to respond in terms of the choices they would make (or have made) were they involved in these situations. The main purpose of the *Interest-A-Lyzer* is to "open up" communication both within the student and between students and teachers. It also is designed to facilitate discussion between groups of students with similar interests who are attempting to identify areas in which they might like to pursue advanced level studies.

Field tests of the *Interest-A-Lyzer* have shown that this instrument can serve as the basis for lively group discussions or in-depth counseling sessions with individual students. Field tests have shown, also, that the self-analysis of interests is an ongoing process which should not be rushed, and that certain steps should be taken to avoid peer pressure that may lead to group conformity or stereotyped responses. An attempt has been made to overcome some of these problems by developing a careful set of directions for the instrument; however, it is important for teachers to allow students maximum freedom of choice in deciding how and with whom they would like to discuss their responses.

Another problem that came to our attention during field tests of the *Interest-A-Lyzer* was that young children often have only limited exposure to certain topics. Item No. 10, for example, deals with a hypothetical situation in which students are asked to indicate their preferences for working

Sample items from the Secondary *Interest-A-Lyzer:*

• *You are fed up with the course offerings at your high school. Your principal has asked you to design the perfect course for people with your same interests. What would the course be called? What would be taught?*

• *Rather than fund a class trip, the board of education has decided to fund each student with an indefinite amount of money for a trip of his or her choice! Where would you go? List three places you would visit and explain what you would do while visiting there.*

• *You have written your first book. What is the title? What is the book about?*

• *Teenagers in your community have been asked to prepare individual time capsules for future generations. You can include 10 personal belongings. What would you include and why?*

To be interested is to be absorbed in, wrapped up in, carried away by, some object. To take an interest is to be on the alert, to care about, to be attentive. We say of an interested person that he has both lost himself in some affair and that he has found himself in it. Both terms express the engrossment of the self in subject.

John Dewey, 1916

on various feature sections of a newspaper. Since many students involved in the field test were unfamiliar with the diversity of feature sections, a brainstorming activity was planned in which students were asked to identify and cut out many different parts of newspapers. The clippings were displayed in the form of a bulletin board collage, and group discussions were used to call attention to the nature and function of each section. This activity helped students to respond to the questionnaire item in a more meaningful way. It is recommended that persons using this instrument consider each item in relation to the age and maturity of youngsters with whom they are working, and that activities such as the one described here be organized whenever there is any doubt as to students' familiarity with the content of the respective items. Teachers may also want to modify or add their own items to the instrument, especially when dealing with very young children or youngsters from culturally diverse populations.

The *Interest-A-Lyzer* is not the type of instrument which yields a numerical score, but rather, is designed in a way that allows for *pattern analysis*. The major patterns or factors that might emerge from the instrument are as follows:

1. Fine Arts and Crafts
2. Scientific and Technical
3. Creative Writing and Journalism
4. Legal, Political and Judicial
5. Mathematical
6. Managerial
7. Historical
8. Athletic and Outdoor Related Activities
9. Performing Arts
10. Business
11. Consumer Action and Environment-Related Activities

It is important to keep in mind that (1) the above factors represent *general* fields or families of interest and (2) numerous ways exist in which an individual may be interested in any particular field. Thus, identifying general patterns is only the first step in interest analysis. General interests must be refined and focused so that students eventually will identify specific problems within a general field or a combination of fields. Additional preferences that we should look for in discussions based on the *Interest-A-Lyzer* are as follows:

- Activities that require precision and accuracy (e.g., editing, scientific experiments, observation, musical conducting)
- Preferences for meeting and dealing with people (e.g., teaching, organizing a "clean-up-the-environment" campaign)
- Activities that show preferences for helping people (e.g., serving as a volunteer at a day care center or kindergarten classroom, becoming a doctor, dentist or veterinarian)
- Preferences for activities that involve color, materials, artistic products that have "eye appeal" and any and all types of design (e.g., costumes, clothing play sets, landscape, jewelry, metal sculpture)
- Preferences for working with machines, tools or precision equipment (e.g., photography, building scenery, refinishing furniture)
- Activities that involve creative expression through music, writing, drawing or movement (e.g., cartooning, play writing, composing, choreography)
- Preferences for leadership, making money or "running things" (e.g., play director, business manager, officer in an organization)
- A concern for legal, moral or philosophical issues (e.g., circulating a petition to start an animal shelter, campaigning for equal participation of girls in sports activities)
- Activities that show a preference for working with computational and numerical problems (e.g., using calculators, computers and slide rules, inventing mathematical games or puzzles, working on "brain teasers")
- Activities that show a preference for outdoor work (e.g., growing things, camping, studying wildlife)

Many interrelationships and areas of overlap exist in the above examples; a great deal of the "art" of good teaching is to sort out interests with the greatest potential for further and, we hope, more intensive follow-up. Information and conclusions that result from the analysis of student interests should be noted on the *Interest-A-Lyzer* or similar document and then placed in the Total Talent Portfolio.

The wisest among the wise is no longer the one who knows more solutions—the erudite—but the one who knows just enough to pose and attack entirely new and fertile systems and has the moral courage to do just that.

M. Bunge, 1967

Style Preferences

Individualization and the Role of Learning Styles

MOST INDIVIDUAL and small group instructional arrangements have focused exclusively on skill or ability levels. An overwhelming amount of research has been directed toward the development of an almost endless number of tests for measuring individual differences in intelligence, achievement, and aptitude. Although these tests have certain obvious benefits as far as grouping, remediation and the individualization of pace are concerned, many conscientious educators have for years questioned the value of these instruments in providing practical and specific programming guidance for the classroom teacher. In more recent years, self-selected and extracurricular activities have called attention to the important role that interests play in motivation and learning; accordingly, a growing number of formal instruments and informal techniques are available to examine personal, occupational and topical interests. Through the use of interest inventories, questionnaires and informal assessments on the parts of teachers and counselors, commendable efforts have been made in discovering the content areas in which particular youngsters seem to have special interest. Many schools are now beginning to pay serious attention to this important dimension of the learner. The result of this expanded respect for students' interests has been a similarly expanded concept of individualization. In other words, instead of devising learning experiences based solely on academic strengths and weaknesses, persons interested in making instruction more meaningful are also considering the topics and areas of study that students would like to pursue.

One of the major assumptions underlying the SEM is that total respect for the individual learner must also take into consideration how the child would like to pursue a particular activity, as well as the rate of learning and the child's preference for a particular topic or area of study. This is not to say that complete freedom of choice can or should exist for all educational activities. On the contrary, there are certain basic skill areas that are taught more appropriately by one approach than another. The number of such cases, however, is more limited than current practices would suggest, and additional steps toward individualization for learning style seem warranted.

Despite a wealth of well-conducted research, schools continue to function in the "dark ages" in terms of the teaching-learning process. Extensive data verify the existence of individual differences among youngsters—differences so extreme that identical methods, resources or grouping procedures can prevent or block learning for a majority of our students.

Rita Dunn & Kenneth Dunn, 1978

Research studies are currently available that support a concept of learning that educators have known about and talked about for years. The concept is that students usually learn more easily and enjoyably when they are taught in a manner consistent with their preferred style(s) of learning. Preferences may vary within the individual according to content area and interest in certain topics; however, if some effort is not made to identify and accommodate these preferences, a valuable opportunity to improve both student achievement and enjoyment for learning will be wasted. As Torrance (1965) has pointed out, "...alert teachers have always been aware of the fact that when they change their method of teaching, certain children who had appeared to be slow learners or even non-learners become outstanding achievers" (p. 253).

A large number of studies have concluded that matching students with various learning environments affects cognitive outcomes and student satisfaction with different types of educational processes (Brophy & Good, 1974; Hunt, 1971; Kagan, 1966; Smith, 1976). Overall, the findings from these investigations suggest that an effort to match teaching strategies to students' learning style preferences can be beneficial. Learning-style-matching approaches were found not only to give students an opportunity to become involved in planning their educational experiences, but also, to enhance students' attitude toward the subject matter under consideration, and, in some cases, to increase scores on end-of-unit examinations. These positive findings, combined with the growing concern about the importance of learning styles, lead us to suggest that a comprehensive model must pay serious attention to the assessment and analysis of styles as well as abilities and interests. This concern is even more relevant today because of greater efforts to organize learning experiences that pay greater attention to multicultural differences among the school population.

Accordingly, the third dimension of the Total Talent Portfolio is a series of indicators of student preferences for learning. They consist of instructional styles preferences, learning environment preferences, thinking styles preferences, and preferences for various types of product styles and formats. These indicators provide information about what individuals are likely to do in a variety of learning situations. Whereas maximum performance indicators and interests are usually specific to a particular aptitude or content domain, preferences for performance cut across content domains,

Adult: Tommy, of all the things your teacher gives you to do in school, which one do you like best and why?

Tommy: Well, I like social studies the best. I like learning about how other people live in different parts of the world. It's also fun because you get to do lots of projects. I like doing projects because you can learn a lot about something on your own. I work hard on my projects, and when I come up with good ideas, I feel good. When you are working on something you thought of, and that's interesting to you, it's more fun to do.

Beth Hennessey & Theresa Amabile, 1988

Teachers must...regard every imperfection in the pupil's comprehension, not as a defect in the pupil, but as a deficit in his or her own instruction, and endeavor to develop in himself or herself the ability to discover a new method [of teaching].

Leo Tolstoy, 1967

interpersonal relations, and various ways in which schools are organized for learning. Preferences represent the characteristic ways in which students adapt and organize the assets they bring to various learning situations. For example, the student mentioned earlier who was interested in dolphins may prefer to pursue this interest through a group project or aquarium internship rather than through a lecture/discussion or simulation format. Although we recognize that it is impossible to accommodate all of these preferences within the context of standard classroom operation, we believe that an understanding of the factors in general, and familiarity with at least some of their manifestations in students, will greatly enhance those opportunities when teachers can introduce enrichment experiences into the schedule. And even within more flexible school structures such as the enrichment clusters and the continuum of special services, it may not be possible to accommodate the full range of individual attributes represented in the four style preference categories of Figure 7. Nevertheless, using as much of this information as possible, whenever possible, should be a major goal of all learning situations. It is only through the use of these types of information that schools can break through the barrier of depersonalization that makes these institutions uninviting places and learning unimportant for so many of our students.

Instructional Styles Preferences

The third column of Figure 7 lists a broad range of instructional techniques that are familiar to most teachers. In some cases, these instructional techniques or styles can also be found in the literature under the title of "learning styles." Although several definitions of instructional styles can be found in the educational and psychological literature (Smith, 1976), the definition we recommend focuses on (1) the specific and identifiable techniques for organizing learning for individuals or for groups of varying size, and (2) the degree of structure inherent in any instructional technique. Our definition and related descriptions of instructional style alternatives have been adopted in an attempt to remove some of the mystery that surrounds the notion of learning styles. By focusing on instructional practices familiar to most teachers, we overcome the drawback of working with a "psychological middleman" that requires teachers to second-guess how certain psychological concepts (e.g., abstract-random learner) might be used in a learning situation. While alternative conceptions have value with respect to stimulating follow-up research that could eventually affect educational practice, our concern is for a theoretically sound, yet practical, approach that has direct and immediate implications for classroom practice.

Examination of the third column of Figure 7 reveals that the several instructional styles listed exist on a continuum, beginning with highly structured approaches to learning and progressing to less structured learning situations. Entire books have been devoted to the study of various instructional techniques, and it is beyond the scope of this book to present a comprehensive analysis of this literature. However, for the purpose of providing a common frame of reference for the discussion that follows, we will present a brief description of the progression from structured to unstructured techniques.

Recitation and Drill. This traditional and widely used approach to instruction involves a teacher asking questions and calling on students to respond with the appropriate information. In contrast to discussion, where students are called upon to think about the relationships among facts, recitation typically entails questions which can be answered by statements of fact. The responses that students provide for these questions are evaluated in terms of the correctness of facts. Recitation is usually preceded by assignment of a topic and rote study on the parts of students.

Programmed Instruction. Programmed instruction is based on students' working alone on material that has been sequenced to teach a particular concept. The material characteristically consists of short statements which terminate with a question or a blank to be filled in. The statements are presented electronically or in a textbook or workbook. Other features of programmed instruction include a provision for immediate feedback, students' determination of their own rates of progress, highly organized content, and low rate of student error. A good deal of computer software has been developed in recent years, and it tends to take one of three forms: tutorial, in which the computer presents new information; drill and practice, in which the computer is used for remediation; and simulations, which involve the learner in relatively complex problem solving.

Peer Tutoring. This technique involves the use of students as teachers of other students. The tutoring situation can be highly structured, i.e., the teacher assigns a tutor to a particular child and defines the content to be covered, or it can be relatively unstructured, i.e., students select their own tutors and cover material that they determine. While peer

It has been estimated that 90 percent of all instruction occurs through the lecture and the question and answer methods, and, yet, only between two and four students in each group of ten learn best by listening.

Rita Dunn & Kenneth Dunn, 1978

Chapter 5

teaching can involve upper grade students tutoring younger children, the practice is usually limited to cooperative arrangements within a classroom.

Lecture. Lecture refers to a verbal presentation in which the teacher or another individual perceived as an expert in a particular area communicates the ideas and concepts to be acquired. The lecture method is usually marked by a lack of discussion or interchange between teacher and students; the teacher "talks to" students. The lecturer organizes and presents the material in the sequence and style he or she prefers.

Discussion. Discussion is characterized by two-way interaction between teacher and students or among students. As opposed to the "straight lecture" method, group discussion involves a greater degree of active participation on the parts of students. Ideally, discussion as a technique requires students to think about the relationships among facts and concepts, to weigh the significance of facts and concepts, and to engage in critical analysis of them. Varying degrees of teacher domination are found, ranging from instances in which the teacher plays a non-directive, mediating role to ones in which the teacher asks most of the questions and provides the agenda and procedures to be followed.

Teaching Games and Simulations. Teaching games are activities that are fun for students to participate in and, at the same time, involve content that the teacher wants students to learn. Teaching games do not need to be realistic to be effective. They can involve the entire class or be geared to individual students or small groups of students. Simulations, on the other hand, are constructed around real-world situations which are used to teach content and skills through role-playing. Generally, a specific concept, problem, or social process is outlined and students are asked to role-play within this context. The student-player must make decisions "on-the-spot." These decisions, in turn, affect the next move of other players. The function of the teacher in this context is generally to coordinate the proposed actions. Realism is a primary concern in the development of simulations. Indeed, the more a simulation reflects "real world" circumstances, the more successful the learning experience will be. The growing concern in recent years to introduce more realism into the curriculum has resulted in greater popularity for this technique and an accompanying increase in the availability of simulation materials. The Interact Company (see the Resource Guide, Chapter 7) is a major publisher of simulations that deal with a broad variety of topics and concepts across

MAYA
A simulation of Mayan civilization during the early seventh century

MAYA invites students to simulate the lives of great rulers of the Mayan culture. Young Indian leaders return to the sweltering jungles of the Yucatan to build their historic cities. Students quickly understand that cooperation between these cities is necessary for a successful Mayan empire to develop.

A simulation developed by Interact for students in grades 5-8.

all grade and subject areas. Interactive computer software has also added new opportunities for problem solving through the use of simulations.

Independent Study. Independent study can be based on independent choice of a topic, independence from the classroom at large, or both. Independent study can be highly structured (as in cases where a course guide, assignments, and proficiency tests are prescribed), or less structured, allowing students to pursue topics or areas of their own choice. Less structured independent study is characterized by freedom from constant supervision, although there is interaction with others when needed. Typically, the student chooses an area of study, develops his or her own approach to gathering information, and produces some kind of outcome, such as an oral presentation or a research paper. If students cover a regular course or unit through independent study, they are usually held accountable to the same evaluation criteria as students who take the course through traditional procedures. A combination of guided and unguided independent study is an excellent way of allowing individuals or small groups to cover material at a faster pace than the pace of a classroom in general. Self-directedness, effective time management skills, and the ability to work cooperatively with others are characteristic of persons who prefer this style of learning.

Projects. The project method, which is also described in the literature as the group investigation model, shares several characteristics with unguided independent study. This method will be dealt with at greater length in our discussion of Type III Enrichment in Chapter 7. The project method is characterized by individual pursuits, and/or by the group of students working together. In some cases the project may fulfill the requirements of an assignment, and students frequently extend their work beyond the original requirements to create a product with real-world application. In other cases the project may originate with the students. In all cases the project results in a final product or service that can be shared with other students. Students work with varying degrees of direction from the teacher or other adults, but typically, the major responsibility for project management rests with students.

Internships, Apprenticeships, and Mentorships. Learning experiences in this category usually involve placing individuals or small groups of students in work-place situations under the direction of adults with high degrees of expertise in a particular profession or area of study. This

---

ZOO
A simulation of caring for animals in a modern zoo

This simulation involves your students in the daily activities of a small, city zoo in Zooland. When the Mayor and members of the city council decide to close Zooland in one year, your students join in the battle to save it. They begin by making a classroom model of Zooland. Then, using this model, they learn how to be zoo keepers. First, they learn the zoo rules and the zoo keeper's responsibilities. Next, they learn how to care for the animals. After passing a brief zoo keepers examination, they begin working on remodeling Zooland. They learn how to design modern barless cages and realistic animal displays. Finally, they use their knowledge to transform Zooland from an old run-down zoo into a modern one with the latest innovations.

A learning activity produced by Interact *for students in grades 3-8.*

approach to learning dates back to ancient times and was the forerunner of formal schools. The degree of structure within these situations varies according to the amount of control exercised by adults with whom young people work; however, use of internships, apprenticeships, and mentorships has been found to be a highly successful method for students who do not adjust well to formal classroom situations and for students who have already developed high levels of interest, motivation, and achievement in a particular area.

The Learning Styles Inventory: A Measure of Student Preference for Instructional Techniques

One of the approaches we have used to gain information about student preferences for instructional techniques is an instrument *entitled, Learning Styles Inventory* (Renzulli & Smith, 1978). This research-based instrument was developed to guide teachers in planning learning experiences that take into account the style preferences of students within their classrooms. The instrument requires approximately thirty minutes to complete and provides descriptive information about student preferences toward the instruction techniques discussed above. As can be seen in the side bar, the Inventory consists of a series of items which describe various classroom learning experiences. Students are asked to read the items carefully and respond in terms of how pleasant they find participating in each one. The directions emphasize that *the Learning Styles Inventory* (LSI) is not a test in the traditional sense of the term, but an instrument that seeks to identify the ways in which individual young people would like to pursue various types of educational experiences. Students are told that there are no "right" or "wrong" answers and that the information gained from the Inventory will be used to help plan future classroom activities.

One of the innovative components of this instrument is the teacher form which accompanies each set of student materials. This form is designed as a tool for teachers to look at the range of instructional strategies used in their own classrooms. The items included on this form parallel those on the student form, but in this case, teachers respond in terms of how frequently each type of instructional practice occurs in their classroom. The profile of instructional styles resulting from this procedure can be compared to individual student preferences and can serve to facilitate a closer match between how teachers instruct and the styles to which students respond most favorably.

Sample Items From The Learning Styles Inventory

Decide how you feel about participating in each of the class activities listed below:

A= *very unpleasant*
B= *rather unpleasant*
C= *neither pleasant nor unpleasant*
D= *rather pleasant*
E= *very pleasant*

- *Having other students who are experts on a topic present their ideas to the class.*

- *Studying on your own to learn new material.*

- *Having a friend help you learn material that you are finding difficult to understand.*

- *Playing a board game that helps you practice one of your school subjects.*

Joseph S. Renzulli & Linda Smith, 1978

All LSI forms are prepared on optical scanning sheets and are scored by computer. Computer analysis results in a variety of easy-to-interpret classroom reports. Scores for individual students contain each student's raw score on the nine dimensions of the instrument. These scores range from 1.00 to 5.00, with a 1.00 indicating a strong negative attitude toward a given learning style dimension and 5.00 indicating a strong preference for a particular style. A student's learning style preferences also indicate the learning style dimensions on which he or she received the two highest and two lowest scores. This analysis serves as a quick summary of student attitudes toward various teaching techniques. This information can be noted on the Learning Style Summary Page by circling the two highest scores in one color and the two lowest scores in a different color. The Summary Page can then be placed in the Total Talent Portfolio. When reviewing large numbers of summary pages, a color-coding approach such as this will save time when decisions are being made as to the most appropriate instructional modifications to initiate for particular students.

A separate analysis of the LSI groups students together according to most and least preferred styles. This information is valuable whenever opportunities arise for forming subgroups within the classroom. The analysis of student data also includes individual and group graphs. In addition, a teacher response form is provided. Teachers should examine closely the results of this instrument to compare the extent to which they use each instructional style and the degree to which the "favored" strategies accommodate individual learning style preferences of their students. Where significant discrepancies exist, the teacher can consider both shifting their general instructional emphasis and planning individual or small group activities that take into account their students' specific learning preferences.

Issues in the Use of the Learning Styles Inventory

Any discussion about learning styles should include some very important cautions. First, every effort should be made to avoid "stamping" a child with a learning style in the manner that some children have been labeled according to intelligence level or disability. Although in rare cases certain students may prefer to pursue most of their studies through a single method such as independent study, what is more nearly the case for the majority of learners is that their preferences for different instructional techniques will vary with age and

"Learning style preferences for individual students...can be included on the Total Talent Portfolio summary page."

123

subject matter. It is, therefore, recommended that the LSI be readministered at various intervals in a student's academic career so that changes in individual preferences can be documented and accommodated more adequately in the classroom.

The second issue relates to the age level for which learning style assessment is appropriate. The LSI was designed for use with students in grades four and higher. Teachers of primary grade students who wish to use the Inventory can do so by making two modifications in the recommended administration procedure. First, items can be read to students and interpreted when the content is not clearly understood. Second, the instrument can be completed in two work sessions rather than in one so as to accommodate the young child's shorter attention span. Teachers should also take into consideration the limited number of teaching/ learning style alternatives to which primary grade students may have been exposed. It would be helpful to involve these students in experiences that incorporate such approaches as independent study, simulation and programmed instruction so they can provide meaningful responses to selected items on the instrument.

"The third and final issue has to do with the degree to which learning style matching is being recommended. It is impossible for teachers to accommodate all students' learning style preferences on all occasions."

The third and final issue has to do with the degree to which learning style matching is being recommended. It is impossible for teachers to accommodate all students' learning style preferences on all occasions. The time and energy required for such a comprehensive effort would be enormous and overburdening for most educators, and even beyond the matter of feasibility, there exists the educational reality that various basic skills can be transmitted more effectively through certain approaches than they can through others. A case in point would be specialized topics in mathematics which might best be taught through lecture or programmed instruction and essentially could not be taught efficiently through a simulation or discussion approach.

The current situation in most classrooms, however, is that learning style preferences are rarely, if ever, considered in the overall planning of educational programs. We are suggesting that this is a serious oversight. And while we do not recommend that instruction be guided solely by learning style preferences, we believe that teachers should make informed decisions about the areas or units within which style differences *can* be incorporated. We also recommend that the LSI be considered as a diagnostic tool for examining a school's staff development needs as far as instructional techniques are concerned. If, for example, the data show that large numbers of a faculty are seldom using a technique such as simulation, this information provides a good rationale for providing workshops on this method of instruction and making available specific materials that are based on the use of simulations.

Learning Environment Preferences

Environmental preferences have not been investigated to the same extent as preferences for instructional style; however, a small body of research and a large measure of common sense suggest that the social and physical aspects of the environment affect various kinds of school performance. Amabile (1983) reviewed research dealing with social and environmental factors that influence creativity in school-age learners. The social contexts within which people operate reflect their preferences for closeness and interaction with others. When one is given freedom of choice, the extent to which she or he pursues group affiliation is almost always an indicator of social style preferences. Some students thrive in small or large peer group situations, others prefer to work with a single partner, and still others prefer to work alone or with an adult. Environmental preferences, like the instructional preferences discussed above, may vary as a function of the material being taught, the nature of the task to be accomplished, and the social relationships that exist within any given group of students. Most modern classrooms provide variations in the learning environment, but these variations are usually offered to students on a one-choice-at-a-time basis. In other words, a teacher may alternate among organizational arrangements such as individual seatwork, cooperative learning groups, and sustained silent reading; however, students are usually not given a choice outside the organizational arrangement selected by the teacher. Although a predominant organizational arrangement may be necessary for purposes of efficiency and classroom control, we recommend that some attention be given to modification or "waivers" when it is clear that some students will benefit from a variation in the learning environment.

Dunn and Dunn (1978, 1992, 1993) investigated factors that affect learners in four general categories. The first categories consist of environmental influences such as sound, light, temperature, and the physical design of the learning environment. The second category consists of emotional factors such as motivation, persistence, responsibility, and the

We have found that there exists a strong and positive link between a person's motivational state and the creativity of the person's performance. And in large part it is certain aspects of the social environment that determines that relationship: People will be most creative when they feel motivated primarily by the interest, enjoyment, satisfaction and challenge of the work itself—not by external pressures.

Beth Hennessey & Theresa Amabile, 1988

"Thinking styles preferences might best be viewed as the bridge between abilities and personality."

degree of structure in learning situations. The third category focuses on the sociological needs of learners and is based on preferences for learning group arrangements (e.g., self, pair, small group, large group, with or without adults). The fourth category comprises factors related to the physical environment such as perceptual modality preferences (e.g., auditory, visual, tactile, and kinesthetic), food intake, time of day, and the amount of mobility that is permitted in the learning environment. A 100-item instrument entitled the *Learning Style Inventory* (Dunn, Dunn, & Price, 1975), provides factor scores and profiles for each of the four categories described above, and the authors have provided numerous practical suggestions for designing educational environments that take maximum advantage of individual learning styles.

A series of instruments designed by Henderson and Conrath (1991) uses a computerized assessment format to provide individual student profiles for modality preferences (visual, auditory, bodily-kinesthetic), group preferences (individual, group), expression preferences (oral, written), and preferences for linear sequential activities or random intuitive activities. A guide to implementation activities (Henderson, Hartnett, & Wair, 1982) provides suggestions for accommodating different learning styles in a variety of classroom situations. Information related to these systems for assessing learning environments is included in the Resource Guide at the end of this chapter.

Thinking Styles Preferences

The fifth dimension of the Total Talent Portfolio provides information about the ways in which learners prefer to use their abilities and aptitudes. Thinking styles preferences might best be viewed as the bridge between abilities and personality; and as such, information about this dimension of the learner provides direction about the ways in which students like to address problems. The discussion that follows is based on the work of Robert J. Sternberg's theory of self-government (1988), which is a derivative of his general triarchic theory of human intelligence (1984). According to Sternberg, "...no matter how much one understands about the mental processes, structures, and representations that underlie intelligence, one cannot fully understand intelligence unless one also understands how it is applied to the everyday world" (1988, pp. 199-200). The theory of mental self-government is based on the assumption that people need to manage their everyday activities, and that whenever possible, people will choose styles of managing themselves with which they are most comfortable.

Sternberg uses the three branches of the U.S. Government as a metaphor for the theory of mental self-government. The *legislative* function of mind is concerned with creating, formulating, and planning. Persons with a legislative style like to create their own rules and ways of doing things, and they prefer less structured problems and constructive, planning-based activities such as writing original works, building things, and designing new projects or enterprises. People with this style enter occupations such as creative writing, science, art, investment banking, policy making, and architecture. The *executive* function is concerned with carrying out or implementing plans or ideas initiated by others. Persons with an executive style prefer to follow rules, figure out ways to get things done, and they like prestructured problems and working within existing structures. The executive style may be the preferred learning style among lawyers, builders, surgeons, policemen, managers, and administrators. The *judicial* function involves monitoring problems and passing judgment over ideas or products. Persons with a judicial style like to evaluate rules, procedures, and existing structures, they like to write critiques, give opinions, and judge people and their work. This style is found in occupations such as judge, critic, systems analyst, admissions officer, and quality control specialist (Sternberg, 1988).

Additional dimensions of Sternberg's government metaphor are the forms, levels, scope, and leanings of mental self-government. "Forms" include monarchic, hierarchic, oligarchic, and anarchic. The *monarchic* form is one in which a single goal, activity, or way of doing things predominates, whereas the *hierarchic* form allows for multiple goals within a prioritized list of alternatives. The *oligarchic* form places equal importance on each goal or activity. And the *anarchic* form resists all rules, guidelines, and standard procedures for pursuing goals and problems. Levels are global and local and refer to the size, complexity, and abstractness of problems with which one chooses to deal. The internal or external nature of problems defines "scope," and by one's leanings is meant where one falls on a continuum of conservative to liberal. Sternberg argues that our attempts to understand academic and job performance solely in terms of intelligence and personality have not been successful because we have neglected to account for thinking styles, which he maintains

I am always ready to learn...but I do not always like being taught.

Winston Churchill

are the "missing link" between intelligence and personality on the one hand, and school and job performance on the other.

Sternberg and Wagner (1991) have developed and carried out research studies on an instrument entitled, *Mental Self-Government Thinking Styles Inventory.* This 128-item, Likert scale questionnaire yields factor scores for each of the following 13 subscales. A sample item from each subscale is included to characterize the types of questions upon which the subscale factors are based.

A thinking style is the way in which intelligence is utilized in thought and action.

Robert J. Sternberg, 1988

Legislative:	I feel happier about a job when I can decide for myself what and how to do it.
Executive:	I like situations in which my role and the way I participate are clearly defined.
Judicial:	When faced with opposing ideas, I like to decide which is the right way to do something.
Global:	I like situations where I can focus on general issues rather than specifics.
Local:	In discussing or writing on a topic, I think the details and facts are more important than the overall picture.
Progressive:	I like to change old ideas or ways of doing things and to seek better ones.
Conservative:	I like tasks and problems that have fixed rules to follow in order to complete them.
Hierarchical:	Before starting a project, I like to know the things I have to do and in what order.
Monarchical:	I have to finish one project before starting another.
Oligarchic:	When there are several important things to do, I choose the ones most important to my peer group.
Anarchic:	I can switch from one task to another easily, because all tasks seem to me to be equally important.

Internal: I prefer situations where I can carry out my own ideas, without relying on others.

External: If I need more information, I prefer to talk about it with others to reading reports on it.

Several aspects of Sternberg's mental self-government theory have implications for its use in the Total Talent Portfolio, as well as for the educational practices recommended in the SEM. First, he points out that "people do not have one style exclusively — rather, they tend to specialize, some people more than others" (1988, p. 204). He also points out that: teachers as well as students have preferred styles; students will seek teachers or activities that are compatible with preferred styles; and that almost any subject can be taught in a variety of styles (Sternberg, 1990). Sternberg believes that programs should be developed to help people modify their styles to make them more adaptable to required tasks of school and work, and that opportunities should be made available that allow students to capitalize upon preferred styles. Teachers and students can use their knowledge of thinking styles in structured, regular curriculum situations to make modifications in assignments, to organize instructional groups, and to develop divisions of labor in group activities. In less structured situations such as the enrichment clusters, where commonality of interest is the rationale for group membership, an understanding of the various thinking styles represented in the group will assist teachers and other adults in forming subgroups and organizing the work of the cluster. Post-learning analysis in both regular curriculum situations and enrichment clusters is designed to help students understand their individual preferences across all four style dimensions of the Total Talent Portfolio, to expand their style repertoire, and to use styles to maximize their effectiveness in a variety of learning situations.

Expression Style Preferences

The final category in the Total Talent Portfolio deals with the ways in which people prefer to express themselves. Most classroom activities depend on written and oral expression; special subject areas such as art and physical education are based on expression styles inherent in their respective disciplines. A knowledge of expression style preferences can help teachers expand the range of learning options for

Sternberg's mental self-government theory has applications for the Total Talent Portfolio:

- *Students do not have just one thinking style, but several among which are one or two that are favored.*

- *Teachers, as well as students, have preferred thinking styles.*

- *Awareness and knowledge about thinking styles can be used by teachers and students to modify the classroom learning environment and the environment of the enrichment clusters. Such modification can maximize the potentials of the school's nuclear family members.*

*Examples of the Ways
Human Beings Express
Themselves*

*Advertisement
Board game
Book cover
Buildings
Charcoal sketch
Coin collection
Costume
Demonstration/March
Diorama
Dress pattern
Editorial
Embroidery
Experiment
Fairy tale
Family tree
Haiku
HyperCard stack
Landscaping
Lecture
Lesson plan
Love letter
Map
Mural
News report
Package for a product
Paper weight
Photo essay
Picture book
Relief map
Rugs
Sand casting
Sculpture
Sit-ins
Song
Sonnet
Terrarium
Textbook
Transparency for an
overhead projector
Travelogue
Video game
Watercolor painting*

individuals and small groups by "legitimizing" a broader variety of the ways in which students express themselves. We all know of students who, for example, may be limited in physical prowess, but who have capitalized on their interest in athletics through related activities such as sports writing, photography, or serving as a team manager. Similarly, students who have difficulty with written assignments can develop language skills and show evidence of subject matter competence through oral presentations; debates; dramatizations; the production of a film, video, or slide show; or participation in simulations that require oral rather than written communication.

Some styles of expression are more participative and leadership-oriented than product-oriented. Organizational, management, and service activities such as starting a club or business, serving as a project or team leader, or participating in community service activities should be explored as alternatives to the traditional written or oral formats that characterize most formal learning activities. These alternatives are especially valuable for students with limited English proficiency, or students who have had difficulty with standard writing or formal speaking skills. For example, we are familiar with a student with learning disabilities in both reading and writing, but with an unusual aptitude and interest in physical science, who won a state science fair by submitting his project in the form of a photographic essay and a series of computer-generated diagrams that explained his research on the spectra of stars. A knowledge of the ways in which young people prefer to express themselves can be a valuable tool for organizing cooperative learning and project groups. By varying responsibilities along the lines of expression styles, a functional rather than random division of labor is established, and more students have an opportunity to contribute in unique strength areas. In one of the companion volumes to this book (Renzulli & Reis, 1985, pp. 413-422) we have listed dozens of "outlet vehicles" that will help teachers and students explore a broadened range of modes of expression. Another way to explore this range is to create a bulletin board around the theme of "How Human Beings Express Themselves." Students should be encouraged to collect as many examples as they can of products (or pictures of products) which have been created by individuals or groups. Discussions about past experiences and speculations about future styles of expression that students might want to explore will help both students and teachers gain a better understanding of expression styles.

Using the Total Talent Portfolio

THE MAIN purpose of the portfolio is to provide as comprehensive a picture as possible about each student's *strengths* in the areas of abilities, interests, and styles. The easiest way to use the portfolio is to prepare a folder for each student, and include in the folder a copy of Figure 7. Simply circling items on this figure that reflect strength areas will provide at a glance a comprehensive picture of strengths that can be capitalized on in various learning situations. Circled items should be "backed-up" by including in the folder examples of student work that are illustrative of the circled items. More detailed profiles can be prepared by simply pasting each of the six columns in Figure 7 on the left-hand side of blank pages, and using the remainder of each page to record anecdotal notes, observations, and references to work samples included in the portfolio. It is important to point out that the categories listed in each column are only guides for recording certain types of information. Additional types of proficiency information may be included as a result of particular learning opportunities that may exist within certain schools or classrooms, or because of certain behavioral strengths displayed by students that fall outside of the categories and items specified in the columns of Figure 7. This figure, or any form derived from it, is designed to call attention to documented student characteristics, to provide an overview of all information in the portfolio, and to serve as the bases for discussions geared toward making programming decisions. Student work, selected by teachers *and* students, should be placed in the portfolio, and examples of particular strengths within a work sample should be marked and annotated with attached notes or marginal comments by the teacher and student. It is recommended that portfolios be reviewed by teams of teachers at least four times a year, and that the portfolios also serve as focal points for meetings with parents. The cover sheet of the portfolio should include summary notations about particular accomplishments within each of the school structures upon which the SEM is targeted. The portfolio should "travel" with a students from year to year, and should serve as the basis for briefing subsequent year teachers about individual student strengths and accomplishments.

In order for the Total Talent Portfolio to achieve maximum effectiveness, it is necessary to avoid three pitfalls that have characterized other systems for gathering and

"Simply circling items in each column of the Total Talent Portfolio that reflect strength areas will provide at a glance a comprehensive picture of student strengths that can be capitalized on in various learning situations."

recording information about student performance. These pitfalls are: (1) the escalation of needless paperwork, (2) the tendency to look at discrete items in student records, and (3) the focus on deficiencies that characterizes so much of school recordkeeping.

Any process for recording information about students can easily turn into another "paperwork nightmare" for teachers. When this happens, the original intent of vehicles such as the portfolio becomes lost in yet another round of recordkeeping overkill and resistance on the parts of teachers to use the information in positive ways. We can avoid this pitfall by not converting the portfolio into another set of boxes, checklists, numerical ratings or percentile scales. Even when the portfolio does include information derived from instruments that yield psychometric scores, we should not take this information too seriously! Most psychometric reporting is based on normative scales that are designed to compare groups of students within categories (e.g., age, grade, gender, socioeconomic level). *The Total Talent Portfolio is intended to look at individual students in a non-comparative way.* We don't want to know how a student "stacks-up" against other students. Rather, we want to know how particular abilities, interests, and styles "stack up" within the student himself or herself; and we want to know this in a very general way. "Liza's best academic area is math," is a statement that allows us to make educational decisions that capitalize on a strength. We don't need complex, comparative statistics to make these decisions for us.

The second pitfall, focusing on discrete items, can best be avoided by noting the interactions among several items in the portfolio that result in a comprehensive picture of student performance and potential. "Liza's best academic area is math, she seems to like science and computers best, she likes to work in small groups, and she likes to draw," is a rich source of information that extends far beyond any one element of the statement individually. A teacher may not be able to accommodate all of these strengths, interests, and preferences all of the time, or even most of the time. But if they are not accommodated at least part of the time, an exceptional opportunity is lost to capitalize on those things that make Liza a unique person and a unique learner. The payoff that results when we make adjustments that accommodate each student's uniqueness is not only in terms of better performance, but it is also reflected in higher motivation and greater enjoyment of learning.

The Total Talent Portfolio is designed to:

- *Focus on the whole student.*

- *Highlight individual strengths and minimize comparisons among students.*

- *Make notations quick and easy.*

A focus on deficiencies is the most serious pitfall of student recordkeeping systems. The Total Talent Portfolio differs from traditional "permanent record folders" in both the use and "the psychology" of the portfolio as well as the information contained in it. Most permanent records are used for class placement in schools where ability grouping is practiced and for placement in skill level groups within-classrooms. They also are notorious for calling attention to learning deficiencies and to personal, social, or family problems. In most instances when a permanent record folder is "pulled" during the school year, it is almost always in connection with a present or impending problem. *We do not want this "psychology of deficit and rehabilitation" to be cast over the Total Talent Portfolio; therefore, we recommend that it not become a part of the traditional permanent record folder.* Nor do we recommend that it become a replacement for existing records. Our focus on positive attributes should remain unmixed from information about problems and deficits because the power of negative information about students always seems to predominate, and, therefore, circumscribe the positive focus that the portfolio is designed to accentuate. *A ground rule when reviewing and discussing portfolios is, therefore, that their only use should be for making decisions about specific and positive actions that will further a student's strength area(s).*

No one is naive enough to believe that in the foreseeable future schools will magically convert from a curricular decision-making process that is externally driven and group-oriented to one that is tailored to the broad range of characteristics documented in the Total Talent Portfolio. The complexity of the educational system, and the many "masters" teachers are required to serve, make it difficult to accommodate the broad array of abilities, interests, and styles that characterize individual learners. But the widespread and well-documented dissatisfaction with schools in general suggests that the opportunity is ripe for experimentation and small steps toward organizing learning environments that are more responsive to the uniquenesses of individual students. Systemic educational reform should begin in the classroom, where learners, teachers, and curriculum interact, rather than in yet another set of regulations or list of standards and outcomes. The Total Talent Portfolio is a tool that can help focus attention on the interactions that represent the act of learning.

No two humans are intrinsically identical. Consequently, all deserve to be seriously evaluated on the basis of individual exclusivity.

As we look to the future...more individuals are going to demand creative outlets. It becomes our responsibility to make available for every individual the opportunities for constructive growth.

Deborah E. Burns, 1994

Chapter 5

Our progress as a nation can be no swifter than our progress in education.

John Fitzgerald Kennedy

---

[1] The interestingness of a task or object is viewed as a property of the task or object rather than a property of the person. Interestingness does, however, have the power to promote personal interests in the learner.

Resource Guide

THE FOLLOWING resources are divided into two categories: Assessment Resources, and Instruments and Inventories. Resources selected for inclusion in the first category are books, articles, technical reports, journals, newsletters and networks which can provide readers with information about the rationale for and design of portfolios. Many of the ideas and strategies provided in the resources can be easily adapted by practitioners to implement The Total Talent Portfolio. To assist practitioners, some of the assessment resources are listed by selected content areas. For those readers needing additional technical support, a list of agencies that provide consulting services related to student assessment is also provided. The first agency listed provides consulting services on assessment and evaluation. The agencies listed thereafter provide technical assistance on a variety of educational issues, including assessment and evaluation, and are listed by geographical area.

The second category in this resource guide, Assessment Instruments and Inventories, provides selected examples of inventories which can be used by practitioners to identify student talents. The instruments are sequenced by type, according to the way they are listed in Figure 2 (i.e., abilities, interests, style preferences). All prices reflect the cost of materials at the time of this writing. A list of publishers' addresses is included at the end of this section as well.

Assessment Resources
Books/Articles
Background Information
Title: Authentic Assessment: What It Means and How It Can Help Schools
Author: Archbald, D.
Description: Authentic Assessment: What It Means and How It Can Help Schools is a 30-page document divided into two parts. In the first, Archbald provides background information related to standardized tests; specifically, the purposes and limitations of standardized tests are discussed. The author then examines what authentic assessments reveal about student knowledge. In the second part of the paper, the author explores the potential of authentic assessments to improve current curriculum and instruction. Finally, the author concludes by describing the feasibility of designing and implementing authentic assessments.

For copies of the article: The University of Wisconsin-Madison, Wisconsin Center for Educational Research, 1025 West Johnson Street, Suite 685, Madison, WI 53706, (608) 263-4730. Price: $8.00

Title: Performance Assessment: Blurring the Edges Among Assessment, Curriculum, and Instruction
Author: Baron, J. B.
Description: This paper begins by providing a brief history of performance assessment in the United States. Baron then examines the reasons performance assessments are being used as an alternative to standardized measures. The author offers an analysis of how performance assessments are being structured in Connecticut in mathematics and science and subsequently, provides a rationale, rooted in cognitive and motivational psychology, for the use of these assessments in classrooms. Baron concludes by exploring insights, provided by teachers, related to the advantages and drawbacks of performance assessments.
Requests for reprints and information: Dr. Joan Boykoff Baron, Connecticut State Department of Education, Room 340, Box 2219, Hartford, CT 06145.

Title: Strategies for the Development of Effective Performance Exercises
Author: Baron, J. B.
Description: This article is divided into four sections. The first examines the values embedded in assessments. The second and third sections explore the properties of effective tasks and the necessity for making assessment tasks engaging and meaningful. Acknowledging the dearth of effective performance assessments available to educators, Baron provides suggestions in the last section for developing tasks which reflect deep understanding of content and process skills.
Requests for reprints and information: Dr. Joan Boykoff Baron, Connecticut State Department of Education, Room 340, Box 2219, Hartford, CT 06145.

English/Language Arts
Title: Assessment and Evaluation in Whole Language Programs
Editor: Harp, B.
Description: Assessment and Evaluation in Whole Language Programs is a 250-page book which not only examines the theoretical base that is developing to support whole language,

but also provides practical suggestions for teachers as they work through some of the realistic and perplexing questions related to student assessment and evaluation. Chapters 1-5 examine the principles of whole language and review past assessment and evaluation practices. Chapters 6-9 are practical and focus on effective ways to use whole language assessment and evaluation in primary and intermediate grades and in special settings, such as bilingual, multicultural, and special education classrooms. Strategies for recordkeeping are discussed in chapter 10, and the concluding chapters, 11 and 12, offer a principal's perspective and a vision for the future of assessment in whole language classrooms, respectively.

Publisher: Christopher-Gordon Publishers, Inc., 480 Washington Street, Norwood, MA 06062, Price: $18.95.

Portfolio Assessment: Getting Started (DeFina, 1992), *Portfolio Assessment in the Reading-Writing Classroom* (Tierney, Carter, & Desai, 1991), and *Portfolios and Beyond: Collaborative Assessment in Reading and Writing* (Glazer & Brown, 1993) are texts designed to help educators begin portfolio assessment in their classrooms. All contain a chapter with a rationale for portfolio assessment, chapters on getting started and sustaining portfolios, recordkeeping, and portfolio assessment. Additionally, they each contain many examples of open-ended assessment questions and assessments requiring extended responses from students.

> *Portfolio Assessment: Getting Started*
> Scholastic, Inc.
> 2931 East McCarthy Street
> Jefferson City, MO 65102
> Price: $10.95.

> *Portfolio Assessment in the Reading-Writing Classroom*
> Christopher-Gordon Publishers
> Norwood, MA 06062
> Price: $18.95.

> *Portfolios and Beyond: Collaborative Assessment in Reading and Writing*
> Christopher-Gordon Publishers
> Norwood, MA 06062
> Price: $18.95.

Title: *Student Assessment: Keys to Improving Student Success*
Author: *Montana State Department of Education*
Description: This brochure is a guide to help educators develop a better match between assessment strategies and learning outcomes: student products and performances. To improve the match, this 62-page document presents a variety of assessment strategies from which educators can select as they develop ways to measure student performance and progress. *For information:* Nancy Keenan, Superintendent, State Capitol, Helena, MT 59620.

Science/Mathematics

Title: *What Do Our Students Know? Assessing Students' Ability to Think and Act Like Scientists Through Performance Assessment*
Author: Baron, J. B., Carlyon, E., Greig, J., & Lomask, M.
Description: Connecticut's Common Core of Learning Assessment Project is designed to develop performance-based assessment tasks for high school students in science and mathematics that teachers can use to determine what students know. The tasks delineated in this document are "bits of curriculum" which the authors believe provide students opportunities to pull their learning together; specifically, each performance task requires students to not only demonstrate an understanding of significant scientific and/or mathematical concepts, but also apply the concepts in real-world contexts. In addition to two performance tasks, the document provides: the Common Core of Learning science objective, generic skills and competencies (e.g., communicating clearly, questioning skills, decision-making skills, synthesizing knowledge from a variety of sources), a list attitudes and attributes performance assessments are designed to foster, criteria of a well-designed performance assessment task, a group and individual scoring rubric, and reaction forms for students and teachers related to the performance assessment tasks.
Requests for reprints and information: Dr. Joan Boykoff Baron, Connecticut State Department of Education, Room 340, Box 2219, Hartford, CT 06145.

History

Title: *CRESST Performance Assessment Models: Assessing Content Area Explanations*
Author: Baker, E., Aschbacher, P., Niemi, D., & Sato, E.
Description: *CRESST Performance Assessment Models: Assessing Content Area Explanations* is a handbook which

presents a performanced-based approach to assessing students' understanding of curriculum content. The material in the report represents the result of five years of research designed to develop alternative assessments in history. By using the writing of expert historians to develop scoring criteria, the authors explain techniques for measuring students' deep understanding of history and scoring their work reliably.

For information: The National Center for Research on Evaluation, Standards, and Student Testing (CRESST), Graduate School of Education, University of California, Los Angeles, Los Angeles, CA 90024-1522, (310) 206-1532. Price: $10.00.

Technical Reports

The National Center for Research on Evaluation, Standards, and Student Testing (CRESST) has developed more than 150 technical reports related to assessment issues in education. The three examples which follow reflect the general nature of the reports and their nominal cost. Technical Report 348 (15 pages), *Accountability and Alternative Assessment: Research and Development Issues,* questions traditional models of evaluation, examines the qualities that good assessment should exemplify, and identifies current research efforts that are underway to produce sound assessment measures ($4.00). Technical Report 337 (45 pages), *Writing Portfolios at the Elementary Level: A Study of Methods for Writing Assessment,* describes an initiative in one elementary school to use portfolios as a way of documenting student writing progress in the classroom and student writing across classrooms in large-scale assessment ($4.00). Technical Report 350 (75 pages), *The Vermont Portfolio Assessment Program: Interim Report on Implementation and Impact, 1991-1992 School Year*, describes the multi-faceted evaluation of Vermont's new assessment initiative ($4.00). *Performance Assessment Handbook* (92 pages) is CRESST's top-selling report. It contains a concise model of alternative assessment, examples of successful CRESST materials, a scoring rubric for performance assessments, and useful benchmark papers ($10.00). These reports, as well as others, are available from: The National Center for Research on Evaluation, Standards, and Student Testing (CRESST), Graduate School of Education, University of California, Los Angeles, Los Angeles, CA 90024-1522, (310) 206-1532.

Journals

Educational Assessment is a new journal, published four times a year, featuring articles on educational assessment and evaluation. Articles in a recent edition included: "Assessment, Testing, Measurement: What's the Difference?", "A National Testing System: Manna from Above", and "Large Scale Testing and Classroom Portfolio Assessments of Student Writing". To subscribe, write: Lawrence Erlbaum Associates, Inc., Journal Subscription Department, 365 Broadway, Hillsdale, NJ 07642, Fax (201) 666-2394. Subscription (individual): $30.00.

Newsletters

The CRESST Line is a quarterly newsletter which is published by the National Center for Research on Evaluation, Standards, and Student Testing, and it features research articles related to assessment practices. Each issue carries an article by one of the co-directors of the research center, and articles are designed to address policy decisions related to new assessment practices. Additionally, issues have a special focus; in Fall, 1992, for example, the theme was portfolio assessment. There is no charge for the publication. Subscribers also receive an additional semi-annual publication, *Evaluation Comment,* which not only lists recent technical reports by the Center, but also contains an article describing current research initiatives. For information: The National Center for Research on Evaluation, Standards, and Student Testing (CRESST), Graduate School of Education, University of California, Los Angeles, Los Angeles, CA 90024-1522, (310) 206-1532.

The FairTest Examiner is a newsletter, published quarterly by the National Center for Fair and Open Testing. Any contribution can be made to become a member of this organization, and memberships include a free subscription to *FairTest Examiner.* For information about membership options: FairTest, 342 Broadway, Cambridge, MA 02139, (617) 864-4810.

Networks

The Association for Supervision and Curriculum Development's Network on Authentic Assessment offers an avenue for interested educators to share, plan, implement, and evaluate performance-based assessments. For more information or to join the network, contact co-facilitators: Kathleen Busick, Pacific Region Education Lab, 1164 Bishop

St., Suite 1409, Honolulu, HI 96813, (808) 532-1900 or Judith Dorsch Backes, Carroll County Public Schools, 55 N. Court Street, Westminister, MD 21157, (410) 876-2208.

Performance Assessment Systems

The Work Sampling System is a performance assessment package that presents an alternative to standardized achievement tests for students Pre-K to Grade 3. The system is grounded in two assumptions: (1) that performances and products are an alternative way of documenting children's social, physical and academic status, and (2) that assessment is necessarily an ongoing process. Accordingly, *The Work Sampling System* consists of: developmental checklists which are criterion-referenced collections of performance indicators by grade level and content domains (i.e., Language and Literacy); forms (i.e., checklists for rating portfolio artifacts, summary forms which document children's progress on the performance indicators three times a year); and a resource guide which describes the components of the Work Sampling System and provides information related to the implementation of the system. For more information: The Work Sampling System; P.O. Box 1746, Ann Arbor, MI 48106-1746, Price: $46.50.

Agencies That Can Provide Technical Assistance Concerning Assessment

Practitioners needing technical assistance may contact:
> The National Center for Research on Evaluation, Standards, and Student Testing (CRESST)
> Graduate School of Education
> University of California, Los Angeles
> Los Angeles, CA 90024-1522
> (310) 206-1532
> Contact: Ron Dietel.

CRESST is a research team that is committed to the research and development of improved approaches to assessment at all levels of education. The organization is composed of a team of researchers from: The UCLA Center for the Study of Evaluation, the University of Colorado, the RAND Corporation, the University of Chicago, the University of Pittsburgh, the University of Santa Barbara, and the University of Southern California. CRESST identifies five major goals:

1. Provide leadership to improve assessment policy and practice at the national, state, and local levels.
2. Improve the quality, sensitivity, and fairness of student performance assessments.
3. Create valid models and indicators for judging the quality of schools.
4. Promote the understanding of assessment development, implementation and effects as they occur in school practice.
5. Advance the comprehension of assessment policy and its contribution to educational improvement.

The following Regional Educational Laboratories also provide technical assistance on a variety of educational issues, including assessment:

Appalachian Region
Appalachian Educational Laboratory
P.O. Box 1348
Charleston, WV 25325
(304) 347-0400
Kentucky, Tennessee, Virginia, West Virginia

Central Region
Mid-Continent Regional Educational Laboratory
2550 South Parker Road, Suite 500
Aurora, CO 80014
(303) 337-0990
Colorado, Kansas, Missouri, Nebraska, North Dakota, South Dakota, Wyoming

Mid-Atlantic Region
Research for Better Schools
444 North Third Street
Philadelphia, PA 19123
(215) 574-9300
Delaware, District of Columbia, Maryland, New Jersey, Pennsylvania

Midwest Region
North Central Regional Educational Laboratory
1990 Spring Road, Suite 300
Oak Brook, IL 60521
(708) 571-4700
Illinois, Indiana, Iowa, Michigan, Minnesota, Ohio, Wisconsin

Northeast Region
The Regional Laboratory for Educational Improvement
of the Northeast and Islands
300 Brickstone Square, Suite 900
Andover, MA 01810
(508) 470-0098
Connecticut, Maine, Massachusetts, New Hampshire,
New York, Puerto Rico, Rhode Island, Vermont, Virgin
Islands

Northwest Region
Northwest Region Educational Laboratory
101 S. W. Main Avenue, Suite 500
Portland, OR 97204
(503) 275-9500
Contact: Susan Smoyer or Dr. Allan Olson
Alaska, Idaho, Montana, Oregon, Washington

Pacific Region
Pacific Region Educational Laboratory
1164 Bishop Street, Suite 1409
Honolulu, HI 96813
(808) 532-1900
American Somoa, Commonwealth of the Northern
Mariana Islands, Federated States of Micronesia,
Guam, Hawaii, Republic of the Marshall Islands,
Republic of Palua

Southeast Region
Southeastern Region Vision for Education
P.O. Box 5367
Greensboro, NC 27412
(919) 334-3211
Alabama, Florida, Georgia, Mississippi, North Carolina,
South Carolina

Southwest Region
Southwest Educational Development Laboratory
211 East Seventh Street
Austin, TX 78701
(512) 476-6861
Arkansas, Louisiana, New Mexico, Oklahoma, Texas

Western Region
Far West Laboratory for Educational Research and Development
730 Harrison Street
San Francisco, CA 94107
(415) 565-3000
Arizona, California, Nevada, Utah

Instruments/Inventories That Can Identify Student Strengths and Preferences
Abilities
Talent Dimensions
Title: Creative Products Scales
Author: Detroit Public Schools
Age Level: Child, adolescent, adult
Purpose: Assesses talent in the arts through product reviews
Description: Nine different types of creative products are reviewed, including: art, music composition, music performance, drama, poetry, short story/novel, oratory, dance (single dance), and dance (group dance). Criteria of excellence are provided for each art form, as are rating scales to assess the degree to which contributions/performances meet each criterion. The scales are sophisticated, and judging requires expertise in the talent area.
Scoring: Judges
Publisher: Detroit Board of Education

Title: Scales for Rating the Behavioral Characteristics of Superior Students (SCRBSS)
Author: Renzulli, J. S., Smith, L. H., White, A. J., Callahan, C. M., & Hartman, R. K.
Age Level: Child, adolescent
Purpose: Assesses behavioral characteristics related to 10 talent dimensions
Description: Pencil-and-paper inventory (95 items) designed originally to identify high ability students. It can also be used to identify the strengths in all students. The following 10 dimensions are evaluated: learning, motivation, creativity, leadership, art, music, dramatics, planning, precise communication, and expressive communication. Teachers and/or parents rate their observations of student behaviors on a 4-point scale from "seldom" to "almost always." The dimensions are separate scales; accordingly, no total score should be derived.
Scoring: Examiner
Publisher: Creative Learning Press, Inc.

Title: *Talent Beyond Words: Identifying and Developing Potential Through Music and Dance in Economically Disadvantaged, Bilingual and Handicapped Children**

Age level: Grades 2-5

Purpose: To develop potential in elementary students through music and dance

Description: The Talent Beyond Words process uses multiple observers, using written observational checklists, to note student behaviors related to music and dance. The observations occur when students are engaged in a variety of activities in the classroom which are designed to elicit general attributes of talent. The checklist does not require expertise to identify potentials in the targeted areas.

For information: Dr. Barry Oreck, Director, ArtsConnection, Murry Bergtraum H.S. Midtown Campus, 120 West 46th Street, New York, New York 10036, (212) 302-7433, Fax: (212) 302-1132.

Achievement

Title: *California Achievement Tests: Forms E and F*

Age Level: Grades K-12

Purpose: Measures student achievement; used to assess educational programming

Description: Assesses students' knowledge in the following areas: reading, language, spelling, mathematics, study skills, science, and social studies.

Scoring: Hand key; computer scoring available

Publisher: CTB/McGraw-Hill

Title: *Iowa Tests of Basic Skills: Forms G and H*

Age Level: Grades K-9

Purpose: Assesses basic skill acquisition. Identifies a student's strengths and weaknesses; evaluates instructional effectiveness

Description: Multiple-choice, paper-and-pencil assessment of basic skills in the following areas: vocabulary, reading, language, work-study, mathematics, science and social studies.

Scoring: Computer

Publisher: The Riverside Publishing Company

Aptitude

Title: *Otis-Lennon Mental Ability Test*

Author: Otis, A. S., & Lennon, R. T.

Age level: Grades K-12

Purpose: Assesses scholastic aptitude

*Note: At the University of Virginia, The National Research Center on the Gifted and Talented has been examining options created by school districts to identify the talents and abilities among culturally diverse, limited English proficient, and at-risk students. A new book, **Contexts for Promise: Noteworthy Practices and Innovations in the Identification of Gifted Students,** *highlights exemplary and innovative practices. Eleven chapters are included in the book, and each features an innovative approach currently being used by practitioners to identify high potential students from different contexts and cultures.*

For information about the publication, write to: The National Research Center on the Gifted and Talented, Curry School of Education, University of Virginia, Ruffner Hall, 405 Emmett Street, Charlottesville, VA 22903

Description: Multiple-item assessment covering a range of cognitive abilities.
Scoring: Hand key; computer scoring available
Publisher: The Psychological Corporation

Title: Raven's Advanced Progressive Matrices
Author: Raven, J. C.
Age Level: Adolescent, adult
Purpose: Assesses capacity for observation, clear thinking or efficiency of intellectual work through nonverbal reasoning tasks
Description: Paper-and-pencil assessment (48 items) in two parts. Part I is practice for Part II. Subjects are presented with a pattern or figure with a missing part and asked to select the correct part from six possible answers.
Scoring: Hand key
Publisher: H. K. Lewis & Co., Ltd.
Distributed in the U.S. by The Psychological Corporation

Title: The Standard Progressive Matrices
Author: Raven, J. C.
Age level: 8-65
Purpose: Assesses intellectual ability
Description: Paper-and-pencil, nonverbal assessment (60 items). It includes five parts, with 12 problems each. The subject is presented with patterns or figures with missing parts and is asked to select the correct part from six possible answers.
Scoring: Hand or machine
Publisher: H. K. Lewis & Co., Ltd.
Distributed in the U.S. by The Psychological Corporation

Title: Wechsler Intelligence Scale for Children-Revised
Author: Wechsler, D.
Age Level: Ages 6-16
Purpose: Assesses intellectual ability
Description: This assessment derives two major scores: verbal and performance. The verbal score is derived from the following subtests: general information, general comprehension, arithmetic, similarities, vocabulary and digit span. The performance section consists of the following subtests: picture completion, picture arrangement, block design, object assembly, coding, and mazes.
Scoring: Examiner
Publisher: The Psychological Corporation

Creativity

Title: Thinking Creatively With Sounds and Words (TCSW)
Author: Torrance, E. P., Khatena, J., & Cunnington, B. F.
Age Level: Grades 3-adult
Purpose: Assesses creativity by measuring the originality of ideas stimulated by abstract sounds and spoken words
Description: Two-test battery assessing creativity by measuring the originality of ideas stimulated by abstract sounds and spoken onomatopoetic words. Two long-playing records provide the stimuli for each level.
Scoring: Examiner with key
Publisher: Scholastic Testing Service, Inc.

Title: Torrance Tests of Creative Thinking (TTCT)
Author: Torrance, E. P.
Age Level: Grades K-adult
Purpose: Measures creativity
Description: Multiple-task, paper-and-pencil measure of an individual's creativity assessing four mental characteristics: fluency, flexibility, originality, and elaboration. Two editions are available: the verbal and figural. Can be administered orally in Grades K-3.
Scoring: Examiner
Publisher: Scholastic Testing Service

Title: The Williams Scale
Author: Williams, F.
Age Level: Grades K-12
Purpose: Assesses student creativity from the parents' and/or teachers' point of view
Description: The scale is a rating scale (3-point: often, seldom, never) used by teachers or parents to evaluate student creativity. Eight factors are assessed including: fluency, flexibility, originality, elaboration, curiosity, imagination, complexity, and risk-taking. A composite score is derived. Four qualitative questions are included which ask parents to explain why their believe their child is creative.
Scoring: Examiner
Publisher: PRO-ED

Interests

Title: Interest-A-Lyzer
Author: Renzulli, J. S.
Age Level: Child, adolescent

Purpose: Assesses the interests, current and potential, of students

Description: The Interest-A-Lyzer, available in 3 forms (elementary, secondary and adult), is a paper-and-pencil instrument designed to identify patterns of student interest.

Scoring: Examiner

Publisher: Creative Learning Press, Inc.

Title: My Book of Things and Stuff

Author: McGreevy, A.

Age Level: Elementary grades

Purpose: Assesses the interests of young children

Description: An interest questionnaire designed to assess the specific interests of young children. Included in this questionnaire are more than 40 illustrated items focusing on the special interests and learning styles of six-to eleven-year-old students. The book also contains a teacher's section, an Interest Profile Sheet, and bibliographies of interest-centered books and magazines for young children.

Scoring: Examiner

Publisher: Creative Learning Press, Inc.

Vocational Interests

Title: Kuder General Interest Survey, Form E

Author: Kuder, F.

Age level: Grades 6-12

Purpose: Assesses student preferences for activities related to a number of occupational areas.

Description: Paper-and-pencil battery (168 items) measuring preferences for 10 occupational areas, including: outdoor, mechanical, scientific, computational, persuasive, artistic, literary, musical, social science, and clerical.

Scoring: Hand key; computer scoring available

Publisher: Science Research Associates, Inc.

Title: Kuder Occupational Interest Survey, Form DD

Author: Kuder, F.

Age level: Adolescent, adult

Purpose: Compares how an individual's interests compare to those of satisfied persons in a number of occupational area.

Description: Paper-and-pencil assessment (100 items) of a participant's interests in a number of areas related to occupations and college majors.

Scoring: Computer

Publisher: Science Research Associates, Inc.

Title: *Strong-Campbell Interest Inventory*
Author: Strong, E. K., Jr., Hansen, J.-I. C., & Campbell, D. P.
Age level: Grade 8+
Purpose: Assesses occupational interests
Description: Paper-and-pencil inventory (325 items) asking subjects to respond to a number of different topics and occupations including, for example, school subjects, activities and types of people. A profile of interests is derived for each subject.
Scoring: Computer
Publisher: Stanford University Press
Distributed by: Consulting Psychologists Press, Inc.

Style Preferences—Instructional Style Preferences
Title: *Learning Styles Inventory: A Measure of Student Preference for Instructional Techniques*
Author: Renzulli, J. S., & Smith, L.
Age Level: Grades 4-12
Purpose: Assesses methods by which students prefer to learn
Description: Paper-and-pencil inventory (65 items) assesses students' attitudes toward nine instructional strategies: projects, drill and recitation, discussion, peer teaching, teaching games, independent study, programmed instruction, lecture and simulation. Teacher form is available and assesses the frequency with which teachers use the nine targeted instructional strategies. Teacher profiles can be matched to student preferences.
Scoring: Examiner
Publisher: Creative Learning Press, Inc.

Style Preferences—Learning Environment Preferences
Title: *Class Activities Questionnaire Class Set*
Author: Steele, J. M.
Purpose: Assesses classroom instructional climate from the teacher's and students' perspective
Description: Assesses the levels of thought processes (Bloom's Taxonomy) and affective factors (openness, independence, divergence and emphasis on grades) that characterize a classroom. The forms included in the Class Set of 30 ask students to provide their perceptions about the level of thought processes and affective characteristics in the classroom. Other forms, ask teachers to indicate what they intend to emphasize in the classroom and predict what students, as a group, will say. The dual perspectives enable teachers' comparisons between what they believe they

emphasize with students' perceptions of goals and expectations.

Scoring: Computer

Publisher: Creative Learning Press, Inc.

Title: Classroom Environment Scale

Author: Moos, R. H., & Trickett, E. J.

Age level: Grades 7-12

Purpose: Assesses the teaching atmosphere of classrooms to evaluate the effects of course content, teaching methods, teacher personality and class composition.

Description: Paper-and-pencil assessment (90 items) measuring nine different dimensions of classroom atmosphere: involvement, affiliation, teacher support, task orientation, competition, rule clarity, order, organization, and innovation. Materials include four forms: The Real Form (Form R) measures students' perceptions of classroom atmosphere; the Ideal Form (I), measures students' conceptions of the ideal classroom atmosphere; and the Expectations Form (Form E), which measures expectations about a new classroom. Forms I and E are not published; rewording instructions are included with items in the manual for Form R.

Scoring: Examiner

Publisher: Consulting Psychologists Press, Inc.

Title: Learning Style Identification Scale (LSIS)-Inter/Intra Personal

Author: Malcom, P. J., Lutz, W. C., Gerken, M. A., & Hoeltke, G. M.

Age Level: Child

Purpose: Assesses the manner in which students prefer to learn

Description: Paper-and-pencil observational instrument (24 items) used to assess classroom behaviors. The scale measures the extent to which a student relies on internal sources of information (feelings, beliefs, and attitudes), and external sources of information (other people, events, social interaction). It also identifies five learning styles based on a student's preferred way of solving problems.

Scoring: Examiner

Publisher: CTB/McGraw-Hill

Title: Learning Styles Inventory (LSI)-Physical Surroundings

Author: Dunn, R., Dunn, K., & Price, G. E.

Age level: Grades 3-12

Purpose: Identifies students' preferred learning environment.
Description: Pencil-and-paper inventory (104 items) assesses the physical conditions under which students prefer to learn. Preferences are measured in the following areas: immediate environment (i.e., sound, heat, light design); emotionality (motivation, persistence, structure); physical needs (perceptual preferences, food intake, time of day, mobility); and sociological needs (self-oriented, peer-oriented, combination).
Scoring: Examiner
Publisher: Price Systems, Inc.

Title: Student Opinion Inventory
Author: National Study of School Evaluation Staff
Age level: Grade 8+
Purpose: Assesses students', parents' and teachers' opinions of the school and its programs
Description: Paper-and-pencil survey in three forms (student, parent and teacher) to measure opinions and attitudes toward school. The student form is in two parts. The first part contains multiple choice items, and the second part is open-ended for students to make recommendations about school. The student form contains six subscales: student-teacher, student-counselor, student-administrator, student-curriculum and instruction, student-participation and student-school image. The student form may be administered separately or in conjunction with the teacher and parent form as part of a more comprehensive analysis.
Scoring: Examiner or machine
Publisher: National Study of School Evaluation

Thinking Style Preferences
Title: Cap-Sol
Author: CAP Associates
Age level: Elementary grades through adult
Purpose: Assesses students' preferred learning styles
Description: Paper-and-pencil instrument (45 items) assessing student preferences for nine learning styles: visual, auditory language, bodily kinesthetic, individual learning, group learning, oral expressive, written expressive, sequential, global.
Scoring: Examiner
Publisher: Process Associates

Publishers' Addresses

Consulting Psychologists Press, Inc.
577 College Avenue
P.O. Box 60070
Palo Alto, CA 94306
(415) 857-1444

Creative Learning Press, Inc.
P.O. Box 320
Mansfield Center, CT 06250
(203) 429-8118

CTB/McGraw-Hill
Publishers Test Service
Del Monte Research Park
2500 Garden Park Road
Monterey, CA 93940
(800) 538-9547

Detroit Board of Education
Research Evaluation and Testing
5057 Woodward Avenue, Rm. 101, School Center Annex
Detroit, MI 48202
(313) 494-2022
Contact: Dr. Linda Leddick

National Study of School Evaluation
5201 Leesburg Pike
Falls Church, VA 22041
(703) 820-2727

Price Systems, Inc.
P.O. Box 3067
Lawrence, KS 66044
(913) 843-7892

PRO-ED
5341 Industrial Oaks Boulevard
Austin, TX 78735
(512) 892-3142

Process Associates
3360 Olivesburg Road
Mansfield, OH 44903
(419) 522-4644

Scholastic Testing Service, Inc.
480 Warner Avenue, Suite 301
Fountain Valley, CA 92708
(312) 766-7150

The Psychological Corporation
Harcourt Brace Jovanovich, Inc.
555 Academic Court
San Antonio, TX 78204
(512) 299-1061

The Riverside Publishing Company
8420 Bryn Mawr Avenue
Chicago, IL 60631
(800) 323-9540

Science Research Associates, Inc.
155 North Wacker Drive
Chicago, IL 60606
(800) 621-0664

Chapter 6
Curriculum
Modification
Techniques

A MAJOR SERVICE DELIVERY component of the Schoolwide Enrichment Model is a series of procedures and recommendations for curriculum modification. These procedures and recommendations fall into two general categories. The first category consists of a step-by-step procedure for modifying existing curriculum. This procedure, entitled "Curriculum Compacting," is a system that can be used to help ensure a better match between the achievement levels of individual learners and the curriculum. It can be used with traditional curriculum in any subject area and grade level, and it can also be used to make modifications in teacher-developed curricular activities.

The second category of curriculum modification techniques consists of three models that can be used as guides by curriculum writers and teachers to create instructional units or sets of coordinated learning activities. These models are: Renzulli's Multiple Menu Model (1988), Kaplan's Grid (1986), and Hayes-Jacobs' Interdisciplinary Concept Model (1989). These models are recommended because they differ from traditional approaches to curriculum development. They differ because they place greater emphasis on blending content and process, they focus on creating a role for learners as more first-hand inquirers rather than "lesson-learners," and they

Going to school and getting an education are two different things; and they don't always happen at the same time.

Dr. Rosa Minoka Hill, First Native American Physician in the United States

include recommendations for dealing with the structure of knowledge and the interconnectedness of disciplines.

Before describing the procedures and suggestions for curricular modification, a brief analysis of the challenge level of textbooks will be presented. This analysis constitutes the rationale for curriculum compacting as well as other curriculum modification techniques described in this chapter.

Rationale for Curriculum Modification

BEFORE INITIATING the curriculum compacting process, it is important to be able to explain and provide a rationale for using this instructional practice. Teachers and administrators who need supporting information about the rationale for compacting can use the following reasons to demonstrate why this procedure should be implemented in most classrooms:

1. Students already know much of their texts' content before "learning it."
2. Textbooks have been "dumbed down."
3. The quality of textbooks has failed to improve significantly.
4. The needs of high-ability students are not often met in classrooms.
5. Curricular modification frees time for more challenging learning experiences.

In the sections that follow, we will summarize the research that provides a very powerful rationale for curriculum compacting. This information can be used to make practitioners, policy makers, and parents aware of the need for curriculum modifications and support their efforts to make them.

Reason One: Students Already Know Much of Their Texts' Content Before "Learning It"

Many parents and educators know that a major problem facing students is the lack of challenge in the work they are assigned in regular classroom settings. One need only enter an American classroom to realize that the work assigned to students is often too easy. Research also supports this claim. In a recent study dealing with average and above-average

When once the child has learned that four and two are six, a thousand repetitions will give him no new information, and it is a waste of time to keep him employed in that manner.

J. M. Greenwood, 1888

readers, Taylor and Frye (1988) found that 78 to 88 percent of fifth- and sixth-grade average readers could pass pretests on basal comprehension skills before they were covered by the basal reader.

Perhaps the repetition of content has been most reported in mathematics textbooks. Since the publication of *A Nation at Risk* (1983), which promulgated the idea that the declining difficulty of textbooks may have had negative effects on students' learning, one prominent theme of complaints about American education is that students fail to demonstrate adequate achievement in problem solving and higher order thinking. For example, the second study by the International Association for the Evaluation of Educational Achievement (IEA) on mathematics, which assessed achievement for eighth-grade students at the end of the 1981-82 school year, found that U.S. students were slightly above the international average in computational arithmetic but well below the international average in problem solving (McKnight, Crosswhite, Dossey, Kifer, Swafford, Travers, & Cooney, 1987). U.S. eighth-graders' achievement in geometry placed in the bottom 25% of participating countries in a sample of which nearly 20% were third-world nations. One possible explanation for these disappointing international comparisons may lie in what U.S. elementary schools emphasize in their instruction (Porter, 1989).

Another distinctive feature of elementary school mathematics is the slowness with which content changes as students progress through the grades. Content overlaps across grades because topics begun at the end of one grade are continued into the beginning of the next grade. To some extent, topics are returned to again and again, each time seeking a greater depth of understanding (Porter, 1989). Flanders (1987) investigated three separate mathematics textbook series to examine just how much new content was presented each year. His primary finding was that a relatively steady decrease occurs in the amount of new content over the years up through eighth grade, where less than one-third of the material taught is new. Overall, students in grades two to five encounter approximately 40% to 65% new content, an equivalent of new material just two or three days per week. By eighth grade, this amount has dropped to 30%, equivalent to just one and one-half days per week. Flanders found that most of the new content in any text is found in the second half of each textbook. In grades seven and eight, where the total new content is lowest, new material occurs in less than

There should be little wonder why good students get bored in mathematics: they do the same thing year after year. Average or slower-than-average students get the same message, and who could blame them for becoming complacent about their mathematics studies? They know that if they don't learn it now, it will be retaught next year.

James Flanders, 1987

Chapter 6

*Our study [to locate challenging curricular materials] has revealed a very bleak materials landscape. With respect to comprehensive curricular materials, we found only one exemplary mathematics curriculum, **Real Math** by Open Court, which was 18 years old. The only comprehensive science curriculum was a Canadian publication, SciencePlus....Clearly, the academic community has grossly underestimated the importance of high quality curricular materials in making schools better.*

Stanley Pogrow, 1993

28% of the first half of the books. Flanders' study shows that the mathematical content of some textbooks is mostly review of previous topics. Flanders states, "The result is that earlier in the year, when students are likely to be more eager to study, they repeat what they have seen before. Later on, whey they are sufficiently bored, they see new material—if they get to the end of the book" (p. 22).

Usiskin (1987) indicates that not only have textbooks decreased in difficulty, but they also incorporate a large percentage of repetition to facilitate learning. Usiskin argues that even average eighth-grade students should study algebra since only 25% of the pages in typical seventh- and eighth-grade mathematics texts contain new content. Usiskin points out that the current practice of spending a great deal of time reviewing work of earlier grades in the same context as the earlier grades is counterproductive. He states, "For the student who does not know the material, the review is simply repeating what they are bad at. We find out what some students do not know and give them little else. It is not the spiral approach winding its way up to the helix of understanding; it is the circular approach going round and round and back to the same place" (p. 432).

Reason Two: Textbooks Have Been "Dumbed Down"

As mentioned earlier, another reason that so many average and above-average students can demonstrate mastery of the regular curriculum is that contemporary textbooks are so much easier than they were only two or three decades ago. The term dumbed down was coined by Terrel Bell, U.S. Secretary of Education, to describe this phenomenon of decreasing difficulty in texts.

Researchers trace the beginning of the dumbing down of textbooks to the late 1920s, when the vocabulary load of reading textbooks decreased with each subsequent edition. Comparative studies document the introduction of fewer and fewer new words and more repetition of them (Chall, 1967). Within a period of ten years, the average number of different words in second-grade readers decreased from 1,147 to 913 (Hockett, 1938). During this same period new words introduced in first-grade readers decreased from 644 to 462 and within the following ten years to 338. This simplification of vocabulary in reading textbooks continued through the 1950s and into the 1960s, during which new words in first-grade readers were repeated on an average of six to ten times immediately following their introduction (Willows, Borwick, & Hayvren, 1981). Reading textbooks for the upper elementary grades also became much easier. The vocabulary in sixth-grade basals decreased consistently from 1947 to 1967, and Gates (1961) described the vocabularies of fourth-grade basals published in the early 1960s as limited enough to be appropriate for average third-grade students.

Changes in the difficulty of subject matter in textbooks beginning in the late 1920s were similar to those found in reading books. Horn (1937) identified this downward trend in difficulty in social studies textbooks as early as the 1930s, and Chall, Conard and Harris (1981) documented a continuation of this trend almost thirty years later. It was not until the 1960s, when national concern that the American educational system might be lagging behind the Soviet Union gained momentum, that educational views on textbook difficulty seemed to change (Elliott & Woodward, 1990). Publishers reacted, and by the middle 1960s, evidence of a reversal of the trend toward simplicity began to appear. Willows, Borwick and Hayvren (1981) noted a fivefold increase in the rate of vocabulary introduction in first-grade readers from 1962 to 1972, and increasing difficulty in sixth-grade readers from 1967 to 1975 was reported by Chall, Conard and Harris (1981). Yet, by the late 1970s, this emphasis on raising challenge for all students was replaced by an overwhelming concern for increasing the scores of our lowest-achieving students. Policy makers thought that the way to "get the scores up" among low achievers was to increase the amount of drill and practice on low-end skills, and textbook publishers followed this trend by replacing challenging material with repetitious exercises. Journalists as well as educators described textbooks as being "dumbed down," a slogan that caught the public's imagination and united various textbook critics. Publishers were accused of lowering academic requirements by oversimplifying or watering down their textbooks (Chall & Conard, 1991).

Chall's and Conard's (1991) research indicates the subject matter textbooks published in the United States represent a rather narrow range of difficulty for each grade level analyzed—more narrow than the range of reading ability found among students. Chall and Conard indicate that this range is also narrower than the range found on standardized tests. "Although the publishers described their textbooks as being developed for 'wide use' or for 'more able' or 'less able' readers, our analysis found them suitable mainly for the middle

Textbooks, for better or worse, dominate what students learn. They set the curriculum, and often the facts learned, in most subjects. For many students, textbooks are their first and sometimes only early exposure to books and reading. The public regards textbooks as authoritative, accurate, and necessary. And teachers rely on them to organize lessons and structure subject matter. But the current system of textbook adoption has filled our schools with Trojan horses—glossily covered blocks of paper whose words emerge to deaden the minds of our nation's youth, and make them enemies of learning.

A. Graham Down in Tyson-Bernstein, 1988

Chapter 6

range of achievement within each grade. Practically none of the content textbooks seemed to be written for the students in the lowest quartile in reading. Further, the books that publishers labeled for less able readers were often more difficult than those labeled for a wide audience or for more able readers" (p. 111).

The lack of challenge in textbooks has been cited by every major content group in our country. In a national report to our nation on the future of mathematics, Lynn Arthur Steen, a professor of mathematics at St. Olaf College, aptly summarized the problems associated with the lack of challenge in mathematics: "In practice, although not in law, we have a national curriculum in mathematics education. It is an 'underachieving' curriculum that follows a spiral of almost constant radius, reviewing each year so much of the past that little new learning takes place" (1989, p. 45).

Ohanian (1987) refers to the basal readers in American classrooms as "homogenized and bowdlerized grade school texts, edited according to elaborate readability formulas and syllable schemes" (p. 20). Ohanian points out another example of "dumbing down" by illustrating how children's literature is altered by textbook companies using the story of Flat Stanley by Jeff Brown. Stanley has gotten himself flattened, and the story describes the very special things that a flat boy can do, including travel across the country by mail. Brown describes Stanley's experience below:

> The envelope fit Stanley very well. There was even room left over, Mrs. Lamchop discovered, for an egg-salad sandwich made with thin bread, and a flat cigarette case filled with milk.
>
> They had to put a great many stamps on the envelope to pay for both airmail and insurance, but it was still much less expensive than a train or airplane ticket to California would have been.

Here is how the description appears in a basal reader:

> The envelope fit Stanley very well. There was even room left over for a sandwich (p. 20).

Harriet Tyson-Bernstein (1985), who has written extensively on the politics of textbook adoption and the mandated use of readability formulas, believes that publishers have been compelled to change textbooks to meet state or local readability formulas. She believes that these formulas have resulted in textbooks that skip from topic to topic and result in what textbook researchers call "mentioning." Tyson-Bernstein (1988) further examined the mentioning problem in social studies textbooks and reported, "The Thirty Years' War will be 'covered' in a paragraph; the Nixon presidency in two sentences....All of the small facts and terms that can be tested on a multiple-choice test will appear in the index, because that is where adoption committees usually check on curricular and test 'congruence' if they check at all (p. 30)." Gagnon (1988) also refers to this problem. Following an extensive content analysis of the five leading American history textbooks, he found the texts "omit or dumb down the Old World background, as though it were of little importance....The Middle Ages, when they are mentioned at all, are dark and stagnant, their people without ideas or curiosity and interested only in life after the grave....Then, suddenly, the Renaissance springs forth, as 'Europe Awakens.' People begin to think for themselves and seek 'new horizons.' Hence, the explorers, and the discovery of America (p. 49)." Further insight is provided by Sewall (1988) in his analysis of one leading elementary-level history textbook as an example of the problem. He states, "Abraham Lincoln warrants two paragraphs, slightly more than Molly Pitcher....Valley Forge goes unmentioned, and World War Two receives about two pages of text, a little more than the Dawes Act and the production of maple syrup." Explanations may simply be absent: "In 1816, James Monroe was elected President. Things went so smoothly that this time is called the Era of Good Feelings" (p. 555).

Sewall (1988) criticizes the readability formulas that plague the textbook industry. He concludes:

> These entrenched, mechanistic, absurd systems claim to measure the readability of a text. Instead, they homogenize and dull down. All good writing has a human voice and makes strong use of verbs, vivid anecdotes, lively quotations, and other literary devices. Textbook buyers should welcome complex sentences and challenging vocabulary, where appropriate, if such writing has style and drama that students can appreciate and remember. Clear expository writing can spur interest, help comprehension, and add to the appreciation of literature, even for less-able students (p. 557).

The most widely adopted elementary social studies textbook series tend to be remarkably uniform, consisting of a compendium of facts....The texts try to cover more topics than they could possibly cover well, and so, rather than organize information coherently around powerful ideas, they present a parade of isolated facts....Even important topics receive superficial coverage, a practice that blurs the distinction between important and small ideas....As if all this isn't bad enough...the material is dry and wooden.

Gerald Bracey, 1993

Bernstein aptly summarizes the problem that current textbooks pose for high ability students: "Even if there were good rules of thumb about the touchy subject of the difficulty of textbooks, the issue becomes moot when a school district buys only one textbook, usually at 'grade level,' for all students in a subject or grade. Such a purchasing policy pressures adoption committees to buy books that the least able students can read. As a result, the needs of more advanced students are sacrificed" (p. 465).

It is safe to conclude that many bright students are using textbooks at least one or two years below their achievement level, and this situation is likely to promote apathy, poor attitudes toward learning, and a habit of doing only what is necessary to survive in the school setting. Students who are not provided with a challenging learning environment often find school too easy and are, therefore, unlikely to learn how to deal with the frustration that is frequently experienced when learning new and difficult skills or concepts.

Reason Three: The Quality of Textbooks Has Failed to Improve Significantly

Since the publication of *A Nation at Risk* (1983), the focus of reports on American education and of school reform efforts has been on the poor performance of students, the low expectations of student achievement, and the school curricula rather than textbook quality (Tyson-Bernstein & Woodward, 1989). Still missing from the reform debate is the acknowledgment that in many cases the textbook defines curriculum and the scope, sequence, and methods of instruction.

At both the elementary and secondary levels, textbooks have been harshly criticized. In 1983, the National Commission on Excellence in Education (NCEE) concluded that textbooks had been "written down," and accordingly, the Commission recommended that "these [textbooks] and other tools of learning and teaching be upgraded to assure more rigorous content and that states and school districts should evaluate texts and other materials on their ability to present rigorous and challenging material" (p. 28).

The recommendations of the NCEE in *A Nation at Risk*—that textbooks become more rigorous and demanding— seem not to have been followed. A thorough examination by Chall and Conard (1991) does not support the suggestions made following the NCEE report that publishers should develop more difficult books. Readability levels did not

If there is a single public school in the United States where there is an official and constitutional provision made for submitting questions of methods, of discipline and teaching, and the questions of curriculum, textbooks, etc., to the discussion of those actually engaged in the work of teaching, the fact has escaped my notice.

Margaret Haley, in Fraser, 1989

change in any appreciable way between the 1979 and 1989 editions. The qualitative analysis done by Chall and Conard indicates that where changes in textbooks were made, they were toward greater ease, not greater difficulty (1991, p. 2).

Earlier studies by Kantor, Anderson and Armbruster (1983) and by Armbruster and Anderson (1984) found texts to be "badly written, rambling, inconsistent, disconnected and inconsiderate (p. 61)." They concluded that students would have difficulty making sense out of the text prose. Armbruster (1984) completed a study in which adults were asked to read twenty paragraphs from several sixth-grade texts, and underline or state the main idea. Adults were unable to state the main idea because of disjointed writing and dumbed down content. Today's textbooks are written by committees and designed to be simplistic and to offend no one, making them incredibly dull. Downey (1980) suggests that one reason for the poor quality of textbooks is that true scholars have little or no role or interest in writing them any longer.

Tyson-Bernstein and Woodward (1989) found that within the last decade, educators themselves have made the greatest contribution to the decline of textbook content. They describe the problem by stating, "As the public began demanding evidence that schools were making good use of their money, educators tried to produce higher student performance on standardized tests. That effort, in turn, has led them to attempt aligning the curriculum, the textbooks and the tests. This self-defeating congruence between the elements of the instructional program rests on the unassailable logic that students will achieve higher scores if they are tested on what they have studied. Following that logic, adoption-state authorities have increasingly begun to specify, in excruciating detail, all the facts, terms and topics that must be included in the textbooks they are willing to buy" (p. 6).

Tyson-Bernstein (1988) points out that publishers of elementary reading books have become concerned with test improvement because their principal customers—teachers—are becoming increasingly nervous about their students' test performance. She explains, "Instead of designing a book from the standpoint of its subject or its capacity to capture the children's imagination, editors are increasingly organizing elementary reading series around the content and timing of standardized tests (p. 26)." Mehlinger (1989) reinforces this position, "Teachers want textbooks to be at or below the reading level of every student in their classes… teachers want textbooks to provide the factual information that will be

Reflections On Good Textbooks:

Does the content grab you? If it doesn't, the book most likely won't grab the students. You should also spot check as extensively as time allows for faulty information and misinformation. Bad writing. Bad information. Neither appears in a quality textbook.

Jean Osborne, Director of the Center for the Study of Reading

An excellent textbook engages students' minds to the extent that they put themselves into it. The book creates new thoughts and responses, even about things not in it.

Michael Hartoonian, Supervisor of Social Studies Curriculum, Wisconsin Department of Public Instruction

An effective mathematics text should be more oriented to thinking and problem solving than rote exercise. Students should be called upon to read, not just do numbers and examples. Textbooks should build problems on real-life settings, using real data to motivate students.

Charles Hamberg, Recipient of a Presidential Award for Excellence in Teaching Mathematics

in S. Conn, 1988

assessed on standardized tests. Since most such tests are multiple choice or short answer, teachers who want their students to look good on tests and to make sure that all topics likely to be covered on the test are covered in the textbook."

Reason Four: The Needs of High Ability Students Are Often Not Met in Classrooms

Two recent studies conducted by The National Research Center on the Gifted and Talented indicate that elementary teachers are not providing major modifications in their classrooms to meet the needs of high ability students. The first study entitled, "The Classroom Practices Survey," (Archambault et al., 1992) was conducted to determine the extent to which high ability students receive differentiated education in regular classrooms. Approximately 7,300 third- and fourth-grade teachers in public schools, private schools and schools with high concentrations of four types of ethnic minorities were randomly selected to participate in this research. The major finding of this study was that classroom teachers make only minor modifications in the curriculum to meet the needs of high ability students in various parts of the country and for various types of communities.

The second study, "The Classroom Practices Observational Study" (Westberg, Archambault, Dobyns, & Salvin, 1992), was conducted to corroborate the findings of the survey, mentioned above. Systematic observations in forty-six third- and fourth-grade classrooms were conducted throughout the United States to determine whether and by what means classroom teachers meet the needs of high achieving students in the regular classroom. Two students, one high achieving student and one average achieving student, were selected as target students for each observation day. The Classroom Practices Record (CPR) was developed to document the types and frequencies of differentiated instruction that high achieving students received through modification in curricular activities, materials, and teacher-student verbal interactions. Descriptive statistics and chi-square procedures were used to analyze the CPR data. The results indicated little instructional and curricular differentiation for high ability students in the regular classroom, including grouping arrangements and verbal interactions. In the course of ninety-two days of observing students in five disciplines, high achieving students received instruction in homogenous groups only twenty-one percent of the time, and, more alarmingly, the target high achieving

He finds himself to be very bored in class. He tells us that he turns it off. He says, "I can't do the science work in class because I'm busy trying to solve pollution problems." And we say to him, "Do the work for class." But in his head he's thinking about the greenhouse effect and the ozone layer, and he's trying to figure out how he could solve them, rather than do the work that was mundane.

Parent of a fifth-grade student, in Purcell, 1993b

students experienced no instructional or curricular differentiation in eighty-four percent of the instructional activities in which they participated.

These findings may account for the fact that many students "turn off" long before secondary school, responding negatively to what they perceive to be a boring and repetitive environment. Students may become behavior problems, dropouts, or, as John Feldhusen suggests, become "systematically demotivated" (1989, p. 58) because our schools have failed to provide them with a challenging curriculum. These students may grow to dislike learning simply because their academic curriculum did not meet their ability level. At the very least, the lack of curriculum compacting can promote "game playing" by bright students who have come to believe that the best way to succeed in school is to do exactly what the teacher asks: nothing less, and nothing more. Educators must ensure that our high achieving students do more than simply mark time in the classroom. In order to promote a love of learning and independent study habits, a drastic change in the academic preparation of higher achieving students is required.

An Overview of Curriculum Compacting

ONE SOLUTION to the lack of challenge in textbooks and curriculum is to write new textbooks. However, the writing, publishing and adoption of new textbooks will take many years. Until such time as new textbooks are available, a system called curriculum compacting can be used to modify existing curriculum to create a better match between the abilities of students and their learning experiences. Curriculum compacting is a system designed to adapt the regular curriculum to meet the needs of students by either eliminating work that has been previously mastered or streamlining work that can be mastered at a pace commensurate with the student's motivation and ability. In addition to creating a more challenging learning environment, compacting helps teachers guarantee proficiency in the basic curriculum and provide time for more appropriate enrichment or acceleration activities. The time provided by compacting is referred to as "compacted time."

Many good classroom teachers already compact the curriculum as part of their daily tasks. For a skill which most

School is a chore, there's no motivation, and both my children hate school. They take no initiative in their work. One of my sons is doing terribly....He's failing and he's one of the brightest kids in the school.

Parent of a capable student, in Purcell, 1993b

students require one or more review worksheets to understand, a teacher may substitute more challenging work for a student who has mastered the skill. This procedure is compacting in its simplest form. This section of the chapter will explain the three steps for implementing compacting.

The Compacting Process

Phase I: Defining Goals and Outcomes. The first of three phases of the compacting process consists of defining the goals and outcomes of a given unit or segment of instruction. This information is readily available in most subjects because specific goals and outcomes usually can be found in teachers' manuals, curriculum guides, scope-and-sequence charts, and some of the new curricular frameworks that are emerging in connection with outcome based education models. Teachers should examine these objectives to determine which objectives represent the acquisition of new content or thinking skills as opposed to reviews or practice of material that has previously been taught. The scope and sequence charts prepared by publishers or a simple comparison of the table of contents of a basal series will provide a quick overview of new versus repeated material. A major goal of this phase of the compacting process is to help teachers make individual programming decisions; a larger professional development goal is to help teachers be better analysts of the material they are teaching and better consumers of textbooks and prescribed curricular material.

Phase II: Identifying Candidates for Compacting. The second phase of curriculum compacting is the identification students who have already mastered the objectives or outcomes of a unit or segment of instruction that is about to be taught. This first step of this phase consists of estimating which students have the potential to master new material at a faster than normal pace. Knowing one's students is, of course, the best way to begin the assessment process. Scores on previous tests, completed assignments, and classroom participation are the best ways of identifying highly likely candidates for compacting. Standardized achievement tests can serve as a good general screen for this step because they allow us to list the names of all students who are scoring one or more years above grade level in particular subject areas.

Being a candidate for compacting does not necessarily mean that a student knows the material under consideration. Therefore, the second step of identifying candidates consists

"Until such time as new textbooks are available, a system called curriculum compacting can be used to modify existing curriculum to create a better match between the abilities of students and their learning experiences."

of finding or developing appropriate tests or other assessment techniques that can be used to evaluate specific learning outcomes. Unit pretests, or end-of-unit tests that can be administered as pretests are ready made for this task, especially when it comes to the assessment of basic skills. An analysis of pretest results enables the teacher to document proficiency in specific skills, and to select instructional activities or practice material necessary to bring the student up to a high level on any skill that may need some additional reinforcement.

The process is slightly modified for compacting content areas that are not as easily assessed as basic skills and for students who have not mastered the material, but are judged to be candidates for more rapid coverage. First, students should have a thorough understanding of the goals and procedures of compacting, including the nature of the replacement process. A given segment of material should be discussed with the student (e.g., a unit that includes a series of chapters in a social studies text), and the procedures for verifying mastery at a high level should be specified. These procedures might consist of answering questions based on the chapters, writing an essay, or taking the standard end-of-unit test. The amount of time for completion of the unit should be specified, and procedures such as periodic progress reports or log entries for teacher review should be agreed upon. And, of course, an examination of potential acceleration and/or enrichment replacement activities should be a part of this discussion.

Another alternative is to assess or pretest all students in a class when a new unit or topic is introduced. Although this may seem like more work for the teacher, it provides the opportunity for all students to demonstrate their strengths or previous mastery in a given area. Using a matrix of learning objectives, teachers can fill in test results and establish small, flexible, and temporary groups for skill instruction and replacement activities.

Phase III: Providing Acceleration and Enrichment Options. The final phase of the compacting process can be one of the most exciting aspects of teaching because it is based on cooperative decision making and creativity on the parts of both teachers and students. Efforts can be made to gather enrichment materials from classroom teachers, librarians, media specialists, and content area or gifted education specialists. These materials may include self-directed learning

---

Preassessment Measures Which Can Be Used to Document Students' Level of Mastery Prior to Instruction

- *Grades*
- *Classwork by the student*
- *Interviews with the student*
- *Interviews with teachers from previous years*
- *Interviews with parents*
- *Recommendations from guidance counselors*
- *Standardized test scores*
- *Performance or authentic assessment*
- *Portfolios*

Chapter 6

Thora

Thora, a high school junior, received consistently high marks in English and literature. She disliked the slow pace of her American History class, and after consultation with the history teacher, Thora was encouraged to pretest out of the history class, chapter by chapter. A great deal of time was gained for Thora, and she decided to work as a mentor with middle school students to create their own literary magazine. Thora met with a small group of middle school students twice a week and by semester's end, she and the students had produced a book of illustrated poetry, Echoes, which was distributed to all students in grades 6-8.

activities, instructional materials that focus on particular thinking skills, and a variety of individual and group project oriented activities that are designed to promote hands on research and investigative skills. The time made available through compacting provides opportunities for exciting learning experiences such as small group, special topic seminars that might be directed by students or community resource persons, community based apprenticeships or opportunities to work with a mentor, peer tutoring situations, involvement in community service activities, and opportunities to rotate through a series of self-selected mini-courses.

Decisions about which replacement activities to use are always guided by factors such as time, space, and the availability of resource persons and materials. Although practical concerns must be considered, the ultimate criteria for replacement activities should be the degree to which they increase academic challenge and the extent to which they meet individual needs. Great care should be taken to select activities and experiences that represent individual strengths and interests rather than the assignment of more-of-the-same worksheets or randomly selected kits, games, and puzzles! This aspect of the compacting process should also be viewed as a creative opportunity for an entire faculty to work cooperatively to organize and institute a broad array of enrichment experiences. A favorite mini-course that a faculty member has always wanted to teach, or serving as a mentor to one or two students who are extremely invested in a teacher's beloved topic are just a few of the ways that replacement activities can add excitement to the teachers' part in this process as well as the obvious benefits for students. We have also observed another interesting occurrence that has resulted from the availability of curriculum compacting. When some previously bright but underachieving students realized that they could both economize on regularly assigned material and "earn time" to pursue self-selected interests, their motivation to complete regular assignments increased. As one student put it, "Everyone understands a good deal!"

The best way to get an overview of the curriculum compacting process is to examine an actual example of how the management form that guides this process is used. A completed example of this form, entitled "The Compactor," is presented in Figure 9. The form is both an organizational and record keeping tool. Teachers should fill out one form per student, or one form for a group of students with similar

INDIVIDUAL EDUCATIONAL PROGRAMMING GUIDE
The Compactor

Prepared by: Joseph S. Renzulli
Linda M. Smith

NAME __Eileen__   AGE __10__   TEACHER(S) __Mr. Cunningham__   Individual Conference Dates And Persons Participating in Planning Of IEP __Oct. 10, 1992__

SCHOOL __Kain Elementary__   GRADE __5__   PARENT(S) __Mrs. Cullan__   __MC__ __JD__ __EF__ __JC__

CURRICULUM AREAS TO BE CONSIDERED FOR COMPACTING Provide a brief description of basic material to be covered during this marking period and the assessment information or evidence that suggests the need for compacting.	PROCEDURES FOR COMPACTING BASIC MATERIAL Describe activities that will be used to guarantee proficiency in basic curricular areas.	ACCELERATION AND/OR ENRICHMENT ACTIVITIES Describe activities that will be used to provide advanced level learning experiences in each area of the regular curriculum.
Language Arts: Holt 14: Units 2-6 Pre-Test Units 2-6 Decoding/encoding skills Language kills	Unit and level tests in Holt Language Arts. Eileen will participate in all Language Arts activity in the classroom except those involving: decoding/encoding skills and language skills already mastered and any kind of "seatwork" (repetitious work).	Advanced Exposure in Language Arts: To read biographies for the purpose of enriching Eileen's background in literature and to see how the following human value applies to her selections: "Determination and courage are often necessary to achieve one's goals."
CTBS Scores: Vocabulary 6.5 Language Mechanics 9.9 Comprehension 9.5 Language Expression 9.9 Total Reading 7.9 Total Language 9.8	Time gained from this will go toward Eileen's advance exposure in Language Arts.	Amelia Earhart Phillis Wheatley Harriet Beecher Stowe Anne Bradstreet Mahalia Jackson Dolly Madison Abigail Adams
		Also, Eileen will choose novels from the Newbury Award series to increase her vocabulary and deepen her understanding of plot structure, introduction, complication, climax, and resolution.
		Advanced Exposure in Science: 8 trips to regional science center for extension, differentiated, and intensive instruction in computers and calculators, chronobiology, and weather. Time to instruct others in class on above topics.
		Resource Room: 5 hours a week. Type I, II, and III activities developing creative thinking, critical thinking, creative and critical problem solving.

☐ Check here if additional information is recorded on the reverse side.

Figure 9. The Compactor.

curricular strengths. Completed Compactors should be kept in students' academic files, and updated on a regular basis. The form can also be used for small groups of students who are working at approximately the same level (e.g., a reading or math group). The Compactor is divided into three sections:

- The first column should include information on learning objectives and student strengths in those areas. Teachers should list the objectives for a particular unit of study, followed by data on students' proficiency in those objectives, including test scores, behavioral profiles and past academic records.
- In the second column, teachers should detail the pretest vehicles they select, along with test results. The pretest instruments can be formal measures, such as pencil and paper tests, or informal measures, such as performance assessments based on observations of class participation and written assignments.
  Specificity is extremely important. Recording an overall score of 85% on ten objectives, for example, sheds little light on what portion of the material can be compacted, since students might show limited mastery of some objectives and high levels of mastery on others.
- Column three is used to record information about acceleration or enrichment options. In determining these options, teachers must be fully aware of students' individual interests and learning styles. We have used two instruments to help us make decisions about replacement activities that place major emphasis on student preferences. The *Interest-A-Lyzer* and the *Learning Styles Inventory* (Renzulli & Smith, 1979) provide profiles of general categories of student interests, and the types of learning activities that students would like to use in pursuing these interests.

The level of the development of a country is determined, in considerable part, by the level of development if its people's intelligence...

Luis Alberto Machado

Eileen: A Sample Compactor Form

Eileen is a fifth grader in a self-contained heterogeneous classroom. Her school, which is very small, is located in a lower socioeconomic urban school district. While Eileen's reading and language scores range between two and five years above grade level, most of her 29 classmates are reading one to two years below grade level. This presented Eileen's teacher with a common problem: What was the best way to instruct Eileen? He agreed to compact her curriculum. Taking the easiest approach possible, he administered all of the appropriate unit tests for the grade level in the Basal Language Arts program, and excused Eileen from completing the activities and worksheets in the units where she showed proficiency (80% and above). When Eileen missed one or two questions, the teacher checked for trends in those items and provided instruction and practice materials to ensure concept mastery.

Eileen usually took part in language arts lessons one or two days a week. The balance of the time she spent with alternative projects, some of which she selected. This strategy spared Eileen up to six or eight hours a week with language arts skills that were simply beneath her level. She joined the class instruction only when her pretests indicated she had not fully acquired the skills or to take part in a discussion that her teacher thought she would enjoy. In the time saved through compacting, Eileen engaged in a number of enrichment activities. First, she spent as many as five hours a week in a resource room for high ability students. This time was usually scheduled during her language arts class, benefiting both Eileen and her teacher, since he didn't have to search for all of the enrichment options himself. The best part of the process for Eileen was she didn't have make-up regular classroom assignments because she was not missing essential work.

Eileen also visited a regional science center with other students who had expressed a high interest and aptitude for science. Science was a second strength area for Eileen, and based on the results of her *Interest-A-Lyzer,* famous women was a special interest. Working closely with her teacher, Eileen choose seven biographies of noted women, most of whom had made contributions in scientific areas. All of the books were extremely challenging and locally available. Three were on an adult level, but Eileen had no trouble reading them. Eileen's Compactor, which covered an entire semester, was updated in January. Her teacher remarked that compacting her curriculum had actually saved him time— time he would have spent correcting papers needlessly assigned! The value of compacting for Eileen also convinced him that he should continue the process. The Compactor was also used as a vehicle for explaining to Eileen's parents how specific modifications were being made to accommodate her advanced language arts achievement level and her interest in science. A copy of the Compactor was also passed on to

The most important single factor influencing learning is what the learner knows. Ascertain this and teach him accordingly.

D. P. Ausubel, 1968

Eileen's sixth grade teacher, and a conference between the fifth and sixth grade teachers and the resource teacher helped to ensure continuity in dealing with Eileen's special needs.

The Multiple Menu Model: A Guide to In-Depth Learning and Teaching

THE SECOND category of procedures covered in this chapter consists of three curriculum models which can be used to create instructional units. They differ from traditional approaches because they place greater emphasis on: (1) content and process, (2) students as first-hand inquirers, and (3) the interconnectedness of knowledge. The Multiple Menu Model (Renzulli, 1988) is a guide that teachers and curriculum writers can use to develop in-depth curriculum units for classroom use. It is based on the work of theorists in curriculum and instruction, including Ausubel (1968), Bandura (1977), Bloom (1954), Bruner (1960, 1966), Gagné and Briggs (1979), Kaplan (1986), Passow (1982), Phenix (1964), and Ward (1961). It consists of a series of six interrelated components (see Figure 10), called menus, because each contains a range of options from which curriculum developers can choose as they create units of study. The six components include: the Knowledge Menu, the Instructional Objectives and Student Activities Menu, the Instructional Strategies Menu, the Instructional Sequences Menu, the Artistic Modification Menu, and the Instructional Products Menu which is composed of two interrelated menus, Concrete Products and Abstract Products Menu. The first menu, the Knowledge Menu, is the most elaborate and concerns the field of selected study (e.g., mythology, astronomy, choreography, geometry). The second through the fifth menus deal with pedagogy or instructional techniques. The last menu, Instructional Products, is related to the types of products that may result from student interactions with knowledge about a domain or interdisciplinary concepts and how that knowledge is constructed by first-hand inquirers. Although it was originally developed as a way of differentiating curriculum for high ability students, the guide can easily be used by teachers who want to encourage first-hand inquiry and creativity among all students.

Intellectual activity anywhere is the same, whether at the frontier of knowledge or in a third-grade classroom.

Jerome Bruner, 1960

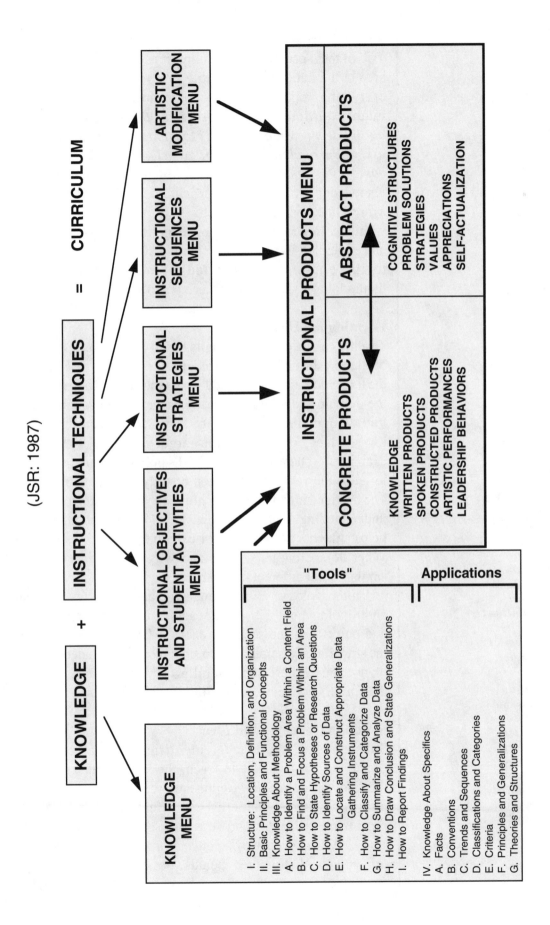

Figure 10. The Multiple Menu Model for developing differentiated curriculum.

Chapter 6

Sample Representative Concepts and Ideas

Literature
Violence
Monsters
Death
Love
Patriotism
Birth
Loyalty
Conflict
Journeys
Heroes
Anti-Heroes

Science
Change
Stability
Equilibrium
Environment
Systems
Interactions
Evolution
Energy
Health
Disease

History
Change
Culture
Dwellings
War
Migrations
Expansionism
Law
Revolution
Equity
Economics
Religion

Mathematics
Measurement
Time
Space
Patterns
Systems
Number
Probability
Chance
Infinity

The Knowledge Menu

Two of the most important assumptions underlying this menu are (1) the belief that it is futile, if not impossible, to teach everything important in a discipline, and (2) the necessity of inquiry. *Rather than focusing on the conclusions of a discipline, the Multiple Menu Model focuses on inquiry itself, asking curriculum developers to select the most important concepts to teach learners.* Accordingly, the first menu, The Knowledge Menu, requires curriculum developers to examine a discipline from four perspectives: its purpose and placement within the larger context of knowledge, its underlying concepts and principles, its most representative topics and contributions to the universe of knowledge and wisdom, and its methodology. This first of these perspectives follows.

Locating the Discipline

Teachers using curriculum units based on the Multiple Menu Model must first locate for students the targeted discipline in the larger domain of knowledge (e.g., the novel is a field within the domain of literature). Teachers and students construct a knowledge tree to illustrate how the selected area of knowledge "fits" within the larger domain. Next, they examine the characteristics of the discipline and subdisciplines to learn the reasons why people study a particular area of knowledge, and what they hope to contribute to human understanding. This first dimension of the Knowledge Menu helps students to examine, for example, What is sociology? What do sociologists study and why? How is sociology similar to and different from other disciplines, e.g., psychology and anthropology? What, then, is social psychology or social anthropology, and How does each fit into the larger picture and purpose of the social sciences? These questions about the structure of disciplines help students gain an understanding of not only where the discipline is located, but also the discipline's connectedness with other disciplines.

Selecting Concepts and Ideas

Subsequently, the teacher identifies and selects basic principles and concepts to teach, the second perspective of the knowledge menu. Representative concepts and ideas consist of themes, patterns, main features, sequences or organizing principles and structures that define an area of study. With respect to science, for example, organizing principles and structures include, not exclusively: change, stability, systems, interactions, energy, chemical composition, volume, light, and color. With respect to the novel, representative elements that cut across all literary contributions include plot, setting, character, and theme. Large concepts exist within each of these elements, as well. For example, the buffoon and tragic hero are archetypal characters who appear in literary contributions throughout time. It is precisely because these concepts and ideas exist across time that they can be used as the bases for interdisciplinary units. Accordingly, curriculum developers must select representative concepts that will most clearly define the discipline being taught.

Selecting Representative Topics

Third, teachers select curricular topics to illustrate the basic principles and representative concepts. In some ways, the selection process is similar to the process that teachers have used in the past; namely, the material must take into consideration the age, maturity, previous study and experiential background of the students. Beyond age, grade, maturity level and experience, however, the Multiple Menu Model selection process is different. Unlike traditional instruction, which asks teachers to cover an entire text by the end of the year or semester, the Multiple Menu Model asks teachers to winnow down all the possible pieces to those few which truly represent the field's principles and concepts. A three-phase approach to the selection of content is recommended that takes into consideration the interaction between intensive coverage and extensive coverage as well as group learning and individual learning situations. The following example points out how the procedure has been used in a literature course.

Phase I. In Phase I (Intensive/Group), a representative concept in literature, such as the genera of tragic heroes, was dealt with through intensive examination of three prototypical examples (e.g., *The Merchant of Venice, Joan of Arc*, and *The Autobiography of Malcolm X*). Selections of more than a single exemplar of the concept allow for both in-depth analysis and opportunities to compare and contrast authors' styles; historical perspectives; ethnic, gender and cultural differences; and a host of other comparative factors that single selections would prohibit. Pre-teaching/learning analysis dealt with an overview of the concept and why it was being studied. Since one of the main purposes is to learn *how* to study tragic heroes, *who* should be studied (i.e., which tragic hero) is less

Another obvious implication, one which only a few people have begun to take seriously, is that we've got to do a lot fewer things in school. The greatest enemy of understanding is coverage. As long as you are determined to cover everything, you actually ensure that most kids are not going to understand. You've got to take enough time to get kids deeply involved in something so they can think about it in lots of different ways and apply it....Now, this is the most revolutionary idea in American education—because some people can't abide the notion that we might leave something out....But we know unambiguously that the way we do things now isn't working, so we have to try something else.

Howard Gardner, in Brandt, 1993

important, as long as the hero is representative of the genera. An emphasis on how rather than who also legitimizes a role for students. The payoff as far as transfer is concerned is to follow the in-depth coverage with a post-learning analysis that focuses on factors that define the representative concept of tragic heroes (e.g., characteristic themes, patterns, etc.). The goal of the post-learning analysis is to help consolidate cognitive structures[1] and patterns of analysis developed through in-depth study of a small number of literary selections so that they are readily available for use in future situations.

Phase II. Phase II (Extensive/Group) consists of the perusal of large numbers of literary contributions dealing with tragic heroes to which similar cognitive structures and patterns of analysis can be applied. In our sample situation, students working in small interest groups, compiled categorical lists and summaries of tragic heroes within their respective areas of special interest. Thus, for example, groups focused on tragic heroes in sports, politics, science, civil rights, religion, the women's movement, arts and entertainment, or other area(s) in which special interests were expressed. Identifying tragic heroes within categories and preparing brief summaries of them developed research and writing skills as well as communication skills for group discussions and oral presentations that were a part of the planned activities. A key feature of this phase of the work was that students were not expected to read entire books about the persons on their lists. Summaries of non-fictional persons were prepared from descriptions found in textbooks or encyclopedias, and fictional tragic heroes were summarized from material found in *Master Plots* or *Cliff Notes*. Although perusal of large numbers is recommended, coverage should be purposefully superficial, *but geared toward stimulating follow-up on the parts of interested individuals or small groups.*

Phase III. Phase III (Intensive/Individual or /Small Group) consists of in-depth follow-up of selected readings based on the personal preferences of students which emerge from Phase II. Phase III in our example was pursued in a variety of ways. Activities included formal study modeled after the procedures used in the Great Books or Junior Great Books study groups, informal discussions about selected tragic heroes by interested groups of students, or simply the more sophisticated appreciation that could now be derived from reading for pleasure or viewing a play or film based on the

Cliff Notes

Advice to the Reader

These notes are intended to be used as a supplementary aid to serious students. They serve to free them from the interminable and distracting note-taking so that they can listen and think intelligently about the work and what the instructor and class is saying. They provide students with the opportunity to make selective notes, secure in the knowledge that they have a basic understanding of the work.

life or exploits of a tragic heroine. Some of this follow-up took place immediately, and in other cases it was deferred until a similar process was followed with other genera. And, of course, it can take place on a personal level at any time in the future. Once students learned how to analyze a particular genus, and after they explored categorical representatives of the genus, they were empowered to apply these skills to future assignments or reading for pleasure.

The three-phase process described above requires that teachers gain an understanding of the pivotal ideas, representative topics, unifying themes, and internal structures that define a field of knowledge or that horizontally cut across a number of disciplines. This is not an easy task for teachers who traditionally have relied on textbooks for curricular decision making. There are, however, excellent resources available to assist in this process. Books such as the *Dictionary of the History of Ideas* (Wiener, 1968) contain essays that cover every major discipline, but the emphasis of the essays is on interdisciplinary, cross-cultural relations. The essays are cross-referenced to direct the reader to other articles in which the same or similar ideas occur in other domains. Similar resources for teachers can be found in books such as the *Syntopicon* (Adler & Hutchins, 1952), which is an organizational structure for the great ideas of the western world.

New curricular materials are also available to assist teachers in the development of in-depth learning units. The recent concern about excellence for all students has prompted the development of new content area standards, such as the new mathematics and science standards. The development of these standards has, in turn, prompted the assessment of curricular materials. Some of these curriculum review initiatives are using criteria aligned with the central concepts of the Multiple Menu Model. Specifically, The Center for Gifted Education at the College of William and Mary reviewed science materials. Unlike traditional review criteria which focused on readability levels and the sheer amount of factual material included within the text, the criteria for this new review were concerned, for example, with the significance of the scientific concepts covered and the amount of practice provided in the processes of scientific inquiry. Information about this initiative is included in the Resource Guide at the end of this chapter.

The principle of appeal to imagination calls for the selection of materials that are drawn from the extraordinary rather than from the experience of everyday life. They should be such as to transform ordinary perspectives rather than to confirm them. Through his studies the student should find himself in a different world from the commonplace one of practical life.

Philip Phenix, 1964

Chapter 6

The Leatherman: Recalling a Legend

A century ago the Leatherman, a legendary wanderer, walked a continuous route through Connecticut and New York, sleeping in caves and rarely speaking. Our reporter, Steve Grant, is planning to retrace the Leatherman's route to discover who he was, where he wandered and why. Steve is interested in whatever information you may have about the Leatherman. If you have correspondence, photographs, maps, other historical material and can help, please call The Hartford Courant.

The Hartford Courant, 1993

A Final Consideration: Appeal to the Imagination

Within the context of in-depth teaching and learning, there is still one additional consideration that should be addressed. Phenix (1964) has termed this concept the appeal to the imagination, and he argues very persuasively for the selection of topics that will lift students to new planes of experience and meaning. Material drawn from the extraordinary allows students to "...see more deeply, feel more intensely, and comprehend more fully" (p. 346). Phenix sets forth three conditions that should guide our thinking with regard to this concept and the role teachers should play in the pursuit of imaginative teaching. First, he points out that the means for stimulating the imagination differ according to the individual, his or her level of maturity, and the cultural context in which the individual is located. Second, the teacher must model the imaginative qualities of mind we are trying to develop in students and be able to enter sympathetically into the lives of students. Finally, imaginative teaching requires faith in the possibility of awakening imagination in any and every student, regardless of the kinds of constraints that may be placed on the learning process.

There are, undoubtedly, different perspectives about how to select content that will appeal to the imagination. Topics with such a focus could easily fall prey to material that deals with seductive details or esoteric and sensational topics. Seductive details are not inherently inappropriate as topics for in-depth study. Indeed, they often serve the important function of stimulating initial interests and creating what Whitehead (1929) called the romance stage with a topic or field of study. But if seductive details and sensational topics become ends rather than means for promoting advanced understanding, then we have traded appeal to the imagination for romanticism and showmanship.

How, then, should we go about selecting curriculum material that appeals to the imagination but that is not based purely on sensationalism? The answer rests, in part, on selecting topics that represent powerful and controversial manifestations of basic ideas and concepts. Thus, for example, the concepts of loyalty versus betrayal might be examined and compared from political, literary, military, or family perspectives, but always in ways that bring intensity, debate, and personal involvement to the concepts. An adversarial approach to ideas and concepts (i.e., loyalty versus betrayal) also guarantees that the essential element of *confrontations with knowledge* will be present in selected curricular topics.

In a certain sense, it would be feasible to write the history of creative productivity as a chronicle of men and women who confronted existing ideas and concepts in an adversarial fashion, and who used existing information only as counterpoints to what eventually became their own unique contributions to the growth of knowledge. It was these confrontations that sparked their imaginations; and it is for this reason that an appeal to the imagination should be a major curricular focus for the coverage of in-depth topics.

Examining the Methodology of the Discipline

Throughout a unit of study, teachers explain, illustrate and involve students in the process of research as defined by the methodology dimension of the Knowledge Menu (e.g., identify a problem area in the study of tragic heroes, focus the problem, state an hypothesis, locate resources, classify and organize data, summarize data, draw conclusions, report findings). The cluster of diverse procedures that surround the acquisition of knowledge—that dimension of learning commonly referred to as "process" or thinking skills—should themselves be viewed as a form of content. It is these more enduring skills that form the cognitive structures and problem solving strategies that have the greatest transfer value. When we view process as content, we avoid the artificial dichotomy and the endless arguments about whether content or process should be the primary goal of learning. Combining content and process leads to a goal that is larger than the sum of the respective parts. Simply stated, this goal is the acquisition of a scheme for acquiring, managing, and producing information in an organized and systematic fashion.

Armed with the tools learned in the knowledge menu and a more mature understanding of the methodology of the field, students are no longer passive recipients of information and are able to begin the process of generating knowledge within the field. With respect to the tragic heroes unit that has been developed, students may want to interview contemporary authors regarding which characteristics they believe define the tragic heroes of today.

The Instructional Techniques Menus

The second, third, fourth and fifth Menus from the model concern pedagogy or instruction. Specifically, these menus provide curriculum developers with a range of options related to how they will present learning activities to students, based on the principles and concepts they have selected. The

It is better to learn a few concepts well and to know how to apply them than to cover long lists of topics for the purposes of recall.

John Goodlad, 1984

One of the most disturbing findings [of a study on classroom practices] is the narrow range of teaching practices used by teachers in our sample....They lectured, monitored seatwork and engaged in activities requiring only rote learning.

John Goodlad, 1984

Instructional Objectives and Student Activities Menu focuses on the thinking and feeling processes (e.g., application, analysis, synthesis) which are used by learners as they construct knowledge about a discipline. It is important that curriculum writers design learning activities that incorporate a balanced variety of these thinking and feeling processes. The balance provides learners with practice in the spectrum of encoding and recoding activities associated with learning new information, concepts and principles. The next menu, the Instructional Strategies Menu, provides a range of specific teaching methods (e.g., discussion, dramatization, independent study) which teachers can use to present new material. A variety of carefully selected instructional strategies from this menu provides students with multiple ways to be engaged with knowledge and to employ the full range of their intellectual abilities and learning styles. Teachers and curriculum writers are provided with a relatively fixed order of events for teaching information through the next component, The Instructional Sequences Menu. For example, teachers open most lessons by gaining the attention of their students, linking the present lesson with previously covered material, and pointing out other applications for what has been introduced. Accordingly, the Instructional Sequences Menu is a rubric which can accommodate any instructional or pedagogical strategy. Finally, the Artistic Modification Menu invites teachers to personalize lessons by sharing an anecdote, observation, hobby, or personal belief about an event, topic or concept. As such, it can be used with any instructional strategy and during any point in the instructional sequence. Personalizing lessons in this fashion generates interest and excitement among students.

The Instructional Products Menu

The Instructional Products Menu is concerned with the outcomes of learning experiences presented by the teacher through the curricular material and pedagogy; but in this case, outcomes are viewed in much more complex learning behaviors than the lists of basic skills typically found in the literature on "outcomes-based education." Two kinds of outcomes emerge: concrete products and abstract products. The concrete products are physical constructions that result from learner interaction with the knowledge, principles and concepts. These physical constructions include, for example, speeches, essays, dramatizations, and experiments. Abstract products include behaviors, such as leadership activities related to an issue, increased self-confidence, and the acquisition of new methodologies, such as interviewing skills. It is important to note that the two kinds of products are mutually reinforcing. As students produce new kinds of concrete products, they will also demonstrate new abstract products, such as methodological skills and self-assurance. As self-confidence and leadership opportunities increase, it is likely that additional physical products will emerge, as well.

Textbook Analysis and Surgical Removal of Unchallenging and Redundant Content

Does a place exist within the Multiple Menu Model and in-depth teaching for the use of traditional textbooks? The answer to this question is an emphatic "yes," provided textbooks are closely examined by teachers prior to their use with curricular units. This scrutiny might best be called "textbook analysis and surgical removal." The procedures for carrying out the textbook analysis and surgical removal are based on the argument that "less is better" when it comes to content selection, but it is necessary to make wise decisions when determining which material will be covered in greater depth. A prerequisite is that teacher groups, working in collaboration with curriculum specialists, must have a solid understanding of the goals and content of a particular unit of study, and the reasons why they are covering given segments of material.

The first step in the process might best be described as "textbook triage." Each unit of instruction is examined to determine (1) which material is needless repetition of previously covered skills and concepts, (2) which material is necessary for review, and (3) which material is important enough to cover in either a survey or an in-depth manner. These decisions obviously require an understanding of the goals and content of the curricular materials being used and some know-how about the use of criteria for making curricular modification decisions. There is a growing body of literature dealing with this process (see, for example, Conn, 1988; Osborne, Jones, & Stein, 1985) that parallels the skills necessary for carrying out effective curriculum compacting. It is recommended that the following five factors be considered by teachers when they make decisions about the suitability of textbooks as resources for units of study constructed around the Multiple Menu Model.

While I do not think a textbook-based curriculum is necessarily wise, I want textbooks to improve, because it would be romantic to think that they are going to go away. They are the curriculum in public schools— whether we like it or not.

Michael W. Apple, in Lockwood, 1992

For instance, the average mathematics textbook has around 220-250 lessons in it. There are 180 days in my contract as a teacher. Unless I'm using surgery on that book to identify what I'm supposed to be teaching out of those 250 lessons, I'll end up teaching the whole book!

Kenneth Komoski, in Lockwood, 1992

1. **Content.** Examine the table of contents.

   • Is the content accurate?
   • Is it representative of themes, concepts, principles and/or structures in the discipline?
   • Are sufficient examples/selections provided to explain and elaborate upon the concept under consideration?
   • Does the content highlight the interrelationships among other curricular areas?

2. **Organization.** Examine the chapters and table of contents.

   • Do the chapters and units address a single concept or theme?
   • Are ideas integrated across lessons and chapters?
   • Is there a forward-moving framework controlling the presentation of content (e.g., simple listing, thematic framework, temporal sequence, problem/ solution format)?
   • Is the framework appropriate for the discipline?

3. **Questions.** Review the chapter and unit questions.

   • Are the questions related to the chapter and unit content?
   • Are they balanced with respect to the levels of thinking and feeling processes (e.g., knowledge, comprehension, application, analysis, synthesis, evaluation)?

4. **Resources.** Examine the reading or resource suggestions in both the teacher's and student's editions.

   • Are the resources correlated with the chapter content?
   • Are they sufficient in number and diverse in nature for the perusal of related works?
   • Do they offer sufficient connections to other disciplines?
   • Do they encourage or facilitate independent investigations?

5. **Adaptability.**
   Students
   - Does the content consider the age, maturity level, experiential background and knowledge base of the student?
   - Can the content be adapted to a range of student ability levels?
   - Does the content provide for varied student interests and learning preferences?
   - Does the content appeal to the students' imagination?
   - Can the material be used by groups and individuals?
   Teachers
   - Does the content encourage teacher initiative and adaptation?
   - Does the content appeal to the teacher's imagination?

What makes the Multiple Menu Model unique is its deep connections with the how-to of disciplines. Other models provide teachers with the skills to enrich curriculum by increasing the amount of material related to a subject, the rate at which it is covered, or by varying the products that emerge from learner interaction with the material in a discipline. *The Multiple Menu Model takes the teacher and student to the very heart of a discipline to examine its location in the domain of information and to understand the methodology employed by those who produce knowledge in the field.* Accordingly, this model enables learners to become first-hand inquirers and *creators* of information, a far more intensive, productive engagement in the school setting than what students experience as consumers of information.

What teachers teach is at the very heart of professional competency. The textbook analysis and surgical removal process offers teachers an opportunity to come together as a group of professionals around specific tasks within and across grade levels and subject areas. Effective group work using this process will undoubtedly contribute to individual teacher growth as far as content mastery is concerned, and this approach has the added benefit of promoting the types of consultation and sharing of knowledge and experience that characterize other professions. In order for this process to occur, however, school leaders need to make available the time and resources for this essential school improvement activity, and teachers must be willing to devote some of their non-teaching professional time to the process. We also believe that creative contributions to curricular modification should

We must ask, then: Are we in the business of creating dead texts or dead minds? If we accept the title of educator—with all of the political and ethical commitments this entails—I think we already know what our answer should be.

Michael W. Apple in Lockwood, 1992

be included in the professional reward structure that is a part of the SEM staff development model presented in Chapter 8.

Interdisciplinary Models

Kaplan's Grid

KAPLAN **(RENZULLI, 1986)** developed a model to guide the construction of curricular units called The Grid (see Figure 11). Although it was written as a model to differentiate instruction for high ability students, it can be used as a model to develop talent among all children. Specifically, The Grid helps curriculum writers make decisions about an overarching theme, the essential elements of curriculum, and the format for the creation of learning experiences.

CONTENTS	PROCESSES	PRODUCT	AFFECTIVE
The subject matter selected for the curriculum reflects knowledge that is mandatory for all students to learn, knowledge that is commensurate with the level of conceptualization and level of knowledge particular to the needs and interests of the students.	The skills and competencies students are expected to master include, but are not limited to, fundamental, rudimentary or basic skills, productive (logic, creative problem-solving and critical-) thinking skills, research skills or the skills of accessing, interpreting, summarizing and reporting information, and personalized skills.	The communication or transmission of the knowledge and skills students have assimilated requires experiences (1) in a variety of media, including the latest forms of technology, and (2) with materials for appropriate and accurate production of the developed work.	The attitudes, appreciation and values introduced to students are an integral feature of, rather than an adjunct to, the curriculum. An understanding of the student as an individual and contributor, who values learning and productivity, and awareness of the roles and responsibility for leadership are some of the affective learnings to be included in the curriculum.

Sandra N. Kaplan

Figure 11. Curriculum development model—The Grid.

Kaplan suggests that curriculum writers begin developing units by identifying themes or concepts, such as power, humor, extinction, the unexpected, or journeys. Like the concept of the tragic hero described earlier, these themes are principles that cut across time and disciplines. It is precisely for this reason that they can be the center of interdisciplinary units. Kaplan suggests that four questions guide the selection of concepts:

Is the theme related to a discipline?
Is it a significant area of study?
Is the theme neither age nor time dependent?
Does the theme allow for a variety of teacher and student
    options for study?

The theme becomes a way to organize and connect individual learning units, thereby providing meaningful connections among the disciplines studied in school.

Once curriculum writers have identified the theme with which they will work for a specified period of time, Kaplan suggests they focus on selecting the content, processes and products for the unit. Content refers to the knowledge or subject matter that is to be taught, and Kaplan believes that the selection of content is the most difficult aspect of curriculum development. She provides specific rules for selecting content. Content should: (1) be related to the theme under consideration, (2) be multidisciplinary (allow for extensions to other disciplines), (3) be consonant with the needs of the learner, and (4) provide a time orientation wherein past, present and future are related. Processes refer to skills or competencies related to the subject matter (e.g., note-taking, interpreting, analyzing) that students will be required to learn. Kaplan recommends that teachers refer to a variety of taxonomies during this phase of the curriculum writing process and that targeted competencies be part of a larger scope and sequence of process skills that students are required to learn. Products refer to the forms of communication students need to learn in order to transmit the knowledge they have assimilated (e.g., essays, debates, dramatizations, computer software applications). The value of the product is twofold, according to Kaplan. First, it is verification that learning has taken place, and second, it is a tool which can be used again and again.

*Curriculum Integration:
The Chemistry of Art*

A teaching team from Duke Ellington School for the Arts in Washington, D.C., is linking the arts and chemistry through a problem in art conservationship. According to the problem scenario, a painting of uncertain value has been discovered in an attic. The painting may be the work of an African-American artist from the Harlem Renaissance era. The student takes on the role of the expert hired to assess the painting. Students must do research in art history, write an essay describing the painting aesthetically, and identify—if possible—the artist, period and value.

Says Shepherd, a science teacher, "we're trying to motivate the students in ways they had never been motivated before." Sue Eddins, a mathematics teacher, said, "If I can find a way to get the students interested, that's exciting enough to get me to give up some of my old habits."

Scott Willis, 1993

Chapter 6

We teach children conservation in physics— that each action produces an equal and opposite reaction—as if it were a law that applied only to billiard balls...without making them aware that the same principle applies to human psychology, to social action, to economics, to the entire planetary system. We bring children up to take their places in a culture that , in reality, no longer exists. The basic skills they learn have little to do with survival in the future. Each academic subject is presented as if it had an existence independent of all others....Yet, if we continue to teach physics separately from ethics, or molecular biology without concern for empathy, the chances of a monstrous evolutionary miscarriage are going to increase. To avoid these possibilities, it is imperative to begin thinking about a truly integrative, global education that takes seriously the actual interconnectedness of causes and effects.

Mihaly Csikszentmihalyi, 1993

The Interdisciplinary Concept Model: A Step-by-Step Approach to Developing Integrated Units of Study

Hayes-Jacobs (1989) also developed an interdisciplinary approach to developing curriculum units and like Kaplan, suggests curriculum writers begin by selecting a theme. Hayes-Jacobs suggests that this first phase be completed collaboratively by teachers and students. Once the topic is selected, she recommends that the theme be explored from all disciplinary angles. To facilitate this exploration, she provides a graphic device: a six-spoked wheel (see Figure 12). Brainstorming is used by students and teachers to generate the discipline-specific questions, topics and issues related to the theme.

Hayes-Jacobs suggests that Bloom's taxonomy guide the next phase of curriculum development: writing activities to explore the questions. To ensure that a balance exists among the learning activities related to the theme, Hayes-Jacobs recommends that each activity be charted under the proper heading of Bloom's taxonomy (i.e., knowledge, comprehension, application, analysis, synthesis, evaluation). At a glance, the content-process matrix of activities provides the curriculum writer with the overall design of the learning experiences. The final phase includes assessment, and Hayes-Jacobs recommends that specific behavioral objectives, embedded into the curricular activities, are critical to the successful measurement of performance assessments.

Kaplan's and Hayes-Jacobs' model are similar; specifically, they both require the identification of a linking theme or concept to provide students with the "big picture" approach to knowledge. Additionally, both provide curriculum writers with methods to select content and process skills. Finally, curricular units designed by using Kaplan's or Hayes-Jacobs' model help ensure talent development among learners for two reasons. First, their thematic approach provides students with a rich foundation from which to make meaningful connections across domains of knowledge. When learners are provided with a larger number of meaningful ways to connect and interact with knowledge, interests are more likely to emerge and to be nurtured. Second, curriculum generated from either model can be individualized to accommodate for student learning styles, interests and ability levels. Adjusting the abstractness of knowledge and levels of process skills, as well as product types to individual learners ensures a match between learners and the curriculum. When optimal conditions for learning are provided, talent development is more likely to occur.

Differences between the models are related to the methodologies for the selection of interdisciplinary topics, the guidelines for selecting content and the taxonomies recommended for selecting process skills. Kaplan leaves the selection of themes to curriculum writers and provides key questions to guide the selection process; Hayes-Jacobs believes theme selection should be a collaborative effort between students and teachers. Similarly, Kaplan provides teachers with guidelines to formulate content; Hayes-Jacobs

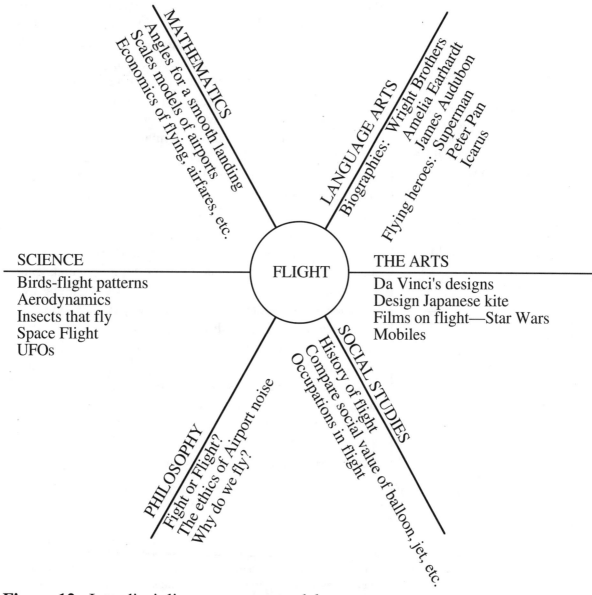

Figure 12. Interdisciplinary concept model
A unit on flight—steps 1 and 2.

provides an open-ended six-spoke wheel graphic organizer to assist students and teachers develop specific content. Finally, Kaplan suggests that several taxonomies be used to articulate the process skills in the curricular unit and integrate them within the larger scope and sequence; Hayes-Jacobs suggests using one taxonomy, Bloom's, to ensure the proper balance of process skills.

By way of summary, we want textbooks to improve, and we believe that the strategies for textbook use and modification described above can serve as a driving force for reconsideration on the parts of textbook publishers. The consumer-driven marketplace will become more responsive to the issue of textbook quality if educators become more sophisticated about the levels of present texts and if they take specific steps to augment or replace existing texts. If, on the other hand, we sit idly by and do nothing, textbooks will continue to the dominant force in the school curriculum. Making changes in the ways we use texts, and in the substitution of in-depth material for mundane textbook content will require three conditions on the parts of teachers and policy makers. First, teachers will need to pursue the kinds of professional growth that will empower them to analyze textbook content and to gain deeper understandings of the material they are teaching. Teachers cannot prepare and teach an in-depth unit on the genera of tragic heroes unless they acquire an in-depth understanding of this topic. Second, school and departmental faculties will have to organize themselves into special purpose teams that focus on increased knowledge and know-how about both content and process, and about improved pedagogy, as well. A discussion about the types of professional improvement process and the role and function of special purpose teams is discussed in the chapter on staff development (Chapter 8). Finally, policy makers and school leaders need to provide the time and staff development resources necessary for curricular modification, and perhaps, most important, for the sincere endorsement of the process.

I am only one,
But still I am one.
I cannot do everything,
But still
I can do something;
And because I cannot
do everything,
I will not refuse to do
The something
That I can do.

Edward E. Hale

---

[1] Cognitive structures are the ways individuals see the physical and social worlds; the ways in which they organize and interrelate facts, concepts, beliefs, and expectations; and the ways they form patterns of interactions between whole/part relationships. A cognitive structure might best be thought of as a mental formula, plan of attack or set of blueprints that a person has stored in his or her brain for use in addressing a familiar or closely-related problem.

Resource Guide

THE RESOURCE guide for Chapter 6 is divided into two sections. The first section contains the names of books, articles and exemplary programs related to the curriculum modification strategies examined in this chapter. The second section contains selected examples of curriculum programs, units or supplementary materials that integrate disciplines, process skills with content, and/or provide students with opportunities to become first-hand inquirers.

Books, Articles and Programs Related to Curriculum Modification

Books
Curriculum Compacting
Title: Curriculum Compacting
Author: Reis, S. M., Burns, D. E., & Renzulli, J. S.
Description: Curriculum Compacting is an easy-to-read book of 170 pages. It is designed for educators who want to free up students' classroom time by eliminating curricular material students already know as well as needless curriculum repetition while, at the same time, promoting educational accountability. The book contains four chapters: History and Rationale for Compacting; An Overview of Curriculum Compacting; Recordkeeping and Enrichment Options; Challenges, Recommendations and Questions. Step-by-step instructions for the curriculum compacting process are included, as are many examples, key forms and lists of resources.
Publisher: Creative Learning Press, P.O. Box 320, Mansfield Center, CT 06250, (203) 429-8118, Price: $24.95.

Title: It's About Time
Author: Starko, A.
Description: It's About Time is a "how-to" guide that describes compacting procedures and provides readers with guidelines for in-service strategies on this topic. Included in the book are simulations and frequently asked questions about curriculum compacting.
Publisher: Creative Learning Press, P.O. Box 320, Mansfield Center, CT 06250, (203) 429-8118, Price: $22.95.

Interdisciplinary Curriculum
Title: Interdisciplinary Curriculum Design and Implementation
Editor: Hayes-Jacobs, H.

This yearbook is published by the Association for Supervision and Curriculum Development. The authors provide a rationale for interdisciplinary teaching, guidelines for selecting and developing interdisciplinary content, and questions which can assist teachers and curriculum writers incorporate process skills into interdisciplinary content.

Publisher: Association for Supervision and Curriculum Development, 1250 N. Pitt Street, Alexandria, VA 22314, (703) 549-9111, Fax: (703) 549-3891, Price: $13.95.

Articles

Title: Civil War Reenactments—"A Real and Complete Image"
Author: RaCocca, C.

Abstract: A Civil War study group is built around 124th New York State Volunteers (famed "Orange Blossoms"), a historic regiment recruited in Orange Country in 1982. Several local high school students have participated in the program by donning authentic military uniforms and civilian dress of the era, conducting primary research, and presenting programs for school and community groups.
Journal: Educational Leadership, 50(7), pp. 42-44.

Title: Courting Controversy: How to Build Interdisciplinary Units
Author: Williams, J., & Reynolds, T. D.

Abstract: By focusing on a polluted river and a visit to a rural Tennessee town, sixth-grade students from suburban Asheville, North Carolina, learned more about this controversy than many of their well-informed parents and teachers. Steps for creating similar interdisciplinary thematic units are described, along with the benefits of team teaching and experiential learning.
Journal: Educational Leadership, 50(7), pp. 13-15.

Title: Global Issues in the 6th Grade? Yes!
Author: Doane, C.

Abstract: Suburban Chicago middle school teachers designed a month-long unit to foster global education, guided by research on integrated, self-selected, and collaborative learning strategies. Teachers initiated brainstorming activities, grouped students by interest, and demonstrated how to be investigative researchers, informative writers, effective

speakers, good listeners, and critical thinkers. An open house program showcased results.
Journal: Educational Leadership, 50(7), pp. 19-21.

Title: Learning History by Doing History
Author: Kobrin, D., Abbott, E., Ellinwood, J., & Horton, D.
Abstract: The traditional way of studying history is unappealing to many students because they rarely perform the historian's tasks: defining essential questions, sorting through available source materials, determining topics, drawing conclusions. Rhode Island high schools have provided students with the skills and resources to create and interpret history.
Journal: Educational Leadership, 50(7), pp. 39-41.

Title: Problem-Based Learning: As Authentic as It Gets
Author: Stepien, W., & Gallagher, S.
Abstract: For three years, the Center for Problem-Based Learning at Illinois Mathematics and Science Academy has been developing innovative programs in various K-12 settings. Students meet an "ill-structured problem" (like thorium waste) before receiving instruction. Teachers act as coaches and tutors, probing findings, hypotheses, and conclusions; sharing their thinking when students need a model; and calling "time-out" discussions on thinking progress.
Journal: Educational Leadership, 50(7), pp. 25-28.

Title: Tackling Society's Problems in English Class
Author: Burke, J.
Abstract: An English teacher's impromptu unit on social problems gave students an opportunity to develop writing skills while expanding concept of community. While gathering data on diminishing rain forests, discussing research in small groups or workshops, interviewing community members, sending letters to political representatives, connecting with environmental organizations, and typing a final report, high school sophomores felt involved and empowered.
Journal: Educational Leadership, 50(7), pp. 16-18.

Title: Taking Word Problems Off the Page
Author: Bottage, B. A., & Hasselbring, T. S.
Abstract: Students do not associate traditional word problems with their own experiences because they describe experiences textually, rather than contextually, and seem artificially geared

Note: Abstracts for the articles included in the Resource Guide for Chapter 6 were obtained from the Education Resources Information Center (ERIC).

to specific number operations and single correct answers. Aided by a state grant, elementary teachers in one Minnesota district are using video anchors to simulate real-life problems, motivate students, and imbue mathematics with real-world value.

Journal: Educational Leadership, 50(7), pp. 36-38.

Interdisciplinary Programs

The Southern Regional High School District, in Manahawkin, New Jersey, implements a schoolwide thematic unit every other year. Initiated by teachers and students who decide upon a theme, the process culminates in a week-long series of interdisciplinary performances and exhibits in which the entire school community participates. The project is currently funded with a grant from the New Jersey State Department of Education. A guidebook, video and computer disc are available that describe the year-long calendar of activities for those who want to implement similar programs.

For information about the project: Jane Plenge, Southern Regional High School District, 75 Cedar Bridge Avenue, Manahawkin, NJ 08050, (609) 597-9481.

Selected Examples of Curricular Materials That Emphasize Interdisciplinary Connections, Content and Process Skills, and Students as First-Hand Inquirers

Math and Science*

Connect is a professional math and science newsletter published by Teachers' Laboratory, Inc. Each of the twelve-page editions is organized around a central theme (e.g., product testing, wetlands, money and economics, patterns), and the eight yearly issues are filled with a wide range of practical, teacher-written articles. All of the contributing authors have the same simple goal: to support teachers and other educators who strive to develop better approaches to hands-on learning and problem solving. Accordingly, the articles reflect diverse ways to engage students in problem solving activities related to the theme under consideration. Additionally, subscribers are provided with current information on outstanding literary connections for each thematic unit. Literature Links, a feature in each issue, is an annotated bibliography of books to expand student learning and extend students' understanding of the theme in other disciplines. Finally, each issue provides detailed information (distributors, etc.) about the equipment and materials featured in each issue.

Publisher: Teachers' Laboratory, Inc., P.O. Box 6480, Brattleboro, VT 05302-6480. $18.00 (1 year); $32.00 (2 years). Phone: (802) 254-3457, FAX: (802) 254-5233. Back issues are available.

Elementary Science Study (ESS) is a series of modules which pose interesting problems in scientific content. The modules are appropriate for students in grades K-9, and examples of modules include: "Eggs and Tadpoles," "Pattern Blocks," and "Balloons and Gases." Modules require different time lines for completion. The one called "Balloons and Gases," for example, is appropriate for students in grades 5-8 and takes from 10-22 weeks to complete. The units focus on hands-on exploration and discovery. Developers of the materials encourage the assessment of student progress on a number of levels, including the level of excitement in class. *Publisher*: Delta Education, Inc., P.O. Box M, Nashua, NH 03061-6012, (800) 258-1302.

Great Explorations in Math and Science (GEMS) are curricular units are designed for "hands-on," in-depth learning in science and mathematics for students in grades K-10. Specifically, each of the more than 30 units is focused on a single topic or theme, and the activities within a unit build upon each other. Additionally, the materials are organized by major concepts and skills. For example, the "Earthworms" unit is focused on the following themes: systems and interaction, stability, effects of temperature, the circulatory system and adaptation. Participating students are provided practice in observing, measuring, experimenting, predicting, averaging, graphing, interpreting data and inferring from data.

A chart is provided to help teachers identify the themes of all the units. Samples of year-long science programs for grades 3, 6 and 8 are also provided to help teachers integrate units into a well-balanced science program. *Publisher*: Lawrence Hall of Science, University of California, Berkeley, CA 94720, (510) 642-5133.

*Note:
The College of William and Mary has created a Consumer's Guide to Science Curriculum *for classroom teachers, curriculum developers and textbook review committees. It is a promising guide because it evaluates*

science curricular materials from three perspectives: (1) the degree to which materials contain standard elements, (2) the degree to which they infuse the practice of the scientific method and promote student skepticism and tolerance for ambiguity, and (3) the degree to which materials provide differentiation for special populations, including students with high abilities, females, minorities and the learning disabled.

The guide reviews three categories of science materials: basal/stand alone texts (i.e., texts designed to be used as the student's total program), modular units (i.e., independent units organized around a large topic or theme), and supplementary materials (i.e., loosely connected activities or fully-developed units that enrich curricula). Each review consists of two sections: a narrative review and a consumer guide rating. The narrative review contains a detailed description of the curriculum materials under consideration along with a critical description of its attributes in the areas of curriculum instruction, issues associated with exemplary science curriculum, and appropriateness for special populations. The Consumer's Rating Guide *encapsulates the fundamental findings on each piece of curriculum so that materials can be compared across categories.*

The two science units recommended above were rated highly by reviewers in the Consumers Guide to Science Curriculum.

For information: College of William and Mary, Center for Gifted Education, P.O. Box 8795, Williamsburg, VA 23187-8795 (804) 221-2185, Fax: (804) 221-2184.

Technical Education Research Center (TERC) is a non-profit education research and development organization dedicated to hands-on mathematics and science learning. The organization sponsors workshops for practitioners in mathematics and science programs engaging students in real world problems and publishes a semi-annual newsletter, *Hands On!* The newsletter contains articles by practitioners who are successfully involving students in hands-on research in mathematics and science. A recent edition of the newsletter contained articles which explained how students could become actively involved in their community in environmental research, how an ozonometer could be used by students to conduct scientific research on the stratospheric ozone, and how secondary science students could investigate indoor air quality with tools they made themselves.

For information: TERC, 2067 Massachusetts Avenue, Cambridge, MA 02140, (617) 547-0430, Fax: (617) 349-3535. A donation is requested to help defray the cost of publication.

Interdisciplinary Learning

Problem-Based Learning is a series of interdisciplinary units created by researchers and teachers at the Center for Problem-Based Learning. The instructional units are loosely-structured problems that provide students with the opportunity to become first-hand professional researchers.

For more information: The Center for Problem-Based Learning, Illinois Mathematics and Science Academy, 1500 West Sullivan Road, Aurora, IL 60506-1000, (708) 907-5956, Fax: (708) 907-5976.

Literature

The Great Books Program, established in 1947, provides reading and discussion programs for children in Grades K-12, and adults. Readings include fiction and nonfiction selections by grade level, and discussions are student-oriented around questions of enduring human significance: Why are there wars? Is there a "real me" apart from the self I present to others? The Great Books Program has a threefold purpose: (1) to build skills in shared inquiry, (2) to encourage reflective and interpretive reading, and (3) to stimulate original thought. Essentially, the program helps teachers and students construct meaning about their lives through literature and the lives of others.

For information about the program and/or training: The Great Books Foundation, 35 East Wacker Drive, Suite 3500, Chicago, IL 60601-2298, (800) 222-5870.

Social Studies/Current Events/Economics

The Wall Street Journal Classroom Edition is a program designed to improve the economic and business literacy of secondary school students. The centerpiece of the program is a full-color student newspaper which is published monthly during the school year, and is made up almost entirely of articles from the daily *Wall Street Journal.* The teacher guide contains many useful lesson plans and activities that emphasize critical thinking, problem solving, practical applications of business and economic principles. Spanish translations of selected articles also appear in the teacher guide.

Of particular interest is the loosely-structured problem that is included in every edition. Related to articles in the same edition, the problem requires that students become first-hand professional investigators. The teacher guide provides a helpful list of reference materials and resources related to the problem.

Teachers can sign up for one semester (five issues) or for a full school year (nine issues). The cost of a classroom set os 30 copies is $90 for one semester or $150 for one year. The Classroom Edition Video (4 per semester) costs an additional $60 for one semester and $120 for one year.

For more information: The Wall Street Journal Classroom Edition, P.O. Box 7019, Chicopee, MA 01021-9940, or call (800) 544-0522.

Mathematics

Zillions: Consumer's Report for Kids is a magazine published every two months for students age 8-14. It is designed by the publishers of *Consumer Reports* to assist youngsters become responsible consumers. To that end, *Zillions* involves its readers directly in consumer issues, such as: "Sneakers: Finding Bargains," "Rating Mechanical Pencils," and "Testing New Board Games." Furthermore, teachers are provided with hands-on research assignments related to consumer issues that students can carry out at home or in the classroom.

Subscription rates: $16/year (six issues), $26/2 years (12 issues), $36/3 years (18 issues). Reduced rates are available to schools, and free subscriptions are available to schools in economically disadvantaged areas.

For information: Rana Arons, Consumers Union, 101 Truman Avenue, Yonkers, NY 10703-1057, (914) 378-2000, Fax: (914) 378-2900.

Chapter 7
Enrichment Learning and Teaching

THIS CHAPTER WILL INTEGRATE a brief discussion about learning theory with practical suggestions for infusing enrichment learning and teaching into the school program. The two approaches to learning theory discussed below in a point/counterpoint format are intended to highlight the essence of *why* schools should create opportunities for enrichment learning and teaching. A subsequent section on the Enrichment Triad Model builds on learning theory concepts, and shows how these concepts have been translated into enrichment practices that are used to organize specific learning activities. The final section deals with how the Triad Model can be applied to enrichment clusters.

Enrichment Learning and Teaching

Two Model Learning Theory
MORE BOOKS, articles, and papers have been written about the process of learning than perhaps any other topic in education and psychology. And when we add the vast amount of material that has been written about models of teaching and theories of instruction, the sheer volume of literature is nothing short of mind boggling! It is not our intention to review this multitudinous literature as background

What we need in America is for students to get more deeply interested in things, more involved in them, more engaged in wanting to know; to have projects that they can get excited about and work on over long periods of time, to be stimulated to find things out on their own.

Howard Gardner, in Brandt, 1993

Chapter 7

Learning is the acquisition of the art of the utilization of knowledge.

Alfred North Whitehead, 1929

for the discussion on enrichment learning and teaching that follows, nor will we argue about the number of unique theories that actually exist, or the advantages and disadvantages of various paradigms for guiding the learning process. We will argue, however, that in spite of all that has been written, every theory of teaching and learning can be classified into one of two general models. There are, obviously, occasions when a particular approach transcends both models; however, for purposes of clarifying the main features of enrichment learning and teaching, we will treat the two main models as polar opposites. Both models of learning and teaching are valuable in the overall process of schooling, and a well-balanced school program must make use of both of these general approaches to learning and teaching.

Although many names have been used to describe the two models that will be discussed, we will simply refer to them as the Deductive Model and the Inductive Model. The Deductive Model is the one with which most educators are familiar and the one that has guided the overwhelming majority of what takes place in classrooms and other places where formal learning is pursued. The Inductive Model, on the other hand, represents the kinds of learning that take place outside of formal school situations. A good way to understand the difference between these two types of learning is to compare how learning takes place in a typical classroom with how someone might learn new material or skills in real world situations. Classrooms are characterized by relatively fixed time schedules, segmented subjects or topics, predetermined sets of information and activity, tests and grades to determine progress, and a pattern of organization that is largely driven by the need to acquire and assimilate information and skills imposed from above and from outside the classroom. The major assumption in the deductive model is that current learning will have transfer value for some future problem, course, occupational pursuit, or life activity.

Contrast this type of learning with the more natural chain of events that take place in inductive situations such as a research laboratory, business office, or film studio. The goal in these situations is to produce a product or service. All resources, information, schedules, and sequences of events are directed toward this goal, and evaluation (rather than grading) is a function of the quality of the product or service as viewed through the eyes of a client or consumer. Everything that results in learning in a research laboratory, for example, is for present use, and, therefore, looking up new information, conducting an experiment, analyzing results, or preparing a report is focused primarily on the present rather than the future. Even the amount of time devoted to a particular project cannot be determined in advance because the nature of the problem and the unknown obstacles that might be encountered prevent us from prescribing rigid schedules.

The deductive model has dominated the ways in which most formal education is pursued, and the "track record" of the model has been less than impressive. One need only reflect for a moment on his or her own school experience to realize that with the exception of basic language and arithmetic, much of the compartmentalized material learned for some remote and ambiguous future situation is seldom used in the conduct of daily activities. The names of famous generals, the geometric formulas, the periodic table and the parts of a plant are quickly forgotten; and even if remembered, they do not have direct applicability to the problems that most people encounter in their daily lives. This is not to say that previously learned information is unimportant, but its relevancy, meaningfulness and endurance for future use is minimized when it is almost always learned apart from real life situations.

Deductive learning is based mainly on the factory model or human engineering conception of schooling. The underlying psychological theory is behaviorism, and the central concept of this ideology is that schools should prepare young people for smooth adjustment into the culture and work force of the society at large. A curriculum based on deductive learning must be examined in terms of both what is taught, and how it is taught. The issue of what is (or should be) taught has always been the subject of controversy ranging from a conservative position that emphasizes a classical or basic education curriculum to a more liberal perspective that includes contemporary knowledge and life adjustment experiences (e.g., driver education, sex education, computer literacy). By and large, American schools have been very effective in adapting what is taught to changes taking place in our society. Recent concerns about the kinds of skills that will be required in a rapidly changing job market have accelerated curricular changes that will prepare students for careers in technological fields and what has been described as a post-industrial society. Nowhere is this change more evident than in the emphasis that is being placed currently on thinking skills and interdisciplinary approaches to curriculum. These changes are viewed as favorable developments so far as schoolwide enrichment is concerned; however, the

To most of us boredom was worse than discipline....The bright were bored stiff, and the dull ones could not help feeling slower in the presence of quick and eager learners...I would often go to bed praying that the school would burn down before morning....Life in the classroom—perhaps it would be more accurate to say the absence of life— accounted for our boredom.

Sidney Hook, 1987

Do not train youth to learn by harshness, but lead them to it by what amuses their minds. Then you may discover the peculiar bent of the genius of each.

Plato

deductive model still places limitations on learning because of restrictions on *how* material is taught.

Although most schools have introduced teaching techniques that go beyond traditional drill and recitation, the predominant instructional model continues to be a prescribed and presented approach to learning. The teacher, textbook, or curriculum guide prescribes what is to be taught, and the material is presented to students in a predetermined manner. Educators have become more clever and imaginative in the teaching models employed, and it is not uncommon to see teachers using approaches such as discovery learning, simulations, cooperative learning, inquiry training, problem-centered learning, concept learning, and a host of variations on these basic models. More recent approaches include simulated problem solving through the use of interactive video discs and computer programs. Some of these approaches certainly make learning more active and enjoyable than traditional, content-based deductive learning, but the "bottom line" is that there are certain predetermined bodies of information and thinking processes that students are expected to acquire. The instructional effects of the deductive model are those directly achieved by leading the learner in prescribed directions. As indicated above, there is nothing inherently "wrong" with the deductive model; however, it is based on a limited conception of the role of the learner, it fails to consider variations in interests and learning styles, and it always places students in roles of lesson learners and exercise doers rather that authentic, first-hand inquirers.

Inductive learning, on the other hand, focuses on the *present use* of content and processes as a way of integrating material and thinking skills into the more enduring structure of the learner's repertoire. And it is these more enduring structures that have the greatest amount of transfer value for future use. When content and processes are learned in authentic, contextual situations, they result in more meaningful uses of information and problem solving strategies than the learning that takes place in artificial, preparation-for-the-future situations. If persons involved in inductive learning experiences are given some choice in the domains and activities in which they are engaged, and if present experience is directed toward realistic and personalized goals, this type of learning creates its own relevancy and meaningfulness.

If we agree that people do, in fact, learn when they are outside of schools and classrooms, in the "real world" as it is sometimes called, then we need to examine the dimensions of this type of learning and the ways that real world learning can be brought into the school. But we must also be extremely cautious whenever we think about "bringing" anything into the school. Our track record in this regard has been one of structuring and institutionalizing even the most innovative approaches to learning. We recall how the much heralded concept of Discovery Learning ended up being what a colleague called "sneaky telling"; and how a focus on thinking skills and creative thinking fell prey to the same types of formulas and prescribed activities that characterized the content-based curriculum which has been criticized so strongly by thinking skills advocates. Even our present fascination with computers and video discs is, in some cases, turning out to be little more than "electronic worksheets."

Enrichment learning and teaching is essentially an inductive approach to learning; however, it draws upon selected practices of deductive learning. Our argument is not an indictment of deductive learning, but, rather, a need to achieve balance between the two major approaches. Introducing inductive learning into the school is important for several reasons. First, schools should be enjoyable places that students want to attend rather than places they endure as part of their journey toward assimilation into the job market and the adult world. Second, schools should be places where students participate in and prepare for intelligent, creative, and effective living. This type of living includes learning how to analyze, criticize, and select from among alternative sources of information and courses of action; how to think effectively about unpredictable personal and interpersonal problems; how to live harmoniously with one another while remaining true to one's own emerging system of attitudes, beliefs, and values; and how to confront, clarify, and act upon problems and situations in constructive and creative ways. Finally, inductive learning is important because our society and democratic way of life are dependent upon an unlimited reservoir of creative and effective people. A small number of rare individuals have always emerged as the thinkers and problem solvers of our society. But we cannot afford to leave the emergence of leaders to chance, nor can we waste the undeveloped talents of so many of our young citizens who are the victims of poverty and the negative consequences that accompany being poor in America. All students must have the opportunity to develop their potentials and to lead constructive lives without trampling on or minimizing the value of others in the process.

The challenge is not simply to adopt innovative teaching techniques or to find new locations for learning, but deliberately to counteract two persistent maladies that make conventional schooling inauthentic: (1) often the work students do does not allow them to use their minds well, and (2) the work has no intrinsic meaning or value to students beyond achieving success in school.

Fred Newmann & Gary Wehlage, 1993

Chapter 7

Perhaps the best way to summarize the difference between deductive and inductive learning is to examine each model in terms of the three components that portray the act of learning. If we place each of these components on a continuum ranging from highly structured learning on the left side to unstructured learning on the right side, what emerges is a contrast such as the type portrayed in Figure 13. There is, obviously, a middle ground for each continuum, and each point on the continua has implications for the ways in which we organize learning situations. We do not believe that all learning should favor the right side of each continuum presented in Figure 13. Some learning situations are undoubtedly more efficient when carried out in structured settings, and even drill and worksheets have value in accomplishing certain goals of learning. But because we believe that schools are first and foremost places for talent development, there are times within the overall process of schooling when we can and should make a conscious commitment to apply enrichment learning and teaching methods to selected aspects of schooling.

The Deductive Model --- **The Inductive Model**
("Direct Frontal Teaching")   **("Enrichment Learning and Teaching")**

The Teacher's Role

Teachers initiate, determine, control, and micro manage learning -- Students pay a leading role in topic/problem selection and pacing

Teachers provide feedback in the form of grades based on normative criteria --- Teachers and students are partners in formative evaluation based on progress toward goals

Teachers as instructors (disseminators of knowledge) --- Teachers as coaches, patrons, resource procurers, probers, editors, ombudsmen, and colleagues

Teachers view content as objective, impersonal, and value free --- Teachers personalize, criticize, and emphasize the value-laden character of content (artistic modification)

The Curriculum

Predetermined by textbooks or courses of study --Derived as a result of individual or small group student interests

Content driven --- Process and product driven

Problems are prescribed, presented, and usually previously solved --- Self-selected, open-ended, real world problems

Information is presented for (possible) future use--- Information is sought only when needed to help solve a present problem

Knowledge is presented as factual material --- Knowledge serves as a vehicle for confrontation with events, issues, ideas, and beliefs

Classroom Organization and Management

Predetermined daily time blocks and the weekly allocation of time are --- Time is determined by the evolving nature of the determined on the size of units of instruction   task, project, or end product

Whole group activities --- Individual and small group activities

Age/grade grouping --- Interest, problem, and common task grouping

Predetermined and usually fixed classroom arrangements --- Classrooms are arranged to facilitate the accomplishment of the task or the completion of products

Classrooms are the places where learning takes place --- Learning takes place wherever relevant information is gathered or experiences are pursued

The Student's Role

Students as lesson learners and consumers of knowledge --- Students as first-hand inquirers and producers of knowledge

Students accumulate and store knowledge for possible future use --- Student confronts and constructs knowledge for present use

Students pursue common tasks and activities --- Students' tasks and activities are based on divisions of labor

Students use knowledge to study *about* problems --- Students use knowledge to *find* and *focus* problems and to *act on* problems

Students passively accept knowledge as objective, factual, and correct --- Students personalize, interpret, criticize, and dissect knowledge

Figure 13. The structured to unstructured continuum of instructional practices.

Enrichment Learning and Teaching Defined

ENRICHMENT LEARNING and teaching is based on the ideas of a small number of philosophers, theorists, and researchers. Although it is beyond the scope of this book to review the work of these eminent thinkers, the following table attempts to summarize the main concepts or ideas that each person has contributed to this approach to learning.

The work of these theorists, coupled with our own research and program development activities, has given rise to the concept that we call "enrichment learning and teaching." The best way to define this concept is in terms of the following four principles:

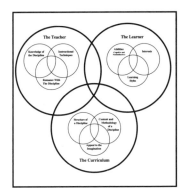

Table 1
Eminent thinkers and their contributions to the enrichment learning and teaching approach

Name	Country and vocation	Life Span	Major Contributions
William James	American psychologist	1842-1910	Proposed that the purpose of education is to organize a child's abilities/talents/powers; organization of the powers begins by wakening the child's interests; nurturing children's interests is central to learning.
John Dewey	American philosopher	1859-1952	Promulgated progressive education; education needs to draw forth the abilities/interests of the child; education is the interaction between thinking *and* doing, emphasis on first-hand inquiry.
Alfred North Whitehead	English philospher	1861-1947	Proposed that learning is essentially cyclical and progresses rhythmically: romance, precision, generalization (Type I, Type II and Type III activities); all three stages need to be present at all times; teachers need to elicit enthusiasm for the essential ideas and the methodology of a subject.
Maria Montessori	Italian physician and educator	1870-1942	Proposed that learning requires self-educating devices specifically designed to enlist the spontaneous interest of the child; child is led to learning and mastery by interest and curiosity; interests are key.
Jean Piaget	Swiss psychologist	1896-1980	Suggested intellectual development occurred in four stages; intelligence matures from the inside, through assimilation and accommodation, and is directed outward; emphasis on the need for a wide variety of experiences to facilitate learning.
Jerome Bruner	American psychologist	1915-	Argued that the inductive method of instruction needs to be the focus of teaching; content can be taught to any student at any level of development; children possess natural curiosity and a desire to become competent at learning tasks; emphasis on methodological training; teachers need to be facilitators.
Philip Phenix	American philosopher and educator	1915-	Reconceptualized content domains based upon fields of human inquiry; selection and organization of content was guided by the degree to which topics (1) represent fields of disciplined inquiry, (2) represent the field as a whole, (3) exemplify methods of inquiry and the modes of understanding in the discipline, and (4) appeal to the imagination of the student (Multiple Menu Model); learning is enhanced to the extent that curriculum follows these guidelines.
E. Paul Torrance	American psychologist	1915-	Brought creativity and its development to the attention of educators, researchers and psychologists; established that instructional programs can increase students' ability to produce many, varied, and original ideas; the *Incubation Model*; emphasis on creative productivity.
Albert Bandura	American psychologist	1925-	Developed a theory of self-efficacy to explain aspects of achievement motivation; specifically, self-efficacy is a psychological mediator, intervening between cognition and action, which may influence a person's choice of activities, the amount of energy expended on a task, and the length of persistence on a task; learning is influenced by internal beliefs about efficacy toward a task; creative productivity of students is enhanced to the extent they see peers involved in first-hand inquiry.
Howard Gardner	American psychologist	1943-	Expanded the concept of intelligence; intelligence is not a single thing, but seven: linguistic, logical-mathematical, spatial, musical, bodily-kinesthetic, interpersonal, and intrapersonal; intelligences are independent of one another; intelligences interact; expanded the definition of talent.
Robert Sternberg	American psychologist	1948-	Expanded the concept of intelligence; proposed the Triarchic Theory of Intelligence: componential subtheory, experiential subtheory, contextual subtheory; intelligence involves recognizing and capitalizing on one's strengths and either compensating for or remediating one's weaknesses; expanded the definition of talent.

1. Each learner is unique, and, therefore, all learning experiences must be examined in ways that take into account the abilities, interests, and learning styles of the individual.
2. Learning is more effective when students enjoy what they are doing, and, therefore, learning experiences should be constructed and assessed with as much concern for enjoyment as for other goals.
3. Learning is more meaningful and enjoyable when content (i.e., knowledge) and process (i.e., thinking skills, methods of inquiry) are learned within the context of a real and present problem,[1] and, therefore, attention should be given to opportunities to personalize student choice in problem selection, the relevance of the problem for individual students at the time the problem is being addressed, and strategies for assisting students in personalizing problems they might choose to study.
4. Some formal instruction may be used in enrichment learning and teaching, but a major goal of this approach to learning is to enhance knowledge and thinking skill acquisition gained through *teacher instruction* with applications of knowledge and skills that result from *students' construction* of meaningfulness.

I am always eager to learn, but I do not always like being taught.

Winston Churchill

The ultimate goal of learning that is guided by these principles is to replace dependence and passive learning with independence and engaged learning. Although all but the most conservative educators will agree with these principles, much controversy exists about how these (or similar) principles may be applied in everyday school situations. A danger also exists that these principles might be viewed as yet another idealized list of glittering generalities that cannot easily be manifested in schools that are overwhelmed by the deductive model of learning. Developing a school program based on these principles is not an easy task. Over the years, however, we have achieved a fair amount of success by gaining faculty, administrative, and parental consensus on a small number of easy-to-understand concepts and related services, and by providing resources and training related to each concept and service delivery procedure. The first two service delivery components (i.e., The Total Talent Portfolio and Curricular Modification) have been discussed in preceding chapters. This chapter will round out the overall Schoolwide

Enrichment Model by describing a model that serves as the core of enrichment learning and teaching. This model, entitled the Enrichment Triad Model (Renzulli, 1977b), was originally developed in the early 1970s as an alternative to didactic models for talent development. In the ensuing years, numerous research studies (Reis & Renzulli, 1994) and field tests in schools with widely varying demographics have been carried out. These studies and field tests provided opportunities for the development of large amounts of practical know-how that are readily available for schools that would like to implement the SEM.

How Can Teachers Learn to Do Enrichment Teaching?

THIS FREQUENTLY-ASKED question probably results from the ways in which we have overly prescribed and organized the work of teachers. Teaching in "a natural way" actually requires very little training! It does, however, require that teachers understand the importance of serving as a facilitator rather than an instructor. This method of teaching has been described in detail in the chapter dealing with Type III Enrichment in the *Schoolwide Enrichment Model* (Renzulli & Reis, 1985, pp. 395-506). This method also requires that teachers know what to do in a situation that purposefully avoids lesson plans, unit plans, and other types of prescribed instructional approaches. Space does not permit a full explanation of this method of teaching, but perhaps some questions will serve as a guide for getting started in an enrichment cluster. Five key questions include:

1. What do people with an interest in this area do?
2. What products do they create and/or what services do they provide?
3. How, and with whom, do they communicate the results of their work?
4. What resources and materials are needed to produce high quality products and services?
5. What steps do we need to take to have an impact on intended audiences?

The teacher's role as a facilitator, for example, included helping the poetry subgroup identify places where they might submit their work for publication. With the help of a librarian,

Reflections on the Benefits of Facilitating Student Research

For me, as their teacher, the benefits were many. First, problem solving with students throughout the unit helped me gain insights into the mental thought processes of 6th graders. Second, taking on the role as their facilitator and guide was rewarding. My gradual releasing of control to the students resulted in outcomes far surpassing all expectations. Finally, I am often reminded that empowering students is one of the most effective maxims for education. Giving students the power and then watching them strive for excellence is an incredible teaching experience.

Catherine Doane, 1993

*The excellent is
new forever.*

Ralph Waldo Emerson

the teacher located a book entitled, *Directory of Poetry Publishers*. This book, which contains hundreds of outlets for poets' work, is one of the kinds of resources that makes the difference between a teacher who teaches poetry in a traditional fashion, and a facilitator who develops talent in young poets.

The most difficult part of being a good enrichment cluster facilitator is to stop teaching, and to replace traditional instruction with the kinds of "guide-on-the-side" responsibilities that are used by mentors and coaches. Persons who fulfill these roles instruct only when there is a direct need to accomplish a task that is part of product development. Many teachers who have served as yearbook advisors, drama club directors, 4-H Club advisors, athletic coaches, and facilitators of other extracurricular activities already have the techniques necessary for facilitating a successful enrichment cluster. The basic characteristics of extracurricular activities are: (1) students and teachers select the area in which they participate, (2) they produce a product or service that is intended to have an impact on a particular audience, (3) they use the authentic methods of professionals to produce their product or service. They may operate at a more junior level than adult professionals, but their goal is exactly the same — to produce as high a quality of product or service as possible within their level of experience and the availability of resources. The teacher's role in an enrichment cluster is to assist in the procurement of methodological resources, and to help students understand how to use the resources. The only time that direct instruction should take place is when the instruction is necessary to help produce and improve the product or service. Thus, for example, students doing a community survey in a social science cluster might receive direct instruction on procedures for developing an authentic questionnaire, rating scale, or survey instrument. A book such as *A Student's Guide to Conducting Social Science Research* can be used for a series of Type II training activities (described in the Resource Guide at the end of this chapter) that are necessary to provide students with the know-how of preparing authentic instruments.

The Enrichment Triad Model

IN **ORDER** for enrichment learning and teaching to be systematically applied to the learning process in the regular classroom, it must be organized in a way that makes sense to teachers and students. An organizational pattern called the Enrichment Triad Model (Renzulli, 1977) is used for this purpose. The three types of enrichment in the model are depicted in Figure 14. Type I enrichment consists of general exploratory experiences that are designed to expose students to topics and areas of study not ordinarily covered in the regular curriculum. Type II enrichment consists of group training in thinking and feeling processes, learning-how-to-learn skills, research and reference skills, and written, oral, and visual communication skills. Type III enrichment consists of first-hand investigations of real problems. Before discussing the role and function of each type of enrichment, it is necessary to discuss three considerations that relate to the model in general.

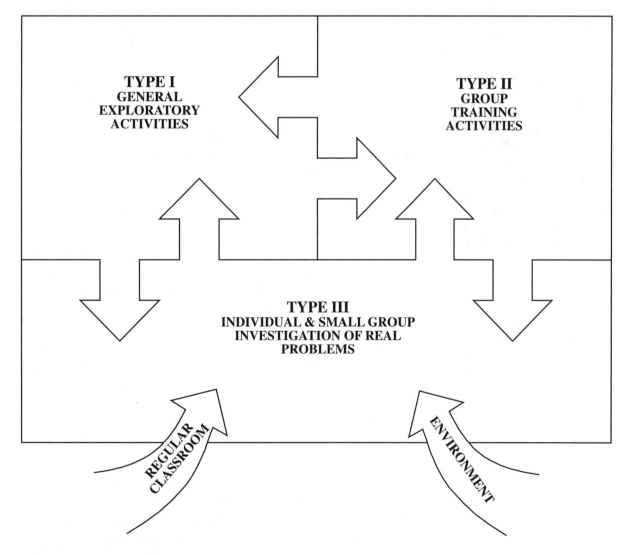

Figure 14. The Enrichment Triad Model.

Chapter 7

Many educational institutions have spent millions of dollars and untold hours of effort revamping their programs without much apparent long-range success....But with little additional cost, medical schools are starting to put students in small groups and help them solve the real problems they will face when treating patients. According to the research data, classroom dynamics change fundamentally, students learn as many facts as those in traditional classes, they enjoy the studies more, and they become lifelong learners (Kaufman, Mennin, Waterman, and Duban, 1989). It is an approach to learning that can happen without a new course of study, a mandate from the state legislature, or a large budget increase. It's a model that all educators can use.

David Aspy, Cheryl Aspy, & Patricia Quinby, 1993

Learning in a Natural Way

The Enrichment Triad Model is based on the ways in which people learn in a natural environment rather than the artificially structured environment that characterizes most classrooms. Just as scientists "look to nature" when they attempt to solve particular types of problems, the process of learning is examined as it unfolds in the non-school world. This process is elegant in its simplicity! External stimulation, internal curiosity, necessity, or combinations of these three starting points cause people to develop an interest in a topic, problem, or area of study. Humans are, by nature, curious, problem solving beings; but in order for them to act upon a problem or interest with some degree of commitment and enthusiasm, the interest must be a sincere one and one in which they see a personal reason for taking action. Once the problem or interest is personalized, a need is created to gather information, resources, and strategies for acting upon the problem.

Problem solving in nature almost always results in a product or service that has a functional, artistic, or humanitarian value. The learning that takes place in real-problem situations is *collateral learning* that results from attacking the problem in order to produce a product or service. Consider a group of pioneers (or engineers, or Boy Scouts or Girl Scouts) who want to build a bridge across a creek or river. They do not stand at the river bank and say, "Let's learn about geometry." Rather, they examine the scope of the problem, what they already know, and what they need to know and do to build the bridge. In the process, they may learn about geometry, strength of materials, planning and sequencing, cooperativeness, structural design, spatial relationships, aesthetics, mechanics, and a host of other things necessary to get the job done. It was precisely this kind of natural problem solving situation that gave rise to the Enrichment Triad Model. The only difference between the natural learning that takes place in real life situations and the use of the Triad Model within the more structured world of the school is that we view products as vehicles through which a wide variety of more enduring and transferable processes can be developed. The products are essential because they give realness, purpose, and hopefully, satisfaction and enjoyment to the present endeavor. The processes developed within the context of real-problem learning are also essential because schools must be concerned with preparation for the future and with the continuity of development in young people over long periods of time. Learning that focuses on the interaction between product and process results in the kinds of learning experiences that enhance both the present and the future.

More Than a Sum of the Parts

A second general consideration about the Enrichment Triad Model is that the *interaction* between and among the three types of enrichment is as important as any type of enrichment or the collective sum of all three types. In other words, the arrows in Figure 14 are as important as the individual cells, because they give the model dynamic properties that cannot be achieved if the three types of enrichment are pursued independently. A Type I experience, for example, may have value in and of itself, but it achieves maximum payoff if leads to Type II or III experiences. In this regard, it is a good idea to view Types I and II enrichment as "identification situations" that may lead to Type III experiences, which are the most advanced type of enrichment in the model. As Figure 14 indicates, the regular curriculum and the environment in general (i.e., non-school experiences) can also serve as pathways of entry into Type III activities. An identification situation is simply an experience that allows students and teachers an opportunity (1) to participate in an activity, (2) to analyze their interest in and reaction to the topic covered in the activity and the processes through which the activity was pursued, and (3) to make a purposeful decision about their interest in the topic and the diverse ways further involvement may be carried out. Type I and Type II are general forms of enrichment that are usually pursued with larger groups of students, and they are oftentimes a prescribed part of enrichment offerings. Methods of presentation span the continuum from deductive to inductive methods of learning. Type III Enrichment, on the other hand, is pursued only on a voluntary and self-selected basis, and the methodology is mainly inductive.

The interactiveness of the three types of enrichment also includes what are sometimes called the "backward arrows" in Figure 14 (e.g., the arrows leading back from Type III to Type I, etc.). In many cases, the advanced work of students (i.e., Type III) can be used as Type I and II experiences for other students. Thus, for example, a group of students who carried out a comprehensive study on lunchroom waste presented their work to other groups for both awareness and instructional purposes, and for purposes of stimulating

Persons whose interests have been engaged and intelligence trained by dealing with things and facts in active occupations having a purpose...will be those most likely to escape the alternatives of an academic and aloof knowledge and a hard, narrow, and merely 'practical' practice. To organize education so that natural tendencies shall be fully enlisted in doing something...is what most needs doing to improve schooling.

John Dewey, 1916

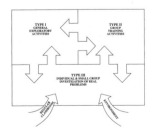

Greg brought Tchaikovsky's "Nutcracker Suite" to his first-grade class. "I've been wondering..." Greg said to his teacher. "There are some parts of this suite that are really sad. Do you think that Tchaikovsky wrote the sad parts when he was really happy? Or do you think that when he was really sad he wrote the happy music to cheer him up and vice versa?" His teacher suggested he find the resource teacher so she could help him find what Tchaikovsky wrote during various periods of his life. Before the year was over, Greg carried out a research project using college-level texts to produce a: "talking" book and tape containing his research and his answer to the questions.

United States Department of Education, 1993

potential new interests on the parts of other students. In this regard, the model is designed to renew itself and to bring students "inside" the pedagogy of the school enterprise rather than viewing learning from a spectator's perspective. We hear a good deal these days about schools becoming a "community of learners," and this model strives to create a role for students that makes them authentic members of a community of both learners and teachers.

Personal Knowledge

A third consideration about the Enrichment Triad Model in general is that it is designed to help students gain personal knowledge about their own abilities, interests, and learning styles. If, as Socrates said, "The unexamined life is not worth living," then we should also consider a corollary to this axiom about life in school: "The unexamined lesson is not worth learning!" While it would be desirable to apply this corollary to all school experiences, the types of enrichment advocated in the Triad Model are excellent vehicles for examining preferences, tastes, and inclinations that will help students gain a greater understanding of themselves.

This corollary is operationalized in the model by recommending debriefings and post-learning analyses (sometimes called meta-learning) about both *what* has been learned, and *how* a particular segment of learning has been pursued. A scenario related to helping students understand learning and teaching style preferences, for example, might begin with the following teacher comment at the beginning of an instructional unit: "We are going to study the economic law of supply and demand by engaging in a *simulation* in which each of you will have control over the buying and selling of major food product groups." The teacher should explain what a simulation is, why it has been selected for use in connection with this topic, and how it compares with other instructional styles through which the topic might be taught. These advanced organizers call attention to the pedagogy of the learning situation as well as to the content and processes to be learned.

Following exposure to a particular instructional style, a careful post-learning analysis should be conducted that focuses on the unique properties of the purposefully selected instructional technique. Students should be encouraged to discuss and record in personal journals their reactions to the instructional technique in terms of both efficiency in learning and the amount of pleasure they derive from the technique.

The goal of the post-learning analysis is to help students understand more about themselves by understanding more about their preferences in a particular situation. Thus, the collective experiences in learning styles should provide: (1) exposure to many styles, (2) an understanding of which styles are the most personally applicable to particular subjects, and (3) and experience in how to blend styles in order to maximize both the effectiveness and satisfaction of learning. The ultimate goal of teaching students about learning styles should be to develop in each student both a repertoire of styles and the strategies that are necessary to modify styles to better fit tasks they will encounter in future learning or career tasks. In much the same way that a golf player examines distance, wind conditions, and obstacles before selecting the appropriate golf club, so also should we teach students to examine learning situations with an eye toward selecting and applying the most appropriate styles.

In a certain sense, the type of training and analysis of styles suggested here might be viewed as a specific form of flexibility training typically associated with the pedagogy used in creative thinking. Although there are undoubtedly a variety of ways in which such training might be organized, the approach recommended in the Enrichment Triad Model focuses on a retrospective analysis of both *what* was learned (i.e., content) and how it was learned (i.e., process). Continued examination of these two aspects of learning helps students develop more concentrated future interests, and it also helps them gain an appreciation for their own learning style preferences on the scale of structured to unstructured learning.

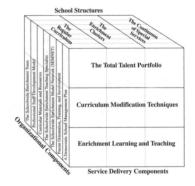

In the sections that follow, each component of the Triad Model will be presented. As you review these sections, it will be helpful to keep in mind the interactions between and among the three types of enrichment, and the ways in which this interaction can be heightened through debriefing and post-learning analysis. It will also be helpful to keep in mind that the Triad Model is part of the service delivery component that is targeted on three school structures: the regular curriculum, the enrichment clusters, and the continuum of special services. In many ways, enrichment learning and teaching can be thought of a transparent overlay which can be applied to these three school structures.

**Methods of Delivering
Type I Enrichment**

*Audio tape
Computer program
Debate
Demonstration
Display
Field trip
Film trip
Guest speaker
Interest center
Learning center
Magazine article
Mini-course
Museum program
Newspaper article
Performance
Photograph
Radio program
Slides
Television program
Video tape*

Type I Enrichment: General Exploratory Experiences

One of the enduring problems of teaching is how to motivate students to such an extent that they will act on their interests in a creative and productive way. The major purpose of Type I Enrichment is to include within the overall school program carefully selected experiences that are purposefully developed to be highly motivational. This type of enrichment consists of experiences and activities designed to expose students to a wide variety of disciplines, topics, ideas, concepts, issues, and events that are not ordinarily covered in the general curriculum. A number of typical Type I methods of delivery are listed in the side bar of this page. Type I can be based on regular curricular topics or innovative outgrowths of prescribed topics, but in order to qualify as a *bona fide* Type I Experience, any and all planned activities in this category must be purposefully designed *to stimulate new or present interests that may lead to more intensive follow-up on the parts of individual students or small groups of students.* An activity can be called a Type I Experience only if it meets the following three conditions: (1) students are aware that the activity is an *invitation* to various kinds and levels of follow-up, (2) there is a systematic debriefing of the experience in order to learn who might want to explore further involvement, and the ways the follow-up might be pursued, and (3) there are various opportunities, resources, and encouragement for diverse kinds of follow-up. An experience is clearly *not* a Type I if every student is required to follow-up an activity in the same or similar way. Required follow-up is a regular curricular practice; and although prescribed follow-up certainly has a genuine role in general education, it almost always fails to capitalize on differences in students' interest and learning styles. The Resource Guide at the end of this chapter provides references to detailed planning guides and strategies for implementing and following up on Type I activities.

Three issues related to Type I experiences need be emphasized. First, Type I experiences should be carefully selected and planned so that there is a high probability that they will be exciting and appealing to students. Visiting speakers, for example, should be selected for both their expertise in a particular area *and* their ability to energize and capture the imagination of students. Persons presenting Type I experiences should be provided with enough orientation about the model to understand the objective described above and the need to help students explore the realms and ranges of opportunity for further involvement that are available within various age and grade considerations. Without such an orientation, these kinds of experiences may be viewed as merely informative; and thus, even a very exciting experience will not have the "feed forward" context that should characterize Type I Enrichment activities.

A second issue related to Type I Enrichment concerns the audiences for whom a given experience is made available and the ascending order of complexity of these kinds of experiences. A majority of Type I activities should be presented to all students in a classroom, grade level, or cross-grade group. The primary purpose of Type I is to introduce students to topics or activities that are new to the majority of the group. Because lack of exposure to the almost unlimited range of topics that can be used for Type I Enrichment, students may not know whether or not they might develop a sustained interest in a particular topic unless they are required to participate. Thus, for example, it may be worthwhile to introduce all middle grade students to a topic such as computer assisted design (CAD) through a demonstration or presentation by a specialist on this topic. Following the activity and an assessment of the levels of interest of all students in the group, an advanced Type I might be planned for highly interested students that pursues the material in greater depth or that involves a field trip to a company or laboratory that uses CAD technology. In this case, there is an interest-based rationale for a special grouping or field trip that is different from offering field trips only to high ability students. A general or introductory Type I should, of course, include all students at given grade(s) levels.

A third issue related to Type I Enrichment is the position of a given experience on the structured to unstructured continuum. Although Type I experiences are, by definition, planned and presented, we can still achieve a fair amount of flexibility by following a few simple guidelines. First, whenever possible, some estimate of general student interests should be obtained as part of the planning for a series of Type I activities. A good menu of Type I experiences should be diversified across many topics and curricular categories. Such diversification improves the probability of influencing broader ranges of student interest, and, accordingly, increasing the number of students that will select an area in which they may like to pursue follow-up activities. Second, even prescribed Type I topics should be planned in a way that encourages

A final critical question about the principle of imagination needs to be considered. Is the imaginative type of general education advocated above really possible for everyone? Is it as applicable to the under-average child in the slum school as to a bright child in a highly favored suburban school? The answer is that imaginative teaching is suitable for everyone and that it is ever more essential in the poor school.

Philip Phenix, 1964

Five General Categories of Process Skills

I. *Cognitive Training*

II. *Affective Training*

III. *Learning-How-To-Learn Training*

IV. *Research and Reference Procedures*

V. *Written, Oral, and Visual Communication Procedures*

maximum student involvement in an activity. Enrichment learning and teaching is more than just presenting unusual topics. Rather, hands-on, problem solving activities, and activities that require discussion, debate, and confrontations with topics and issues are much more effective in prompting the kinds of affective reactions that help students to personalize a topic and to make a commitment to more intensive follow-up. The Type I dimension of the Enrichment Triad Model can be an extremely exciting aspect of overall schooling because it creates a legitimate "slot" within the school for bringing the vast world of knowledge and ideas that are above and beyond the regular curriculum to students' attention. It is also an excellent vehicle for teams of teachers, students, and parents to plan and work together on a relatively easy-to-implement component of the model. Type I Enrichment is an excellent vehicle for getting started in an enrichment cluster. For example, a group of students in a film making cluster used the suggestions of a local professional in this area to explore options and to determine the kinds of films they could produce within the time, budget, and equipment constraints to which they were bound. Specific procedures and planning guides for organizing and implementing Type I Enrichment are included in related publications listed in the Resource Guide at the end of this chapter.

Type II Enrichment: Group Training Activities

If there is one area of school improvement about which virtually all educators agree, that area is the need to blend into the curriculum more training in the development of higher order thinking skills. In this section, we will discuss a systematic approach for organizing a process skills component within the overall Schoolwide Enrichment Model. Type II Enrichment consists of instructional methods and materials that are purposefully designed to develop a broad range of process skills in the following five general categories: (1) Cognitive Training, (2) Affective Training, (3) Learning-How-To-Learn Training, (4) Research and Reference Procedures, and (5) Written, Oral, and Visual Communication Procedures. We will use the term "process skills" to include all of these categories. Examples of specific skills within each of these four general categories (and related subcategories) can be found in a taxonomy that is included in Appendix B. In a Chapter 8, we will describe the Enrichment Materials Data Base that can be used to help locate materials by content area, process skill, and grade level cluster.

Type II Enrichment also serves a motivational purpose similar to that discussed in connection with Type I activities. The sections that follow will discuss two general considerations that should be taken into account in developing a schoolwide plan for Type II Enrichment. These considerations are (1) levels and audiences for Type II activities, and (2) the objectives and strategies for implementing this component of the Enrichment Triad Model.

Levels and Audiences

Within each category of Type II Enrichment, the targeted skills exist along a continuum ranging from very basic manifestations of a given skill to higher and more complex applications of any given process. Thus, for example, skills such as conditional reasoning or recording data from original sources can be taught to students at any grade, but the level and complexity of the specific activities will vary according to students' developmental levels. Primary grade students, for instance, can learn observational and data gathering skills by counting and recording the number of times that different kinds of birds come to a bird feeder during a given period of time. These data might be presented by using simple tallies or pictograms. Older students can develop the same skills at higher levels by, for example, observing and recording pulse and blood pressure measures while controlling for factors such as age, height/weight ratios, and specified periods of exercise. And the advanced mathematics and computer skills of older students might enable them to engage in more sophisticated statistical analyses of their data.

Teachers' knowledge of students' developmental levels, together with students' and previous experiences in using a particular thinking skill, are important considerations when selecting materials and activities for Type II training. One of the ongoing activities of teachers and curriculum specialists using the SEM is to be continually searching for and examining enrichment materials that might enhance regular curriculum topics, or that might serve as useful resources for enrichment clusters or special service situations. Professional journals, publishers' catalogs, and displays of materials at conferences are good sources of new materials.

There are three different methods for presenting Type II Enrichment. The first method consists of planned, systematic activities that can be organized in advance for any unit of instruction within the general curriculum. These are the kinds of Type II activities that are planned in advance,

"Primary grade students can learn observational and data gathering skills by counting and recording the number of times that different kinds of birds come to a bird feeder during a given period of time. These data might be presented by using simple tallies or pictograms. Older students can develop the same skills at higher levels by, for example, observing and recording pulse and blood pressure measures while controlling for factors such as age, height/weight ratios, and specified periods of exercise."

and are a part of an ongoing framework to develop a comprehensive "scope and sequence" of process-oriented activities that parallel regular curriculum topics. The main criterion for selecting Type II activities in this category is that the activity bears a direct or indirect relationship to the subject matter being taught. For example, an activity entitled *Gold Rush: A simulation of life and adventure in a frontier mining camp* (Flindt, 1978), can be used in connection with a social studies unit on westward expansion in United States history. This activity is designed to develop decision making and creative writing skills within the context of the historical period covered in the unit. Activities in this category are ordinarily used with all students in a classroom, although advanced-level follow-up or related Type II training should take student interests and learning styles into account.

The second method for presenting Type II Enrichment consists of activities that can *not* be planned in advance because they grow out of students' reactions to school or non-school experiences. In other words, this dimension is characterized by responsiveness to student interests rather than preplanning. Thus, for example, a group of students who developed an interest in investigative reporting were provided with advanced training in questioning and interviewing techniques, verifying information sources, and other skills related to this area of specialization. The interest resulted from a Type I presentation by a local journalist; however, the interest could also have been an outcome of a unit on journalism in the language arts curriculum, or a reaction to an important local or national news event. Enrichment in this dimension can also fulfill the motivational goal of the model by stimulating interests that may lead to more intensive follow-up in the form of Type III Enrichment.

Type II Enrichment in this category can also be used to provide direction for students in a particular enrichment cluster. Because a cluster is composed of students and teachers who have already declared interests in particular areas of study, Type II training that provides methodological skills within the area will help the group generate problems to which the methods can be applied. For example, a group of students who expressed strong interests in environmental issues was provided with a mini-course that taught them how to analyze the chemical properties of soil and water. A brainstorming and problem focusing session resulted in making contact with a state agency, meeting with water pollution specialists, and eventually conducting a very professional study on acid rain

*Mark is investigating gun control, an issue he and his partner, Welles, are concerned about. They have researched their topic at the school and local library. The school librarian taught them how to use the computer terminal and **Info Track** to search for and locate articles about gun control.*

Additionally, they interviewed local police, a lobbyist who lives in town, and wrote to their congresspersons. Their teacher provided them with training in interviewing skills and letterwriting.

in their geographic area. This is a good example of how learning the methodology first provided the impetus for the extended work of the cluster that followed.

The third method for presenting Type II Enrichment consists of activities that are used within the context of already initiated Type III investigations. Activities used in this way represent the best application of inductive learning. Simply stated, an individual or group learns a process skill because they need the skill to solve a real and present problem. In the section on Type III Enrichment later in this chapter, we will discuss ways of finding resources especially relevant to this use of Type III Enrichment.

Objectives and Strategies for Type II Training

The Type II component of the Enrichment Triad Model is designed to provide students with training opportunities to improve a wide variety of process skills not normally taught within the grade level curriculum. Teachers or other adults who provide Type II training do so for diverse purposes, in multiple settings, with varied teaching strategies and resources, and for a wide range of students. Seven major objectives for students participating in Type II training are as follows:

1. Improve their ability to use higher order cognitive skills to organize, analyze, and synthesize new information;
2. Improve their leadership and interpersonal skills;
3. Improve their ability to gather, organize and analyze raw data from appropriate primary and secondary sources;
4. Improve their ability to use a wide range of sophisticated reference materials and techniques when searching for answers to their personal research questions;
5. Demonstrate a more organized and systematic approach to research, experimentation and investigation;
6. Improve the quality and appropriateness of the products that they create in conjunction with real world problem solving; and
7. Use the methods and techniques of various adult professionals to find problems, gather and organize data, and develop products.

In general, the goals of Type II training are to provide students with various learning opportunities designed to

The traditional way of studying history doesn't feel authentic to many students because they rarely perform the historian's tasks: defining essential questions, sorting through available primary source material, determining topics, drawing conclusions, and presenting them persuasively.

David Kobrin, Ed Abbott, John Ellinwood, & Davis Horton, 1993

improve their independent learning skills as well as the quality of their personal assignments, projects and research. Type II Enrichment also includes a broad range of affective training activities designed to improve interpersonal and intrapersonal skills and to promote greater degrees of cooperativeness and mutual respect among students. By placing this instruction within the framework of the regular curriculum or the enrichment clusters, teachers can offer these valuable training activities without the risk of having the training viewed as an end in and of itself.

The Type II Taxonomy and Resource Database

Since the need for Type II training with a specific skill varies from student to student, from grade to grade, and from one subject area to another, there is no finite list of skills that "should" be taught as part of the Type II component. The developers of the Schoolwide Enrichment Model have, instead, used the objectives listed above as category labels to collect and organize a set of over 400 process skills within a document called the Type II Taxonomy (Renzulli & Reis, 1985). This taxonomy can be used by teachers to gain a holistic perspective on the Type II component and its comprehensive nature. The Taxonomy can also be used as a "menu" to help teachers select the most appropriate Type II skills for their students.

In some districts, a committee of faculty members has used this list to create a scope and sequence document that specifies which Type II skills will be taught through large group instruction in the regular classroom or within enrichment clusters or other multiage groupings. The scope and sequence document also ensures that their SEM program is offering a comprehensive set of training opportunities within all grade levels and to all students in the school. The seventeen skill categories within the Type II Taxonomy have also been used to create a data base of selected commercial materials for the teaching of process skills (Burns & Reis, 1991). Although many teachers may prefer to create their own Type II lessons and units, many of these commercial materials can be used for supplementary activities or as resources for teachers who are unfamiliar with Type II instructional techniques.

The Who, When, Where, and How Decisions

Type II training can be offered as a result of observed student need, as a follow-up to a Type I exploration, as a result of expressed student interest, or within the parameters of a

Heidi, Mark, and Erica are researching the homeless issue. As part of this study, they interviewed an authority on homelessness, uncovering many misconceptions about the issue. They also volunteer at a soup kitchen.... In evaluating the entire experience, students spoke freely about their projects and certain phrases and words kept popping up: "a meaningful assignment," "it was hard work that taught me a lot," "the volume of resources available in libraries and in the community," "the chance to work with a different kind of teacher," and the value of "having a real audience to teach others" what they had learned.

Catherine Doane, 1993

student's individual Type III investigation. It is extremely important to ensure that a specific Type II skill is offered at the appropriate time, in the appropriate setting, with the appropriate teaching strategies, and for the appropriate students. Teachers or faculties should use their knowledge of students and curriculum to make the best decisions possible about which students will receive specific kinds of Type II training, and which settings and teaching strategies will be most advantageous.

Some classroom teachers who have modified their textbook-based curriculum and are designing their own curriculum units (Conn, 1988; Osborne, Jones, & Stein, 1985; Renzulli, 1988) may integrate or infuse Type II training within these units as a way of teaching related process skills (e.g., teaching students how to conduct oral history interviews during a unit on the Vietnam War). At other times, classroom teachers may prefer to develop a stand-alone unit that focuses exclusively on a single Type II skill to ensure that novice learners receive explicit instruction in how to acquire and use this skill process (e.g., teaching a unit on creative problem solving). Still, other Type II skills can be embedded within students' investigations or research projects and taught only when they are needed for specific and immediate purposes (e.g., a student wants to learn how to recognize the trees in the woods behind the school because she is creating a nature trail).

In addition to varying the nature of the instructional strategy used to teach Type II skills, teachers should also vary the audience of students who will receive this training. Some Type II lessons can and should be taught to all students in a class or grade level, some skills can be taught in a small group setting to only those students who have not already acquired the skill, and other skills might be taught to only those students interested in learning them. Teachers who sponsor or facilitate interest clusters may also find their students need or request Type II training as a result of their common interest in a subject area or local problem. A cluster of students interested in journalism might receive training in editing, proofreading, layout or advertising techniques. An interest cluster concerned with environmental problems might receive Type II training in how to draft a petition, how to lobby effectively, how to write an editorial or how to write a letter to key government officials.

The resources for teaching these Type II skills can also vary. Although many classroom teachers will assume responsibility for teaching specific Type II skills to all students,

Type II Taxonomy Skill Categories

Cognitive Training
1. *Analysis Skills*
2. *Organizational Skills*
3. *Critical Thinking Skills*
4. *Creativity Skills*

Affective Training
5. *Intrapersonal Skills*
6. *Interpersonal Skills*
7. *Dealing With Critical Life Incidents*

Learning-How-To-Learn Training
8. *Listening, Observing, Perceiving*
9. *Notetaking and Outlining*
10. *Interviewing and Surveying*
11. *Analyzing and Organizing Data*

Developing Advanced Research and Reference Procedures
12. *Preparing for Type III Investigations*
13. *Library Skills*
14. *Using Community Resources*

Developing Written, Oral, and Visual Communication
15. *Written Communication Skills*
16. *Oral Communication Skills*
17. *Visual Communication Skills*

or small groups of students within their class, enrichment specialists can also schedule a variety of mini-courses for interested students. This approach facilitates multiclass and multiage groupings and allows teachers to progress to advanced levels because of heightened student interests. Community resources (doctors, gardeners, lawyers, dietitians, etc.) can also be recruited to offer Type II training to interested groups of students. Content area teachers or specialists from the faculty or among the student population can also be recruited to teach Type II lessons. In addition, learning centers, computer software, pamphlets, videos and how-to books can be used by individual students who prefer self-instruction for selected Type II skills. Care should be taken, however, to ensure that Type II training is offered on an as-needed basis as often as possible. Teachers must be aware that some students have already acquired many of the Type II skills through modeling or informal learning opportunities; other students require a great deal of time, explicit teaching and coaching in order to master new skills; and still others won't be ready to learn a given Type II skill until they see the immediate relevance for the skill's use.

"Whether Type II skills are infused in the content curriculum, taught explicitly, or embedded in a student's interest exploration or problem solving endeavor, all students who participate in Type II training should have numerous extension opportunities to transfer and apply their learned skills to new academic content, to their own research questions or to their product development efforts."

Whether Type II skills are infused in the content curriculum, taught explicitly, or embedded in a student's interest exploration or problem solving endeavors, all students who participate in Type II training should have numerous extension opportunities to transfer and apply their learned skills to new academic content, to their own research questions or to their product development efforts. Although process skill training has been a staple of gifted education programs for many years, our research has shown that this kind of training can be used with all students. While it may be true that not all students will use their newly acquired skills for personal research, experimentation or investigation, all students can apply these skills to new and challenging academic content. When successful, Type II training helps students improve their academic achievement by showing them how to acquire and assimilate new content more rapidly and effectively, and these skills also have important transfer value to subsequent learning and the world of work.

Type III Enrichment: Individual and Small Group Investigations of Real Problems
The Assembly Plant of the Mind
Type III Enrichment consists of investigative activities and the development of creative products in which students

assume roles as first-hand investigators, writers, artists, or other types of practicing professionals. Although students pursue these kinds of involvement at a more junior level than adult professionals, the overriding purpose of Type III Enrichment is to create situations in which young people are thinking, feeling, and doing what practicing professionals do in the delivery of products and services. Type III Enrichment experiences should be viewed as vehicles in which students can apply their interests, knowledge, thinking skills, creative ideas, and task commitment to self-selected problems or areas of study. In addition to this general goal, there are four objectives of Type III Enrichment:

1. To acquire advanced-level understanding of the knowledge and methodology used within particular disciplines, artistic areas of expression, and interdisciplinary studies.
2. To develop authentic products or services that are primarily directed toward bringing about a desired impact on one or more specified audiences.
3. To develop self-directed learning skills in the areas of planning, problem finding and focusing, organizational skills, resource utilization, time management, cooperativeness, decision making, and self-evaluation.
4. To develop task commitment, self-confidence, feelings of creative accomplishment, and the ability to interact effectively with other students and adults who share common goals and interests.

Type III Enrichment should be viewed as the vehicle within the total school experience through which everything from basic skills to advanced content and processes "comes together" in the form of student-developed products and services. In much the same way that all of the separate but interrelated parts of an automobile come together at an assembly plant, so, also, do we consider this form of enrichment as the assembly plant of mind. This kind of learning represents a synthesis and an application of content, process, and personal involvement. The student's role is transformed from one of lesson learner to first-hand inquirer, and the role of the teacher changes from an instructor and disseminator of knowledge to a combination of coach, resource procurer, mentor, and, sometimes, a partner or colleague. Although products play an important role in

Nadia Ben-Youssef

Eight-year-old Nadia Ben-Youssef, a Sidney, Montana third grader, has always had a passion for music and poetry. In fact, her mother remembers her singing and humming little melodies to herself before she could even talk!

As she grew, she added words to her songs, beautiful lyric words conveying deep faith and insight, as well as amusing thoughts. It wasn't until June, 1991 that her parents realized that her many songs were originals. They had always assumed that Nadia had heard them from friends or at school or from watching television. With that discovery, however, her mother began to record the lyrics of her songs, which are the basis for this book.

This is Nadia's first book. Her dream is to sing professionally, a dream she captures beautifully in her poem, "My Voice."

My Voice

When I was a child, God fell into me.
He put his heart into my dignity.
God made me the best that I could be.
When I grow up, I know what I will be.
I'll make him proud of what I should be,
Hoping he will keep on helping me.
I'll try my best, for me to sing.
To make my voice richer than a king.
I'll sing for people, to make the world smile again.
The voice that God gave me, will then not come to an end.

September 1, 1991
Reprinted with the author's permission.

For several reasons, we have found a controversial local issue makes a good topic. First, it ignites student interest in ways that other studies can't. Students begin to examine the needs of their own community through previously unexplored sources of information and find ways of becoming involved and making a contribution.

Jackie Williams & Terry Deal Reynolds, 1993

creating Type III Enrichment situations, a major concern is the development and application of a wide range of cognitive, affective, and motivational processes.

Since this type of enrichment is defined in terms of the pursuit of real problems, it is necessary to define this term at the outset of our discussion. The term "real problem," like many other concepts in education, gets tossed around so freely that after a while it becomes little more than a cliché. Research on the meaning of a real problem (Renzulli, 1982) did not produce a neat and trim definition, but an examination of various connotations of the term yielded four characteristics that will serves as the basis for our discussion. First, a real problem must have a personal frame of reference for the individual or group pursuing the problem. In other words, it must involve an emotional or internal commitment in addition to a cognitive or scholarly interest. Thus, for example, stating that global warming or urban crime are "real problems" does not make them real for an individual or group unless they decide to do something to address the problem. These concerns may affect all people, but until a commitment is made to act upon them, they are more properly classified as "societal issues." Similarly, telling a person or group that "you have a problem" does not make it real unless the problem is internalized and acted upon in some way.

A second characteristic of real problems is that they do not have existing or unique solutions for persons addressing the problem. If there is an agreed-upon, correct solution or set of strategies for solving the problem, then it is more appropriately classified as a "training exercise." As indicated earlier, it is not our intent to diminish the value of training exercises. Indeed, many of the activities that make up the Type II dimension of the Triad Model are exercises designed to develop thinking skills and research methods. They fail, however, to qualify as real problems because they are externally assigned, and there is a predetermined skill or problem-solving strategy that we hope learners will acquire. Even simulations that are based on approximations of real world events are considered to be training exercises if their main purpose is to teach content or thinking skills.

The third characteristic of a real problem is best described in terms of why people pursue these kinds of problems. The main reason is that they want to bring about some form of change in actions, attitudes, or beliefs on the parts of a targeted audience, or they want to contribute something new to the sciences, arts, or humanities. The word "new" is used here in a local rather than global way; therefore, we don't necessarily expect young people to make contributions that are new "for all mankind." But even replications of studies that have been done many times before are new in a relative sense if they are based on data that have not been gathered previously. Thus, for example, if a group of young people gathered data about television watching habits across grade levels in their school or community, these data and the resulting analysis would be new in the sense that they never existed before.

The final characteristic of real problems is that they are directed toward a real audience. Real audiences are defined as persons who voluntarily attend to information, events, services, or objects. A good way to understand the difference between a real and contrived audience is to reflect for a moment on what students might do with the results of a local oral history project. Although they might want to practice presenting the material before their classmates, an authentic audience would more properly consist of members of a local historical society or persons who choose to read about the study in a local newspaper, magazine, or shopping guide. The practicing professional, upon whose work Type III Enrichment is modeled, almost always begins his or her work with an audience in mind. Audiences may change as the work evolves, but they serve as targets that give purpose and direction to the work.

Essential Elements of Type III Enrichment

The preceding discussion of characteristics of real problems may appear to be a hairsplitting one, but it is necessary if we are to avoid common misconceptions of the term and resulting activities that are only approximations of real problems. For example, the difference between students operating a school store that is authentic in every way, versus a play store with toy money and empty soup cans is equivalent to the difference between lightning and a lightning bug! There is nothing inherently wrong with using a play store to teach mathematics and other skills to young children, but it should not be confused with the authenticity of a business that must succeed according to real world economic principles and practices. In this section, we will discuss how the characteristics of real problems, coupled with our earlier examination of inductive learning, can be used to guide teachers and students in the Type III process. The discussion that follows is organized around five essential elements of Type III Enrichment.

When Sean and Jim return to class, their enthusiasm is obvious. They tell me that they talked to "some guy" who wants to send them all sorts of "stuff" on the rainforest. All year, these two students have been passive participants in the class as we have studied literature and tried to learn new writing skills. Suddenly, finding themselves in charge of this project, needing to communicate with "real people" in this community, they are into it and eager to share what they are learning.

Jim Burke, 1993

The whole process of education should be thus conceived as the process of learning to think through the solutions of real problems.

John Dewey, 1916

A Personal Frame of Reference

The first essential element is that problems being pursued through this type of learning experience must be based on individual or group interests. Teachers and other adults can certainly provide guidance and some creative steering toward the formulation of a problem, but they must avoid at all costs crossing the line from suggestion to prescription. If a problem is forced upon students, we endanger the personal frame of reference discussed above, and the kind of affective commitments that result in a willingness to engage in creative and demanding work. The Resource Guide at the end of this chapter lists books that describe specific techniques for spotting action information that might lead to student-selected problems, and for assisting students in problem finding and focusing. These resources also describe how students in a given group can become involved in different ways within the same problem or problem area. In most cases, the division of labor that takes place in group Type III situations causes a broader range of talents to be developed and promotes the kinds of real-world cooperativeness and mutual respect that we are attempting to achieve in the SEM. In addition to allowing for various types of involvement, problems that require a diversity of specialties also create opportunities for more personalization on the parts of individuals in the group. When each person feels that she or he "owns" a part of the problem, the first characteristic of a real problem is met.

A Focus on Advanced-Level Knowledge

The second essential element of Type III Enrichment is that it should draw upon authentic, advanced-level knowledge. If we want young people to approximate the roles of practicing professionals, then it is important to examine the characteristics of persons who have displayed high levels of expertise in their respective domains of knowledge. During the past two decades, cognitive psychologists have devoted much research to the topic of experts and expertise, and the role of knowledge in attaining expert performance. Studies ranging from the characteristics of chess masters to the acquisition of routine tasks in unskilled or semi-skilled jobs (e.g., taxi driving) have uncovered a number of generalizations across the various domains that have been studied. Glaser (1988) has summarized some of the key characteristics of experts' performance, and these characteristics can be used to provide guidance for this dimension of the Enrichment Triad Model.

Experts mainly excel in their own domain, and they spend much more time than novices analyzing information within their respective fields of study. Experts also perceive large, meaningful patterns in their domain and they have an understanding of how knowledge is organized in their domain. They tend to represent problems at deeper levels by creating conceptual categories rather than categories based on surface or superficial features, they are goal-oriented, and they access knowledge mainly for its applicability to present problems. Finally, experts develop self-regulatory skills such as judging problem difficulty, apportioning their time, asking questions, reviewing their knowledge, and predicting outcomes.

High levels of expertise in a topic or domain obviously emerge from extensive experience gained over long periods of time. If we contrast this characteristic of expert performance with the forty-two minute period, traditionally found in schools, and the rapid march through numerous topics at superficial levels, the first hint that can be derived from the research on expertise is that we must radically extend the amount of time that young people are allowed to work on problems that have a personal frame of reference. Time allocations for individual or small group Type III investigations, whether in enrichment clusters, regular classes or other organizational arrangements, should be unbounded and expandable, as long as motivation remains high and progress toward goals is clearly evident.

The amount and complexity of knowledge available to students pursuing advanced studies and investigations must also be expanded. Guidelines for identifying both advanced-level content and methodology were presented in our discussion of the Multiple Menu Model in Chapter 6, and the subject area standards carried out by various professional associations, such as the National Council of Teachers of Mathematics, provides another vehicle for identifying advanced-level content. Finally, there has been a significant movement within teacher education programs to emphasize subject area competency as well as pedagogy. When all is said and done, the amount of advanced level knowledge that teachers possess will be a major determinant of the level of the courses they teach.

A Focus on Methodology

The third essential element of Type III Enrichment is the use of authentic methodology. This characteristic is essential because one of the goals of Type III Enrichment is to help

In the absence of an environment that inspires and engages, inmates and students soon ask, "Is this all there is?" For inmates it comes soon after the shock of incarceration is replaced by a numb throbbing in the soul. Having suffered as much self-loathing as he or she can stand, an inmate finally asks, "Now what do I do? Spend the next five years staring at a wall?" For students, it comes with the realization that most courses are driven by the same flat, grey routines. The student says, "I'm supposed spend how many years doing this? You are kidding, right?...."

I used to laugh when a kid said, "This place is like a prison." I won't ever laugh at that again. Rather, I'll wonder why so many schools treat students as prisoners when they haven't committed any crimes."

Eliot Wigginton, 1994

There is no more reliable fact in the study of creative lives than this: Important creative achievements result from prolonged work, from protracted and repeated encounters of the creative person with the task he or she has undertaken.

Howard E. Gruber, 1986

youngsters extend their work beyond the usual kinds of reporting that often results when teachers and students view "research" as merely "looking up" information. Some reporting of previous information is a necessary part of most investigations. Indeed, the pursuit of new knowledge should always begin with a review of what is already known about a given topic. The end result of a Type III investigation, however, should be a creative contribution that goes beyond already existing information that is typically found in encyclopedias and other all-about-books.

Every field of organized knowledge can be defined, in part, by its methodology, and the methodology of most fields can be found in certain kinds of guidebooks or manuals. These "How-To" books are the key to escalating studies beyond the traditional report writing approach that often passes for research. We have described some of these books at length in the Resource Guide, and a separate SEM data base, is devoted to methodological guidebooks.

Every field of knowledge can also be partly defined by the kinds of data that represent the "raw material" of the field. New contributions are made in a field when investigators apply well-defined methods to the process of making sense out of random bits and pieces of information. Although some investigations require levels of sophistication and equipment that are far beyond the reach of younger investigators, almost every field of knowledge has entry level and junior level data gathering opportunities.

We have seen scientifically respectable questionnaire studies on food and television preferences carried out by primary grade students. A group of middle grade students gathered and analyzed water samples as part of a large regional study on the extent and effects of acid rain. This work was so thoroughly and carefully done that the students' findings were requested for use by a state environmental agency. Another group of elementary students used very professional techniques in every aspect of producing a weekly television show broadcast by a local cable television company. A fifth-grade student wrote a guidebook that was adopted by his city's government as the official historical walking tour of the city; a group of high school students engaged in a very sophisticated community research and citizens' action project that resulted in the appropriation of $200,000 for a citywide system of bike paths. The success and high level of product development reflected in these examples can be traced to the proper use of authentic methods and techniques, even if these techniques were carried out at a somewhat junior level than those used by adult inquirers.

The teacher's role in providing methodological assistance is to help students identify, locate, and obtain resource materials and/or persons to provide assistance in the appropriate use of investigative techniques. In some cases, it may be necessary to consult with librarians or professionals within various fields for advice about where and how to find methodological resources. Professional assistance may also be needed in translating complex concepts into material students can understand. Although methodological assistance is a major part of the teacher's responsibility in Type III Enrichment, it is neither necessary nor realistic to expect teachers to have mastered a large number of investigative techniques. A good general background and orientation toward the overall nature of research is necessary, but the most important skill is the ability to know where and how to help students obtain the right kind of material and the willingness to reach out beyond the usual school resources for specialized kinds of materials and resource persons.

Sense of Audience

The fourth essential element of Type III Enrichment is that products and services resulting from this kind of involvement are targeted on real audiences. The magic key that has unlocked the success of so many Type III projects is the "sense of audience" that students have developed in connection with their work. It is this sense of audience which helps give students a reason for wanting to improve the quality of their products and develop effective ways of communicating their results with interested others. A sense of audience is also a primary contributor to the creation of task commitment and the concern for excellence and quality that has characterized so many Type III investigations.

If the Type III dimension of our model is to have maximum value in the overall development of young people, major attention must be given to helping them find appropriate outlets and audiences for their most creative efforts. This concern is modeled after the *modus operandi* of creative and productive individuals. If we could sum up in a few words the *raison d'etre* of creative and productive people, it would certainly be *impact upon audience*. Type III Enrichment provides natural opportunities for the kinds of personal satisfaction and self-expression that result from bringing an important piece of work to fruition. Writers hope to influence

Steps for Guiding Students Though a Type III

1. *Assess, find or create student interests.*

2. *Conduct an interview to determine the strength of the interest.*

3. *Help find a question to research.*

4. *Develop a written plan.*

5. *Help locate multiple resources.*

6. *Provide methodological assistance.*

7. *Provide managerial assistance.*

8. *Help identify the final product and outlets.*

9. *Provide feedback and escalate the process.*

10. *Evaluate, with the student, the process and product according to appropriate criteria.*

Chapter 7

**Possible Type III
Products and Audiences**

Literary
School Newspapers
Local Newspapers
Literary Magazines
*Folklore and Legends of the
Town*
School/Town Calendars
Yearbooks
Library Story Hours

Artistic
Greeting Cards
Wrapping Paper
Grocery Store Bags
Illustrated Books
Animated Movies
Cartoon Books

Historical/Social Sciences
School/Local Newspapers
*Oral History Interview
Series*
*Historical Walking Tours of
a City*
Historical Plays
Debates
Awareness Campaigns

Scientific
Science Journals
*Daily Meteorological
Postings*
School Museums
Acid Rain Studies
*Local Town Butterfly
Gardens*

Town Nature Walks

Mathematical
*School Mathematical
Magazines*
*Mathematics Consultants for
Schools*
*Software Applications
Related to Mathematics*
Original Tessellations
*Fibonacci Numbers in
Nature: An Exhibit*

thoughts and emotions, scientists do research to find better ways to contribute new knowledge to their fields, and artists create products to enrich the lives of those who view their works. Teachers can help young people to acquire this orientation by encouraging them to develop a sense of audience from the earliest stages of a Type III investigation.

The teacher's role regarding outlets and audiences requires helping students take one small but often neglected first step in the overall process of product development. This important step is to consider *what* people in a particular field produce, and *how* they typically communicate their results with other interested persons. Once again, we can look to the activities of practicing professionals and the How-To books for guidance. In most cases, young artists and scholars will be restricted to local outlets and audiences, but there will be occasions when products of unusual excellence can be shared with larger audiences. Examples of vehicles that have been used regularly in programs organized around the Triad Model can be found in books listed in the Resource Guide for this chapter; and a data base of young people's publishing opportunities, described in Chapter 8, is a part of the resources for the SEM.

Although school and local audiences are obvious starting points in the search for outlet vehicles, teachers should always help students gain a perspective for more comprehensive outlet vehicles and audiences beyond local opportunities. Many organizations, for example, prepare newsletters and journals at the state and national levels, and they are usually receptive to high-quality contributions by young people. Similarly, state and national magazines oftentimes carry outstanding work by young people. The search for more widespread audiences should only be encouraged when student work is high in quality and when it has achieved recognition locally. Exploring external audiences will help young people develop standards of quality, and it will also provide them with "real world" experiences about the rigors and challenges of reaching out to wider audiences. Exploring external audiences involves an element of "risk-taking" and the chances of not having work accepted in the wider arenas of publications and dissemination. But by beginning a search for audiences at the local level, an element of success is likely to be achieved.

Authentic Evaluation

The fifth essential element of Type III Enrichment is that work carried out using this approach to learning is evaluated in an authentic rather than artificial manner. The ultimate test of quality in the world outside the school is whether or not products or services achieve a desired impact on clients or selected audiences. *For this reason, Type III products should never be graded or scored.* This traditional school practice is antithetical to the ways in which work is evaluated in the real world. Students can be provided with categorical feedback using a guide such as the *Student Product Assessment Form* (Renzulli, 1981), but even this instrument should only be used to help students refine and improve their work. Teachers and other adults should view their role in the feedback process as that of a "resident escalator." Sensitive and specific recommendations about how particular aspects of the work can be improved will help students move slowly but surely toward higher and higher levels of product excellence. Every effort should be made to pinpoint specific areas where suggested changes should be implemented. This approach will help avoid student discouragement and reconfirm a belief in the overall value of their endeavors.

Applying the Type III Process to Enrichment Clusters

The enrichment clusters are ideal places to implement Type III Enrichment. By using information from the Total Talent Portfolio to form the clusters, we are assured of at least some commonality of interest on the parts of students in the various clusters. Mutual interests are a good starting point for accelerating motivation and promoting harmony, respect, and cooperation among group members. Getting an enrichment cluster started is not an easy task for students or teachers who have not had previous experience in these types of inductive situations. Teachers often feel vulnerable without a lesson plan in hand, and students frequently become wary if the traditional rules of learning are changed. The most important message to students during the early meetings of an enrichment cluster is that the cluster is more like a club or extracurricular activity than a regular class. An orientation session should emphasize the objectives and essential elements of Type III Enrichment and the characteristics of a real problem. Experience has shown that students catch on quickly to this approach to learning if teachers are consistent in their transformed role as coach and mentor rather than conventional instructor.

The biggest single problem in implementing enrichment clusters is getting started! *Type III Enrichment represents qualitatively different learning experiences, and it is important*

An inventor fails 999 times, and if she succeeds once, she's in. She treats her failures simply as practice shots.

Charles Kettering

*Good, better, best,
Never let it rest,
Until the good is better,
And 'til the better is best.*

229

It's amazing what ordinary people can do if they set out without preconceived notions.

Charles Kettering

The game is well worth the candle that may have to be burned far into the night. There's no feeling like the feeling of success.

J. Paul Getty

for teachers to realize that they themselves must engage in some activities which differ from the traditional activities that define the traditional teacher's role. This point cannot be overemphasized. It is impossible to foster *differential* types of learning experiences through the use of ordinary teaching methods. If we want young people "to think, feel and do" like practicing professionals (or first-hand inquirers), then teachers must also learn how to raise a few of the questions that professionals ask about the nature and function of their own work. In other words, teachers must go one step beyond the questions that are ordinarily raised in problem solving situations. This step involves *problem* focusing and *product* focusing. This kind of focusing is how practicing professionals begin their work. Almost everything that young people do in traditional classrooms casts them in the role of lesson learners. Even when working on so called "research reports," students nearly always perceive their main purpose as that of "finding out about...." One need only ask youngsters *why* they are working on a particular report. Invariably, they reply: To find out *about* the eating habits of the gray squirrel; *about* the exports of Brazil; *about* the Battle of Gettysburg. There is nothing wrong with finding out about things—all student and adult inquirers do it, but the big difference is that practicing professionals do it for a purpose *beyond* merely finding out about something for its own sake. This purpose, which we might refer as the application purpose, is what Type III Enrichment is all about. Thus, the key to helping youngsters feel like first-hand inquirers rather than mere absorbers of knowledge is to explore with them some of the questions that professionals raise. The three essential questions that should be used at the outset of an enrichment cluster are the following:

1. What do [ecologists, film makers, historians, puppeteers, etc.] produce?
2. How do they produce it?
3. How and to whom do they communicate the results of their work?

Exploration of these questions can be pursued in a variety of ways. Type I experiences in the form of visiting speakers, discussions of career education materials, displays of typical products from the field(s) around which a cluster is organized, or videos of professionals at work can provide a picture of the products, services, and activities that characterize various fields of study. A library trip organized around a scavenger hunt format is a good way to help students broaden their perspective about the products and communication vehicles associated with various areas of inquiry.

Type II activities that provide direct or simulated experiences of typical pursuits in a particular field are also useful in helping young people to answer the above questions. How-To books are an especially valuable source for locating such activities. Thus, for example, a social science cluster can experience data gathering and analysis methods by using one of the sample activities on surveying, observing, or developing a research hypothesis that can be found in the book, *A Student's Guide to Conducting Social Science Research* (Bunker, Pearlson, & Schultz, 1975). This entire book can be used at the introductory stages of a cluster to provide know-how and to generate ideas that will help students identify their own research interests. It is important, however, for students to be informed in advance that planned, deductive activities are preparatory for the self-selected, inductive work that should be the primary focus of an enrichment cluster.

A combined brainstorming and webbing technique such as the one pictured in Figure 15 can also be used to explore the types of products and communication vehicles that characterize given fields of study or topical interests. This activity can be done by individuals or small groups, after which the responses of the entire group can be entered on a wall chart. An activity such as this can be enhanced by asking students to interview local professionals, obtain career-related literature from professional societies and associations, and to explore library products within selected fields and topics.

The teacher's role in the above situations is three-fold. First, teachers should organize and guide, but not dominate, the exploration process. Second, teachers should assist in the location of methodological resource materials such as a book on puppet making or presenting data in graphic or tabular forms. In this regard, the teacher functions as a *methodological resource person*. The third role of the teacher is to open doors for "connecting" student products with appropriate audiences. This role involves activities such as: telephoning a day care or senior citizens' center to ask if a puppet show can be presented; meeting with a shopping mall manager to ask if a student display can be set up; arranging transportation to a radio or television station; and helping students locate a book such as *The Directory of Poetry*

I don't cause teachers trouble,
my grades have been okay.
I listen in my classes,
and I'm in school every day.

My teachers think I'm average,
my parents think so too.
I wish I didn't know that
cause there's lots I would like to do.

I would like to build a rocket.
I have a book that tells you how,
or start a stamp collection.
Well, no use trying now.

Cause since I've found I'm average,
I am just smart enough you see
to know there is nothing special
that I should expect from me.

I am part of that majority
that hump part of the bell
who spends his life unnoticed
in an average kind of hell.

Anonymous Student

231

Publishers (Fulton, 1993). Our experience has shown that when teachers assume these different kinds of responsibilities, students develop an entirely new attitude toward both their work and their teachers. There is one overriding goal to developing learning opportunities based on the concept of Type III Enrichment. This goal is larger than the products students prepare or the methods they learn in pursuing their work. The largest goal is that students begin to think, feel and do like creative and productive individuals. This component of the SEM is designed to develop an attitude that has reinforced the work of effective people since the beginning of time: I can do...I can be...I can create.

[1] In a later section we will provide a brief discussion of the topic, What Makes a Problem Real?

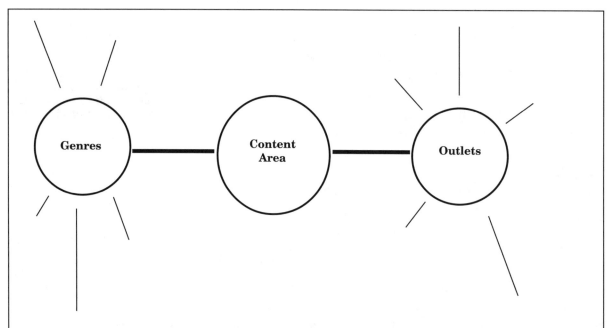

When used as a "worksheet," this combined webbing/brainstorming activity follows a very easy-to-use scenario. A group of students and teachers with a common interest in this general area came together to address five questions: What do people with an interest in this area do? What products do they create and/or what services do they provide? How, and with whom, do they communicate the results of their work? A number of exploration activities (e.g., interviews, library searches, surveys) were used over a two-week period to address these questions. After dividing into subgroups by genre, they then addressed the last two questions: What resources and materials do we need to produce high-quality products and services? What steps do we need to take to have an impact on intended audiences? These last two questions help to define the role of teachers (or other adults) in the cluster.

Figure 15. Example of a web to identify products and outlets associated with a content area.

Resource Guide

THIS RESOURCE guide is divided into four sections. Each section is designed to provide practitioners with specific information that will assist in the implementation of enrichment learning and teaching. The first section, Background Information, includes books that provide helpful background reading for those unfamiliar with the Enrichment Triad Model and the Schoolwide Enrichment Model. The second section, Type I Activities, includes information and know-how related to the creation and implementation of exploratory experiences. An annotated bibliography of selected methodological resource books to help with Type II Enrichment is contained in the third part of this Resource Guide. It serves as a beginning list for teachers interested in purchasing how-to books for their districts. This third section also includes an annotated bibliography of how-to books that may be useful to facilitators initiating enrichment clusters. The final section, Type III Activities, contains selected examples of Type III activities that have been completed by students. They are part of the SEMNET data base, Type III Activities, described more fully in Chapter 8.

Background Information

Title: The Enrichment Triad Model
Author: Renzulli, J. S.
Description: In this book Dr. Renzulli addresses some of the age-old questions that haunt persons attempting to develop defensible programs for exceptional youth. He draws a distinction between enrichment activities that are good for all children and those that are relatively unique to those with high abilities. Three types of enrichment (Type I, Type II, and Type III) are introduced in this book, along with recommendations for their use in the school setting.
Publisher: Creative Learning Press, P.O. Box 320, Mansfield Center, CT 06250, (203) 429-8118. Order No. 658, Price: $9.95.

Title: The Schoolwide Enrichment Model: A Comprehensive Plan for School Change
Author: Renzulli, J. S., & Reis, S. M.
Description: This book is about schools and how they can change to achieve the much-sought-after goal of excellence. Essentially, the concept of enrichment for highly able students is used to develop enrichment programs on a schoolwide basis.

These programs seek to establish an atmosphere of excellence by building upon the strengths and interests of school staffs and by focusing on the delivery of five services to students: (1) identifying student strengths, (2) curriculum compacting, (3) general exploratory activities, (4) group training activities to develop higher level thinking and affective skills, and (5) individual and small group investigations of real problems.

What makes this book truly unique is the practical, step-by-step guidance that is offered to supplement the theory that underlies this model. The authors have developed a series of action forms and in-service training materials that have been field-tested in schools throughout the United States. Useful materials include, for example:

- Checklists for long- and short-term planning
- Procedures for developing schoolwide enrichment teams
- Strategies for creating program ownership and faculty involvement
- Sample letters, memos, and announcements for students, parents, and faculty members
- Instruments for assessing students' strengths, interests, learning styles
- Guidelines for developing interest development centers
- A taxonomy of over 150 thinking skills and affective processes
- Sample evaluation questionnaires and forms
- Descriptions of advanced level resource books for students
- Guidelines for developing a faculty/community mentor system

Publisher: Creative Learning Press, P.O. Box 320, Mansfield Center, CT 06250, (203) 429-8118. Order No. 691, Price: $42.95.

Title: The Schoolwide Enrichment Model: A Videotape Training Program for Teachers
Description: This videotape training program is based on the Schoolwide Enrichment Model and features Drs. Joseph Renzulli and Sally Reis. It consists of nine tapes in which various components of the model are described. Each tape is approximately 25-30 minutes long and can easily be incorporated into any workshop program.

Tape 1(26 Minutes): Orientation and Overview of The Schoolwide Enrichment Model

Tape 2 (35 minutes): The Conception of Giftedness Underlying The Schoolwide Enrichment Model

Tape 3 (23 minutes): Forming the Talent Pool in a Schoolwide Enrichment Program

Tape 4 (28 minutes): Introduction and Overview of Curriculum Compacting

Tape 5 (25 minutes): An In-Depth Look at Curriculum Compacting

Tape 6 (30 minutes): Type I Enrichment: General Exploratory Activities

Tape 7 (30 minutes): Type II Enrichment: Group Training Activities

Tape 8 (30 minutes): Type III Enrichment: Investigations Into Real Problems

Tape 9 (26 minutes): Implementing The Schoolwide Enrichment Model at the Secondary Level

Publisher: Creative Learning Press, P.O. Box 320, Mansfield Center, CT 06250, (203) 429-8118. Order No. MR09, Price: $1,800.00 for the entire program; $200.00 each tape; shipping and handling is $25.00 per order.

Type Is

The General Approach to Type I Planning*

There are two ways to approach Type I planning, although in reality, both approaches almost always proceed simultaneously. The first approach is to identify various topics that might serve as important subjects of Type I without immediate consideration each one's method of delivery (e.g., video tape, mini-course, guest speaker, interest center). For example, the group of teachers might decide that the topic, the influence of Harriet Beecher Stowe's book, *Uncle Tom's Cabin*, would be an important supplementary enrichment topic for students studying the Civil War. Listing the topics does not immediately tell us what the ultimate method of delivery might be. The important issue at this point is to obtain consensus among the group that this topic is indeed important enough to be included in our planning of enrichment topics

*Source: *The Schoolwide Enrichment Model: A Comprehensive Plan for School Change*, pp. 255-258.

related to the Civil War. Later on, we can explore various ways in which the topic may be delivered to our students. We might subsequently review film or video catalogues, examine our list of faculty and community resource persons, or check with the History or English departments at a nearby college or university to determine if they have a person who specializes in this topic.

The second approach to organizing Type I experiences is to begin with already existing methods of delivery. For example, we might not have the topic of *Uncle Tom's Cabin* in mind beforehand, but this might emerge as we review film catalogues or lists of faculty and community resource persons and their areas of interest or specialization. We might, for example, discover that a nearby college professor specializes in this topic. One of the responsibilities of the Enrichment Team (a small group of teachers and parents who oversee the development, implementation, and evaluation of Type I and Type II Experiences) is to then make contact with the person and set up a date for a lecture on the topic in question. Or we may discover an audio cassette that can serve as the focus of a classroom discussion or debate on the role that Harriet Beecher Stowe's book played in events leading up to the Civil War.

It may be useful to set some target objectives regarding the number of experiences that might be desirable in connection with any given topic or subject matter area and some target objectives with regard to the diversity that will be employed using various methods of delivery. For example, a secondary social studies department might decide before instruction that they would like to have at least one Type I for each social science covered in the curriculum. Similarly, they might also decide that they want to include at least six or eight various methods of delivery in order to accommodate differences in learning styles among students. Although this two-fold approach is optimally desirable, what is oftentimes the case is that the availability of resources will dictate the method of delivery for any given topic.

Guidelines for Identifying Sources of Type I Enrichment
A major factor in determining the success of the Type I dimension of the curriculum will be the extent to which the teachers can identify a large number and variety of resources that are specifically designed to expose the students to topics and areas of study not ordinarily covered in the regular curriculum. Fortunately, there are literally thousands of sources to draw upon, and our major task in pursuing the Type

I objectives is to identify and organize the sources so that they can be effectively utilized by all members of the nuclear school family. In the sections that follow, we have attempted to identify the major categories of sources and to provide some examples of important sources that have been identified already.

An important factor to keep in mind as you begin work on identifying Type I sources is that this is a developmental approach that should be accomplished over a long period of time. In other words, work should begin on a modest scale and attempt to added to continuously over a long period of time. This work is most effectively accomplished by assigning specific tasks to members of the Enrichment Team and subgroups of teachers who should be asked to volunteer to identify sources in areas of specialized interest. For example, a subgroup of science teachers or teachers in the arts might be asked to serve as special groups for the identification of Type I sources in their respective areas of interest.

As the number of Type I sources increases over the years, procedures for disseminating information about this dimension of the curriculum should be formalized so that eventually a "Type I Source Guide" can be published and distributed on a regular basis throughout all schools in the district. The Type I dimension can be a very exciting aspect of the school program because it will bring into the learning community an almost unlimited number and variety of experiences that are not ordinarily found in the general curriculum. Further, it provides a remarkable opportunity to bring into the schools community members who will, in the process, learn more about the schoolwide enrichment program. This approach holds promise of increasing the number of supporters and advocates of enrichment programming and, therefore, its payoff can be both in terms of public relations and support as well as the many educational experiences that will be provided for students.

Human Resources

In a previous section, we have discussed procedures for surveying faculty and community resources and recording information for easy and efficient retrieval and dissemination of these resource persons. There are a number of other ways in which human resources can be recruited and the following represents a partial list of "places" that should be explored for the purposes of identifying Type I resources. These include the following:

1. *College and University Catalogs.* These catalogs are always well organized by department ,and, in many cases, we can determine the specialty of individual faculty members by the titles of the courses they teach. Many universities also maintain a public service speakers bureau, and a telephone call to the university's office of public information will ordinarily enable you to learn about the extent of already existing procedures for obtaining speakers as well as other services that might be available such as visitations, departmental lecture series, artistic presentations, and other events sponsored by colleges and universities. You might also want to request a copy of the college or university faculty directory so that you can make direct contact with individual faculty members. Many universities are interested in offering services to schools because such involvement not only helps universities in fulfilling a community service function, but it also provides an opportunity for universities to familiarize young people with programs and faculty members that might result in the later enrollment of undergraduate students. In a certain sense, this "recruitment function" provides a benefit to the college or university as well as an important service to the schools seeking the assistance of resource persons. In recent years, universities have become more competitive in the recruitment of potential students, and, therefore, they frequently have expanded their community service function in an effort to familiarize young people with opportunities for higher education.

2. *Professional Organizations and Societies.* Many professional organizations and societies will provide assistance in identifying resource persons in a local area or within a state or region. An excellent resource for obtaining the names of such organizations is *The Encyclopedia of Associations* (Gale Research, Inc., 835 Penobscot Building, Detroit, Michigan 48226). This book, which can be found in most college and university libraries, might be the major starting point for making contact with the several thousand professional societies and organizations included in the encyclopedia. Some of the organizations listed in this book already have

prepared categorical lists of community resource opportunities. For example, the American Association for the Advancement of Science (1776 Massachusetts Avenue, N.W., Washington, DC 20036) has published a booklet called "Out of School Programs in Science." This booklet, which is organized on a state-by-state basis, lists numerous science museums, environmental educational centers, archaeological field sites, and state and local scientific organizations that have already existing resources for young people. An introductory section describes how the book can be used in identifying local, national and regional resources as well as Junior Academies of Science. These academies are programs coordinated by state academies of science and offer various opportunities for students in almost every state of the union.

In a similar fashion, many state historical societies, commissions or councils on the arts, and other special interest groups maintain directories of local organizations that can serve as an invaluable source of Type I experiences. Since most of the state-level organizations are located in the capital cities of the respective states, the search can begin by looking in the Yellow Pages of the telephone directory under the guideword of "Associations." The Hartford, Connecticut telephone directory, for example, lists approximately one hundred different professional organizations, hobby groups, and other special interest groups. The Blue Pages also list a wide variety of governmental organizations that might be highly viable sources of speakers, films, demonstrations, field trip opportunities, and other resources that might be highly effective Type I experiences for students.

3. *Senior Citizens' Centers and Groups.* A valuable source of human resources can be found among the oftentimes overlooked interests and talents that can be found within any group of senior citizens. Almost every city, town, or county has some type of organized senior citizens' center, and the coordinators of such centers can easily be identified by checking in the Blue Pages of the telephone directory. The use of senior citizens as Type I resources not only provides a wide diversity of

occupations, hobbies, talents, and other areas of interest, but it also can serve as a ready-made audience for several of the presentations and Type III products developed by students.

4. *Interest Development Centers (IDC)* A major source of Type I experiences consists of teacher-developed centers specifically designed to stimulate new interests in young people. The main difference between an Interest Development Center and the traditional kinds of "learning centers" found in many classrooms is that IDCs do not focus primarily on skill development, the completion of worksheets, or other activities that are primarily designed to develop basic skills. For this reason, IDCs ordinarily do not contain task cards, worksheets or "Skill Builders."

   Interest Development Centers provide teachers with an opportunity to pursue their own interests and exercise their own creativity by producing dynamic collections of materials and activities that are purposefully designed to achieve the objectives of Type I Enrichment. Although the Triad Model does not require teachers to be the writers and developers of their own curriculum, the IDC represents one of the opportunities within the model whereby interested teachers can make use of curriculum development interests and skills. We believe that any activity related to curriculum development should be voluntary rather than required, but we also have found from experience that IDCs represent a specific approach to curriculum planning that has had a great deal of appeal to teachers who like to translate their own interests and creative ideas into purposeful activities for young people.

5. *Additional Sources.* There are a number of other ways that we can identify valuable resources for Type I experiences. Brief presentations about the enrichment program at local service clubs followed by requests for Type I speakers or presentations have proven to be an effective way of recruiting persons for the Type I directory. Examination of the separate sections of newspapers (community events, arts columns, community announcements and other special feature sections) will bring to your attention

various persons in the community who are involved in a variety of professional activities, artistic presentations and hobby and recreational groups. And, of course, a category-by-category analysis of the Yellow Pages of the telephone directory will give you a fast overview of the many different occupations and areas of specialization that are available in your community. Contact should also be made with museums, art galleries, planetariums, outdoor education centers and science centers. These organizations frequently have regularly scheduled programs and also sponsor periodic events that can serve as valuable sources of Type I experiences. Each center or organization should be contacted and requests made to place the enrichment program on their mailing list. Large corporations, military installations, and other organizations (both private and public) oftentimes have specially designated persons or divisions that provide free or inexpensive services to schools and community groups. Many of these places also provide excellent opportunities for field trips, and they may even be sources of mentors for students who develop a highly specialized interest in some of the activities that take place within such organizations and centers.

Media
An almost endless supply of Type I experiences can be obtained through the careful analysis of catalogs that describe films, filmstrips, audio and video cassettes, slides and other forms of non-print media. Almost every state department of education publishes an annual guide of instructional television programs and resources; both commercial and public television frequently provide Viewer's Guides for several of their programs that are of special interest to young people. Enrichment team members can review these viewing guides on a regular basis and alert faculty members to programs that hold promise as Type I experiences for students.

Books Related to the Development of Type I Activities
Title: Change for Children
Author: Kaplan, S., Kaplan, J., Madsen, S., & Gould, B.
Age level: Grades K-6
Description: Change for Children is a guidebook designed to assist primary and elementary teachers tailor instruction

for classroom members through the use of interest centers. Interest centers can be used as one way to provide Type I activities for students, and this resource contains over 21 ready-to-use centers, as well as practical instructions on how to construct them based upon students' interests. The guide includes step-by-step procedures for changing the classroom environment to accommodate the centers, developing and placing learning activities in the room, and devising plans and schedules of student and teacher time. Ideas for record-keeping and evaluation are also included.

Publisher: Scott, Foresman and Company. Price: $14.95.

Type IIs
Communication

Title: How to Make Visual Presentations
Author: McBride, D.
Age level: Grades 7-12
Description: This guidebook provides information about and tips regarding visual presentations in a variety of contexts. It includes sections on: overhead projectors, charts, slides and movies/video. General tips are provided about charts, graphs, diagrams and illustrations, as well as lettering. Order #229, Price: $7.95.

Title: How to Write and Give a Speech
Author: Detz, J.
Age level: Grades 7-12
Description: This guidebook takes students from the beginning of the speech writing process to the nitty-gritty details of the presentation. Included are sections on assessing the audience, researching and writing the speech, style, uses of humor, delivery, and preparing for the delivery. Order #258, Price: $14.95.

Title: Joining In: An Anthology of Audience Participation Stories & How to Tell Them
Author: Miller, T.
Age level: Grades 4-11
Description: This book is an anthology for those who are interested in audience participation stories. Eighteen classic stories are included, each containing the teller's recommendations about actions and strategies for dealing with audience responses. Historical perspectives are provided on each story. Order #253, Price: $14.95.

Note: All of the books listed in this section are available from:

Creative Learning Press
P.O. Box 320
Mansfield Center, CT 06250
(203) 429-8118

Title: *The Knowhow Book of Puppets*
Author: Philpott, V., & McNeil, M. J.
Age level: Grades 3-6
Description: This book explains how children can make their own puppets, how to make them move, create special effects and work backstage. Instructions detail how students can construct finger puppets, sock creatures, mouth monsters and stick puppets. Order #231, Price: $8.95.

Title: Writing for Film and Television
Author: Bronfeld, S.
Age level: Grades 3-6
Description: Written by a professional writer of films and television scripts, this book includes how-to advice on writing for the visual media. The author explains how to create stories, characters and dialogue, and provides tips on scenecraft and camera concerns, as well as the packaging and selling of a script. Order #252, Price: $10.95.

Title: Writing for Kids
Author: Benjamin, C. L.
Age level: Grades 3-6
Description: This guidebook contains clear explanations on how children can come up with ideas, choose words, move from sentences to paragraphs to finished works and edit their own writing. Directions are included for making books of various sizes. Order #251, Price: $16.95.

Research Methodology
Title: Chi Square, Pie Charts and Me
Author: Baum, S., Gable, R. K., & List, K.
Age level: Grades 4-12
Description: This book is designed for students and teachers because it provides easy-to-understand descriptions of the research process, types of research, management plans, and statistical techniques. Examples of research done by students are provided. Order #526, Price: $14.95.

Title: The Craft of Interviewing
Author: Brady, J.
Age level: Grades 8-12
Description: The author of this book provides tips about interviewing. Along with traditional suggestions about background research, taping and note-taking, he gives insider tips on how to get interviews, develop rapport, ask questions

to promote interesting responses, get tough, and verify and write the final report. Order #519, Price: $10.95.

Title: How to Conduct Surveys: A Step-by-Step Guide
Author: Fink, A., & Kosecoff, J.
Age level: Grades 8-12
Description: This guidebook contains information about all aspects of conducting surveys. Included are chapters on survey design, data analysis and presentation of results. Examples are provided to illustrate positive and negative examples of points being made. Order #521, Price: $18.95.

Title: How to Think Like a Scientist
Author: Kramer, S. P.
Age level: Grades 2-5
Description: Designed for young children, this book includes an explanation of the scientific method in simple terms. The author provides examples of the five steps in the scientific method, illustrates the concept of control groups and provides a chapter which helps children identify questions they might want to answer. Order #513, Price: $15.95.

Title: Looking for Data in All the Right Places
Author: Starko, A., & Schack, G.
Age level: Grades 3-12
Description: The author of this book invites students to go out into the real world to gather and analyze data and share their results. Chapters are devoted to steps in the research process and include: finding a problem, focusing a problem, formulating research questions and hypotheses, choosing research designs, gathering data, analyzing data and sharing results. Order #958, Price: $18.95.

Title: A Student's Guide to Conducting Social Science Research
Author: Bunker, B., Pearlson, H. B., & Schultz, J. W.
Age Level: Grades 5-10
Description: The authors of this guidebook ground their work by relating research to real life experiences. Subsequently, they provide information about research design, testing hypotheses, surveys, observation and experiments. Finally, the authors provide several hands-on, ready-to-use activities. Order #508, Price: $18.95.

Title: Students and Research: Practical Strategies for Science Classrooms and Competitions
Author: Cothron, J. H., Geise, R. N., & Rezba, R. J.
Age level: Grades 3-12
Description: This is a hands-on guidebook, and the authors present field-tested strategies to help teachers develop sophisticated research skills with students of all ages. Through involvement with the activities and reflection afterwards, students gain an understanding about hypothesis formation, experimental design, gathering and analyzing data and communicating findings. Order #530, Price: $21.95.

Social Action
Title: It's A Free Country: A Young Person's Guide to Politics and Elections
Author: Samuels, C. K.
Age level: Grades 5-9
Description: The author invites student participation in elections and politics in two ways. First, she provides stories of men and women in politics. Second, she explains what is involved in the process of nomination, campaigning, and election. Order #318, Price: $15.95.

Title: The Kid's Guide to Social Action
Author: Lewis, B.
Age level: Grades 4-12
Description: This guidebook explains "power skills"—letter writing, interviewing, speech-making, fund raising and media coverage—which can be used by students to make a difference. Examples of real students who have been successful in campaigns related to social issues are included. Samples of actual projects and blank forms help others get started. Order #320, Price: $17.95.

Title: Like It Was: A Complete Guide to Writing Oral History
Author: Brown, S. C.
Age level: Grades 6-12
Description: The author's history of the civil rights movement serves as a backdrop to this guidebook. Clear directions are included about using a recorder, conducting the interview, transcribing and developing a product, such as short articles and full-length biographies. Order #324, Price: $14.95.

Title: Save the Earth: An Action Handbook for Kids
Author: Miles, B.
Age level: Grades 4-12
Description: This resource book for teachers provides examples of ways students can make a difference in the areas of land, atmosphere, water, energy, plants and animals, and people. Each chapter suggests problems for students as well as examples of actions taken by students. Order #321, Price: $9.95.

Science
Title: Making Your Own Nature
Author: Alford MacFarlane, R.
Age level: Grades 3-8
Description: This resource book explains ways to make displays without killing organisms, by using evidence of animals, plants, photographs, drawings, and rubbings. Additionally, the author provides illustrations and a list of supply companies. Order #434, Price: $14.95.

Title: Math Projects for Young Scientists
Author: Thomas, D.
Age level: Grades 7-12
Description: The author of this guidebook presents almost 100 intriguing math problems in combinatorics and probability, Fibonacci numbers, number theory, sequences and series, geometry and topology, and dynamical systems, Julia sets and fractals. Order #436, Price: $8.95.

Title: The Whole Cosmos Catalog of Science Activities
Author: Abruscato, J., & Hassard, J.
Age level: Grades 3-9
Description: This oversized guidebook provides readers with puzzles and games related to a variety of science topics. Sections include life sciences, earth sciences, physical sciences, aerospace sciences, and science fiction. Order #440, Price: $14.95.

How-To Books Especially Appropriate for Enrichment Clusters
Enrichment Cluster: The Young Astronomers' Society
Title: Usborne Guide: The Young Astronomer
Author: Snowden, S.
Age level: Grades 5-9
Description: A great book for those who aspire to be astronomers! Following a brief introduction to observing and

different types of observational equipment, the author provides information about constellations, stars, galaxies, nebulae, planets, comets, meteors, the moon, the sun and eclipses. The observation tips, sky maps, and a chart of astronomical sights provided by the author promote first-hand involvement. Order #423, Price: $8.95.

Enrichment Cluster: The Young Meteorologists' Research Team
Title: Making and Using Your Own Weather Station
Author: Tannenbaum, A. J., & Tannenbaum, H.
Age level: Grades 4-12
Description: Along with information about air, moisture, winds, clouds, and storms, each chapter includes suggested activities and directions for making a different weather instrument, including: barometer, thermometer, sling psychrometer, rain/snow gauge, wind vane, and anemometer. Order #437, Price: $14.95.

Enrichment Cluster: An Environmental Protection Association
Title: Usborne Guide: The Young Naturalist
Author: Mitchell, A.
Age level: Grades 2-6
Description: The guidebook is filled with suggestions and instructions for observing and experimenting with plants, birds, insects, mammals, ecosystems and wildlife. It also contains excellent ideas for making collections that involve evidence of living things, such as bones, shells, sounds, plaster casts, etc. Order #402, Price: $8.95.

Enrichment Cluster: Creative Greeting Cards Guild
Title: How to Make Pop-Ups
Author: Irvine, J.
Age level: Grades 3-12
Description: Clear directions and illustrations characterize this guidebook which details pop-up strategies for making different kinds of cards. Material lists are supplied as are tips on getting started. More advanced activities include the creation of a pop-up book. Order #254, Price: $9.95.

Enrichment Cluster: The Young Geologists' Guild
Title: Understanding and Collecting Rocks and Fossils
Author: Branwell, M.
Age level: Grades 6-12

Description: This book is full of interesting and informative illustrations explaining the forces continually changing the earth's surface. Many experimental activities are included to stimulate and challenge the minds of young geologists, such as identifying minerals and fossils, making time charts, showing how geological processes work and establishing collections. Order #420, Price: $7.95.

Enrichment Cluster: The Architecture for Learning Research Team
Title: Carpentry for Children
Author: Walker, L.
Age level: Grades 4-12
Description: This resource guide starts with chapters on using tools and building a workshop. Subsequent chapters deal with one-day projects, such as a tugboat or birdhouse, and weekend projects, including a lemonade stand. This book provides the enrichment cluster facilitator with the foundation necessary for experimental activities with students. Order #801, Price: $13.95.

Enrichment Cluster: The Future Fashion Research Institute
Title: Usborne Guide to Fashion Design
Author: Everett, F.
Age level: Grades 6-12
Description: The author of this guide books takes readers behind the scenes to learn how clothes are designed, made and sold. In addition to learning about the business and artistic aspects of fashion design, readers will learn about the materials and skills used by fashion illustrators. Order #812, Price: $9.95.

Enrichment Cluster: The Creative Cartographers' Guild
Title: How Maps Are Made
Author: Baynes, J.
Grade level: Grades 4-12
Description: This guidebook contains information about different kinds of map's and the author discusses mapmaking techniques such as scale, signs, grid references, surveying and cartographic tools. The book contains many color photos and drawings. Order #325, Price: $15.95.

Enrichment Cluster: The Video Production Company
Title: Kid Vid: Fundamentals of Video Instruction
Author: Black, K.
Grade level: Grades 4-12
Description: Nine easy lessons are contained in this book about video production. Topics include scripting, story boarding, program treatment, production, editing, and evaluation. Appendices provide useful items, including sample scripts, storyboarding sheets, video production proposals and suggested materials for the classroom. Order #255, Price: $16.95.

Enrichment Cluster: The Visual Artists' Workshop
Title: How to Draw and Paint What You See
Author: Smith, R.
Age level: Grades 7-12
Description: Aspiring artists are taken step-by-step through a variety of projects. The author gives precise directions for projects so the reader can concentrate on techniques being taught. Sample projects include: the use of black and white, color and elements of picture-making, landscapes, still lifes, and portraits. Order #810, Price: $31.95.

Title: Usborne Guide to Pottery
Author: Potter, T.
Age level: Grades 3-12
Description: Bowls, jewelry and race cars are just a few of the projects beginners can learn about in this resource book. The author provides clear explanations for potters and teaches basic pottery techniques along the way. Later chapters contain information about glazes and how to design and market artists' work. Order #821, Price: $7.95.

Title: The Kid's Multicultural Art Book
Author: Terziam, A. M.
Age level: Pre-K to Grade 5
Description: This guidebook introduces young children to art and craft experiences from around the world. Using materials commonly found at home, the book provides directions for making more than 100 projects which represent African, American, Eskimo, Indian, Asian, Hispanic and Latino cultures. Order #443, Price: $12.95.

Resources for Teachers: Identifying Student Abilities

Title: Thinking Smart: A Primer of the Talents Unlimited Model

Author: Schlichter, C. L., & Palmer, W. R.

Description: Talents Unlimited is a classroom-based model designed to develop creative and critical thinking skills. It is based on the work of Calvin Taylor's multiple talent theory which proposes that students have talents in creative and productive thinking, decision making, planning, forecasting, communication and academic talents. In this handbook, thirteen chapters explain various aspects of the model including: theory and research, classroom and school applications, evaluations and new directions for the model. This book is designed to help teachers develop talents in all students. Order #961, Price: $23.95.

Type IIIs

Resources for Teachers: Problem Finding and Problem Focusing

Title: Pathways to Investigative Skills: Instructional Lessons for Guiding Students from Problem Finding to Final Product

Author: Burns, D. E.

Grade level: Elementary-Junior High

Description: This is an all-in-one teacher resource book written by one of the nation's leading experts on thinking skills. It consists of ten step-by-step lessons designed to teach children about interest finding, problem finding, topic webbing, topic focusing, and creative problem solving. The numerous resources provided in this notebook are the following:

- 28 slides and a script for a slide show featuring Type III projects completed by students.
- 9 classroom posters (11"x17").
- A pathways planning sheet that keeps students on target and helps them visualize their goals.
- Blackline masters needed in each lesson.
- A 273-item interest-finder form.
- A one-page summary of each lesson with goals, key ideas, and materials needed.

Order #951, Price: $49.95.

Enrichment Material	Science-By-Mail

Author	Museum of Science	1991
Publisher\Contact		800 729-3300; 617 589-0437
Address	Museum of Science Boston MA 02114-1099	

Format
- ☐ Macintosh Software ☐ Textbook ☐ Video ☐ Activity cards
- ☐ IBM Software ☒ Simulation ☐ Book ☐ Teacher Guidebook
- ☐ CD ROM ☒ Kit ☐ Game ☐ Curricular Activities

ISBN Number

Price

Target Audience
- ☒ Practitioners/Teachers ☐ Parents
- ☐ Administrators ☒ Students
- ☐ Board of Education Members

Content Area
- ☐ Reading/Language Arts ☐ Mathematics ☐ Industrial Arts/Design & Technology
- ☐ Literature/Humanities ☐ Visual Arts ☐ Physical Education
- ☒ Science ☐ Performing Arts ☐ Home Economics
- ☐ Social Studies/History ☐ Computer Science

Grade Level ☐ Pre-K ☒ Primary ☒ Elementary ☒ Middle School ☐ High School

Orientation ☐ Student-focused, Content ☒ Student-focused, Process ☒ Teacher-focused

Student Involvement ☒ Needs guidance ☐ Self-explanatory

Grouping ☒ Whole class ☒ Small groups ☒ Individual

Preparation Time ☐ Necessary ☒ Not necessary

Description Science-By Mail is designed to be noncompetititve and nonjudgemental. It focuses on problem solving and the scientific process. The highlight of the program is that it provides a forum for correspondence between children and professional scientists. One of the goals of the program is to increase children's awareness of the importance of science in their everyday lives, as well as to introduce them to scientists as real people doing real jobs that children may want to pursue later in their lives.

Three times during the year children receive packets from Science-By-Mail, and each packet covers a different topic which allows children to provide open-ended responses. Included in the packets are activities to develop students' thinking skills and to help them learn more about the target topic, as well as tools to help them do the activities.

Sample entry from SEMNET DataBase, Enrichment Materials

Learning How-To-Learn	☐ Listening, Observing and Perceiving ☒ Notetaking and Outlining ☐ Interviewing and Surveying ☒ Organizing and Analyzing Data
Cognitive and Affective Training	☒ Analytical Reasoning Skills ☒ Organizational Thinking Skills ☐ Critical Thinking Skills ☒ Creative Thinking Skills ☐ Affective Thinking Skills
Using Advanced Research Skills and Reference Materials	☐ Preparing for Type III Investigations ☐ Library Skills ☐ Using Community Resources
Developing Written, Oral and Visual Communication Skills	☐ Visual Communication ☐ Oral Communication ☒ Written Communication
Methodological Resources	☐ Reading/Language Arts ☐ Literature/Humanities ☒ Science ☐ Social Studies/History ☐ Mathematics ☐ Visual Arts ☐ Performing Arts ☐ Computer Science ☐ Industrial Arts/Design & Technology ☐ Physical Education ☐ Home Economics

Sample entry from SEMNET DataBase, Enrichment Materials (continued)

Chapter 8
Organizational Components of the Schoolwide Enrichment Model

THIS CHAPTER WILL DISCUSS the following six organizational components of the Schoolwide Enrichment Model (SEM): the Schoolwide Enrichment Teaching Specialist; the Schoolwide Enrichment Team; the Professional Development Model; the Schoolwide Enrichment Model Network; Parent Orientation, Training, and Involvement; and a Democratic School Management Plan. These organizational components consist of practical strategies and resources that support the direct delivery of services to students. The components described in the sections that follow are based on several years of developmental work in programs that have used the SEM. The practicality of the components is reflected in the planning guides, lists of enrichment materials, sample letters, and teacher training materials that can be found in the companion volumes and data bases that have been developed over the years to assist in the implementation of the SEM. Resources of this type are always in the process of being updated, revised, and modified to reflect new developments in the model, changes that are taking place in general education, and creative contributions being made by persons using the model. Thus, for example, new concerns in American education for the inclusion of multicultural perspectives and environmental issues have resulted in extended searches for curricular materials on these topics. And the availability of electronic

*If your plan is for one year, plant rice;
If your plan is for ten years, plant trees;
If your plan is for 100 years, educate children.*

Confucius

bulletin boards and interactive satellite broadcast capabilities for staff development have brought a new dimension to the professional development component of the model. Some of the organizational components are at more mature stages of development than others; however, all of the components are "real" in the sense that they are actually being used in one form or another in schools that use the SEM. As will be pointed out in a later section, a vehicle entitled the Schoolwide Enrichment Model Network (SEMNET) has been established to allow schools greater access to these resources and to allow schools in the network to share resources with one another.

The Schoolwide Enrichment Teaching Specialist

AN ESSENTIAL ingredient for a successful enrichment program is a person within a school who is responsible for (1) direct services to students, and (2) leadership in program development, staff development, and the infusion of enrichment know-how and materials into the school. The role of the schoolwide enrichment teaching specialist evolved from practical experience gained in schools that expanded their traditional gifted programs into programs based on the SEM. Many of these specialists formerly served as teachers of the gifted and talented; their background and training proved to be valuable assets in making the transition to an expanded, schoolwide model. We do not view this position as a separate or additional position in schools that employ teachers of the gifted. Rather, we view the position as one that encompasses a broader application of many of the skills and responsibilities of gifted education specialists, some additional leadership responsibilities, and a commitment to apply "gifted program know-how" to all of the school structures toward which the SEM is targeted.

The Three-Fifths Solution to Allocating an Enrichment Specialist's Time

Among the most frequently asked questions about the SEM are: What does the schoolwide enrichment teaching specialist do? And, with whom does he or she work? We have divided the work of these specialists into two categories: direct services to students, and resource and leadership responsibilities. Figure 16 is intended to convey the *approximate* proportions of time spent pursuing

We know where most of the creativity, the innovation, the stuff that drives productivity lies— in the minds of those closest to the work. It's been there in front of our noses while we've been running around chasing robots and reading books on how to manage like the Japanese.

John F. Welsh, chairman General Electric Company

responsibilities in each category. Direct services to students are divided into two subcategories. One of these subcategories is face-to-face work with students in individual teaching, mentoring, and counseling situations. The other subcategory consists of arranging for services that will be carried out in cooperation with, or under the direction of, other faculty members, community resource persons or agencies, or faculty members at nearby colleges and universities. These arrangements, which are part of the continuum of special services, also include local, state, and national programs such as the Westinghouse Science Talent Search, the Young American Newsmagazine for Kids, and the International Science and Engineering Fair. Activities in the resource and leadership category include: general enrichment program administration and coordination, dissemination of information about enrichment materials and methods, staff development and demonstration teaching, peer coaching, public relations and communication, and program monitoring and evaluation. This broad range of duties could easily be overwhelming for a single person, and it is for this reason that we have built into the model a support group in the form of a schoolwide enrichment team. The role and responsibilities of this team

Direct Services to Students		**Resource and Leadership Responsibilities**	
Face-To-Face Activities	**Services provided Through Arrangements with Other Persons and Organizations**	Peer Coaching and Staff Development	Demonstration Teaching
• Individual and small group teaching and mentoring.	• Providing teachers with materials to use with a specific group or individual.	Working with Enrichment Teams	Reviewing Materials
• Direct coaching and supervision of Type III Enrichment projects that are extensions of regular classes, enrichment clusters, or non-school initiated interests.	• Coordinating mentorships with individual faculty or community resource persons and agencies.	Public Relations	Communications (Newsletters, Parent Meetings, ect.)
• Counseling and referring students about issues such as multipotentiality, underachievement, and other special needs.	• Organizing programs such as Odyssey of the Mind or the Artifact Box Program. • Arranging for students to attend summer programs in their talent areas.	Program Evaluation, Monitoring	General Administration

Figure 16. Responsibilities of The Schoolwide Enrichment Teaching Specialist. (The 3/5 Solution)

Chapter 8

will be described in the section that follows. Although allocations of the enrichment specialist's time should be more or less guided by the proportions of time depicted in Figure 16, adjustments will need to be made in accordance with local school conditions and the degree of *active* participation on the parts of enrichment team members. Our experience has shown that in cases where enrichment specialists covered more than one school, the enrichment team was a crucial factor in providing the continuity necessary to ensure program success.

Direct Services to Students

This section will describe the rationale underlying the allocation of the specialist's time, and some important "ground rules" will be discussed. A number of practical and political realities must be taken into account when recommending support for any school position beyond those of existing classroom teachers and traditional administrative positions. Budgetary issues are always a major concern, and reluctance is growing to fund positions that focus on special services to relatively small proportions of school populations. Unless a supplementary position is defined in terms of services that will have an impact on the entire student body, less likelihood exists that such positions will be initiated and supported on a continuing basis. And even when such positions are approved, it is nothing short of essential for these persons to demonstrate their *usefulness* to the entire school program. It is for this reason that we have defined the position of schoolwide teaching specialist in terms of both direct services to students, and as a series of leadership responsibilities.

Another political reality is that schools are being criticized for being administratively "top heavy." Both teachers and the general public are skeptical about creating additional layers of administration, especially during times when tightened school budgets result in increased class size and the elimination of other personnel and services. By including the word *teaching* in the job description of the enrichment specialist, we are attempting to emphasize the teaching responsibilities of persons in specialists' positions rather than duties they will fulfill in the resource and leadership portion of their jobs.

There are, of course, other reasons why it is important for enrichment teaching specialists to maintain as much direct contact with students as possible. Developing talent in all students means that there will be times and circumstances when the performance, or the potential for performance in some young people, escalates to such a degree that they require very concentrated and intense support. This support may be in the form of individual or small group instruction, guidance and counseling, apprenticeship or mentorship opportunities, or participation in out-of-school courses, cultural institutions, business or professional work places and agencies. There are two ground rules that should guide decisions about direct services provided by the enrichment teaching specialist. First, these services must be tied to *specific* areas in which high levels of talent potential have clearly been demonstrated. If, for example, a schoolwide enrichment teaching specialist teaches a cross-grade cluster group of advanced mathematics students for a few hours a week, a legitimate rationale exists for bringing this group together—the development of their advanced math talent. But if a group is brought together on a regular basis only because they have been preselected on the basis of general ability test scores, then we may be falling back into the traditional practice of designating one group of students as "the gifted" (or, in more recent terminology, "the truly gifted").

This practice has, by and large, resulted in what can only be described as *un*differentiated gifted programs. By "undifferentiated," we simply mean that the programs have focused usually on preselected topics or units of instruction, the direct teaching of general process skills, a large measure of "fun and games" activities, and field trips and visiting speakers. Since these activities ordinarily are not tied directly to a specific area of talent development for a particular individual or small group, they should be made available to all students through the regular curriculum or the enrichment clusters. A field trip to a newspaper office, for example, is an excellent experience for students studying journalism as part of their language arts curriculum, or for an enrichment cluster that is actually producing a newspaper. But to take a group on such a trip merely because they have been designated as "the gifted" is to conjure up all the criticisms that have been leveled at special programs by persons from both within and outside the field of gifted education, as well as by the general public.

Our experience has shown that enrichment teaching specialists are more effective and accepted by all members of the school community when the direct service portion of their work concentrates on specific, high level talent development activities that ordinarily cannot be accomplished in larger

DATELINE: NEW LONDON, CONNECTICUT

The Gifted Don't Need the Extras

One of the most refreshing proposals in education in some time is up for approval in East Lyme: Getting rid of the "gifted-and-talented" program. Now that's progressive, even if the motivation is budgetary. What the promising "few" (finally identified after generations of anonymity and repression) will do without the field trips to, say, the Metropolitan Museum of Art or the Bronx Zoo, I don't know. But at least the rest of the student body won't have to watch the "gifted" being treated to yet another adventure while everybody else remains behind in the class for the crime of being the lowest form of suburban life— merely average.

Steven Slosberg, 1990

Reprinted with permission of the author and the **New London Day**

Small changes can produce big results—but the areas of highest leverage are often the least obvious.

Peter M. Senge, 1990

group situations (i.e., regular classrooms and enrichment clusters). Very positive attitudes toward the enrichment teaching specialist have been observed in situations where she or he helped extend the work of classroom teachers. A third grade teacher, for example, asked the enrichment specialist to work individually with a student who had remarkable poetry writing ability. Curriculum compacting allowed the student to leave the regular classroom during reading and language arts periods. The two teachers worked out a mutually agreeable schedule that resulted in approximately one hour of individual assistance each week.

The second ground rule is that the work of enrichment teaching specialists must focus on talent development at the "high-end" of students' work rather than remedial assistance or tutorial extensions of classroom assignments. Worst-case scenarios result when teachers view enrichment specialists as persons who fulfill the same role as teachers' aids or remedial specialists. Since enrichment and remedial specialists share common strategies when working with individuals or small groups, it is best to define the enrichment specialist's role in terms of the level of product rather than the instructional strategies. There is a subtle but important distinction between: "Will you please help this student who is having trouble with his term paper," and, "This paper may be good enough to submit to the state essay contest, but it still needs major revisions and rewriting." We note in this second statement implications for the kinds of assistance that will lead to the development of a Type III product; and it is precisely this kind of assistance that should define the enrichment specialist's major responsibilities. An extension of work that may have originated in the regular classroom is certainly a legitimate domain for enrichment specialists; however, these extensions should be directed toward extraordinary levels of talent development.

These two ground rules will help to clarify the role of schoolwide enrichment personnel as talent development specialists, and they will set parameters for the kinds of direct contact specialists have with students. They should not be interpreted, however, as an indication that only enrichment specialists are responsible for talent development, or that the only purpose of the SEM is to concentrate resources on a select group of students. Many classroom teachers have guided the development of outstanding Type III products, both within regular classes and in the enrichment clusters. And, in numerous instances, the training and experience of *both* enrichment specialists and classroom teachers have been combined to produce maximal benefits for students. Talent development is everybody's job, and the enrichment teaching specialist, faculty and other personnel, have a collective responsibility for developing talent to the highest level possible in every student.

Resource and Leadership Responsibilities
The resource and leadership responsibilities of the enrichment specialist generally fall into the following four categories:

1. Gaining a familiarity with the vast amount of enrichment materials available, and collecting, reviewing, and disseminating information about these materials to administrators, faculty members, students, and parents.
2. Providing staff development and demonstration teaching sessions in the use of enrichment materials and general strategies for enrichment learning and teaching.
3. Preparing communication vehicles for parents and professionals, creating support through public relations activities, and maintaining contact with a network of schoolwide enrichment specialists.
4. Overseeing the organization, administration, and evaluation of the program and organizing the various subgroups and schoolwide enrichment teams that have responsibilities for implementing particular components of the model.

Growth, change, and ultimately evolution occur as individuals, organizations, and society increase the depth of their relationships by continually broadening and strengthening their interdependent connection.

G. Laud & B. Jarman, 1992

In one of the companion volumes (Renzulli & Reis, 1985) that contains detailed information about implementing the SEM, a separate chapter (Chapter 4, pp. 85-177) is devoted to the roles and responsibilities of coordinating a schoolwide enrichment program. This chapter includes guidance for organizing staff development sessions, providing orientation for parents and students, developing handbooks and other communication vehicles for teachers and parents, preparing public relations and community awareness information. The chapter also includes sample letters and descriptive information that can be modified for local use; sample schedules of enrichment specialists' allocation of time; sample parent, student, and teacher questionnaires; and reproducible teacher training simulations. The chronological steps for program development, and an outline for a five year plan are

People often have great difficulty talking about their vision, even when the visions are clear. Why? Because we are acutely aware of the gaps between our vision and reality....These gaps can make a vision seem unrealistic or fanciful. They can discourage us or make us feel hopeless. But the gap between vision and current reality is also a source of energy. If there was no gap, there would be no need for any action to move toward the vision. Indeed, the gap is the source of creative energy. We call this gap creative tension.

Peter M. Senge, 1990

included. As is the case with all material developed in connection with the SEM, we encourage local adaptation according to the unique nature of individual programs, the availability of resources, and the specific ways in which the schoolwide enrichment teaching specialist allocates his or her time. Information related to these aspects of the SEM is included in the Resource Guide at the end of Chapter 7 and Chapter 8.

Enrichment specialists are the sparkplugs that ignite most of the enrichment activities in a school, and they are the conceptual and practical adhesive that holds together the many dimensions of an SEM school. But the job is far too complex to be carried out effectively by one person, and, therefore, an organizational component has been built into the model that provides the enrichment specialist with a support system essential for the maximum delivery of services. This component is described in the section that follows.

The Schoolwide Enrichment Team

ONE OF the best ways to expand the full range of enrichment services to all students is through the development of a schoolwide enrichment team. An enrichment team is not a policy making body or an advisory committee, but, rather, a working group of faculty members and parents who have specific responsibilities for organizing the overall enrichment effort for an entire school. Enrichment team members serve as representatives of their grade level or department, and one of their responsibilities is to promote faculty involvement in schoolwide enrichment activities. Organizing an enrichment team will develop a sense of faculty and community ownership in the SEM. We have found that when classroom teachers are encouraged to become actively involved in enrichment team activities, they eventually come to regard efforts to develop talent as a joint venture to be shared by all faculty members. Our experience has also shown that faculty members at large are frequently interested in planning and organizing enrichment activities, as well as in the direct delivery of services. Over the last several years we have worked with many school districts that have implemented outstanding enrichment programs. In almost every case, the first step after the SEM was adopted and administrative support assured was an orientation for all staff members about the components of the model *and* the establishment of an enrichment team.

Who Should Be on the Enrichment Team?

We have found the most effective way to organize an enrichment team is to recruit members from various segments of the school and community. We, therefore, suggest that the enrichment team include parents, community resource persons, administrators, classroom teachers who represent all grade levels, art, music, physical education and other special subject teachers, and the librarian or media specialist. At the secondary level, a general enrichment team includes representatives from each department; separate enrichment teams can be organized within departments, as well. We have also found that it is extremely effective to include students on the enrichment team. One reluctant community resource person, for example, told us that he could have easily refused an adult's invitation to present a 45-minute workshop on his specialty area, but it was impossible for him to refuse the request when it was made by an excited fifth-grader!

An invitation to serve on the enrichment team should be extended to all faculty members. In one school system where all staff members were required to select two instructional objectives on which to be evaluated at the end of the school year, principals encouraged faculty members to select participation on the schoolwide enrichment team as an objective.

The number of team members can vary. We have seen effective teams that have only three active members (in smaller schools) and teams of ten or twelve (in larger schools). It is also important to mention that in some school districts, negative, outspoken faculty members have been invited to serve on the enrichment team and, indeed, have been personally recruited by the principal and/or the enrichment specialist. In many cases, negative energy has been channeled into a more positive direction by simply including this kind of teacher on the team. We should caution, however, that as few as two negative persons can become a strong enough coalition to block positive action through the strength they gain from each other.

We recommend that the superintendent of schools write a "letter of appointment" to the individuals serving on the enrichment team, telling them how important their task is and commending them for volunteering. This practice exemplifies administrative support, and it also lets team members know that the chief school officer is aware of their additional effort and involvement. We also recommend that, whenever possible, some type of budget be given to the team. Although the great majority of the enrichment experiences typically

People with a high level of personal mastery live in a continual learning mode. They never arrive. Sometimes, language, such as the term, "personal mastery," creates a misleading sense of definitiveness, of black and white. But personal mastery is not something you possess. It is a process. It is a lifelong discipline. People with a high level of personal mastery are acutely aware of their ignorance...their growth areas. And they are deeply self-confident. Paradoxical? Only for those who do not see that the "journey is the reward."

Peter M. Senge, 1990

used in the SEM do not require supplementary funds, there may be occasions when a cost is involved. If the enrichment team has even a small budget with which to work, a great number of avenues may be opened up for the exploration of possible enrichment activities. Additionally, access to even limited funds helps to legitimize the importance of the team in the eyes of the school community.

Finally, no one should ever be forced to serve on the enrichment team. We strongly advocate the inclusion of a building principal even if he or she attends meetings only on a periodic basis. But no one should serve on the team who truly does not want to be involved. We have found that once the benefits of the various types of enrichment experiences become obvious, more faculty members become interested in joining the team in subsequent years.

Who Should Serve as the Chairperson of the Enrichment Team?

If a schoolwide enrichment teaching specialist is available, it is advisable to have this person serve as chairperson of the team and to organize *regular* meetings. This approach is recommended because a resource teacher often has a more flexible schedule than classroom teachers. The chair should preside over a democratic decision-making process that leads to subdividing duties so that the responsibilities are shared among team members and the general faculty members whom they represent. The key to successful functioning of the enrichment team is specificity of tasks and a division of labor among team members. A series of "Action Forms" (Renzulli & Reis, 1985, see the side bar) have been developed to assist in this process. Since team members can devote only relatively small portions of their time to this endeavor, it is essential that tasks be broken down into targeted activities that can be carried out with minimal expenditures of time. If a resource teacher or enrichment specialist is not present in the school, we recommend the election or appointment of a chairperson who is organized, efficient, and gets along with other faculty members. We strongly advise that this person have some release time for organizing the enrichment team's work in addition to his or her regularly scheduled planning time. Two or three hours a week that an administrator can arrange for the chairperson to use as planning time communicates a very important message to the chairperson and the entire faculty. Simply, that message is: We value what you are doing, and we support your efforts to complete this task.

How Often Should the Team Meet and What Should It Accomplish?

For teams that are just beginning, we recommend regular weekly meetings for the first month or two of school. At these initial meetings, the logistical questions that face all enrichment teams should be discussed. These questions include, but are not limited to the following:

1. When is the best time of the week to organize regular enrichment experiences?
2. Should most enrichment activities be conducted in regular classroom settings? In the enrichment clusters? In the continuum of special services?
3. How can we orient the faculty to realize that enrichment experiences are wide and varied and include more than speakers?
4. How can enrichment experiences be implemented to allow for equal representation across subject matter areas?
5. How many enrichment experiences should be organized for a given period of time?
6. How can we organize these activities with minimal disruption to the regular school day?
7. How can we involve as many faculty members as possible?
8. How can we recruit parents and community members and agencies?
9. How can we evaluate the effectiveness of enrichment activities?
10. How do we (the enrichment team) get started?

These and other logistical questions will require more organizational time for the enrichment team at the beginning of the year. We have found that the answers to the above questions vary from school to school, depending upon many factors including the size of a school, availability of space for enrichment experiences, flexibility of the faculty, administrative attitudes toward the enrichment program, and the time that the enrichment team is able to spend working together. The companion volumes to this book, referenced in the Resource Guide at the end of this chapter, provide practical advice for addressing these and other questions related to the role and functioning of the enrichment team.

Selection Criteria for Team Membership

- *Commitment to change*

- *A reputation for innovation*

- *An ability to make things happen*

- *Evidence of energy and persistence*

- *Evidence of some capacity for leadership based on past performance or the perception of others*

- *Patience*

Gene Maeroff, 1993

Goal 3 of the Schoolwide Enrichment Model

"To promote continuous, reflective, growth-oriented professionalism on the parts of all school personnel."

The Professional Development Model

ALTHOUGH SCHOOLS are supposed to be the major formal agencies for learning in our society, when it comes to the education of persons within the teaching profession, we consistently violate what is known about how people learn most effectively and the conditions under which they apply their knowledge to new situations. If, as John Goodlad tells us, today's schools bear a striking resemblance to schools at the turn of the century (Goodlad, 1983, 1984), then we must reexamine the ways in which we prepare teachers in direct relation to the types of schools we are trying to create. In our discussion of Goal 3, a rationale for a different kind of professional development model was presented; it was argued that the "old style" in-service training, which focused almost exclusively on one-shot, skill-oriented workshops, is inadequate for bringing about real and lasting improvements in schools. But the history of professional development, and the enormity of the task of improved professionalism, require that proposals for change must be approached with caution and parsimony and an understanding of the process of change itself. The almost endless amount of time spent in poor quality training, the external restrictions that limit application of newly acquired methods, and the roles that teachers have played as recipients rather than decision makers about their own training, have produced a quiet skepticism about the entire issue of professional development. We will not attempt to "rewrite the book" on professional development because we do not believe there are any magical solutions to the complex problem of improving the professionalism of all school personnel. We will, however, offer some common sense suggestions that have proven to be effective in bringing about school improvement within the context of the SEM.

The professional development model for the SEM is built around a three-phase process that includes: (1) substantive examinations of theoretical, pedagogical, and curricular knowledge, (2) skill-oriented training that focuses on the know-how of implementing a particular teaching method or set of curricular materials, and (3) opportunities to apply knowledge and know-how in a relatively unrestricted and non-threatening experimental setting. A graphic representation of this model is presented in Figure 17, and the sections that follow describe procedures for using the professional development model. A group within the school should serve as a steering committee for making decisions about issues that will be the focus for professional development, and this group should gather suggestions from individuals and other teams that represent various subgroups of faculty, administration, and parents. A major criterion for determining which topics will become focus issues is how a particular topic relates to one of the components of the SEM. Thus, for example, the larger issue of curriculum modification and related theoretical and research information about curriculum compacting can serve as a focus issue for faculty discussion.

Knowledge Seminars

The knowledge component of the model is ordinarily the starting point of the staff development process, and it consists of selecting an idea, topic, curriculum issue, or teaching method that will be the *focus* of a particular school improvement initiative. This may be a macro-change initiative such as the exploration of the SEM, which, if adopted, can be followed by micro-change professional development activities. Following an introduction to the topic and the distribution of an economical set of background material for individual reading, small group seminars are conducted to discuss the full range of ramifications the topic generates.

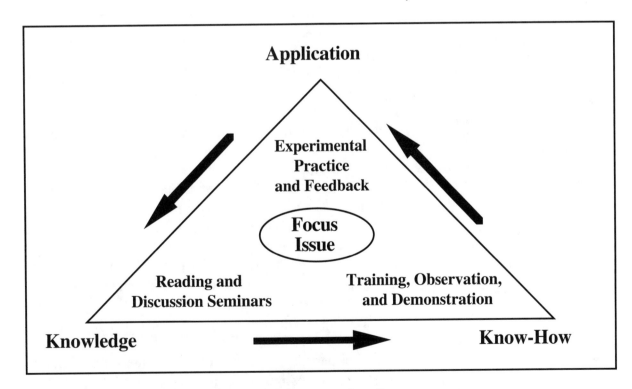

Figure 17. The professional development triangle.

DATELINE: NEW YORK CITY

Teachers Feel Left Out of Reform, Study Says

Despite widespread and urgent calls over the last decade for school reform, nearly 60 percent of the nation's school teachers say they have yet to see major changes...."I think what this study shows is that teachers need to be at the table in the discussions of school reform," said Dr. Allison Bernstein, director of the Ford Foundation's Education and Cultural Division, which financed the poll. "Contrary to public opinion, teachers are not resistant to reform. And I think in the final analysis, the top-down strategy simply won't succeed."

Samuel Weiss, 1993

Persons organizing the seminar should also provide easy access to related research and theoretical literature about the topic, bibliographies of related material, and an open invitation for all persons to contribute background material of their own choosing. The seminars should have two inviolable ground rules. First and foremost, the seminar should be viewed as a "community of professional scholars" who are coming together to examine the theoretical and pedagogical merits of the focus issue. The main questions should be: "Will it [i.e., method, curricular material, management procedure, grouping alternative, etc.] improve learning?" "Will it help to make a difference in the lives of students?" "Will it help to make our school a better place?" By focusing on theoretical issues, we avoid getting mired down in the "toxic details" of implementation and the admonitions of naysayers who so often prevent any new idea from ever having the remotest chance of being considered. The negativism that exists on the parts of many teachers is, in part, the result of not having opportunities to discuss important issues that lead to decision making. Our profession has had a tradition of bringing in the persons who will be charged with the responsibility for implementing a change only *after* theoretical issues have been considered by policy makers, and *after* decisions have been made about new initiatives. Little wonder that so many teachers and building administrators take a negative stance toward proposed changes, and in some cases, even go so far as to undermine changes that they believe have been imposed upon them.

Another tradition in education is that teachers go to "teacher workshops," administrators go to "administrator workshops," etc. This tradition has perpetuated the us-and-them syndrome and is clearly the best way to ensure poor communication and a lack of understanding of the problems and agendas of the respective groups. We believe that teachers, administrators, and supervisory personnel should be involved in all three phases of this professional development process. Recent research by Maeroff (1993, see the Resource Guide in Chapter 8) reports on the benefits of collaboration between administrators and teachers. Not only can teaming of administrators and teachers lead to "shared convictions and a fresh willingness on the part of participants to accept part of the burden of leadership, it also helps to minimize the possibilities of miscommunication" (p. 87).

In order for the process to work effectively, another important ground rule must be followed. This second ground rule is that everyone's opinion must be valued and respected. If administrative personnel, union representatives, or high status teachers "pull rank," or if overt or subtle messages minimize the teachers' role in the group, then the process will be undermined from the very outset. Similarly, if teachers put out negative messages about how administrators "don't truly understand the nuts and bolts of the real classroom," then the process will take on the same battle lines that have hindered past attempts at school improvement.

The knowledge seminars are, indeed, a part of the process for addressing practical problems and solutions, but the main purpose of this component of the professional development process is to provide a vehicle for the kinds of intellectual and creative thinking that are largely absent from so much of the work of practicing school personnel. We have experimented with these types of seminars with teachers and administrators involved in professional development related to the SEM, and two observations are immediately apparent. First, practitioners have consistently said that dealing with ideas and concepts about theoretical issues is a refreshing departure from the kinds of "teacher training" in which they are ordinarily involved. One teacher's comment typifies the reactions of many: "This is the first time since college that anyone expected me to actually use my *mind!*" Another teacher said, "They are always asking us to do something different, but we are never given an opportunity to deal with *why* we are doing it or what the research says about the benefits of doing it."

Second, far more teachers and administrators than we expected "rose to the occasion" of the intellectual challenges that were required for the discussion of theoretical and pedagogical issues. The degree of preparation and participation clearly indicates that we may have been underestimating teachers' interest in and ability to engage in the kinds of dialogue that tradition has generally restricted to policy makers and administrators, or to college courses that are often disconnected from school improvement activities. To be certain, the process did not take place easily and naturally in its early stages. Limited opportunities, and, therefore, experience, in engaging in this kind of interaction is a tradition that frequently turns teachers' meetings into gripe sessions and causes suspicion about the motivation for promoting this kind of professional involvement. These traditions will require time and hard work to overcome. But when teachers view an examination of theoretical issues in

DATELINE: LOUISVILLE, KENTUCKY

Student Gains, Intensive Restructuring Linked, Study Finds

Jefferson County Public School/Gheens Professional Academy in Louisville has gained a national reputation for linking the professional development of teachers and administrators directly to innovations in individual schools. Across all levels of education (42 schools—18 elementary schools, 12 middle schools and 12 high schools), schools engaged in systemic reform (i.e., Group I schools) outperformed both sets of comparison schools:

- *Group I schools increased the percentage of students scoring at or above the 50th percentile on the C.T.B.S. 88 percent of the time, compared with 50 percent of the time for students in Group II schools and 58 percent for those in Group III schools.*

- *Students in Group I schools improved at an average rate of 8.3 percent a year in the C.T.B.S., compared with 2.6 percent for those in Group II and 5.5 for those in Group III.*

- *Rates of student attendance, parent and student satisfaction, and parental involvement increased—and student suspension and retention rates decreased—83 percent of the time in Group I schools. In Groups II and III schools, the rates improved 44 percent and 50 percent, respectively.*

Lynn Olson, 1992

The context in which educational change is pursued is everything. Many policies are based on assumptions about contexts for reform that do not take into account the alternatives that networks offer. Instead of targeting individuals and attempting to provide them with new skills or perspectives, networks concentrate on building communication among teachers/learners. It is thus critical that policy makers and others approach teacher networks not from the standpoint of management and control, but from that of the norms and agreements of communal relations.

Ann Leiberman & Milbrey W. McLaughlin, 1992

the larger context of decision making, and as a prelude to possible follow-up of a more practical nature, the knowledge seminars take on a more important role in overall professional development. The education profession has generally underestimated the conceptual role of teachers; by so doing, we have not only missed opportunities to nurture and use local intelligence and creativity, but we have also turned the profession into a rank-and-file organization that replaces self-motivation with greater and greater amounts of supervision. Complicated teacher evaluation systems have been adopted by some states and districts that give higher ratings to persons adhering to formula-driven teaching-by-prescription than to creative and responsive, student-centered teaching! In one state that adopted such an evaluation system, several teachers who were acknowledged to be among the very best in a particular district actually earned the lowest ratings because they did not use the prescribed steps in every lesson. The knowledge seminars provide opportunities for enhancing the professionalization of teaching by allowing practitioners to study and to examine the theoretical issues and research findings that are the foundation of their work.

Know-How Workshops

This dimension of the professional development triangle is probably the most familiar to teachers and other educational personnel. Know-how workshops usually focus on the acquisition of new skills, teaching and management techniques, and the use of specified sets of instructional materials. Most of the training in this area has been carried out by having persons present information in workshop settings. Equally valuable, but less frequently used approaches, are observations of particular techniques in classrooms where the technique has been perfected, or participation in demonstration lessons in which adult audience members assume the roles of students. The effectiveness of all three approaches can be enhanced by using them in conjunction with one another; and effectiveness will be further enhanced if know-how workshops include, whenever possible, demonstration teaching and opportunities for participants to practice a particular technique.

One of the more fortunate results of the school improvement initiative has been a rapidly growing body of staff development materials. The use of video training tapes and interactive satellite communication links has made high levels of professional training available to schools that cannot afford expensive consultants or schools that lack the local expertise necessary for new initiatives. The Resource Guides that have been included in this book are also a source of training materials for know-how workshops; however, the professional development steering committee should solicit suggestions from all faculty members for both topics and recommended persons or training packages that will provide training in particular areas of teacher interest.

Professional development that focuses on the acquisition of know-how has been a mainstay of teacher training, and it has also been the subject of a fair amount of criticism and wasted time! There are few teachers who cannot add their own personal "horror stories" to the list of tales about disappointing workshops, boring presenters, and forced attendance at training sessions on topics in which they had little interest. Although it will be difficult, if not impossible, to overcome all of the criticism about in-service training, there are at least four specific issues to be considered if we are to avoid past mistakes, therefore, increasing the impact of training recommended for the know-how dimension of the staff development model. First, all persons in the school community should be involved in planning in-service training, either directly or indirectly through the representatives of their respective teams. Second, input about the quality of a trainer or training package should be sought from individuals or groups who have had first-hand experience with the trainer or training package being considered. Third, time should be made available for a post-learning analysis of the training session in order to consider the value of the training within the overall context of the school's goals. Finally, administrators and parents, as well as teachers, should participate in the know-how workshops, and teacher and parent representatives should participate in workshops that are specifically targeted for administrators.

Two ground rules should guide all know-how workshops. First, a workshop should be offered only if it "fits in" with an already-adopted model or larger plan for school improvement. This ground rule will help prevent schools from falling prey to the flavor-of-the-month approach to staff development. Our profession has been plagued by slick-talking consultants who blitz into town for a few hours with yet another panacea or lists of "noble shoulds," but with little follow-up on the know-how required for implementation and the methods and materials necessary for putting their ideas into practice. This ground rule helps to guarantee continuity

Investments in teacher learning are what ultimately fuel student learning.

Ann Leiberman, Linda Darling-Hammond, & Diane Zuckerman, 1991

Systems change when enough kindred spirits coalesce in the same direction. This is why top-down structural change does not work. You can't mandate what matters because there are no shortcuts to changes in systems' cultures. But like-minded people, pushing for change, do add up.

Michael Fullan, 1993

and integrity to a comprehensive approach to school improvement rather than an *ad hoc* approach to staff development.

A second ground rule is that any know-how training must be recommended by the steering committee and approved by a majority of the faculty within a given building. This ground rule guarantees staff involvement rather than top-down decision making, and it helps to link the knowledge seminars with know-how workshops. When an entire faculty examines training opportunities within the context of a general plan or model, and when there is a perceived need based on discussions of theoretical and pedagogical issues, there is greater likelihood that professional development will have the kind of payoff that we have hoped for, but seldom achieved.

The "fit" or need for in-service can be assessed in a dialogue among educators or with the assistance of inventories. Schlichter and Olenchak (1992) developed an instrument for identifying in-service needs in schools using the SEM. Through extensive interviews and reviews of literature on the model and on enrichment teaching practices, the authors developed an item pool which they field tested subsequently in three schools. Measures of central tendency and dispersion were calculated, and a factor analysis was conducted to determine the number of significant factors and the loadings defining each factor. Four areas were identified as major categories that should be considered in preparing for staff development. These areas are: Preparing for School Change, Focusing Type III Investigations, Organizing and Providing Enrichment for All Students, and Stimulating the Interests of Each Individual Student. The research resulted in a final instrument consisting of 24 items based on a 5-point Likert response format. The instrument, entitled *Schoolwide Enrichment Teachers' Ratings of Appraised In-service Needs* (SE-TRAIN) is included in Appendix C. In addition to this model-specific approach to examining in-service needs, general approaches such as the Concerns-Based Adoption Model (CBAM) (Hall, George, & Rutherford, 1979) can be customized to provide direction to staff development needs. CBAM uses a 35-item survey instrument, *Stages of Concern Questionnaire,* to examine the following seven stages of concern with regard to adopting new practices: awareness about the practice; information about what the uses of the practice entail; personal concerns and uncertainties; management concerns about time and logistics; consequence concerns about the impact upon students; implications about collaboration; and refocusing concerns about new ideas to replace or alter the practice. The instrument yields an individual profile that can be used for diagnostic purposes about both the adoption of a new practice and the nature of support required during the implementation of an innovation.

Application Situations

Our efforts to improve teaching have profoundly violated what we know about learning by failing to provide teachers with opportunities to apply what they have learned about good teaching. Almost every teacher has been subjected to hundreds of hours of training, and, yet, very little of that training has produced lasting changes in what takes place in classrooms. External regulations, the influence of textbooks and standardized testing, and the tendency of our profession to jump on almost every fad and bandwagon that comes down the road are undoubtedly reasons for the limited impact of training. But another reason we do not make use of newly acquired skills over longer periods of time is that limited opportunities exist in the present school structure to practice and refine new skills in a supportive and non-threatening environment. Using a metaphor called "polishing the stone," Stigler and Stevenson (1991) report that one of the characteristics of successful Asian teachers is that they devote time to refining and honing their lessons to a high state of perfection. Furthermore, not only do they discuss with their colleagues the art and science of good teaching, and engage in a continuous inquiry about their own teaching activities, but also "national television in Japan presents programs that show how master teachers handle particular lessons or concepts" (Stigler & Stevenson, 1991, p. 46).

The third dimension of the SEM professional development model is designed to provide application situations and opportunities to discuss concerns and issues related to newly initiated teaching methods. This type of *reflective teaching* capitalizes on the knowledge base and know-how phases discussed above, and it draws upon the same principles of learning that are advocated for students. One vehicle for application situations is built into the SEM in the form of the enrichment clusters. Our own experience, and the experience of numerous teachers with whom we have worked over the years, provided the clue for this connection between reflective teaching and the lack of structure that characterizes enrichment clusters. Anyone who has ever

The full realization of how little time American teachers have when they are not directly in charge of children became clear to us during a meeting in Beijing. We were discussing the teachers' workday. When we informed Chinese teachers that American teachers are responsible for classes all day long, with only an hour or less outside the classroom each day, they looked incredulous. How could any teacher be expected to do a good job when there is no time outside of class to prepare and correct lessons, work with individual children, consult with other teachers, and attend to all the other matters that arise during the day!...The situation is similar in Japan. According to our estimate, Japanese elementary school teachers are in charge of classes only 60 percent of the time they are at school.

James Stigler & Harold Stevenson, 1991

Reflection is the practice or act of analyzing our actions, decisions, or products....Reflection-on-action is reflection on practice and on one's actions and thoughts, undertaken after action is completed. Reflection-in-action is reflection on phenomena and on one's spontaneous ways of thinking and acting in the midst of action....Reflection-for-action is the desired outcome of both previous types of reflection. We undertake reflection, not so much to revisit the past or to become aware of the metacognitive processes one is experiencing,...but to guide future action. Reflection, then, is a process that encompasses all time designations...[to] generate knowledge that will inform our future actions.

Joellen Killon & Guy Todnem, 1991

taught in a special program (e.g., Saturday enrichment classes, 4-H program, preparation for science fairs, play or musical production), or who has served as a leader or coach in an extracurricular activity, operates by a different set of rules from those present in formal classroom instruction. First, the major goal is to produce a high-quality product or service. Second, there are no mastery tests or grading requirements hanging over the teacher's heads. Third, the adult's role is more like that of a guide and compatriot rather than a direct frontal instructor. These types of situations result in qualitatively different relations between young people and adults,[1] and they require that a different kind of learning paradigm be used. Many of our colleagues have reported that teaching in such an environment has enabled them to develop skills that are readily applicable to regular classroom teaching situations. Because the enrichment clusters are purposefully designed to provide a different "brand" of learning, they can also serve as true laboratories for teachers to practice and refine new skills in a climate free from the constraints usually placed on the regular curriculum.

There is, however, one additional component that is necessary to capitalize on these laboratory situations, and to ensure that they are a systematic, rather than random, part of professional development. Teachers need an opportunity to discuss and reflect upon all of their teaching practices. To do this, time must be made available, and procedures initiated so that discussions about one another's teaching can be carried out in an open and trusting atmosphere. This is a difficult task, especially in a profession that historically has treated what goes on in "the privacy of one's own classroom" as a very personal matter. We have already discussed the two major taboos of teaching: "Thou shall not enter thy neighbor's classroom while she or he is teaching," and "Thou shall not discuss craft with one's colleagues." There are no formulas or easy solutions for overcoming these ancient taboos; however, a number of specific strategies are emerging from recent studies on team building that provide guidance for creating a nucleus of committed people in each school that can lead the way toward more consultation and sharing between and among members of the faculty.

In a book entitled, *Team Building for School Change: Equipping Teachers for New Roles,* Maeroff (1993) suggests that one reason for the failure of school reform is the tendency of reform efforts to overlook the role of teachers in the change process. Maeroff compares school reformers to designers of new cars "who seek to overhaul the automobile without paying attention to the impact of the person who will sit behind the steering wheel" (p. 2). To jump start meaningful and lasting educational change, Maeroff suggests that designated teachers and a building principal be trained as a team to deal with the changes that will be required to improve schools. This guidebook explains how team members are selected and trained, the stages through which teams evolve as they develop lives of their own, and how to analyze the obstacles the new team will encounter as it works to bring about changes. Maeroff's work is an example of the practice-related research that is needed in education; it leads to a much deeper understanding of change, the dynamics of change in the educational setting, and contains practical suggestions for those who wish to utilize teams to encourage change in their district. Most important, Maeroff's work is one of the few works to recognize teachers as the essential element in school improvement.

Team building is an excellent way of overcoming the isolation and sense of inconsequentiality that many teachers experience. Teams can consist of two persons such as the type recommended in the peer coaching model (Glatthorn, 1987; Joyce & Showers, 1982; Showers, Joyce, & Bennett, 1987), or they can be slightly larger based on individual preferences. The most important consideration in forming teams that focus on the teaching process is that persons have a choice in determining their own team's make-up. This approach will help to overcome problems usually associated with school committees that are formed along traditional lines. Since the function of the teams is to examine the most personal part of our professionalism, i.e., our teaching, it is essential that persons be on a team with people they trust!

This approach to school improvement is based, in part, on lessons that have been learned from successful practices in business and industry, where teams have been formed to tackle difficult problems related to efficiency, effectiveness, and motivation. Although a good deal of the emerging literature on democratic school governance focuses on policy and management issues, the team approach is especially applicable to the direct improvement of teaching. The major reality that catapulted team building to the forefront of private and public organizations is that persons closest to the work know best how to perform and improve the work they are doing. At the heart of the work of schools, and of the SEM, is the act of learning. In a later section, we will discuss team

Everyone needs opportunities for self-renewal, but those responsible for developing other human beings need them most of all. Thinking deeply about what we are doing leads us to ask better questions, break out of fruitless routines, make unexpected connections, and experiment with fresh ideas.

Ron Brandt, 1991

Restoring Professionalism to Teaching: Reflections from Inside a Dryer*

The pathology of teaching, according to Roland Barth, is the "resonating helplessness, anger, frustration and sense of defeat" that has sapped the curiosity, enthusiasm, and self-assurance from many of today's teachers. The helplessness is due, in part, to the turbulent demands and worklife conditions that exact burdensome tolls on those who lead classrooms. Most important, Barth believes that the anger and sense of defeat stem from teachers' feelings related to loss of control over their environment and the new belief that they are merely old tennis shoes in "hot, bumpy, dark and congested dryers." Clearly, teachers no longer believe that their visions of schools as exciting and powerful places are meaningful and valued.

The only way to restore teachers' generative power and the professionalism to teaching, Barth claims, is for teachers to do something for themselves, and he describes this revitalization as a three-stage process. First, teachers need to reawaken their deeply concealed visions of schools. Second, they must bring their personal visions of school to the classroom and experiment with curriculum and pedagogy in order to realize their vision. Teachers must examine and re-examine their content and teaching strategies, take risks, and even become revolutionaries. When teachers reflect upon, scrutinize and challenge their own practices, the most effective ones will emerge to make visible the richness of their lost professionalism. Third and finally, teachers must share their artistry and inform the restructuring of schools.

Adapted from: A. T. Lockwood, (1992). Becoming School Leaders. In Focus in Change, 9, 8-11.

building issues related to democratic school governance. Although there are commonalities in all processes based on the use of teams, our concern here is with the application of team strategies to the learning process. The Resource Guide at the end of this chapter includes references to peer coaching and team building that are especially applicable to the ways in which teachers can work cooperatively to improve their teaching.

Another Kind of Professionalism

Although we have advocated a gentle and evolutionary approach toward school improvement, one of the issues related to professional development is a somewhat bolder recommendation for promoting growth among the teachers who would like to play an expanded role in school improvement. This recommendation relates to the reward structure that most commentators on total quality management have indicated is an essential ingredient for improving the effectiveness of services to clients. The discussion that follows about the use of a reward structure within the context of the SEM is based on two principles of total quality management. The first principle is that improvements in worker performance are best approached by utilizing the experience and know-how of persons who are closest to the work being carried out. Our experience has shown that there is a remarkable amount of unrecognized and underutilized expertise within the teaching profession, but this talent has remained largely undeveloped because the roles of teachers are often conceptualized in terms of what they do *inside* their own classrooms. Most educators view professional leadership as something that "belongs" to persons who fulfill official leadership roles (e.g., administrators, supervisors, staff development specialists) or persons with status based on their professional activities (e.g., researchers, professors, outside consultants). Although these persons may possess expertise that can improve the teaching and learning process, the roles they fulfill usually place them at some distance from the day-to-day operation of what goes on in classrooms. If we truly believe that persons closest to the work know best how to perform and improve the work they are doing, then we must examine specific vehicles for creating opportunities that will encourage teachers to pursue leadership activities that focus directly on the learning process.

A second principle of total quality management is that persons should be rewarded for notable contributions to the overall operation of their respective organizations. "Notable contributions" means more than simply improving one's own performance on the assembly line. Rather, it means devising ways to make the assembly line work better, or making suggestions for the improvement of *everyone's* performance. Unfortunately, our profession has not had a tradition of providing incentives for teachers who want to develop high levels of expertise targeted on improving the work of other teachers or creating materials or organizational structures designed to improve the school as a whole. Whenever we talk about the "professional growth of teachers," we are almost always referring to teachers as *recipients* of training that they will apply within the confines of their own classrooms.

There have, indeed, been attempts within the profession to provide incentives in the form of merit pay or "career ladders," but these attempts have met with limited success. And in some cases, these approaches have had nothing short of devastating results on faculty morale and the personal relations that exist among teachers. The complexity and demands of teaching, the diversity of the clientele teachers serve, the subjectivity of observational information, and the wide variety of conditions in which teachers work make it almost impossible to devise an equitable system for awarding merit pay based on a teacher's performance in the classroom. But there is another approach to providing incentives and rewards for teachers that is modeled somewhat on reward systems used for years to supplement the salaries of athletic coaches and persons who have taken on supplementary responsibilities in addition to their regular teaching assignments. In this case, however, the reward system is targeted toward teachers willing to develop high degrees of expertise in areas that make them indispensable to the improvement of the quality of learning that takes place in a school or district.

The procedure recommended here is best understood by examining two levels of professionalism within the field of education. A Level 1 professional is a qualified, accomplished specialist who conforms to the technical or ethical standards of a field or occupation. All teachers are expected to achieve this level of professionalism, and it is almost trite to say that persons who do not conform to the technical and ethical standards of the field should probably be removed from the profession.

A Level 2 professional is a person who conforms to the technical and ethical standards of a field or occupation, but

> *The tired and worn-out school staffing and teacher personnel practices of past decades must be scrapped. The single salary schedule cries out for enhancements that will compensate our great teachers on a level commensurate with their worth. This problem keeps coming up on the reform agenda. It won't go away, because our current practices hamstring our efforts to build a truly great teaching profession. In higher education there are teaching assistants, a variety of academic ranks, distinguished professorships, and endowed chairs....The worn and weary personnel patterns will begin to disappear soon— and the sooner, the better.*
>
> *Terrel H. Bell, 1993*

Today was something different. We worked on a grant-writing project and are submitting a building grant proposal. We are so excited about it we can hardly see straight.

Teacher, in Wilson, 1993

A number of us feel that the most significant thing we ever did was arrange to have lunch outside the faculty lounge....We ate and talked in an environment where everybody had given you permission to be elated about the things that worked and cry about the things that didn't. The end result was that it created relationships that made possible a lot of sharing and encouragement to try things when you were nervous.

Teacher, in Wilson, 1993

---

who also contributes in a creative and productive way to the growth of the field. Examples of contributions to the teaching profession might be developing innovative curricular materials, conducting demonstration teaching lessons that exemplify new teaching strategies, developing high levels of expertise in staff development, or providing ground-breaking leadership in matters related to developing special programs and services, organizing innovative scheduling techniques, and creating specific vehicles for collaboration with non-school agencies, businesses, or cultural institutions. In many respects, this level of professionalism represents the same type of undertaking recommended for students who are involved in Type III Enrichment. But in order for this type of involvement to have built-in quality control mechanisms, it must follow the "market competition" model that is used to evaluate product quality in the competitive world of business and industry. Perhaps a negative example will point out the ways in which such a procedure should *not* be pursued.

A school district had some staff development money "left over" that needed to be spent by the end of the fiscal year! A group of teachers was given a summer stipend to "write curriculum" related to the development of thinking skills. They were not required to prepare a proposal for review, seek approval prior to beginning their work, nor were provisions made for an external review, evaluation, and field testing of the materials prior to their publication and distribution by the district. The materials were seldom used, and even the persons who developed them expressed little enthusiasm for what they had produced. The persons preparing the materials were paid for the work they did without any concern for the quality of the material produced. Thus, there was very little motivation to follow the *modus operandi* of "real authors" whose work must adhere to market-place standards of quality that make it competitive in real-world publishing situations.

Let us now examine a positive example of how this process worked in connection with a teacher who wanted to make a professional leadership contribution in the area of staff development. A middle school teacher developed a high degree of enthusiasm for the process of curriculum compacting because she felt it would help increase the level of challenge for large numbers of students in her school. A proposal was prepared that outlined the rationale, related research, and procedures underlying compacting, and a workshop scenario was written that included handouts, visual display materials, and simulated training activities for teachers. The proposal was reviewed by the principal and curriculum coordinator, both of whom attended the one-hour workshop. A formal evaluation questionnaire was distributed at the conclusion of the workshop, and, based on the positive reactions of almost all persons who attended this session, the district "contracted" with the teacher to conduct training with numerous other groups of teachers throughout the district. In addition to being provided with release time for each training session, the teacher was also given a stipend for each presentation.

This scenario is an excellent example of the ways in which we can provide motivation for those persons who would like to contribute to the growth of the profession. Rather than putting teachers into competition with one another about how they operate their respective classrooms, this approach is based on the ways in which persons might like to contribute to the improvement of schools, and it follows the market competition approach of rewarding only contributions that have been judged to be valuable according to external criteria. This is the dimension of our profession that we have not made available to those persons who would like to contribute in these more creative and productive ways. To be certain, making contributions at Level 2 is not for everyone. But if a variety of the types of opportunities for this kind of professionalism are available (in-service training, curriculum development, etc.), more teachers will explore vehicles that capitalize on their own strengths. And when this type of creative contribution becomes a reality and a part of the culture of the school, more teachers will view themselves as wanting to be a part of it.

A question usually raised when this suggestion is put forward to school officials is, "How are we going to pay for it?" By setting aside a portion of the staff development budget for this plan, it is conceivable that money might actually be saved over the course of time. In many cases we have spent unusually large amounts of money to employ outside consultants and big-name speakers, and we have not devoted similar resources to developing the talents of our own faculties. The approach recommended here will not only help a school district to capitalize on local professional expertise, but it will also pay off in other ways such as improved morale and the self-image of teachers, extended motivation for teachers to invest in themselves and in their profession and, most important, improved learning for students.

I created materials that we then passed out to everybody who was teaching that subject in my department. I have a personal interest in digging out information that I think may be helpful to somebody else, even if I can't use it at a particular moment.

Teacher, in Wilson, 1993

The Schoolwide Enrichment Model Network (SEMNET)

ONE OF the advantages of a school improvement process based on a unified model is that categorical components of the model can be shared among model users in an organized rather than random fashion. To facilitate this process we have developed a Schoolwide Enrichment Model Network (SEMNET) that allows teachers and administrators to share a wide variety of SEM know-how such as instructional materials, program development tips and tactics, and professional development resources. Communication vehicles include newsletters, a computer bulletin board, training institutes, video tapes, teleconferences, and a set of model-specific electronic data bases. The data bases have been developed around categorical descriptions of enrichment materials; materials that promote multicultural awareness; practitioner-friendly research reports; professional development materials; sites to visit; a regional and national consultant bank; publishing and other outlet opportunities for young people; state and national opportunities for summer programs, competitions, internships, mentorships, and special schools; and information about how and where to obtain financial assistance for higher education. Brief descriptions of several SEMNET data bases follows. Sample printouts of records from selected data bases are included in Chapter 4 and in the Resource Guide of Chapter 7.

- *The Enrichment Materials Data Base* contains the names and descriptions of books, videos, software, CD Roms, simulations, and games that can be used by practitioners or parents to enhance curricula/ home-related projects and make learning more meaningful for school-aged youths. For user convenience, the enrichment materials can be sorted by additional categories, including: content area, grade level, preparation time, grouping (i.e., whole class, small group or individual) or thinking skill (i.e., Cognitive and Affective Training, Using Advanced Research Skills and Reference Materials, Developing Written, Oral and Visual Communication Skills, Learning-How-to-Learn, and Methodological Training).

From crude cave drawings to instant global communication by satellite and computer, what has distinguished humans from all other species is their ability to share information and ideas with one another.

Author Unknown

- *The Fairs, Competitions, and Publishing Outlets Data Base* provides members with the names and descriptions of publishing opportunities that can be used to encourage creativity and real products among students. Members may request that information from this data base be sorted according to: the submission format (i.e., essay, short story, poem, drawing, play, poster, photograph, experiment), content area, grade level, grouping strategy, and the existence or non-existence of an entry fee.

- Exemplary Type III projects, self-selected authentic student investigations, are the subject of the *Type IIIs Data Base* and will provide practitioners with ideas for jump-starting similar projects among their students. Practitioners will receive the name of the Type III, the content area of the investigation, as well as the triggering "A-HA!," the resources used, the methodological training provided, the services provided by the resource person and a listing of the difficulties encountered by the student and facilitator.

All schools enrolled in SEMNET are provided with blank entry forms for each data base. New material from practitioners and information gathered by the SEMNET manager are entered regularly into the data bases so that periodic updates can be made available to network members. Newsletters and the electronic bulletin board will allow network members to exchange information, to share resources, and to arrange for contacts among students who are pursuing similar research interests.

Parent Orientation, Training, and Involvement

A GROWING body of literature points out the crucial role that parents need to play in their children's education. Accordingly, we have developed and acquired materials and procedures that promote the parental advocacy and support system necessary for improved cooperation between home and school. Print and audio-visual materials have been developed that provide orientation for parents about

SEMNET DATABASES

- *Assessment*

- *Electronic Learning*

- *Enrichment Materials*

- *Fairs, Competitions and Publishing Outlets*

- *Parenting*

- *Restructuring*

- *Satellite Distance Learning*

- *School and University Partnerships*

- *Site Visit Data Base*

- *Type IIIs*

The best inheritance that parents can give their children is a few minutes of their time each day.

Ancient Chinese proverb

My mother told me if I wanted to be a soldier, I would become a general; If I wanted to be a monk, I would become Pope; I wanted to be an artist, so I became Picasso.

SEM concepts such as curriculum compacting, the role of interest and effort in learning, the overall goals and components of the model, and ways in which parents can become involved in their own children's work as well as in various aspects of the enrichment program in general. Vehicles such as the *Community Talent Miner* (Renzulli & Reis, 1985) are designed to query parents about special areas of expertise, cultural experiences, and know-how that can serve as enrichment resources to the school. Guidebooks and audio-visual material have been identified that provide parental training in such diverse topics as homework assistance, family television viewing, and the location of financial support for higher education. Some of these resources are listed in the Resource Guide at the end of this section, and a more extensive collection is available in the resource data bases that have been developed to support the Schoolwide Enrichment Model.

Our goal in this organizational component is to integrate parents and other community resources into the educational program rather than simply using parents for "around-the-edges" busy work. Improved communication with parents is the key to making better connections between the home and school cultures, but it is also necessary to have an organizational plan for building the parent component of the model. The plan that we have developed focuses on the following three dimensions of parent involvement: parent orientation about schoolwide enrichment and roles that parents can play in decision making processes that affect their children's education, direct involvement with their children at home, and involvement in enrichment activities at school. This plan is based on parent involvement programs that have proven to be successful in various types of schools around the country.

One such plan is James Comer's model (1988, 1990), developed specifically to help parents and teachers in inner-city schools work together to overcome barriers created by rigid school structures and limited cooperation between and among parents, schools, and other social service agencies and specialists. Because poor minority children from nonmainstream families often feel disconnected from schools, Comer emphasized psychological development and interpersonal factors rather than traditional reform initiatives which tend to favor curriculum and instruction. The program supports children's learning and development by building bonds among children, parents, and school personnel. Social gatherings help to promote better relations between parents and staff, and life-skill training programs for students help them to develop mainstream social skills for interacting with peers and adults.

The center of Comer's plan is a core management team for each school that includes community-elected parents and teachers, the principal, a mental-health specialist, and a member of the classified support staff. The principal has ultimate authority, but consensus is encouraged and the focus is on problem solving rather than accusing and blaming others for past problems. Each school also has an intervention team consisting of a teacher, psychologist, and social worker. The team identifies patterns of troublesome behavior in individual students, and intervention strategies are based on total team input that takes into consideration the personal and social needs of the developing child as well as academic needs. Although initial problems and resistance to this innovative plan were experienced in the early stages of implementation, parents and staff realized the benefits of solving school problems by overcoming the misalignment between home and school, and positive results began to emerge. Follow-up studies (Comer, 1988) of schools using Comer's model showed that participating schools improved in achievement and attendance, and there was a decrease in the incidence of behavior problems.

A five-state study conducted by the Southwest Educational Development Laboratory used key informants, site visits, and evaluation questionnaires to examine factors that contributed to successful programs of parent involvement. "The programs identified as 'promising' featured several types of parent involvement and included many roles for parents: audience, home tutor, program supporter, co-learner, advocate and decision maker" (Williams & Chavkin, 1989, p. 18). Some of the programs were affiliated with national coalitions such as the National School Volunteer Program, and others were described as small, "homegrown" efforts. Regardless of size and affiliation, however, all of the promising programs had the following seven essential elements:

1. Written policies that legitimize parent involvement and frame the context for program activities;
2. Administrative support in the form of funds, resources (materials, meeting space, duplication and communication equipment), and designated people to carry out program efforts;

DATELINE: CONNECTICUT

Frustrations on the Board

As a newly elected representative to my town's board of education, I received a letter of "deepest personal condolences" from a colleague. Now I know why....

- *I am caught between the ever increasing number of state mandates and ever diminishing funding. This would be tolerable if Congress or any elected body determined that the benefits of its mandated programs were worth the expense, but no such evaluation is made. Congress and the state have abrogated their responsibility by refusing to make hard choices. They won't and local officials can't.*

- *In the critical matter of teacher performance, school boards are restricted statutorily by the state and contractually by the teachers' union.*

- *Another problem is the decreasing ability of the schools to discipline. Unlike private schools, which can expel those who don't conform, the public system must take everyone....*

It's not the inordinate hours nor the lack of public appreciation, but the inability to effect change that creates the overwhelming frustration often felt by board members and the lack of desire to serve a system badly in need of change.

Johanne Asslin Presser, 1993 Reprinted with permission of the author and **Newsweek** *magazine*

> *[O]ne of the biggest barriers blocking the development of successful [parent involvement] programs is that groups that must work together have different understandings of the concept. Administrators often equate parental involvement with fund raising or with participation on school advisory groups. Teachers think of parent involvement as sending children to school on time, attending parent/ teacher conferences, helping with homework, and responding to teacher requests. Parents want to be kept better informed about their children's progress, and would like to be welcomed openly at school and in the classroom.*
>
> *Janet Chrispeels, 1991*

3. Ongoing training for the development of parenting skills, and training on skills for teacher and parent cooperation;
4. A "partnership approach" to joint planning, goal setting, defining roles, setting school standards, developing instructional and school support efforts, and program assessment;
5. Two-way communication that allowed parents to feel comfortable coming to school, sharing ideas, and voicing concerns;
6. Networking with other schools with parent involvement initiatives in order to share information, resources, and technical expertise; and
7. Regular (formative) evaluation activities at key stages so that modifications and revisions can be made when needed rather than waiting until the end of the year (Williams & Chavkin, 1989, pp. 18-20).

Parent Involvement in Decision Making

Although everyone talks about parent involvement in decision making, very little guidance exist in the literature about specific procedures for promoting this kind of involvement; to be very frank, the education establishment has paid only lip service to opening doors to important decision making on the parts of parents. Boards of education are *supposed* to be major policy making bodies, but in reality, most of the decisions they make are carefully crafted and steered within limited boundaries set by external regulations and district administrators. Persons in positions of power and authority at state and district levels and in collective bargaining units determine almost all of what happens in today's classrooms. It is not our intent to minimize the roles that these forces should play in the overall education of young people; however, if we are sincere about parent involvement, then it is necessary to create honest vehicles for parental participation in decision making as well as functionary activities. And, just as parents must learn about the techniques and responsibilities for decision making, so also must professional educators learn the know-how of sharing power with non-professional groups and individuals.

There is no "easy formula" for creating a more viable role for parents in school decision making, but some of the materials listed in the Resource Guide at the end of this chapter are designed to provide guidance for both parents and professional educators in the delicate task of opening up the school to a more meaningful role for parents. These materials include books and articles by leaders at the national, state and local level who are creating new partnerships between schools and families.

The best efforts to improve our schools will not be maximally effective unless parents become more directly involved in their children's education. We are not recommending that parents fulfill the role of teacher-at-home, nor do we expect parents to master the subject matter that their children are expected to learn. Parents can, however, provide the physical environment and psychological support at home that is necessary for improved school performance. Obvious support activities such as a fixed time and place to study, a daily routine that ensures both the completion of homework and a parental review of each day's assignments, periodic visits to school, and becoming acquainted with teachers are far less common in our society than they were a century ago. In order to assist parents in taking a more active part in their children's education, the school must also take a more active role in providing specific services and resources for parents. Some of these resources are listed in the Resource Guide, and a SEMNET data base will provide a continuous update of new materials as they become available.

A Democratic School Management Plan

NATIONAL, STATE, and local concerns for school improvement, perhaps for the first time in the history of education, have opened the door to more democratic school governance procedures. Everyone who has a stake in effective schools realizes that practical strategies for attracting, organizing, and making the best use of human resources are, without question, the hallmark of successful organizations. Many of these strategies originated in the private sector and in overseas corporations, but they are rapidly being embraced by North American schools. Although we have not adopted a single model for school management, a set of criteria for democratic management has been developed (see Goal 5), and we will recommend the essential components of a plan for initiating a democratic school management process.

The Seven Cs of School Change

The essence of this plan is built around what we will call the Seven Cs of School Change, and the use of these Cs by a

Three ways the minority community can encourage academic striving among its children:

1. *Teach children to separate attitudes and behaviors that lead to academic success from attitudes and behaviors that lead to a loss of academic identity....*
2. *Provide children with concrete evidence that its members value academic success.*
3. *Teach children to accept responsibility for their school adjustment and performance.*

John Ogbu, 1992

Goal 5 of the Schoolwide Enrichment Model

To implement a democratic school governance procedure that includes appropriate decision-making opportunities for students, parents, teachers, and administrators.

The Seven Cs of School Change

- *Consensus*
- *Compromise*
- *Communication*
- *Collegiality*
- *Commitment*
- *Creativity*
- *Courage*

---

school governing council. The council should consist of the principal, an equal number of elected teachers and parents, an appointed member from the special service staff (e.g., school psychologist, social worker, nurse), and an appointed member of the non-professional staff (e.g., custodian, security guard, cafeteria worker). The principal should chair the council and be responsible for setting up a regularly scheduled meeting and soliciting agenda items from all staff members and parents of students in the school. There also may be times when agenda items are solicited from students or members of the community at large. The first, and perhaps most important C for the council to consider is *consensus*. The difficult task of sharing power and decision making must begin with a willingness to establish a governance group in each school that honors the opinions of all members of the council. A second, but related C is *compromise*. Each group (teachers, parents, administrators) brings "to the table" its own agenda and accumulated history of grievances that it is prone to blame on one or more of the other groups. Many school improvement initiatives have faltered or become ineffective because ground rules were not established to ensure consensus and compromise at the very outset of the governance process. One of the first decisions that the council should make is whether or not it should obtain professional assistance in learning how to conduct a democratic governance process that is based on consensus and compromise. Suggestions for where this kind of assistance can be obtained are listed in the Resource Guide at the end of this chapter.

The third C is *communication*. All council meetings should be open to the staff and public, and a summary of the minutes of meetings should be included in a regularly published newsletter. A budget for communication, reproduction, and distribution services should be made available to the council, and a council work space should be provided so that parents feel they have a home base when they come to the school. Each newsletter should have a clip-and-mail coupon that encourages readers to react to actions by the council and to make suggestions about issues or services that readers would like the council to consider. The fourth C, *collegiality*, should help define the larger mission of the council. This mission transcends the traditional constituencies of school organizations (i.e., parents representing parents, teachers representing teachers, etc.). Collegiality means that members of the council are tied together in the larger mission of working together to make a difference in the lives of students. Colleagues are persons who talk with one another and collaborate in order to better serve the interests of their common clients. Far too many school organizations and legislative bodies have failed to make significant and lasting changes because members have viewed themselves as representatives of vested interest peer groups rather than participants who share a common vision. All council activities should address the questions, "Is this good for our students?" or" Is this good for our school?" rather than questions relating to the satisfaction of one's fellow teachers, parents, or administrators. Admittedly, this is a difficult transition for any leadership group to make; however, all of the adults associated with a school should know beforehand that the council will have this kind of orientation.

The fifth and sixth Cs are *commitment* and *creativity.* Involvement on a school council that is going to accomplish anything important requires a commitment of time and energy that goes beyond the time spent in meetings. Background reading, meetings with subgroups, attendance at leadership training activities, preparing material for distribution to others, writing proposals, and working one-on-one with reluctant individuals are all commitments of time that persons should be willing to make if they choose to serve on a school council. We all have our favorite jokes about useless committees and time wasted in committee meetings. And we are all familiar with people who are good talkers "at the table" but who do little or nothing between meetings! The most effective meetings are those that draw upon activity that has taken place in preparation for the meeting.

Persons who become involved in school councils should also be willing to explore ways of expanding their own creative ability. One of the main reasons that schools haven't changed is because we have tried to address present-day school concerns and problems with endless variations of the same solutions. The quotation by Einstein at the beginning of this book reminds us that, "Problems cannot be solved at the same level of consciousness that created them." As schools have become more structured and subjected to an endless proliferation of regulations, we have used these very structures and regulations as defenses against change. "We can't change the schedule because it won't meet state requirements." "The teachers' union will never let you have a staff development session that is not over by 4:20." "Who will pay the custodians if we have a Saturday morning enrichment program?" "If it doesn't cover one of the 'outcomes' on the list, the director of

There's no such thing as the perfect solution. Every solution, no matter how good, creates new problems.

Author Unknown

You miss 100 percent of the shots you never take.

Wayne Gretsky, 1991

curriculum will never buy it." None of the above is an insurmountable problem; however, we often *act* as if they are as inevitable and omnipresent as the phases of the moon! The result has been that we tinker with the *status quo* rather than use our imaginations to change it.

In the first chapter mention was made of Edward de Bono's (1985) planned strategy for improving the efficiency of meetings (see the Resource Guide at the end of this chapter). De Bono's plan is also built around his work in the area of creativity training. We recommend that the school council consider engaging in some type of systematic creativity training such as de Bono's Six Thinking Hats model, or other approaches that are listed in the Resource Guide at the end of this section. It would be unthinkable to put together a talent development program for students without a creative thinking and problem solving component; and we believe that such a component is equally important for adults who are responsible for both program development and for overcoming the traditional roadblocks that have stood in the way of most efforts to improve schools.

The last C in our Seven Cs of School Improvement is *courage*. The activities described above, and, indeed, throughout this book, are not radical or revolutionary; but they do require that some people have the courage to examine what is widely recognized as one of the most intransigent and bureaucratized public service agencies in our society. Radical changes have taken place in our society during the last quarter of the twentieth century. The emergence of a global economy and the transfer of manufacturing jobs to other nations, the development of sophisticated communication systems and information technologies, the rise of feminism, multiculturalism, and concerns for planetary ecosystems have all played a part in bringing about massive cultural changes. As this trend accelerates, the ways that we modify our education system become one of the most crucial factors in determining whether schools will play a role in shaping society or whether they will become obsolete. It is not easy to question the basic assumptions that have guided educational thought or to rethink what has generally been a system operating on automatic pilot for decades, if not centuries. If we are to change the system, even through a gentle and evolutionary process, persons at all levels of involvement will need to summon up the courage to think and act in ways that may be discomforting.

Creating More Effective Leadership and Management Techniques

School leadership and management are the "hottest" new topics to emerge from present efforts to restructure schools. Buzz words about structural changes such as teacher empowerment, total quality management, site-based management, and transformational leadership jump off the pages of ream after ream of educational publications, and leadership training has become the most recent cottage industry in a field that is prone to throwing words at problems rather than substantial actions. The critical importance of leadership and management is indisputable, but if real and lasting change is to take place, it is necessary to devise specific and practical ways of implementing the structural changes that are being popularized in the exploding school improvement literature. In spite of this literature, most schools seem to operate in much the same way they have operated over the past several decades. As Murphy (1991) has pointed out:

> The evidence accumulated so far suggests that there are insufficient data to link the structural components of restructuring with student learning outcomes. In many ways, this should not be surprising. To begin with, efforts at reorganization—despite the prevailing rhetoric—often have more to do with politics than with greater efficiency and enhanced quality....Structural changes in and of themselves never have and never will predict organizational success, i.e., student learning in this case....Instead of embracing structural change that may or may not enhance student learning, schools should look behind classroom doors and determine factors that contribute to the kinds of interactions between students and teachers that promote achievement. (Murphy, 1991, pp. 76-77)

With so much material about educational leadership and management "out there," and with conflicting and unsubstantiated approaches to contend with, it is difficult to draw any firm conclusions from what has become a mindboggling mountain of recommendations. To be certain, clichés, and formulas, and lists of "principles" abound; there is, indeed, a good deal of leadership craft that can be learned by selecting carefully from among the rapidly growing literature on leadership and school management. Some of

In the final analysis, someone, a person or two in formal or informal leadership roles, has to step forward, take the risk, and take the criticism that inevitably follows the initiation of the kind of change we envision.

Martin Maehr, in National Center for School Leadership, 1993

this literature that we have found to be particularly helpful is listed in the Resource Guide at the end of this chapter. We will not attempt to reinvent this literature, nor give new names to concepts or practices that are already defined in various books, articles, and reports. We will, however, describe three major considerations that must be addressed when examining present and possible future leadership activities necessary for the successful operation of an SEM program.

Focus on the Act of Learning

The first consideration is that all leadership activities must be directly related to the act of learning. A focus on the act of learning, which, along with the goals discussed in Chapter 2, is the centerpiece of the SEM. Adoption of this model means that a majority of the school community has reached consensus on a common purpose and a shared vision about learning. Every decision should be examined by asking: How will this affect what happens in the interaction that takes place between and among learners, teachers, and curriculum? Conventions such as traditional scheduling, budgeting, single textbook adoption, school hours, large scale testing, grading policies, tenure rules, decisions about staff development, and collective bargaining agreements should be subjected to the act-of-learning question rather than administrative expedience or mere convenience. Even state regulations should be questioned, and waivers should be sought if they impinge upon a school's act-of-learning mission. As the responsibility for improved student performance is moved closer to classrooms where actual learning takes place, power and authority should also be moved down the bureaucratic pipeline into the hands of those responsible for producing agreed-upon results. Leadership training in the use of authority must be provided, just as training should be provided to those persons who must learn how to share authority and power with others. All of the Seven Cs of school change mentioned above will be required to bring about the evolution of shared decision making necessary to focus on learning rather than organizational expediency, but certainly the courage to venture into uncharted waters will be an essential ingredient.

Your School and the Mineral Metaphor

A second consideration is a school's "personality" and the ways in which a school collectively views itself. One of the best ways to begin a systemic improvement process is for members of the school's nuclear family to "get a fix" on the

It is today that we must create the world of the future.

Eleanor Roosevelt

**Goal 2
of the Schoolwide
Enrichment Model**

To improve the academic performance of all students by engaging them in meaningful and enjoyable learning.

school's desire for change versus the desire to create the appearance of change. Sternberg (in press) has studied the modifiability of organizations within varying contexts; and using individual schools as a unit of analysis for examining change potential, he developed a mineral metaphor to describe alternative school contexts. A summary of characteristics for eight types of schools and their potential for modifiability is presented in Table 2. Although the probability for change varies from one "mineral" school type to another, we believe that an honest appraisal of predominant characteristics is a necessary starting point for school improvement.

There are two almost pathological school syndromes that Sternberg's metaphor should cause us to reflect upon. The first has to do with adopting any school improvement plan based on ideas that originated outside the school. Schools with high self-esteem but low desire for actual change feel that they will "lose face" if the idea isn't their own; and heaven

Table 2

A theory of contextual modifiability

Description	Desire for Actual Change	Desire for Appearance of Change	Self-Esteem	Significant Modifiability	Surface Deep Modifiability
Rusted Iron	L	L	L	L	L
Granite	L	L	H	L	L
Amber (with Internal Insects)	L	H	L	L	ML
Opal	L	H	H	L	ML
Cubic Zirconium	H	L	L	L	ML
Slightly Imperfect (SI) Diamond	H	L	H	ML	MH
Lead	H	H	L	ML	MH
Diamond in the Rough	H	H	H	H	H

L = Low   M = Medium   H = High

[W]e need to shift our thinking about what it means to be a strong superintendent or principal. We need to develop some gentler, more feminine images of leadership to accompany our tough masculine images....[S]uperintendents need to pay more attention to the unheroic dimensions of leadership if they are to promote local autonomy and professionalism. Superintendents and principals must not only have personal vision, but they must also work with others to develop shared vision and to find the common ground; they must not only have answers, but also ask the right questions, they must not only persuade, but also listen carefully and consult widely before making decisions; they must not only wield power, but also depend on others and develop caring relationships; they must not only exercise leadership, but also nurture the development of leadership throughout the school district. In this view, the real heroes are not the highly visible superintendents at the top, but the less visible professionals and parents throughout the system who work directly with students.

J. T. Murphy, 1989

forbid that they should follow in the footsteps of another school, regardless of how effective that school may be. This syndrome results in competition between schools to come up with something different, even if what they come up with is of questionable value. In most cases, this kind of one-upmanship competition is mainly for "show," or what Sternberg describes as a desire for the *appearance* of change.

The second pathological syndrome is usually found in schools that have both low and high self-esteem, but that also have a low desire for actual change. In low self-esteem schools it might best be described as the "It-Won't-Work-Here" syndrome. In high self-esteem schools it is manifested in the "We're-Already-Doing-That" syndrome. In both cases, the hidden message to persons who want to bring a plan for change to the attention of the school's nuclear family is, "Keep your ideas to yourself!" Fear of "looking bad" by calling attention to possible modifications in the *status quo* has caused more than one individual or group to actually conceal, misrepresent, or even subvert the efforts of persons who want to examine a school improvement process.

The personalities of entire schools do not change easily; we would be fooling ourselves if we thought than any model or plan for school improvement could overcome the accumulated history that results in the schools portrayed in the mineral metaphor. It is, however, worthwhile for schools to examine themselves within the context of a metaphor such as the one provided by Sternberg. Even if the probability for real change is low, an honest appraisal of a school's personality and level of self-esteem will at least place the issue about readiness for change on the table. A confrontation with a difficult problem or issue is always the first step toward alternative courses of action, and, therefore, we recommend that all schools take the time to examine the kind of mineral they resemble.

What Happens When Democratic Management Is Absent?

The third leadership consideration necessary for implementing the SEM (or any other model, for that matter) addresses two issues that everyone "knows about," but that are seldom covered in polite conversation or the written material about school improvement. These issues are the personalities of individuals, especially those in positions of power and authority, and the politics of self-protection, job enhancement, or the exercise of power for egotistic (or even pathological) reasons. Anyone who has worked in schools or other bureaucracies knows that competence, initiative, creativity, service to clients, and the stated goals of the organization are not always the criteria upon which decisions are made and resources allocated. Almost everyone can add her or his own "horror story" to the list of questionable practices and decisions that have been made because politics and personalities have overshadowed actions that are in the best interest of students. One of the best enrichment programs we have ever observed was eliminated almost overnight when a new assistant superintendent arbitrarily decided to cut the program from the budget. A subsequent investigation by interested teachers and parents revealed that the assistant superintendent harbored a grudge against the program director dating back to the time when they were both students in high school!

Unfortunately, personalities and the politics of self-protection and enhancement will always be present in organizations; they are, unquestionably, the most complex variables in the change process. Equally unfortunate is the sad but true reality that even the most noble goals and worthwhile practices don't change personalities. It is for this reason that a democratic governance process is necessary. Programs that earn their merit following a reasonable experimental period should be protected from capricious and arbitrary decisions at the policy level. The essence of a democratic system of governance is that no single individual can circumvent the interests of the majority or the reasoned interests of a minority not fairly represented in governing bodies. And the role of policy in an organization is to "take a stand" on matters of importance so that they are not subject to the whim or will of persons with temporary influence or an idiosyncratic axe to grind. Policies should be enacted only after considered study, dialogue, and debate, and final policy should be adopted only following experimental or pilot periods during which changes in practice are field tested and evaluated.

Although democratic management is a goal that will help create the motivation and commitment necessary for bringing about *any* change in our schools, we would be less than realistic if we assumed this goal could be achieved in all schools and districts. Personalities, politics, and vested interests are not stronger than good ideas, but they have a way of gaining control of power over the decision making process that influences so much of what happens in our schools

"As its name implies, the end run strategy is designed to go around a road block; and more than anything, it requires courage on the parts of persons who are advocating a school improvement model."

"[This] example does point out that when persons in positions of authority fail to be responsive to the sincere interests of their constituents, there is recourse to higher authority."

and classrooms. What happens when a majority of the school's nuclear family wants to implement the SEM, but they come up against a "road block" of an authority person(s) unwilling to support the plan? It is at this point that only two alternatives are available to scrapping the plan and returning to business as usual. The first alternative is "friendly persuasion." We may need to redouble efforts to inform and influence authority figures about the rationale, feasibility, and advantages of pursuing a model that has the support of a significant majority of persons in the nuclear family. This is the best alternative because everything will operate more effectively and harmoniously if persons in positions of authority are at least willing to accept the plan on an experimental basis for a specified period of time.

The second alternative, called "the end run strategy," is recommended *only* when all efforts to achieve support through the Seven Cs of school change have failed. As its name implies, the end run strategy is designed to go around a road block; more than anything, it requires courage on the parts of persons who are advocating a school improvement model. We will illustrate the end run strategy by presenting an actual case study that involved a dictatorial and recalcitrant school superintendent whom we will call Moe Steel. Moe can best be described as a clever, street smart, and very articulate administrator who surrounded himself with "yes men," and who managed to keep a fairly sophisticated school board under his control by feeding them contemporary jargon and educational double-talk. Many board and community members respected Moe because he ran a "tight ship," kept school costs down and problems contained, and could tell you at a moment's notice enrollment projections, the basket ball team's record, and the best vendors from whom to buy toilet tissue! Moe said that any changes in "his schools" would be based only on his beliefs, which were essentially a regimented, one-size-fits-all curriculum. He defended his beliefs by talking about "uniform standards," "curriculum alignment," and other flavor-of-the-month terms that he used to justify the *status quo*.

A group of parents and teachers in the district expressed an interest in the SEM, and a building principal said that she would be interested in piloting the model in her school. But because they feared recriminations, the teachers and principal said that they wanted to keep a "low profile" until Moe gave permission for the plan to proceed. Moe, of course, stopped the plan dead in its tracks, using every bureaucratic ploy in his bag of tricks. At this point, the parents and two courageous teachers approached a school board member, and began to provide him with information about the SEM. The board member enthusiastically supported the plan and assumed the role of champion[2] of the group. Following an effective presentation to the board that was arranged by the supportive board member, it looked as though there was enough support to gain a favorable vote for a pilot SEM program. When Moe sensed that the vote might go against him, he invoked one of his favorite ploys: "Let's do a study to see if we really need this program!"

The board followed Moe's advice, and a consultant was retained to conduct a needs assessment study. Two local newspapers reported the story, and up to this point, everyone involved received favorable comments from the press. The newspaper stories also resulted in more parent and teacher support for suggested changes in the school program. Although it was clear that the study was initiated by the board rather than the administration, Moe immediately began to conspire so that he could steer and micro-manage the study. Fortunately, the consultant in charge of the study did not buckle under to Moe's demands and intimidation tactics, but Moe used his position to sabotage the study and intimidate school personnel. He would not allow questionnaires to be distributed unless he edited them, and he would not allow teachers to be interviewed unless administrators were present. These activities were reported by the consultant at a subsequent board meeting, and this time both the board and the press questioned Moe's actions. A reprimand was issued, the study was completed without additional interference, and the SEM was eventually implemented at a number of schools in the district. A year later, Moe Steel moved on to a new job.

We do not consider this case history of an end run strategy to be a "success story." Many people were caught in the cross fire and the intrigue that resulted from differences of opinion which could have been negotiated and minimized through communication and compromise. But the example does point out that when persons in positions of authority fail to be responsive to the sincere interests of their constituents, there is recourse to higher authority. If a democratic management plan had been in place prior to the events described above, a good deal of unpleasantness and wasted energy would have been avoided, and that would have been the best success story of all!

First, I cannot stress enough that personal purpose and vision are the starting agenda. It comes from within, it gives meaning to work, and it exists independent of the particular organization....Second, personal vision in teaching is often too implicit and dormant....Teachers should be pursuing moral purpose with greater and greater skill, conceptualizing their role on a higher plane than they currently do. Third, once it gets going, personal purpose is not as private as it sounds. Especially in moral occupations like teaching, the more one takes the risk to express personal purpose, the more kindred spirits one will find.

Michael Fullan, 1993

Goal 1
of the Schoolwide
Enrichment Model

To develop the talent potentials of young people by (a) systematically assessing their strengths, (b) by providing enrichment opportunities and resources to develop their strengths, and (c) using a flexible approach to curricular differentiation and the use of school time.

Goal 2
of the Schoolwide
Enrichment Model

To improve the academic performance of all students in all areas of the regular curriculum and to blend into the standard curriculum activities and will engage students in meaningful and enjoyable learning.

Concluding Thoughts

The issues raised in the case history of Moe Steel are a subset of issues related to democratic school governance. They are also tied to the professionalism objectives of SEM: the need to promote continuous, reflective growth among the members of the nuclear school family and the need to create a community of learners. Furthermore, these goals are related to the first two goals of this plan for school improvement: enhancing the creative productivity and achievement levels of students (see the sidebar). Specifically, systematic reform begins when all members of the school family are treated as equal partners pursuing a common mission. The work among the equal partners must be based on the premise that all involved strive for continuous improvement, actively seek job-related knowledge, and share, though collaboration, their experiences and expertise. When members of the nuclear school family learn to trust and respect each other, encourage and challenge one another to stimulate optimal performance, share a common vision and choose to work together, educational opportunities for students will improve. And when educational opportunities for students improve, talent development for all students becomes a realistic goal. Roland Barth (1990) captured the essence of the meaning of collaboration when he wrote: "The relationships among the adults in schools are the basis, the precondition, the *sine qua non* that allow, energize, and sustain all other attempts at school improvement. Unless adults talk with one another, observe one another, and help one another, very little will change" (p. 32).

With collaboration as both a goal and a process, the nuclear school family can initiate long-sought, systemic reforms by freeing and allocating school time to the two essential elements discussed in this realistic plan for school improvement: teachers and students. Teachers need time to collectively recreate a vision of schools as places for talent development and time to plan learning activities that will engage, and re-engage, students. Students need time within the framework of enrichment clusters to discover that they can be producers of knowledge by adopting the role of the first-hand inquirer. By beginning with these steps, this plan for talent development focuses on those aspects of learning and development over which the schools have the most control, thereby providing the nuclear school family with the highest probability of achieving success.

In closing, we acknowledge the limitations that confront systemic school reform. Society's faith in the capacity of the nation's schools to improve the conditions of people, individually and collectively, is misplaced hope. Changing family structures, de facto segregation, insufferable housing conditions, poor nutrition and health care, limited employment and economic opportunities, and unfair treatment of women and minorities are all factors that contribute to inferior schools. We believe, therefore, that other institutions in society must share in the responsibility for addressing the multi-faceted problem of developing the talent of all children. At the same time, we believe also that schools can do something now by concentrating on improving the quality of experiences for nuclear school family members provided between the opening and closing bells of the school day, and by working with parents on matters that affect student performance in school. Schools may not be powerful enough to restructure society, but they do have the potential to be powerful forces in the lives of young people.

---

[1] It is interesting to note that studies of college graduates found that extracurricular activities were more consequential in determining adult accomplishments than were traditional academic predictors, including test scores, high school grades and college grades (Munday & Davis, 1974).

[2] Conventional wisdom in politics says that action within a decision making body, especially if the action is related to changes in the *status quo*, is much more likely to take place if one or more persons become "champions" of a particular cause or action.

This Bridge

This bridge will only take
you halfway there
To those mysterious lands you
long to see:
Through Gypsy camps and
swirling Arab fairs
And moonlit woods where
unicorns run free.
So come and walk awhile
with me and share
The twisting trails and
wondrous worlds I've known.
But this bridge will only take
you halfway there–
The last few steps you'll have
to take alone.

Shel Silverstein
A Light in the Attic, *1981*

Resource Guide

THIS RESOURCE guide provides lists of exemplary materials related to school governance and management and contains six sections: Educational Change, Team Building and Collaboration, Staff Development, the Schoolwide Enrichment Model, Parent and School Partnerships, and School Governance. The prices listed reflect the prices at the time of writing.

Educational Change
Books
Title: *Change Forces in Education*
Author: Fullan, M.
Description: In his latest book, Fullan proposes that we are at the edge of a quantum leap—a paradigm breakthrough—in the way we think about and act in relation to change. He proposes eight lessons which, if learned, can harness the change forces through a system of checks and balances. Based upon the conviction that people change systems, not vice versa, Fullan argues that pre-service and in-service are vehicles for inspiring teachers to become moral change agents.
Publisher: The Falmer Press. Price: $24.50.

Title: *The Copernican Plan: Restructuring the American High School*
Author: Carroll, J. M.
Description: Carroll's thinking is very specific and imaginative about restructuring secondary schools. He restructures the way schools use time through altering the school schedule, making smaller classes, focusing on individualized learning and changing teaching methods.
Publisher: The Regional Laboratory for Educational Improvement of the Northeast and Islands. Price: $14.95.

Title: *The Fifth Discipline: The Art and Practice of the Learning Organization*
Author: Senge, P. M.
Description: Senge is concerned with building learning organizations that can overcome obstacles and recognize new opportunities. He argues that five disciplines (vital human dimensions) will distinguish learning organizations from the more traditional controlling organizations: systems thinking, personal mastery, mental models, building shared vision, and

team learning. Although Senge's book is philosophical and his work has been with corporations, *The Fifth Discipline* has value for educators and school communities. If schools are going to make the changes which many agree are necessary, they will have to become more like the learning organizations Senge describes.
Publisher: Doubleday/Currency. Price: $25.00.

Title: *Making School Reform Happen*
Author: Bullard, P., & Taylor, B. O.
Description: Unlike other books that talk about the change process, this book recounts personal stories about those who played major roles in reforming their schools with the assistance of The National Center for Effective Schools. Teachers, principals, and parents talk about how the change process began, the turmoil that changes created, and the triumphant successes which resulted. Most impressive are the narratives which chronicle how the change process in each school or district began; the common thread among the vignettes is one person with extraordinary courage and commitment.
Publisher: Allyn and Bacon. Price: $24.95.

Title: *Restructuring Schools: Capturing and Assessing the Phenomenon*
Author: Murphy, J. T.
Description: The purpose of Murphy's book is to chronicle what has been learned about restructuring. The first two chapters of the book review the rationale for restructuring and develop a model for this process that is explored in later chapters. Chapters 3-5 examine the major components of educational restructuring: work redesign, organization and governance structures and the core technology of schools. Murphy's final chapter explores factors which will need to be addressed if restructuring is to be successful in schools.
Publisher: Teachers College Press. Price: $16.95.

Articles

Title: Finding the Way: Structure, Time, and Culture In School Improvement
Author: Donahoe, T.
Abstract: This article describes Donahoe's reflections after four-years involvement in restructuring schools. He is struck by the failure of those involved with changing educational institutions and concludes that all attempts have been "fatal

half-measures." The remainder of the article examines three critical factors which must change to accommodate school reforms: school organization, the structure of time, and school culture. The author describes strategies, implemented in California school districts, to change the way faculties' and students' time is utilized to facilitate educational change.
Journal: *Phi Delta Kappan, 75*(4), pp. 298-305.

Title: The Time Dilemma in School Restructuring
Author: Watts, G. D., & Castle, S.
Abstract: The authors of this article describe what schools involved in restructuring have done to reconceptualize time. They categorize solutions into five strategies: freed-up time, restructured or rescheduled time, common time, better-used time, and prescribed time. The authors conclude with several important considerations for those who plan on dealing with the issue of school time.
Journal: *Phi Delta Kappan, 75*(4), pp. 306-310.

Title: Unlocking the Lockstep High School Schedule
Author: Canady, R. L., & Rettig, M. D.
Abstract: The high school schedule is the focus of this article on restructuring school time. Canady and Rettig propose three plans, the 75-75-30 plan, the alternate-day block plan, and the combined plan. Advantages of the plans are considered.
Journal: *Phi Delta Kappan, 75*(4), pp. 310-314.

Instruments
Concerns Based Adoption Model (CBAM)
Author: Hord, S. H., Rutherford, W. L., Huling-Austin, L., & Hall, G. E.
Age level: Adult
Purpose: Assesses teachers' attitudes toward educational innovation
Description: CBAM is a collection of three diagnostic tools, Stages of Concern Questionnaire (SoCQ), Levels of Use, and Innovation Configuration, which provide information regarding how teachers feel about an innovation. The SoCQ assesses 7 distinct concerns teachers may have when they implement a new practice: awareness, information, personal, management, consequence, collaboration and refocusing.
Publisher: Southwest Educational Development Laboratory 211 East Seventh Street, Austin, TX 78701, (512) 476-6861.

Taking Charge of Change is An ASCD yearbook publication which describes CBAM at some length.
Association for Supervision and Curriculum Development
1250 N. Pitt Street
Alexandria, VA 22314-1403
(703) 549-9110
Price: $13.95.

Organizations Concerned With Restructuring
The National Center for Effective Schools

The National Center for Effective Schools is a grant-funded organization housed within the School of Education at the University of Wisconsin-Madison, and its mission is to assist all students receive a high-quality education. The Center's goals are threefold: (1) to empower school leaders to implement and sustain school improvement, (2) to facilitate educators' use of computer software so that information related to learning and student progress is available at the school and/or classroom level, and (3) to disseminate publications about cutting-edge reforms.

Current research practices are highlighted in the Center's quarterly, *Focus in Change* and its companion, *Research in the Classroom*. For more information: National Center for Effective Schools, 1025 West Johnson Street, Suite 685, Madison, WI 53706, (608) 263-4730

Resource Center for Redesigning Education

Founded in April, 1993, the Resource Center for Redesigning Education has two goals: to facilitate a rethinking of the role of schooling in the postindustrial society and to encourage dialogue among educators to provide a more thorough understanding of learner-centered education. The Center produces a resource catalog featuring books and videos on innovative approaches to elementary and secondary education and plans to provide workshops and retreats to facilitate educational dialogue. For more information: Great Ideas in Education, P.O. Box 818, Shelburne, VT 05482, (800) 639-4122

Team Building and Collaboration
Books

Title: Roadmap to Success 2000
Author: Information Technology Foundation.
Description: Roadmap to Success 2000 is the result of an initiative to improve education, K-12, in the United States.

What makes this book unusual is that it is written for business leaders as a guidebook to initiate and sustain business partnerships with local school districts. The organization of the guidebook is straightforward and sequential and includes four sections: Getting Started, Customizing the Program Initiative, Implementing the Program, and Appendices. The most well-developed section, Customizing the Program, details four levels of cooperation with the educational community: Educational Policy, Working with Students, Working With Teachers and Administrators and Working With Families. The descriptions under each of the four levels contain numerous strategies businesses can use to initiate partnerships with the targeted population. For example, the authors list 10 partnering strategies to enhance student learning and/or productivity: tutoring and mentorship programs, speakers bureaus, tours of facilities, science and engineering fairs, career and job fairs, career guidance, internships and summer work, scholarships, sponsorship of student activities, and student award programs.

One of the greatest strengths of this guidebook is its realistic understanding of the nature of change in public education. The authors state clearly that change in education will take time: "partnering ventures must be long term" (p. 5). Furthermore, their work is based upon the premise that partnering is essential to effect the deep and systemic reforms that are required to change the essential elements of schooling: learning and teaching. The document is free and may be photocopied.

Publisher: Information Technology Association of America. Requests for copies should be made to Diane Greer, Information Technology Foundation, 1616 N. Meyer Drive, Suite 1300, Arlington, VA 22209-3106, (703) 284-5307.

Title: Six Thinking Hats for Schools
Author: de Bono, E.
Description: Edward de Bono, pioneer in the field of teaching thinking in education, has a new series of resource books for teaching thinking in all areas of the curriculum. The six thinking hats represent different modes of thinking, and all are valuable; none is inferior to the others. The red thinking hat represents emotional thinking, the yellow hat represents benefit thinking, the black hat represents judgmental thinking, while the green, white and blue hats represent creative, informational and organizational thinking, respectively. The six hats method is also a valuable tool for helping groups

understand the team concept. Specifically, each member of the group is valued for the perspective and thinking style he or she offers.

Publisher: Perfection Learning. Price: $16.95

Title: Team Building for School Change.
Author: Maeroff, G. I.
Description: Few would argue that although students have changed considerably over the last half century, schools continue to operate in much the same way as they did 50 years ago. This status quo condition related to the operation of schools remains in spite of massive school reform efforts in the last decade. Gene Maeroff, in his new book entitled, *Team Building for School Change: Equipping Teachers for New Roles*, suggests that one reason for the failure of school reform is the tendency of reformers and reform efforts to overlook the role of teachers in the change process. Maeroff compares school reformers to designers of new cars "who seek to overhaul the automobile without paying attention to the impact of the person who will sit behind the steering wheel" (p. 2).

To jump start meaningful and lasting educational change, Maeroff suggests that designated teachers and a building principal be trained as a team to deal with the changes that will be required to improve schools. His new book is not only a guidebook that explains how team members are selected and trained, but also an examination of the stages through which teams evolve as they develop lives of their own and an analysis of the obstacles the new team will encounter as it works to bring about changes in its respective district. Chapters include: Selecting Teams, Bonding and Growing, The Team and the Principal, The Team Returns, Making Time for Teams and Obstacles to Teams.

Maeroff's work leads to a deeper understanding of change, the dynamics of change in the educational setting, and contains some practical suggestions for those who wish to utilize teams to encourage change in their district. Most important, Maeroff's work is one of the few works to recognize teachers as the essential element in school improvement.

Publisher: Teachers College Press. Price: $16.95.

Articles

Title: Consultation and Teaming: Problem-Solving Among Educators, Parents, and Support Personnel

Author: Elliott, S. N., & Sheriden, S. M.

Abstract: Elliott and Sheriden examine the use of consultation and school-based multidisciplinary team conferences in the delivery of educational and psychological services for mainstreamed handicapped children. Step-by-step illustrations of problem solving in a consultative relationship are extended to team problem solving.

Journal: Elementary School Journal, 92(3), pp. 315-338.

Title: Designing Systems to Facilitate Collaboration: Collective Wisdom from Colorado

Author: Adams, L., & Cessna, K.

Abstract: This article describes efforts in Colorado to develop collaborative relationships to better meet the needs of students with disabilities. The authors stress the importance of developing common understanding, developing a full array of services within the delivery system, and addressing school scheduling issues.

Journal: Preventing School Failure, 35(4), pp. 37-42.

Title: Essential Collaborative Consultation Competencies for Regular and Special Educators

Author: West, J. F., & Cannon, G. S.

Abstract: Using a Delphi technique, a 100-member interdisciplinary, expert panel from 47 states identified 47 competencies in eight categories as essential to collaborative consultation between special and regular educators. Highest ratings were given to interactive communication, collaborative problem solving, and personal characteristics.

Journal: Journal of Learning Disabilities, 21(1), pp. 56-63, 68.

Title: Principles for the Practice of Collaboration in Schools

Author: Cook, L., & Friend, M.

Abstract: The authors of this paper clarify vocabulary in the area of collaboration in schools, describe characteristics of collaboration, and outline a set of principles related to the strategy. The principles, the authors explain, are not prerequisites in most school programs, may occur informally, require time to develop, and are not panaceas.

Journal: Preventing School Failure, 35(4), pp. 6-9.

Instruments
Title: *Teachers' Perceptions Toward Collaboration*
Author: Leppien, J.
Age level: Adult
Purpose: Assesses teachers' attitudes toward collaboration
Description: Paper-and-pencil instrument in two parts that examines teachers' attitudes toward collaboration. Collaboration is defined as an interactive process which enables people with diverse areas of expertise to generate creative solutions to mutually-defined problems. The first part, 9 Likert scale items, assesses the degree to which subjects believe collaboration is supported in their school. The second part, 13 Likert scale items, assesses teachers' self-efficacy with respect to collaboration. A copy of this instrument is included in Appendix C.
Scoring: Machine
For additional information, write: Dr. Jann Leppien, The National Research Center on the Gifted and Talented, 362 Fairfield Road U-7, The University of Connecticut, Storrs, CT 06269-2007, (203) 486-3741.

Staff Development
Peer Coaching
Books/Articles
Title: The Coaching of Teaching
Author: Joyce, B., & Showers, B.
Abstract: Teachers, like athletes, are more likely to adopt new ways of doing their jobs if they are coached, and they are also likely to get worse before they get better. This article describes the coaching of teachers and includes an interview with a football coach to illustrate the parallel with athletics.
Journal: *Educational Leadership, 40*(1), pp. 4-8, 10.

Title: Cooperative Professional Development: Peer-Centered Options for Teacher Growth
Author: Glatthorn, A. A.
Abstract: Cooperative professional development is a process by which teams of teachers work together for their own professional development. Types of cooperative development described include the following: professional dialogue, curriculum development, peer supervision, peer coaching and action research.
Journal: *Educational Leadership, 45*(3), pp. 31-35.

Title: Synthesis of Research on Staff Development: A Framework for Future Study and a State-of-the-Art Analysis
Author: Showers, B., Joyce, B., & Bennett, B.
Abstract: A meta-analysis of nearly 200 research studies, plus a review of the literature on staff development, point to the importance of staff development program design in providing insights that teachers can use in their classrooms.
Journal: Educational Leadership, 45(3), pp. 77-87.

The Reflective Practitioner
Books/Articles
Title: Finding Time for Collaboration
Author: Raywid, M. A.
Abstract: Many schools throughout the country are experimenting with creative ways to find time for shared reflection. The authors share examples from 15 school districts around the country.
Journal: Educational Leadership, 51(1), pp. 30-34.

Title: The Virtues of Not Knowing. In E. Duckworth, *The Having of Wonderful Ideas and Other Essays on Teaching and Learning*
Author: Duckworth, E.
Description: In this article Duckworth focuses attention away from the importance of knowing the right answer (which she believes is a passive virtue), and focuses on the virtues of not knowing. After all, she concludes, "what you do about what you don't know is, in the final analysis, what determines what you will ultimately know" (p. 68). If educators are going to make a difference in students' intellectual thoughts, they must relinquish the one-right-answer mentality and help children develop curiosity, patience, honest attempts, puzzlement and wrong outcomes as legitimate elements in learning.
Publisher: Teachers College Press. *Price:* $15.95.

Title: The Reflective Practitioner: How Professionals Think in Action
Author: Schon, D.
Description: Schon argues that competent practitioners know more than they can say. He documents this belief with vignettes of practitioners who demonstrate reflection and intuitive knowing in the midst of action. Schon also argues that teachers must embark on the course of reflective practice, even though it may cause confusion and uncertainty, because

the reflections ultimately increase teachers' capacities to contribute to student and organizational learning.
Publisher: Jossey-Bass. *Price:* $17.00.

Schoolwide Enrichment Model
Books
Title: The Complete Triad Trainers In-service Manual
Author: Renzulli, J. S., & Reis, S. M.
Description: Based on *The Enrichment Triad Model* and *The Schoolwide Enrichment Model,* this book offers helpful advice and organizational tips that will assist practitioners conduct successful workshops in any subject or field.
Publisher: Creative Learning Press, P.O. Box 320, Mansfield Center, CT 06250, (203) 429-8118. Order No. 957. Price: $22.95.

Title: The Triad Reader
Author: Renzulli, J. S., & Reis, S. M.
Description: This resource book is a collection of articles, background information, and practical ideas about implementing enrichment programs for students. Included in this publication are articles on teacher training, curriculum compacting, how-to-do-it books, learning styles, mentorship programs, community resources, program evaluation, secondary enrichment programs and schoolwide enrichment teams.
Publisher: Creative Learning Press, P.O. Box 320, Mansfield Center, CT 06250, (203) 429-8118. Order No. 957. Price: $22.95.

Instruments
Title: Schoolwide Enrichment Teachers' Ratings of Appraised In-service Needs (SE Train)
Author: Olenchak, F. R., & Schlichter, C. L.
Age level: Adult
Purpose: Assesses teachers' perceptions regarding in-service needs related to the Schoolwide Enrichment Program
Description: Paper-and-pencil instrument (24 items) designed to assess teachers' perceived levels of efficacy related to the components of the Schoolwide Enrichment Model (see Appendix D).
Scoring: Evaluator
For additional information, write:
Dr. F. Richard Olenchak
University of Alabama

College of Education
P.O. Box 2592
Tuscaloosa, AL 35487-2592
(205) 348-1448

Parent and School Partnerships
Books/Monographs
Title: America's Smallest School: The Family
Author: Barton, P., & Coley, R.
Description: This report addresses the available research on the home as a learning environment. National and international data are presented about 8 home factors related to student learning: parent-pupil ratio, the home library, reading at home, television viewing habits, homework, absenteeism, parental involvement and family resources. One way to increase the academic achievement of students, the authors claim, is to make homes into child-centered environments where children are encouraged to explore and discover. The report explains several strategies parents can use to increase the learning opportunities in all homes.
Publisher: Educational Testing Service. To order a copy of the report, send a check or money order for $5.50 to: Policy Information Center, ETS, Mail Stop 04-R, Rosedale Road, Princeton, NJ 08541-0001. Refer to publication number 204851 and make checks payable to Educational Testing Service. The brochure, *Publications for Parents*, describes the Department of Education's series of booklets on learning activities for parents. For a free copy, send your name and address to OERI, Department EIB, 555 New Jersey Avenue, NW, Washington, DC 20208-564. Ask for publication #PIP 91-920.

Title: Awakening Your Child's Natural Genius
Author: Armstrong, T.
Description: This book provides parents with strategies for bringing out the very best in their children. The author, a columnist for *Parenting Magazine*, divides his book into four parts. In the first section he deals with the learning environment of home and school. In the second and third part, Academics the Natural Way and Growing Through Arts and Leisure, he explores ways families can explore and learn about academic content in enjoyable ways. In the final section of the book, Armstrong examines different strategies that will assist parents maintain their children's uniqueness in school. The format for each of the chapters is practical. At the end of

each chapter are tips for parents and lists of resources (i.e., organizations, books, articles) that parents can use to help develop the talents in their children.
Publisher: Jeremy P. Tarcher, Inc. Price: $12.95.

Title: *College Comes Sooner Than You Think: The Essential Planning Guide for High School Students and Their Families*
Author: Featherstone, B. D., & Reilly, J. M.
Description: This book is written on the premise that few families take enough time to "shop" for colleges. Accordingly, students and parents are encouraged to act as consumers when they plan this important step in an adolescent's career. The chapters take families from defining priorities to planning the finances for the student's years in college. The planning forms are especially helpful as is the resource list in Chapter 14. Also included is a complete list of references to related topics, including: applications, athletes' information, career guidance, financial aid, résumé preparation and testing.
Publisher: Ohio Psychology Press. Price: $12.95.

Title: *Developing Talent in Young People*
Author: Bloom, B. S.
Description: One hundred and twenty men and women who had reached the highest levels of accomplishment in their selected fields were interviewed by a University of Chicago research team. Those selected were accomplished in music and art, athletics, and mathematics and science. Based on the results of their research, the authors provide perspectives on the nature of talent development.
Publisher: Out of print.

Title: *How to Help Your Child With Homework*
Author: Radencich, M. C., & Schumm, J. S.
Description: This book is based on the premise that homework doesn't have to be unpleasant. The authors offer specific tips and techniques that can make homework more bearable for all who are involved. Separate chapters are devoted to academic areas (i.e., reading, spelling and writing, mathematics, science and social studies) and each chapter contains specific strategies for working in the discipline. Additionally, other chapters are devoted to research projects and family games. A final chapter provides resources as well as forms, lists, charts, and game boards to help parents help children with homework.
Publisher: Free Spirit Publishing. Price: $12.95.

Title: The MegaSkills Workshop Program
Author: The Home and School Institute
Description: *The MegaSkills Workshop Program* empowers parents and teachers to develop critical learning skills to help children achieve in school. Workshop training is provided to interested teachers and parents, and activity-oriented guidebooks encourage the development of ten skills related to scholastic achievement: confidence, motivation, effort, responsibility, initiative, perseverance, caring, teamwork, common sense, and problem solving. Although the authors recommend that teachers, parents and schools work collaboratively to foster these skills in students, the guidebooks can be used separately by parents or teachers. Materials are available in Spanish as well as English.
Bright Idea-A book in comic-strip form which teaches children problem-solving strategies to daily life situations: communication, health, money and household organization. Price: $7.00.

MegaSkills-An activities book that provides activities designed to teach the 10 skills related to academic achievement. It includes responses from parents and teachers who have used the activities and a special section about the importance of grandparents. Price: $12.95.

Special Solutions-A book of home activities designed to give extra help for children in reading, writing, mathematics, science and social studies. Price: $7.00.

Publisher: The Home and School Institute, Special Projects Office, 1201 16th Street, N.W., Washington, DC 20036 (202) 466-3633.

Title: *Parenting the Very Young Gifted Child (Research Monograph No. 9308)*
Author: Robinson, N. M.
Description: Although this monograph is about young high ability children, many of the topics and suggestions developed by Robinson can be used by parents to develop talent in all children. Two sections are especially useful: How do Adults Promote the Development of Gifted Children? And What Other Aspects of Development Need Attention?
Publisher: The National Research Center on the Gifted and Talented, Storrs, CT. To order: Send check (payable to The University of Connecticut) or money order to: Dawn Guenther,

Dissemination Coordinator, The University of Connecticut, The National Research Center on the Gifted and Talented, 362 Fairfield Road, U-7, Storrs, CT 06269-2007 Price: $15.00.

Title: Reading With Young Children (Research Monograph No. 9302)
Author: Jackson, N. E., & Roller, C. M.
Description: This monograph has a number of purposes. First, it summarizes the research literature about literary development. One of the important conclusions of the research is that children's reading and writing skills develop unevenly. Accordingly, the second part of this document contains recommendations and suggestions to enhance the reading skills of children at all stages of literacy development. The authors answer questions including, for example: What should adults do when they read with a child? Should talking be part of reading with a child? What kind of talk occurs during story reading? What kind of book choices make good reading? What do children learn from reading with adults?
Publisher: The National Research Center on the Gifted and Talented, Storrs, CT. To order: Send check (payable to The University of Connecticut) or money order to: Dawn Guenther, Dissemination Coordinator, The University of Connecticut, The National Research Center on the Gifted and Talented, 362 Fairfield Road, U-7, Storrs, CT 06269-2007. Price: $15.00.

Title: Some Children Under Some Conditions: TV and the High Potential Kid (Research Monograph No. 9206)
Author: Abelman, R.
Description: Abelman addresses controversial issues in this monograph: How much TV is too much? and Is TV harmful? The author examines the relationship between high ability children and their television watching habits and presents these findings in the report. Equally important, he provides guidelines for parent decision making related to children's television viewing.
Publisher: The National Research Center on the Gifted and Talented, Storrs, CT. To order, send check (payable to The University of Connecticut) or money order to: Dawn Guenther, Dissemination Coordinator, The University of Connecticut, The National Research Center on the Gifted and Talented, 362 Fairfield Road, U-7, Storrs, CT 06269-2007. Price: $15.00.

Articles

Title: California's Policy on Parent involvement
Author: Solomon, Z. P.
Abstract: California state initiatives designed to involve parents fall into four categories: government, client services, parents as teachers, and parents as parents. These initiatives, aligned with the state's curriculum reform strategies, require a five-year action plan for enabling school districts to develop local policies and plans that would involve all families.
Journal: Phi Delta Kappan, 72(5), pp. 359-362.

Title: District Leadership in Parent involvement: Policies and Action in San Diego
Author: Chrispeels, J. H.
Abstract: The new state and district policy initiatives in California recognize that effective parent involvement is multifaceted and requires schools' active efforts. The San Diego County Office of Education has served as information clearinghouse, source of direct services to parents, and provider of staff development and planning assistance.
Journal: Phi Delta Kappan, 72(5), pp. 367-371.

Title: Educating Poor Minority Children
Author: Comer, J. P.
Abstract: In this article Comer argues that money and effort expended for educational reform will be of little benefit as long as underlying developmental and social issues of students remain unaddressed. Beginning in 1968, he began work with two urban elementary schools to address students' needs and improve their scholastic achievement. By working collaboratively with a governance team, a parents' program and a mental health team, students' behavioral problems declined, relations between parents and staff improved, and student achievement had improved.
Journal: Scientific American, 259(5), pp. 42-48.

Title: The Illinois Experience: State Grants to Improve Schools Through Parent involvement
Author: Chapman, W.
Abstract: In 1987, the Illinois State Board of Education committed itself to adopt and expand policies, procedures and programs addressing the problems of at-risk children and youths. To address issues involving early intervention, early childhood education, minority achievement, urban education,

truancy preventions and alternative education, the Board created the Urban Education Partnership Grants program.
Journal: Phi Delta Kappan, 72(5), pp. 355-358.

Title: Parent involvement in the States: How Firm is the Commitment?
Author: Nardine, F. E., & Morris, R. D.
Abstract: According to two recent state surveys, much existing state legislation pays only lip service to the importance of parent participation. Staffing and funding levels are inadequate. Despite decades of federal legislation and support for parental involvement, most states have not passed enabling legislation, developed policies or written guidelines.
Journal: Phi Delta Kappan, 72(5), pp. 363-366.

Title: Parents in Touch: District Leadership for Parent involvement
Author: Warner, I.
Abstract: Parents in Touch, the umbrella program for parental involvement in the Indianapolis Public Schools, was established to facilitate the kind of two-way communication that enables parents to become partners in their children's education. This program uses various approaches, including parent/teacher conferences, a dial-a-teacher assistance program, and a homework hotline.
Journal: Phi Delta Kappan, 72(5), pp. 372-375.

Title: Paths to Partnerships: What We Can Learn From Federal, State, District, and School Initiatives
Author: Epstein, J.
Abstract: Leaders at the national, state and district levels are following new paths to partnership between schools and families. Most programs make teachers' jobs easier and should continue throughout childhood and adolescence and include all families.
Journal: Phi Delta Kappan, 72(5), pp. 344-349.

Title: Schools Reaching Out: Family, School, and Community Partnerships for Student Success
Author: Davies, D.
Abstract: In the family support movement, three themes are central: providing success for all children, serving the whole child, and sharing responsibility. The Institute for Responsive Education used these themes to develop a national project

(Schools Reaching Out) designed to redefine and expand parent involvement as part of urban school reform.
Journal: Phi Delta Kappan, 72(5), pp. 376-382.

Places to Send for More Information About Parent and School Partnerships
Title: Family Education and Training: From Research to Practice. Report No. 14.
Author: Kagan, S. L., Neville, P., & Rustici, J.
Price: $5.40
For Information: Publications Office, Center on Families, Communities, Schools and Children's Learning
The Johns Hopkins University
3505 North Charles Street
Baltimore, MD 21218

Council of the Great City Schools
1413 K Street, N.W., 4th Floor
Washington, DC 20005
(202) 6355431

National Coalition for Parent involvement in Education
119 North Payne Street
Alexandria, VA 22314
(703) 683-6232

National Congress of Parents and Teachers
1201 16th Street., N.W., #619
Washington, DC 20036
(202) 822-7878

Parent involvement Center
Chapter I Technical Assistance Center
RMC Research Corporation
400 Lafayette Road
Hampton, NH 03842
(603) 926-8888

Southwest Educational Development Laboratory
211 E. Seventh Street
Austin, TX 78701
(512) 476-6861

School Governance
Articles

Title: A Changing Context Means School Board Reform
Author: Kirst, M. W.

Abstract: Kirst reports that the last major reported change in the role of local school boards occurred over 70 years ago and he uses this rationale for the remainder of his article which chronicles recent trends and changes in local educational governance. The changes he cites include: (1) the inclusion of minority representation on boards, (2) the participation of teacher unions in board elections, (3) the ceding of board control to specialized personnel within the district as well as state legislation, and, accordingly, (4) a shrinking of the area over which local boards have control. Kirst concludes that school boards can no longer control their agenda and proposes a rethinking of the role of school governance organizations to revitalize their policy-making role.
Journal: Phi Delta Kappan, 75(5), pp. 378-382.

Title: The Changing Local Community School Board
Author: Shannon, T. A.

Abstract: Shannon argues that no support for ending or substantially limiting the control of public schools by local electorates exists. To the contrary, he states that a democratic society will continue to demand local representative governance. To ensure that only the most highly qualified men and women are elected to governance positions, he calls upon local leaders for assistance.
Journal: Phi Delta Kappan, 75(5), pp. 387-390.

Title: Defining the Leadership Role of School Boards In the 21st Century
Author: Campbell, D. W., & Greene, D.

Abstract: The authors of this article begin by identifying core decision-making functions that are so fundamental to a school system's accountability to the public that they can be performed only by an elected governing body. Content functions of the elected governing body include: ensuring a long-term vision and a climate for excellence, superintendent appointment and evaluation, budget adoption and fiscal accountability, curriculum development and program accountability, governance and policy, collective bargaining, and advocacy. The extent to which board members are able to complete their content-related functions depends upon board members' proficiency in "boardmanship," claim the

authors. Campbell and Grenne believe the tenets of boardmanship include: a clear understanding of a board member's duties and powerful role, teamwork, the adoption of a positive attitude toward board business, respect for the roles of others in the school community, trust, fairness, and an understanding of the importance of open and clear communication.
Journal: Phi Delta Kappan, 75(5), pp. 391-395.

Title: Governing the Nation's Schools
Author: Danzberger, J. P.
Abstract: In this article Danzberger examines the reasons commonly cited by critics for the failure of local school governance organizations. To support these reasons, she cites evidence from three studies conducted by the Institute for Educational Leadership (IEL). In the concluding section of the article, the author provides specific strategies community members can initiate to restructure school boards as well as specific guidelines state legislators can enact to reinforce the role of local boards as policy makers.
Journal: Phi Delta Kappan, 75(5), pp. 367-373.

Title: Reinventing Urban Public Education
Author: Hill, P. T.
Abstract: Hill opens his article by stating that gridlock exists in the big city school systems and that "the enemy is us." He proposes that schools need a true alternative form of governance that allows them to be operated by a variety of public and private organizations. A school system, the author claims, would hold many different contracts–some for high schools, some for grade schools, some for highly distinctive schools and others for more conventional schools. The remainder of Hill's article is devoted to explaining how the contracting might work, delineating the advantages of contracting, and enumerating some of the steps necessary to ensure a smooth transition to contracting.
Journal: Phi Delta Kappan, 75(5), pp. 396-401.

Title: The Relationship Between School Boards and General Purpose Government
Author: Usdan, M. D.
Abstract: This article about the need for change in school governance is grounded on the premise that schools and local governance organizations can no longer unilaterally resolve the complex and interrelated issues confronting growing

numbers of needy children and their families. The author proposes that school boards are vital to the development of alternative governance structures and/or closer intercommunity collaborations designed to meet the needs of children in marginal circumstances.
Journal: *Phi Delta Kappan, 75(5),* pp. 374-377.

Title: Urban Education: A Board Member's Perspective
Author: Wilson, J. C.
Abstract: Wilson's primary concern is with the problem-plagued urban city school districts. He believes that school boards are more necessary than ever before to cut through state mandates and the mountains of reading material that distract administrative attention away from the needs of schools. Most important, the author believes school board representatives will be the only members of the school community to advocate consistently for the needs of children who are disadvantaged and helpless.
Journal: *Phi Delta Kappan, 75(5),* pp. 382-286.

Appendix A

**Summary of Research on The Schoolwide Enrichment Model (SEM) and
Related Models (i.e., Enrichment Triad Model, Talents Unlimited Model)***

*Adapted from: Renzulli, J. S., & Reis, S. M. (1994). Research related to the Schoolwide Enrichment Triad Model. *Gifted Child Quarterly 38*(1), 7-20.

Author & Date	Title of Study	Samples*	Major Finding
Effectiveness of SEM as Perceived by Teachers, Administrators, and Parents			
Reis, 1981	An analysis of the productivity of gifted students participating in programs using the Revolving Door Identification Model	P, E	Teachers preferred the Revolving Door identification procedures over more traditional methods of identification; teachers reported that a high level of involvement with the program influenced their teaching practices.
Olenchak, 1988	The Schoolwide Enrichment Model in elementary schools: A study of implementation stages and effects on educational excellence	E	SEM contributed to improved teachers', parents' and administrators' attitudes toward education for high ability students.
Cooper, 1983	Administrator's attitudes toward gifted programs based on the Enrichment Triad/Revolving Door Identification Model: Case studies in decision-making	8 districts	Administrator perceptions regarding the model included: greater staff participation in education of high ability students, more positive staff attitudes toward the program, fewer concerns about identification, positive changes in how the guidance department worked with students, more incentives for students to work toward higher goals.
Creativity and SEM-Quality of Products			
Reis, 1981	An analysis of the productivity of gifted students participating in programs using the Revolving Door Identification Model	P, E	Products of above average students were equally as good as the products completed by students who were identified for the program using traditional methods.
Gubbins, 1982	Revolving Door Identification Model: Characteristics of Talent Pool students	E	Students who did not generate self-selected projects (Type IIIs) attributed the lack of product development to time management difficulties and difficulty in generating product ideas.
Creativity and SEM-Effects of Training			
Burns, 1987	The effects of group training activities on students' creative productivity	E	Students receiving process skill training were 64% more likely to initiate self-selected projects (Type IIIs) than the students who did not receive the training.
Newman, 1991	The effects of the Talents Unlimited Model on students' creative productivity	E	Students with training in the Talents Unlimited Model were more likely to complete independent investigations (Type IIIs) than students who did not receive the training.

*P=Primary grades, K-2; E=Elementary grades, 3-5; M=Middle grades, 6-8; S=Secondary grades, 9-12.

Author & Date	Title of Study	Samples	Major Finding
SEM and Creativity-Investigations of Student Creative and Productive Behaviors			
Delcourt, 1988	Characteristics related to high levels of creative/ productive behavior in secondary school students: A multi-case study	S	Students completing self-selected investigations (Type IIIs) displayed changes in the following: personal skills required for project completion (e.g., writing), personal characteristics (e.g., increased patience, decisions related to career choices.
Starko, 1986	The effects of the Revolving Door Identification Model on creative productivity and self-efficacy	E	Students who became involved with self-selected independent studies in SEM programs more often initiated their own creative products both inside and outside school than did students who qualified for the program but did not receive services.
SEM and Personal and Social Development			
Delisle, 1981	The Revolving Door Identification and Programming Model: Correlates of creative production	E	Students with high academic self-concepts tended to revolve into the program, tended to initiate projects (Type IIIs), and internalized their academic successes.
Olenchak, 1991	Assessing program effects for gifted/learning disabled students	E	SEM, when used as an intervention, was associated with improved attitudes toward learning among elementary, high ability students with learning disabilities. Furthermore, the same students, who completed a high percentage of Type III projects, made positive gains with respect to self-concept.
SEM and Social Acceptability			
Skaught, 1987	The social acceptability of talent pool students in an elementary school using The Schoolwide Enrichment Model	E	Students identified for an SEM program were positively accepted by their peers.
Heal, 1987	Student perceptions of labeling the gifted: A comparative case study	E	SEM was associated with a reduction in the negative effects of labeling.
SEM and Underachievement			
Emerick, 1988	Academic underachievement among the gifted: Students' perceptions of factors relating to the reversal of academic underachievement patterns	H+	Reasons attributed to the reversal of academic underachievement included: the use of curriculum compacting, exposure to Type I activities, opportunities to be involved in Type III independent investigations and a close match between the unique learning modes of students and a teacher who understands the modes.

320

Author & Date	Title of Study	Samples	Major Finding
SEM and Underachievement, continued			
Baum, Renzulli & Hébert (in preparation)	Reversing underachievement through pursuit of student interests	E, M	A positive gain in classroom performance was made by underachieving students who undertook a self-selected independent investigation (Type III).
Taylor, 1992	The effects of The Secondary Enrichment Triad Model on the career development of vocational-technical school students	S	Secondary vocational-technical students who undertook Type III investigations changed college plans from attending 2.6 years to attending 4.0 years of post-secondary education.
SEM and High Ability/Learning Disabled Students			
Baum, 1988	An enrichment program for the gifted learning disabled student	E	The Type III independent study, when used as an intervention with high ability, learning disabled students, was associated with improvement in the students' behavior, specifically the ability to self regulate time on task; improvement in self-esteem; and the development of specific instructional strategies to enhance the potential of high potential, learning disabled students.
SEM and Self-Efficacy			
Schack, 1986	Creative productivity and self-efficacy in children	E, M	Self-efficacy was a significant predictor of initiation of an independent investigation, and self-efficacy at the end of treatment (a mini-course on research methodology) was higher in students who participated in Type III projects.
Starko, 1986	The effects of The Revolving Door Identification Model on creative productivity and self-efficacy	E	The number of creative products completed in school (Type IIIs) was a highly significant predictor of self-efficacy.
SEM and Learning Styles			
Stewart, 1979	Learning styles among gifted/talented students: Preferences for instructional techniques	E	High ability students tend to prefer instructional methods that emphasize independence while students in the general population prefer instructional methods with more structure.
SEM and Curriculum Compacting			
Reis, et al., 1992	Technical report of The Curriculum Compacting Research Study	P, E	Ninety-five percent of teachers were able to identify high ability students in their classes and document students' strength areas; teachers were able to eliminate an average of 45%-50% of curriculum for high ability learners across content areas.

Author & Date	Title of Study	Samples	Major Finding
SEM and Longitudinal Research			
Delcourt, 1993	Creative productivity among secondary school students: Combining energy, interest, and imagination		Students who participated in Type III projects, both in and out of school, maintained interests in college and career aspirations that were similar to those manifested during their public school years.
Hébert, 1993	Reflections at graduation: The long-term impact of elementary school experiences in creative productivity		Type III interests of students affect post-secondary plans; creative outlets are needed in high school; the Type III process serves as important training for later productivity.

Appendix B

Taxonomy of Type II Process Skills
Deborah E. Burns, 1994

I. **COGNITIVE TRAINING**

A. **Analysis Skills**

Identifying characteristics
Recognizing attributes
Making an observation
Discriminating between same and different
Comparing and contrasting
Categorizing
Classifying
Criteria setting
Ranking, prioritizing, and sequencing
Seeing relationships
Determining cause and effect
Pattern finding
Predicting
Making analogies

B. **Organization Skills**

Memorizing
Summarizing
Metacognition
Goal setting
Formulating questions
Developing hypotheses
Generalizing
Problem solving
Decision making
Planning

C. **Critical Thinking Skills**

Inductive thinking
Deductive thinking
Determining reality and fantasy
Determining benefits and drawbacks
Identifying value statements
Identifying points of view
Determining bias
Identifying fact and opinion
Determining the accuracy of presented information
Judging essential and incidental evidence
Determining relevance
Identifying missing information
Judging the credibility of a source

Determining warranted and unwarranted claims
Recognizing assumptions
Recognizing fallacies
Detecting inconsistencies in an argument
Identifying ambiguity
Identifying exaggeration
Determining the strength of an argument

D. **Creativity Skills**

Fluent thinking
Flexible thinking
Original thinking
Elaborational thinking
Developing imagery
SCAMPER modification techniques
Attribute Listing
Random Input
Brainstorming
Creative problem solving
Synectics

II. AFFECTIVE TRAINING

A. **Intrapersonal Skills**

Analyzing strengths
Clarifying values
Developing a personal framework for activism
Developing a sense of humor
Developing an ethical framework
Developing moral reasoning
Developing resiliency
Developing responsibility
Developing self-efficacy
Developing self-esteem
Developing self-reliance
Developing task commitment
Understanding integrity
Understanding self-management
Understanding image management
Understanding learning styles

B. **Interpersonal Skills**

Developing environmental awareness
Developing etiquette and courtesy
Developing multicultural awareness
Developing social skills
Understanding assertiveness
Understanding and developing leadership skills
Understanding conflict resolution
Understanding cooperation and collaboration
Understanding nonverbal communication
Understanding stereotypes
Understanding tolerance, empathy, and compassion

C. **Dealing With Critical Life Incidents**

Coping with loss
Dealing with change
Dealing with dependency
Dealing with failure
Dealing with stress
Dealing with success
Making choices
Planning for the future
Understanding perfectionism
Understanding risk-taking

III. **LEARNING HOW-TO-LEARN SKILLS**

A. **Listening, Observing, and Perceiving Skills**

Following directions
Noting specific details
Understanding main points, themes, and sequences
Separating relevant from irrelevant information
Paying attention to whole-part relationships
Scanning for the "big picture"
Focusing on specifics
Asking for clarification
Asking appropriate questions
Making inferences
Noting subtleties
Predicting outcomes
Evaluating a speaker's point of view

B. **Notetaking and Outlining Skills**

Notetaking Skills

Selecting key terms, concepts, and ideas
Disregarding unimportant information
Noting what needs to be remembered
Recording words, dates and figures to aid in recall
Reviewing notes and highlighting the most important items
Categorizing notes in a logical order
Organizing notes so that information from various sources can be
added later

Outlining and webbing

Using outlining skills to write material that has unity and coherence
Selecting and using a system of notation (e.g., Roman numerals)
Deciding whether to write topic outlines or sentence outlines
Stating each topic or point clearly
Developing each topic sufficiently

C. **Interviewing and Surveying–Developing and Practicing the Use of:**

Identifying information being sought
Deciding on appropriate instruments
Identifying sources of existing instruments
Designing instruments (e.g., check-lists, rating scales, interview
schedules)
Developing question wording skills (e.g., factual, attitudinal, probing,
follow-up)
Sequencing questions
Identifying representative samples
Field testing and revising instruments
Developing rapport with subjects
Preparing a data-gathering matrix and schedule
Using follow-up techniques

D. **Analyzing and Organizing Data–Developing and Practicing the Use of:**

Identifying types and sources of data
Identifying and developing data gathering instruments and techniques
Identifying appropriate sampling techniques
Developing data-recording and coding techniques
Classifying and tabulating data
Preparing descriptive (statistical) summaries of data (e.g., percentages,
means, modes, etc.)
Analyzing data with inferential statistics

Preparing tables, graphs, and diagrams
Drawing conclusions and making generalizations
Writing up and reporting results

IV. USING ADVANCED RESEARCH AND REFERENCE MATERIALS

A. Preparing for Type III Investigations:

Developing problem finding and focusing skills
Identifying variables
Stating hypotheses and research questions
Identifying human and material resources
Developing a management plan
Developing time management skills
Selecting appropriate product formats
Obtaining feedback and making revisions
Identifying appropriate outlets and audiences
Developing an assessment plan

B. Library Skills:

Understanding library organizational systems
Using information retrieval systems
Using interlibrary loan procedures
Understanding specialized types of information in reference books, such as:
    abstracts
    almanacs
    annuals
    anthologies
    atlases
    bibliographies
    books of quotations, proverbs, maxims, and familiar phrases
    concordances
    data tables
    diaries
    dictionaries and glossaries
    digests
    directories and registers
    encyclopedias
    handbooks
    histories and chronicles of particular fields, organizations
    indexes
    manuals
    periodicals
    reader's guides
    reviews

source books

surveys

yearbooks

Understanding the specific types of information in nonbook reference
materials, such as:

art prints

audio tapes

charts

data tapes

CD Roms

film loops

films

filmstrips

filmstrips with sound

flashcards

globes

maps

microforms

models

pictures

realia

records

slides

study prints

talking books

transparencies

video tapes, discs

C.   **Community Resources**:

Identifying community resources, such as:

art and theater groups

clubs, hobby, and special interest groups

college and university services and persons

governmental and social service agencies

museums, galleries, science centers, places of special interest or
function

private and community colleges

private business and individuals

private individuals

professional societies and associations

senior citizen groups

service clubs

universities

V. DEVELOPING WRITTEN, ORAL, AND VISUAL COMMUNICATION TECHNIQUES

A. **Visual Communication–Developing Skills in the Preparation of:**

Audio tape recordings
Filmstrips
Motion pictures
Multimedia images
Overhead transparencies
Photographic print series
Slide series
Video tape recordings

B. **Oral Communication–Developing and Practicing the Use of:**

Organizing material for an oral presentation
Vocal delivery
Appropriate gestures, eye movement, facial expression, and body movement
Acceptance of the ideas and feelings of others
Appropriate words, quotations, anecdotes, personal experiences, illustrative examples, and relevant information
Appropriate use of the latest technology
Obtaining and evaluating feedback

C. **Written Communication:**

Planning the written document (e.g., subject, audience, purpose, thesis, tone, outline, title)
Choosing appropriate and imaginative words
Developing paragraphs with unity, coherence, and emphasis
Developing "technique" (e.g., metaphor, comparison, hyperbole, personal experience)
Writing powerful introductions and conclusions
Practicing the four basic forms of writing (exposition, persuasion, description, and narration)
Applying the basic forms to a variety of genre (i.e., short stories, book reviews, research papers, etc.)
Developing technical skills (e.g., proofreading, editing, revising, footnoting, preparing bibliographies, writing summaries, and abstracts)

Appendix C

Teachers' Perceptions Toward Collaboration

Teachers' Perceptions Toward Collaboration

Jann H. Leppien
The University of Connecticut

About this Instrument: This study focuses on your perceptions of collaboration in a school environment. You can help us learn more about this concept by taking a few minutes to complete this survey. Be assured that your answers will be kept strictly confidential and that all reporting will be done at the group level. Thank you very much for your time.

Directions: The following survey contains statements that address teachers' perceptions regarding collaboration. For the purposes of this study, collaboration is defined as an interactive process that enables people with diverse expertise to generate creative solutions to mutually defined problems. The major purpose of collaboration is to provide comprehensive and effective programs for all students.

Please complete the following demographic statements:

1. Gender   ☐ Male   ☐ Female

2. Years of Teaching Experience

     ☐ 0-5 Years
     ☐ 6-10 Years
     ☐ 11-15 Years
     ☐ 16-20 Years
     ☐ 21+Years

3. Current Position

     ☐ Elementary
     ☐ Middle/Junior High School
     ☐ High School

4. Staff Membership Classroom Teacher

     ☐ Specialist (i.e., School Psychologist, Special Education, Gifted/Talented, Art, P.E.)
     ☐ Other

PART I

Instructions: Please read each statement below and circle the appropriate response to indicate the extent that you agree with each statement. The words that correspond to the letters are as follows:

(SD)	(D)	(U)	(A)	(SA)
Strongly Disagree	Disagree	Undecided	Agree	Strongly Agree

STATEMENTS:

1. My colleagues are committed to working together to improve student learning.   SD   D   U   A   SA

2. When I have a student concern, I feel comfortable discussing the issue with my principal.   SD   D   U   A   SA

3. I get sufficient support from other teachers when I am having difficulty with a student.   SD   D   U   A   SA

4. My principal supports teachers' efforts to work together to address student concerns.   SD   D   U   A   SA

5. My principal empowers staff to make decisions regarding students.   SD   D   U   A   SA

6. In this school, teachers value cooperating with each other.   SD   D   U   A   SA

7. My principal provides time for teachers to meet with each other to discuss student concerns.   SD   D   U   A   SA

8. My principal encourages teachers to work together to discuss student concerns.   SD   D   U   A   SA

9. Colleagues in this school respect one another's opinions.   SD   D   U   A   SA

PART II

Instructions: Below is a list of collaborative tasks. How much confidence do you have in doing these tasks? Rate your confidence using this scale:

1	2	3	4	5
VERY LITTLE				QUITE A LOT

10. Organizing and planning the implementation of an idea.　　1　2　3　4　5

11. Interpreting non-verbal communication.　　1　2　3　4　5

12. Sharing ideas or opinions honestly with colleagues about student issues.　　1　2　3　4　5

13. Evaluating the effectiveness of a possible solution to a student problem.　　1　2　3　4　5

14. Crediting colleagues for their ideas.　　1　2　3　4　5

15. Listening to the concerns expressed by colleagues.　　1　2　3　4　5

16. Making decisions related to student issues.　　1　2　3　4　5

17. Generating many ideas about solving student problems.　　1　2　3　4　5

18. Analyzing student problems.　　1　2　3　4　5

19. Identifying specific student problems.　　1　2　3　4　5

20. Implementing a new idea.　　1　2　3　4　5

21. Managing conflict and confrontation skillfully.　　1　2　3　4　5

22. Communicating ideas about students to colleagues.　　1　2　3　4　5

Appendix D

Schoolwide Enrichment Teachers' Ratings of Appraised In-service Needs (SE Train)

SE-TRAIN

Schoolwide Enrichment Teachers' Rating of Appraised In-service Needs

INSTRUCTION: The following statements should be considered as they relate to *you* and to *your perceptions* regarding In-service needs connected to the Schoolwide Enrichment Program with which your school has been involved. Please rate each item on the scale of A (strongly agree) to E (strongly disagree). Although the demographic information is needed to assist in analyzing the results of this survey, all responses are anonymous. The results of the information provided through this survey will be used to help your school formulate future Schoolwide Enrichment training programs that are based on actual needs of teachers and other instructional staff members in your school.

DEMOGRAPHIC INFORMATION

Your role in school (*circle the ONE that BEST pertains*)

Classroom teacher	Special program teacher	Instructional aide
Media/librarian	Counselor	Administrator

Other instructional position _____

Grade level you *primarily* serve (*circle the ONE that BEST pertains*)

Preschool	Kindergarten	1st
2nd	3rd	4th
5th	6th	All of the above
K-2	3-5	3-6

Other levels _____

Total years you have worked in education (teacher, administrator, counselor, media/librarian, therapist, specialist, aide, etc.)

_____ Year(s)

SE-TRAIN (1990) Olenchak & Schlichter

The highest degree/course work you held (*circle the **ONE** that **BEST** pertains*)

Diploma	AD	BA
BS	BA plus	BS plus
MA plus	MS plus	Specialist
Specialist plus	EdD	PhD

Training you have had in education of the gifted and talented (*circle the **ONE** that **BEST** pertains*)

undergraduate course(s)	1 course	2 courses	3 or more courses
graduate course(s)	1 course	2 courses	3 or more courses
In-service session(s)	1 session	2 sessions	3 or more sessions

Training you have had in Schoolwide Enrichment as either the *entire* content or *potential* content of the course(s) or session(s) (*circle the **ONE** that **BEST** pertains*)

undergraduate course(s)	1 course	2 courses	3 or more courses
graduate course(s)	1 course	2 courses	3 or more courses
In-service session(s)	1 session	2 sessions	3 or more sessions

SE-TRAIN (1990) Olenchak & Schlichter

Strongly agree   Strongly disagree
      A ------------ B ------------ C ------------ D ------------ E

1. I am able to show other teachers
    how to use curriculum compacting.   A   B   C   D   E

2. Encouraging students to do original
    work is important to me.   A   B   C   D   E

3. Good teachers are able to guide students
    into Type III activities.   A   B   C   D   E

4. The debriefing technique is a crucial
    skill for classroom teachers to use.   A   B   C   D   E

5. Students' interests are used as means
    for developing exploratory activities.   A   B   C   D   E

6. I try to use a variety of instructional
    strategies to address different learning
    styles of students.   A   B   C   D   E

7. Students who are really gifted are able
    to identify outlets for their interest
    without a lot of teacher attention.   A   B   C   D   E

8. My teaching reflects attention to
    development of a wide array of
    thinking skills.   A   B   C   D   E

9. Curriculum compacting is viewed as a
    priority by the principal in our school.   A   B   C   D   E

10. My knowledge and skill in using a
    specific thinking skills model is a key
    to my success in providing Type IIs.   A   B   C   D   E

11. I can identify student behaviors suggesting
    the need for an Action Information Message. A   B   C   D   E

12. I can help students find a variety of
    outlets for their independent projects.   A   B   C   D   E

13. Type IIIs often necessitate instruction
    in specific process skills.   A   B   C   D   E

SE-TRAIN (1990) Olenchak & Schlichter

Strongly agree   Strongly disagree
        A ----------- B ----------- C ----------- D ------------ E

14. Type I enrichment is aimed at inviting
    students to do more than explore.   A   B   C   D   E

15. I am comfortable in my ability to
    identify students for the Talent Pool.   A   B   C   D   E

16. Type IIs include a variety of skills,
    some of which have been addressed
    in schools for years.   A   B   C   D   E

17. I can explain the nature and purpose
    of Type I enrichment to others.   A   B   C   D   E

18. Even though there's always room for
    improvement, I feel I know how to
    stimulate students to pursue interests
    beyond an introductory level.   A   B   C   D   E

19. All students can benefit from regular
    instruction in thinking skills.   A   B   C   D   E

20. Children best get identified for gifted
    programs when teachers and parents
    work together.   A   B   C   D   E

21. I think it's important to be able to
    explain the three-ring conception
    of giftedness.   A   B   C   D   E

22. Students in my classes can identify
    procedures for decision making,
    planning, and predicting.   A   B   C   D   E

23. Compacting should be offered to any
    student who can demonstrate mastery
    in an area of the curriculum.   A   B   C   D   E

24. I have developed some ways to help
    students keep on task with their
    investigations.   A   B   C   D   E

SE-TRAIN (1990) Olenchak & Schlichter

344

Bibliography

Adler, M. J., & Hutchins, R. M. (1952). *The great ideas: A syntopicon of great books of the western world.* Chicago: Encyclopedia Britannica.

Albert, R. S., & Runco, M. A. (1986). The achievement of eminence: A model based on a longitudinal study of exceptionally gifted boys and their families. In R. J. Sternberg & J. E. Davidson (Eds.), *Conceptions of giftedness* (pp. 332-357). Cambridge: Cambridge University Press.

Altbach, P. G., Kelly, G. P., Petrie, H. G., & Weis, L. (1991). *Textbooks in American society.* Albany, NY: State University of New York Press.

Amabile, T. M. (1983). *The social psychology of creativity.* New York: Springer-Verlag.

Apple, M. (1992). The text and cultural politics. *Educational Researcher, 21*(7), 4-11.

Applebee, A. N., Langer, J. A., & Mullis, I. V. S. (1989). *Crossroads in American education.* Princeton: Educational Testing Service.

Bibliography

Archambault, F. X., Westberg, K. L., Brown, S., Hallmark, B. W., Zhang, W., & Emmons, C. (1992). Regular classroom practices with gifted students. *Journal for the Education of the Gifted, 16*(2), 103-119.

Armbruster, B. B. (1984). The problem of inconsiderate text. In G. Duffy, L. Roehler, & J. Mason (Eds.), *Comprehension instruction* (pp. 202-217). New York: Longman.

Armbruster, B. B., & Anderson, T. H. (1984). Structures of explanation in history textbooks, or so what if Governor Stanford missed the spike and hit the rail? *Educational Leadership, 41*(2), 18-20.

Aspy, D., Aspy, C., & Quinby, P. (1993). What doctors can teach teachers about problem-based learning. *Educational Leadership, 50*(7), 22-24.

Atkin, J. M., & Karplus, R. (1962). Discovery or invention. *Science Teacher, 29*(5), 45-51.

Ausubel, D. P. (1968). *Educational psychology: A cognitive view*. New York: Holt, Rinehart and Winston.

Bandura, A. (1977). Self efficacy: Toward a unifying theory of behavioral change. *Psychology Review, 84*(2), 191-215.

Baron, J. B., Carlyon, E., Greig, J., & Lomask, M. (1992). *What do our students know? Assessing students' abilities to think and act like scientists through performance assessment*. Hartford, CT: The Connecticut State Department of Education.

Barth, R. (1990). *Improving schools from within: Teachers, parents, principals can make a difference*. San Francisco, CA: Jossey-Bass.

Baum, S. (1988). An enrichment program for the gifted learning disabled students. *Gifted Child Quarterly, 32*(1), 226-230.

Baum, S., Renzulli, J. S., & Hébert, T. P. (in preparation). Reversing underachievement through pursuit of student interests.

Bell, T. H. (1993). Reflections one decade after - A nation at risk. *Phi Delta Kappan, 74*(8), 592-600.

Bishop, J. H. (1989). Is the test score decline responsible for the productivity growth decline? *The American Economic Review, 79*(1), 178-179.

Blanton, M. (1993, October 7). Parent's Odyssey. *Education Week*, p. 33.

Bloom, B. S. (1985). *Developing talent in young people.* New York: Ballantine Books.

Bloom, B. S. (Ed.), (1954). *Taxonomy of educational objectives. Handbook I: Cognitive domain.* New York: Longman.

Boyd, W. L. (1987). Public education's last hurrah?: Schizophrenia, amnesia, and ignorance in school politics. *Educational Evaluation and Policy Analysis, 9*(2), 85-100.

Bracey, G. W. (1993). Elementary curriculum materials: Still a long way to go. *Phi Delta Kappan, 74*(8), 654-656.

Brandt, R. (1993). On teaching for understanding: A conversation with Howard Gardner. *Educational Leadership, 50*(7), 4-7.

Brophy, J. E., & Good, T. L. (1974). *Teacher-Student relationships: Causes and consequences.* New York: Holt, Rinehart & Winston.

Bruner, J. S. (1960). *The process of education.* Cambridge, MA: Harvard University Press.

Bruner, J. S. (1966). *Toward a theory of instruction.* Cambridge, MA: Harvard University Press.

Bunge, M. (1967). *Scientific research 1: The search for system.* New York: Springer-Verlag.

Bunker, B. B., Pearlson, H. B., & Schultz, J. W. (1975). *A student's guide to conducting social science research.* New York: Human Sciences Press.

Burke, J. (1993). Tackling society's problems in English class. *Educational Leadership, 50*(7), 16-18.

Burns, D. E. (1987). *The effects of group training activities on students' creative productivity.* Unpublished doctoral dissertation, The University of Connecticut, Storrs, CT.

Burns, D. E., & Reis, S. M. (1991). Developing a thinking skills component in the gifted education program. *Roeper Review, 12*(2), 72-78.

Carroll, J. M. (1989). *The Copernican Plan: Restructuring the American high school. Andover,* MA: The Regional Laboratory for Educational Improvement of the Northeast and the Islands.

Chall, J. S. (1967). *Learning to read: The great debate.* New York: McGraw-Hill.

Chall, J. S. (1983). *Learning to read: The great debate* (2nd ed.). New York: McGraw-Hill.

Chall, J. S., & Conard, S. S. (1991). *Should textbooks challenge students?: The case for easier or harder textbooks.* New York: Teachers College Press.

Chall, J. S., Conard, S. S., & Harris, S. H. (1981). *An analysis of textbooks in relation to decline in SAT scores.* New York: College Entrance Examination Board.

Chrispeels, J. H. (1991). District leadership in parent involvement: Policies and actions in San Diego. *Phi Delta Kappan, 72*(5), 367-371.

Clay, M. M., & Cazden, C. B. (1992). A Vygotskian interpretation of reading recovery. In C. B. Cazden (Ed.), *Whole language plus* (pp. 114-135). New York: Teachers College Press.

Clune, W. H. (1993). Systemic educational policy: A conceptual framework. In S. H. Fuhrman (Ed.), *Designing coherent educational policy: Improving the system* (pp. 125-140). San Francisco: Jossey-Bass.

Comer, J. P. (1988). Educating poor minority children. *Scientific American, 259*(5), 42-48.

Comer, J. P. (1990). Home, school and academic learning. In J. I. Goodlad & P. Keating (Eds.), *Access to knowledge: An agenda for our nation's schools* (pp. 23-42). New York: College Entrance Examination Board.

Conn, S. (1988). Textbooks: Defining new criteria. *Media and Methods, 24*(4), 30-31.

Cooper, C. (1983). *Administrator's attitudes toward gifted programs based on the enrichment triad/revolving door identification model: Case studies in decision-making.* Unpublished doctoral dissertation, The University of Connecticut, Storrs, CT.

Corbett, H. D., & Wilson, B. (1990). *Testing, reform and rebellion.* Norwood, NY: Albex.

Csikszentmihalyi, M. (1993). *The evolving self: A psychology for the third millennium.* New York: HarperCollins Publishers.

Cuban, L. (1990). Four stories: About national goals for American education. *Phi Delta Kappan, 72*(4), 265-271.

Darling-Hammond, L., & Goodwin, L. (1993). Progress toward professionalism in teaching. In G. Cawelti, (Ed.), *Challenges and achievements of American education* (pp. 19-52). Alexandria, VA: 1993 Yearbook of the Association of Supervision and Curriculum Development.

de Bono, E. (1985). *Six thinking hats.* Boston: Little Brown and Company.

Delcourt, M. A. B. (1988). *Characteristics related to high levels of creative/product behavior in secondary school students: A multi-case study.* Unpublished doctoral dissertation, The University of Connecticut, Storrs, CT.

Delcourt, M. A. B. (1993). Creative productivity among secondary school students: Combining energy, interest and imagination. *Gifted Child Quarterly, 37*(1), 23-31.

Delisle, J. R. (1981). *The revolving door identification and programming model: Correlates of creative production. of behavioral change.* Unpublished doctoral dissertation, The University of Connecticut, Storrs, CT.

Dewey, J. (1913). *Interest and effort in education.* New York: Houghton Mifflin.

Dewey, J. (1916). *Democracy and education.* New York: The Free Press.

Dismuke, D. (1992, November). Four-Day week comes to school. *NEA Today,* p. 15.

Doane, C. (1993). Global issues in 6th grade? Yes! *Educational Leadership, 50*(7), 19-22.

Downey, M. T. (1980). Speaking of textbooks: Putting pressure on the publishers. *History Teacher, 14*(1), 61-72.

Dunn, R., & Dunn, K. (1978). *Teaching students through their individual learning styles: A practical approach.* Englewood Cliffs, NJ: Prentice-Hall.

Dunn, R., & Dunn, K. (1992). *Teaching elementary students through their individual learning styles: Practical approaches for grades 3-6.* Boston: Allyn and Bacon.

Dunn, R., & Dunn, K. (1993). *Teaching secondary students through their individual learning styles: Practical approaches for grades 7-12.* Boston: Allyn and Bacon.

Dunn, R., Dunn, K., & Price, G. E. (1975). *Learning style inventory.* Lawrence, KS: Price Systems.

Educational Testing Service. (1991). *Performance at the top.* Princeton: Educational Testing Service.

Elliott, D. L., & Woodward, A. (1990). Textbook and schooling in the United States. *Eighty-ninth yearbook of the National Society for the Study of Education.* Chicago, IL: The University of Chicago Press.

Ellis, D. (1992, June 8). Knowledge for sale. *Time*, pp. 69-71.

Emerick, L. J. (1988). *Academic underachievement among the gifted: Students' perceptions of factors relating to the reversal of the academic underachievement pattern.* Unpublished doctoral dissertation, The University of Connecticut, Storrs, CT.

Feldhusen, J. F. (1989). Why the public schools will continue to neglect the gifted. *Gifted Child Today, 12*(2), 55-59.

Flanders, J. R. (1987). How much of the content in mathematics textbooks is new? *Arithmetic Teacher, 35*(1), 18-23.

Flindt, M. (1978). *Gold Rush: A simulation of life and adventure in a frontier mining camp.* Lakeside, CA: INTERACT.

Floden, R. E., Porter, A. C., Schmidt, W. H., Freeman, D. J., & Schwille, J. R. (1981). Responses to curriculum pressures: A policy-capturing study of teacher decisions about content. *Journal of Educational Psychology, 73*(2), 129-141.

Flynn, J. R. (1984). The mean IQ of Americans: Massive gains 1932 to 1978. *Psychological Bulletin, 95*(1), 29-51.

Fostnot C. T. (1993). Preface. In J. G. Brooks and M. G. Brooks (Eds.), *In search of understanding: The case for constructivist classrooms.* Alexandria, VA: Association for Supervision and Curriculum Development.

Fraser, J. W. (1989). Agents in democracy: Urban elementary schools teachers and the conditions of teaching. In D. Warner (Ed.), *American teachers: History of the profession at work* (pp. 118-156). New York: MacMillan.

Frymier, J. (1987). Bureaucracy and the neutering of teachers. *Phi Delta Kappan, 69*(1), 9-14.

Fullan, M. G. (1993). *Change forces*. New York: Falmer Press.

Fullan, M. G. (1991). *The meaning of educational change*. New York: Teachers College Press.

Fullan, M. G., & Miles, M. B. (1992). Getting reform right: What works and what doesn't. *Phi Delta Kappan, 73*(10), 745-752.

Fulton, L. (Ed.), (annual). Directory of Poetry Publishers (9th ed.). 1993-1994. Paradise, CA: Dustbooks.

Gagné, R. M., & Briggs, L. J. (1979). *Principles of instructional design* (2nd ed.). New York: Holt, Rinehart and Winston.

Gagnon, P. (1988). Why study history? *Atlantic, 262*, 43-66.

Gardner, H. (1983). *Frames of mind*. New York: Basic Books.

Gates, A. I. (1961). Vocabulary control in basal reading material. *Reading Teacher, 15*(2), 81-85.

Gearhart, M., Herman, J. L., Baker, E. L., & Whittaker, A. K. (1992). *Writing portfolios at the elementary level: A study of methods for writing assessment*. (Report No. 337). Los Angeles, CA: National Center for the Study of Evaluation, Standards, and Student Testing (CRESST).

George, P. S. (1988). Tracking and ability grouping: Which way for the middle school? *The Middle School Journal, 20*(1), 21-28.

Glaser, R. (1990). Expert knowledge and the thinking process. *Chemtech, 20*, pp. 394-397.

Glatthorn, A. A. (1987). Cooperative professional development: Peer-centered options for teacher growth. *Educational Leadership, 45*(3), 31-35.

Glazer, S. M., & Brown, C. S. (1993). *Collaborative assessment in reading and writing*. Christopher-Gordon, Norwood: MA.

Goodlad, J. I. (1984). *A place called school*. New York: McGraw Hill.

Gruber, H. E. (1986). The self construction of the extraordinary. In R. J. Sternberg & J. E. Davidson (Eds.), *Conceptions of giftedness* (pp. 247-263). Cambridge: Cambridge University Press.

Gubbins, E. J. (1982). *Revolving door identification model: Characteristics of talent pool students*. Unpublished doctoral dissertation, The University of Connecticut, Storrs, CT.

Gutiérrez, R., & Slavin, R. E. (1992). *Achievement effects of the nongraded elementary school: A retrospective review*. Baltimore, MD: Center for Research on Effective Schooling for Disadvantaged Students. (ERIC Document Reproduction Service No. ED 346 996)

Hall, G. E., George, A. A., & Rutherford, W. L. (1979). *Measuring stages of concern: A manual for the use of the Stages of Concern Questionnaire*. Austin: Research and Development Center for Teacher Education, University of Texas.

Hayes-Jacobs, H. (1989). The Interdisciplinary Model: A step-by-step approach for developing integrated units of study. In H. Hayes-Jacobs (Ed.), *Interdisciplinary curriculum: Design and implementation* (pp. 53-66). Alexandria, VA: Association for Supervision and Curriculum Development.

Heal, M. M. (1989). *Student perceptions of labeling the gifted: A comparative case study analysis*. Unpublished doctoral dissertation, The University of Connecticut, Storrs, CT.

Hébert, T. P. (1993). *An ethnographic description of the high school experiences of high ability males in an urban environment*. Unpublished doctoral dissertation, University of Connecticut, Storrs, CT.

Hébert, T. P. (1993). Reflections at graduations: The long-term impact of elementary school experiences in creative productivity. *Roeper Review, 16*(1), 22-28.

Henderson, H., & Conrath, J. M. (1991). *CAPSOL style of learning assessment.* Mansfield, OH: Process Associates.

Henderson, H., Hartnett, W., & Wair, R. (1982). *Learning styles... An alternative for achievement. A guide to implementation.* Mansfield, OH: Madison Local Schools.

Hennessey, B. A., & Amabile, T. M. (1988). The conditions of creativity. In R. J. Sternberg (Ed.), *The nature of creativity* (pp. 11-37). Cambridge: Cambridge University Press.

Herbart, J. F. (1965) General theory of pedagogy, derived from the purpose of education. In J. F. Herbart (Ed.), *Writing an education, Vol. 2* (pp. 9-155). Dusseldorf: Kuepper (Original work published in 1806).

Herbart, J. F. (1965) Outline of education lectures. In J. F. Herbart (Ed.), *Writing an education, Vol. 1* (pp. 157-300). Dusseldorf: Kuepper (Original work published in 1841).

Hockett, J. A. (1938). The vocabularies of recent primers and first readers. *Elementary School Journal, 39,* 112-115.

Hook, S. (1987). *Out of step: An unquiet life in the twentieth century.* New York: HarperCollins.

Hoover, S. M., Sayler, M., & Feldhusen, J. F. (1993). Cluster grouping of gifted students at the elementary level. *Roeper Review, 16*(1), pp. 13-15.

Horn, E. (1937). *Methods of instruction in the social studies.* New York: Charles Scribner's Sons.

Hunt, D. E. (1971). *Matching models in education: The coordination of teaching methods with student characteristics.* Canada: Ontario Institute for Studies in Education.

Husén, T., & Tuijnman, A. (1991). The contribution of formal schooling to the increase in intellectual capital. *Educational Researcher, 20*(7), 17-25.

Jaeger, R. M. (1992). World class standards, choice and privatization: Weak measurement serving presumptive policy. *Phi Delta Kappan, 74*(2), 118-128.

James, W. (1890). *The principles of psychology.* London: MacMillan.

Joyce, B., & Showers, B. (1987). The coaching of teaching. *Educational Leadership, 45*(3), 4-10.

Kagan, J. (1966). Reflection-impulsivity: The generality and dynamics of conceptual tempo. *Journal of Abnormal Psychology, 71*(1), 17-24.

Kantor, R. N., Anderson, T. H., & Armbruster, B. B. (1983). How inconsiderate are children's textbooks? *Journal of Curriculum Studies, 15*(1), 61-72.

Kaplan, S. N. (1986). The Grid: A model to construct differentiated curriculum for the gifted. In J. S. Renzulli (Ed.), *Systems and models for developing programs for the gifted and talented* (pp. 180-193). Mansfield, CT: Creative Learning Press.

Kaufman, A. S., Mennin, S., Waterman, R., & Duban, S. (1989). The New Mexico Experiment: Educational innovation and institutional change. *Academic Medicine, 64*(6), 285-294.

Killon, J. P., & Todnem, G. R. (1991). A process for personal theory building. *Educational Leadership, 48*(6), 14-17.

Kirst, M. W. (1982). How to improve schools without spending more money. *Phi Delta Kappan, 64*(1), 6-8.

Kobrin, D., Abbott, E., Ellinwood, J., & Horton, D. (1993). Learning history by doing history. *Educational Leadership, 50*(7), 39-41.

Krapp, A. (1989). The importance of the concept of interest in education research. *Empirische Paedagogik, 3,* 233-255.

Kulik, J. A. (1992). *An analysis of the research on ability grouping: Historical and contemporary perspectives.* (Research Monograph No. 9204). Storrs, CT: The National Research Center on the Gifted and Talented.

Kulik, J. A., & Kulik, C.-L. C. (1982). Effects of ability grouping on secondary school students: A meta-analysis of evaluation findings. *American Educational Research Journal, 19*(3), 415-428.

Kulik, J. A., & Kulik, C.-L. C. (1987). Effects of ability grouping on student achievement. *Equity and Excellence, 23*(1-2), 22-30.

Lampert, M. (1984). Thinking about teaching and teaching about thinking. *Journal of Curriculum Studies, 16*(1), 1-18.

Laud, G., & Jarman, B. (1992). *Break-point and beyond.* New York: Harper Business.

Lawson, A. E. (1978). The development and validation of a classroom test of formal reasoning. *Journal of Research in Science Teaching, 15*(1), 11-24.

Le Carre, J. (1989). *The Russia House.* New York: Knopf.

Leiberman, A., Darling-Hammond, L., & Zuckerman, D. (1991). *Early lessons in restructuring schools.* New York: National Center for Restructuring Education, Schools, and Teaching / Teachers College.

Leiberman, A., & McLaughlin, M. W. (1992). Networks for educational change: Powerful and problematic. *Phi Delta Kappan, 73*(9), 73-77.

Leming, J. S. (1992). The influence of contemporary issues curricula on school-aged youth. *Review of Research in Education, 18*, 111-161.

Linn, M., Chen, B., & Thier, H. (1977). Teaching children to control variables: Investigation of a free choice environment. *Journal of Research on Science Teaching, 14*(3), 249-255.

Lockwood, A. T. (1992). Whose knowledge do we teach? *Focus in Change, 6,* 3-7.

Madaus, G. F., West, M. M., Harmon, M. E., Lomax, R. G., & Viator, K. A. (1992). *The influence of testing on teaching math and science in grades 4-12.* Chestnut Hill, MA: Center for the Study of Testing, Evaluation and Educational Policy.

Maeroff, G. I. (1993). *Team building for school change: Equipping teachers for new roles.* New York: Teachers College Press.

Mathematical Sciences Education Board. (1986). Report prepared for fall meeting, mimeo.

McCaslin, M., & Good, T. (1992). Compliant cognition: The misalliance of management and instructional goals in current school reform. *Educational Researcher, 21*(4), 4-17.

McGreevey, A. (1982). *My book of things and stuff: An interest questionnaire for young children.* Mansfield Center, CT: Creative Learning Press.

McKnight, C. C., Crosswhite, F. J., Dossey, J. A., Kifer, E., Swafford, J. O., Travers, K. J., & Cooney, T. J. (1987). *The underachieving curriculum: Assessing the U.S. mathematics from an international perspective.* Champaign, IL: Stipes.

McLaughlin, M. W., & Talbert, J. E. (1993). *Contexts that matter for teaching and learning.* Stanford, CA: Center for Research on the Context of Secondary School Teaching.

Mehlinger, H. (1989). American textbook reform: What we can learn from the Soviet experience? *Phi Delta Kappan, 71*(1), 29-35.

Meisels, S. J. (1993). Remaking classroom assessment with the Work Sampling System. *Young Children, 48*(5), 34-40.

Munday, L. A., & Davis, J. C. (1974). *Varieties of accomplishment after college: Perspectives on the meaning of academic talent.* Research Report No. 62. Iowa City, IA: American College Testing Program.

Murphy, J. T. (1989). The paradox of decentralizing schools: Lessons from business, government and the Catholic Church. *Phi Delta Kappan, 70*(10), 808-812.

Murphy, J. T. (1991). *Restructuring schools: Capturing and assessing the phenomenon.* New York: Teachers College Press.

National Center for School Leadership. (1993, Summer). It begins with a question: What is the role of school leadership? Urbana, IL: Author.

National Commission on Excellence in Education. (1983). *A nation at risk: The imperative of educational reform.* Report to the nation and the Secretary of Education. Washington, DC: U.S. Government Printing Office.

National Council on Education Standards and Testing. (1992). *Raising Standards for American Education: A report to Congress, the Secretary of Education, the National Goals Panel, and the American People.* Washington, DC: U.S. Government Printing Office.

Newman, J. L. (1991). *The effects of the talents unlimited model on students' creative productivity.* Unpublished doctoral dissertation, The University of Alabama, Tuscaloosa, AL.

Newmann, F. M., & Wehlag, G. G. (1993). Five standards of authentic instruction. *Educational Leadership, 50*(7), 8-12.

O'Neil, J. (1993). Can separate be equal? *Curriculum Update*, June 1993. Alexandria, VA: Association for Supervision and Curriculum Development. 1-2.

Oakes, J. (1985). *Keeping track: How schools structure inequality.* New Haven, CT: Yale University Press.

Ogbu, J. U. (1974). *The next generation: An ethnography of education in an urban neighborhood.* New York: Academic Press.

Ogbu, J. U. (1985). Research currents: Cultural-ecological influences on minority school learning. *Language Arts, 62*(8), 860-868.

Ogbu, J. U. (1987). Variability in minority school performance: A problem in search of an explanation. *Anthropology and Education Quarterly, 18*(4), 312-334.

Ogbu, J. U. (1991). Immigrant and involuntary minorities in comparative perspective. In M. A. Gibson & J. U. Ogbu (Eds.), *Minority status and schooling: A comparative study of immigrant and involuntary minorities* (pp. 3-33). New York: Garland Publishing.

Ogbu, J. U. (1992). Understanding cultural diversity and learning. *Educational Researcher, 21*(8), pp. 5-14.

Ohanian, S. (1987). Ruffles and flourishes. *Atlantic, 260,* 20-22.

Olenchak, F. R. (1988). The schoolwide enrichment model in the elementary schools: A study of implementation stages and effects on educational excellence. In J. S. Renzulli (Ed.), *Technical report on research studies relating to the Revolving Door Identification Model* (2nd ed.). Storrs, CT: Bureau of Educational Research, The University of Connecticut.

Olenchak, F. R. (1991). *Assessing program effects for gifted/ learning disabled students.* In R. Swassing & A. Robinson (Eds.), NAGC 1991 research briefs. Washington, DC: National Association for Gifted Students.

Olson, L. (1992, September 9). Fed up with tinkering, reformers now touting "systemic" approach. *Education Week,* pp. 1, 30.

Osborne, J. H., Jones, B. F., & Stein, M. (1985). The case for improving textbooks. *Educational Leadership, 42*(7), 9-16.

Paine, S. C., Bellamy, G. T., & Wilcox, B. (1984). *Human services that work: From innovation to standard practice.* Baltimore, MD: Brooks Publishing.

Paris, S., Lawton, T., Turner, J., & Roth, J. (1991). A developmental perspective on standardized achievement tests. *Educational Researcher, 20*(5), 12-20.

Passow, A. H. (1982). *Differentiated curricula for the gifted/talented.* Ventura, CA: Leadership Training Institute on the Gifted and Talented.

Pea, R. D. (1987). Socializing the knowledge transfer problem. *International Journal of Educational Research, 11*(6), 639-663.

Phenix, P. H. (1964). *Realms of meaning.* New York: McGraw-Hill.

Piaget, J. (Ed.), (1981). *Intelligence and affectivity: Their relationship during child development.* (Trans.) Annual Reviews Monograph. Palo Alto, CA: Annual Review.

Pogrow, S. (1993). Where's the beef: Looking for exemplary materials. *Educational Leadership, 50*(8), 39-45.

Porter, A. (1989). A curriculum out of balance: The case of elementary mathematics. *Educational Researcher, 18*(5), 9-15.

Prager, K. (1992, Fall). Estimating the extent of school restructuring. *Brief to Policy Makers, 4.* Madison,WI: Center on Organization and Restructuring Schools.

Purcell, J. H. (1993a). *The program status study: An analysis of the factors that influence the retention and elimination of programs for high ability students in a sample of twenty states.* Unpublished doctoral dissertation, University of Connecticut, Storrs, CT.

Purcell, J. H. (1993b). The effects of the elimination of gifted and talented programs on participating students and their parents. *Gifted Child Quarterly, 37*(4), 177-187.

Raywid, M. A. (1993). Finding time for collaboration. *Educational Leadership, 51*(1), 30-35.

Reis, S. M. (1981). *An analysis of the productivity of gifted students participating in programs using the Revolving Door Identification Model.* Unpublished doctoral dissertation, University of Connecticut, Storrs, CT.

Renninger, K. A. (1989). Individual patterns in children's play interests. In L. T. Winegar (Ed.), *Social interaction and the development of children's understanding* (pp 147-172). Norword, NJ: Ablex.

Renninger, K. A. (1990). Children's play interests, representations and activity. In R. Fivush & J. Hudson (Eds.), *Knowing and remembering in young children* (pp. 127-165). Emory Cognition Series (Vol. 3). Cambridge, MA: Cambridge University Press.

Renzulli, J. S. (1977a). *The enrichment triad model. A guide for developing defensible programs for the gifted.* Mansfield Center, CT: Creative Learning Press.

Renzulli, J. S. (1977b). *The Adult Interest-A-Lyzer.* Mansfield Center, CT: Creative Learning Press.

Renzulli, J. S. (1978). What makes giftedness? Reexamining a definition. *Phi Delta Kappan, 60*(3), 180-184, 261.

Renzulli, J. S. (1988). The Multiple Menu Model for developing differentiated curriculum for the gifted and talented. *Gifted Child Quarterly, 32*(3), 298-309.

Renzulli, J. S. (1992). A general theory for the development of creative productivity through the pursuit of ideal acts of learning. *Gifted Child Quarterly, 36*(4), 170-181.

Renzulli, J. S., & Reis, S. M. (1985). *The schoolwide enrichment model: A comprehensive plan for educational excellence.* Mansfield Center, CT: Creative Learning Press.

Renzulli, J. S., & Reis, S. M. (1994). Research related to the schoolwide enrichment model. *Gifted Child Quarterly, 38*(1), 7-20.

Renzulli, J. S., & Smith, L. H. (1978). The learning styles inventory: *A measure of student preference for instructional techniques.* Mansfield Center, CT: Creative Learning Press.

Renzulli, J. S., Hébert, T. P., & Sorenson, M. F. (1994). *Secondary Interest-A-Lyzer.* Mansfield Center, CT: Creative Learning Press.

Renzulli, J. S., Smith, L. H., Callahan, C., White, A., & Hartman, R. (1977). *Scales for rating the behavioral characteristics of superior students.* Mansfield Center, CT: Creative Learning Press.

Rogers, K. B. (1991). *The relationship of grouping practices to the education of the gifted and talented learner.* (Research Monograph No. 9101). Storrs, CT: The National Research Center on the Gifted and Talented.

Rothman, R. (1990, March 7). Choice claims overstated, A.S.C.D. panel concludes. *Education Week,* p. 8.

Schack, G. D. (1993). Involving students in authentic research. *Educational Leadership, 50*(7), 29-31.

Schack, G. D. (1986). *Creative productivity and self-efficacy in children.* Unpublished doctoral dissertation, The University of Connecticut, Storrs, CT.

Schiefele, U. (1989). Motivated conditions of text comprehension. *Zeitschrift Paeodgogik, 34,* 687-708.

Schlichter C. L., & Olenchak, F. R. (1992). Identification of in-service needs among Schoolwide Enrichment schools. *Roeper Review, 14* (3), 159-162.

Sedlack, M., Wheeler, C., Pullin, D., & Cusick, P. (1986). *Selling students short: Classroom bargains and academic reform in the American high school.* New York: Teachers College Press.

Senge, P. M. (1990). *The Fifth Discipline.* New York: Doubleday.

Sewall, G. T. (1988). American history textbooks: Where do we go from here? *Phi Delta Kappan, 69*(8), 554-558.

Shanker, A. (1993, January 31). Where we stand: The debate on grouping. *The New York Times*, p. 7.

Showers, B., Joyce, B., & Bennett, B. (1987). Synthesis of research on staff development: A framework for future study and a state-of-the-art analysis. *Educational Leadership, 45*(3) 77-87.

Silverstein, S. (1981). *Light in the attic.* New York: Harper & Row.

Singal, D. J. (1991). The other crisis in American education. *The Atlantic Monthly, 268*(5), 59-74.

Sizer, T. R. (1992). *Horace's compromise: The dilemma of the American school.* Boston, MA: Houghton Mifflin.

Skaught, B. J. (1987). *The social acceptability of talent pool students in an elementary school using the schoolwide enrichment model.* Unpublished doctoral dissertation, The University of Connecticut, Storrs, CT.

Slavin, R. E. (1987). Ability grouping and school achievement in elementary schools: A best-evidence synthesis. *Review of Educational Research, 57*(3), 293-336.

Slavin, R. E. (1990). Ability grouping in secondary schools: A response to Hallinian. *Review of Educational Research, 60*(3), 505-507.

Smith, L. H. (1976). *Learning styles: Measurement and educational significance.* Unpublished doctoral dissertation, University of Connecticut, Storrs, CT.

Smith, M. (1991). Put to the test: The effects of external testing on teachers. *Educational Researcher, 21*(4), 4-17.

Smith, M. S. & O'Day, J. (1990). Systemic school reform. In S. H. Fuhrman & B. Malen (Eds.), *The politics of curriculum and testing* (1990 Yearbook of the Politics of Educational Association, pp. 233-267). London: Taylor & Francis.

Stacy, R. D. (1990). *Managing the unknowable.* San Francisco, CA: Jossey-Bass.

Starko, A. J. (1986). *The effects of the revolving door identification model on creative productivity and self-efficacy.* Unpublished doctoral dissertation, The University of Connecticut, Storrs, CT.

Steen, L. A. (1989). *Everybody counts: A report to the nation on the future of mathematics education.* Washington, DC: National Research Council of the National Academy of Sciences.

Sternberg, R. J. (1988). Mental self-government: A theory of intellectual styles and their development. *Human Development, 31,* 197-224.

Sternberg, R. J. (in press). Human intelligence: Its nature, use and interaction with context. In D. Detterman (Ed.), *Current directions in human intelligence.* Norwood, NJ: Ablex.

Sternberg, R. J. (1984). Toward a triarchic theory of human intelligence. *Behavioral and Brain Sciences, 7,* 269-287.

Sternberg, R. J. (1990). Thinking styles: Keys to understanding student performance. *Phi Delta Kappan, 71*(5), 366-371.

Sternberg, R. J., & Wagner, R. K. (1991). *Mental self-government thinking styles inventory.* New Haven, CT: Authors.

Stevenson, H. W., & Stigler, J. W. (1992). *The learning gap: Why our schools are failing and what we can learn from Japanese and Chinese education.* New York: Summit Books.

Stevenson, H. W., Chen, C., & Lee, S. Y. (1993). Mathematics achievement of Chinese, Japanese, and American children: Ten years later. *Science, 259,* 53-58.

Stevenson, H. W., Lee, S. Y., & Stigler, J. W. (1986). Mathematics achievement of Chinese, Japanese, and American children. *Science, 231,* 693-669.

Stewart, E. D. (1979). *Learning styles among gifted/talented students: Preferences for instructional techniques.* Unpublished doctoral dissertation, The University of Connecticut, Storrs, CT.

Stigler, J. W., & Stevenson, H. W. (1991). How Asian teachers polish each lesson to perfection. *American Educator, 15*(1),12-20, 43-47.

Taylor, B. M., & Frye, B. J. (1988). Pretesting: Minimize time spent on skill work for intermediate readers. *The Reading Teacher, 42*(2), 100-103.

Thorndike, E. L. (1935). *Adult interests.* New York: MacMillan.

Tittle, B. M. (1992, Winter). From drop-out to out-standing. *Educating Able Learners,* 14-16.

Toepfer, C. F. (1990). Heterogeneous grouping in middle school levels: Leadership responsibilities for principals. *Schools in the middle: A report on trends and practices.* Reston, VA: National Association of Secondary School Principals.

Tolstoy, L. (1967). On teaching rudiments. In L. Weiner (Ed.), *Tolstoy on education* (pp. 34-62). Chicago: University of Chicago Press.

Torrance, E. P. (1965). *Rewarding creative behavior.* Englewood Cliffs, NJ: Prentice-Hall.

Tyson-Bernstein, H. (1985). The new policies of textbook adoption. *Phi Delta Kappan, 66*(7), 463-466.

Tyson-Bernstein, H. (1988). *A conspiracy of good intentions: America's textbook fiasco.* Washington, DC: Council for Basic Education.

Tyson-Bernstein, H., & Woodward, A. (1989). Nineteenth century policies for 21st century practice: The textbook reform dilemma. *Educational Policy, 3*(2), 95-106.

United States Department of Education. (1993). *National Excellence: A case for developing America's talent.* Washington, DC: Office of Educational Research and Improvement, U.S. Department of Education.

Usiskin, Z. (1987). Why elementary algebra can, should and must be an eighth-grade course for average students. *Mathematics Teacher, 80*(6), 428-438.

Vermont Department of Education. (1991a). *"This is my best:" Vermont's writing assessment program*, pilot year 1990-1991. Montpelier, VT: Author.

Vermont Department of Education. (1991b). *Vermont mathematics portfolio project: Resource book.* Montpelier, VT: Author.

Vermont Department of Education. (1991c). *Vermont mathematics portfolio project: Teacher's guide.* Montpelier, VT: Author.

Vygotsky, L. S. (1962). *Thought and language.* Cambridge, MA: M.I.T. Press.

Walberg, H. W. (1984). Improving the productivity of America's schools. *Educational Leadership, 41*(8), 19-27.

Ward, V. S. (1961). *Educating the gifted: An axiomatic approach.* Columbus, OH: Merrill.

Wechsler, D. (1990). Parkinson's Law 101. *Forbes, 145*(13), 52-56.

Weiss, S. (1993, September 26). Teachers feel left out of reform, study says. *The New York Times,* p. 34.

Westberg, K. L., Archambault, F. X., Dobyns, S. M., & Salvin, T. J. (1992). The classroom practices observational study. *Journal for the Education of the Gifted, 16*(2), 120-146.

Whitehead, A. N. (1929). The rhythm of education. In A. N. Whitehead (Ed.), *The aims of education* (pp. 46-59). New York: MacMillan.

Wiener, P. P. (Ed.). (1973). *Dictionary of the history of ideas* (Vol. 1). New York: Charles Scribner.

Wigginton, E. C. (1993). A song of inmates. *Educational Leadership, 51*(4), 64-71.

Williams, D. L., & Chavkin, N. F. (1989). Essential elements of strong parental involvement programs. *Educational Leadership ,47*(2), 18-20.

Williams, J., & Reynolds, T. D. (1993). Courting controversy: How to build interdisciplinary units. *Educational Leadership, 50*(7), 13-15.

Willis, S. (1993). Curriculum integration: Chemistry of art. *ASCD Update, 35*(5), 2.

Willows, D. M., Borwick, D., & Hayvren, M. (1981). The content of school readers. In G. E. MacKinnon and T. G. Waller (Eds.), *Reading research: Advances in theory and practice* (pp. 100-175). New York: Academic Press.

Wohlstetter, P., & Mohrman, S. A. (1993). School-based management: Strategies for success. *Consortium for Policy Research in Education Finance Briefs.* FB-02-1/93. pp. 1-9.

Yakes, N., & Akey, D. (Eds.). (annual). *Encyclopedia of associations.* Detroit, MI: Gale Research Company.

Bibliography

Author Index

Subject Index